VOL. 18
Action Edition

Story and Art by
RUMIKO TAKAHASHI

English Adaptation by Gerard Jones

Translation/Mari Morimoto
Touch-Up Art & Lettering/Bill Schuch
Cover and Interior Graphics & Design/Yuki Ameda
Editor/Avery Gotoh
Supervising Editor/Michelle Pangilinan

Managing Editor/Annette Roman
Editor in Chief/Alvin Lu
Production Manager/Noboru Watanabe
Sr. Dir. of Licensing and Acquisitions/Rika Inouye
VP of Sales/Joe Morici
VP of Marketing/Liza Coppola
Executive VP/Hyoe Narita
Publisher/Seiji Horibuchi

© 1997 Rumiko Takahashi/Shogakukan, Inc. First published
by Shogakukan, Inc. in Japan as "Inuyasha."

Printed in Canada.

Published by VIZ, LLC
P.O. Box 77010
San Francisco, CA 94107

Action Edition
10 9 8 7 6 5 4 3 2
First printing, June 2004
Second printing, July 2004

store.viz.com

www.viz.com

INUYASHA

VOL. 18   Action Edition

STORY AND ART BY
RUMIKO TAKAHASHI

CONTENTS

THE STORY THUS FAR

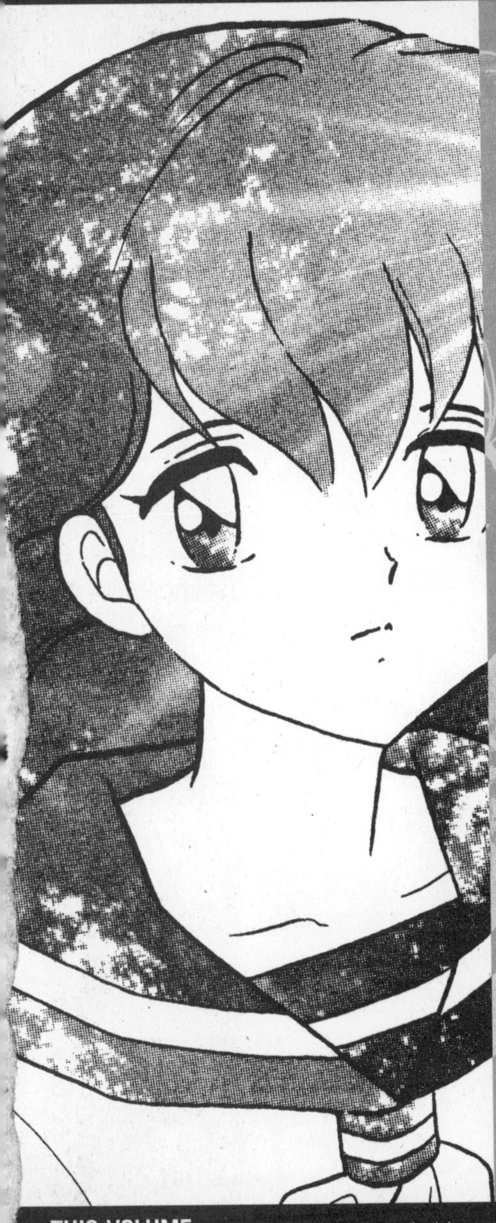

Long ago, in the "Warring States" era of Japan's Muromachi period (*Sengoku-jidai*, approximately 1467-1568 CE), a legendary doglike half-demon called "Inu-Yasha" attempted to steal the Shikon Jewel—or "Jewel of Four Souls"—from a village, but was stopped by the enchanted arrow of the village priestess, Kikyo. Inu-Yasha fell into a deep sleep, pinned to a tree by Kikyo's arrow, while the mortally wounded Kikyo took the Shikon Jewel with her into the fires of her funeral pyre. Years passed.

Fast-forward to the present day. Kagome, a Japanese high-school girl, is pulled into a well one day by a mysterious centipede monster, and finds herself transported into the past, only to come face to face with the trapped Inu-Yasha. She frees him, and Inu-Yasha easily defeats the centipede monster.

The residents of the village, now 50 years older, readily accept Kagome as the reincarnation of their deceased priestess Kikyo, a claim supported by the fact that the Shikon Jewel emerges from a cut on Kagome's body. Unfortunately, the jewel's rediscovery means that the village is soon under attack by a variety of demons in search of this treasure. Then, the jewel is accidentally shattered into many shards, each of which may have the fearsome power of the entire jewel.

Although Inu-Yasha says he hates Kagome because of her resemblance to Kikyo—the woman who "killed" him—he is forced to team up with her when Kaede, the village leader, binds him to Kagome with a powerful spell. Now the two grudging companions must fight to reclaim and reassemble the shattered shards of the Shikon Jewel before they fall into the wrong hands...

THIS VOLUME Inu-Yasha makes a delicate decision to pledge his love and devotion to his special one (at the expense of someone else's feelings for him), while Sango's love for her long-lost little brother jeopardizes the group's safety as the demon Naraku inches closer.

CHARACTERS

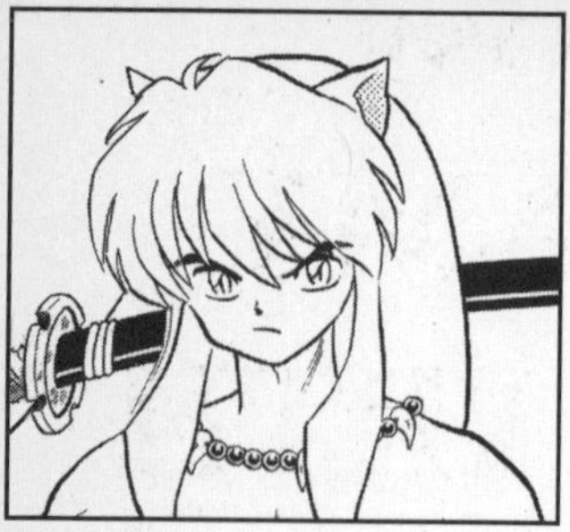

INU-YASHA
Half-demon hybrid, son of a human mother and demon father. His necklace is enchanted, allowing Kagome to control him with a word.

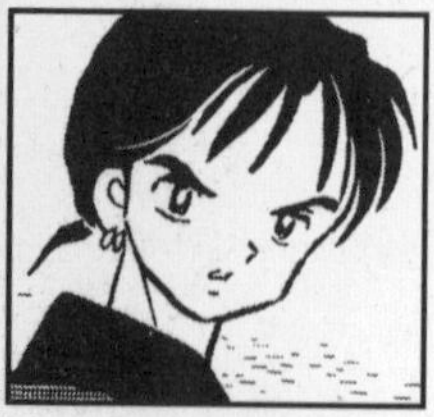

MIROKU
Lecherous Buddhist priest cursed with a mystical "hellhole" in his hand that's slowly killing him.

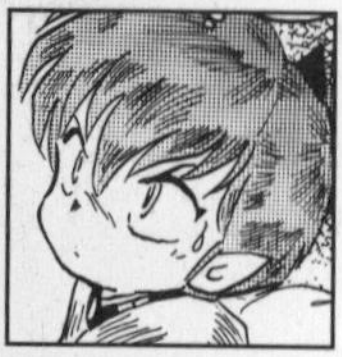

SHIPPO
Orphaned young fox-demon who likes to play shape-changing tricks.

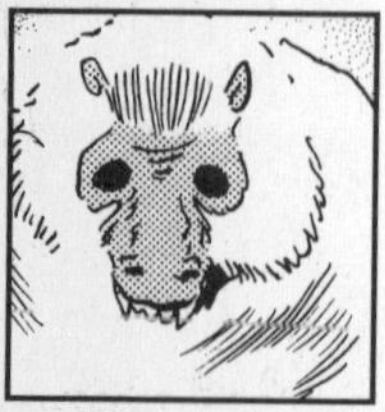

NARAKU
Enigmatic demon-mastermind behind the miseries of nearly everyone in the story.

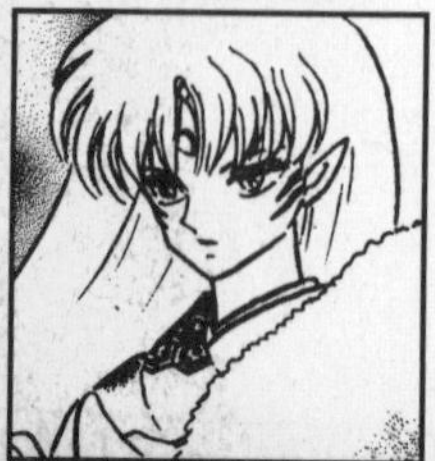

SESSHO-MARU
Inu-Yasha's half-brother, Sessho-Maru is the full-demon son of the same father.

KAGOME
Modern-day Japanese schoolgirl who can travel back and forth between the past and present through an enchanted well.

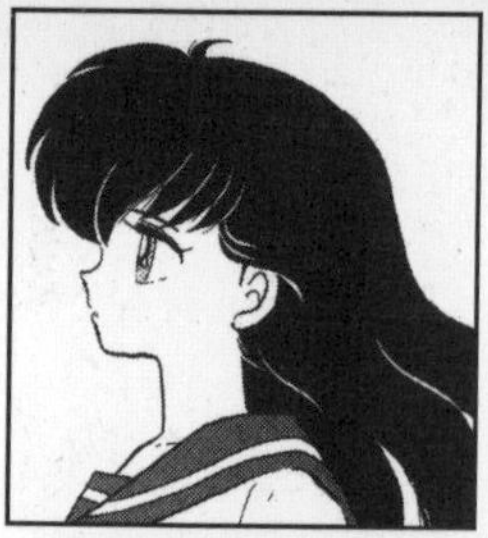

KOHAKU
Killed by Naraku—but not before first slaying both his own and Sango's father—now he's back again in a newer...if somewhat *slower*...form.

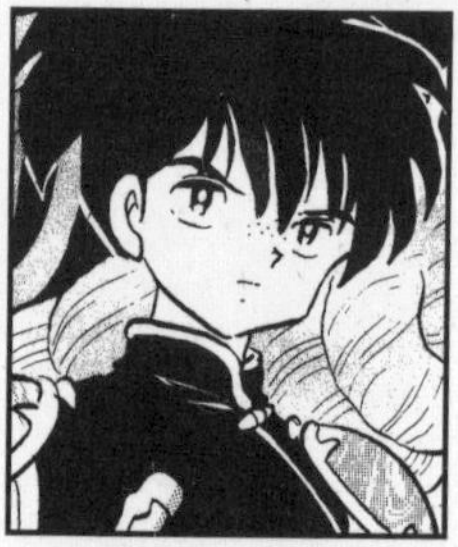

SANGO
"Demon Exterminator" or slayer from the village where the Shikon Jewel was first born.

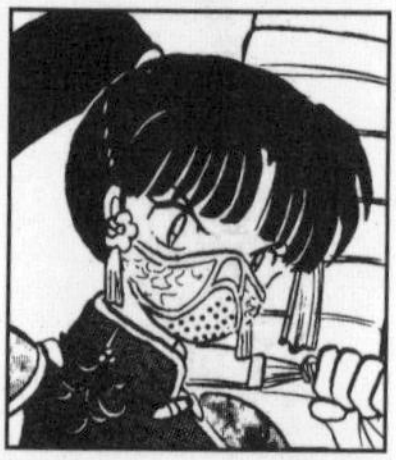

KAGURA
Created by Naraku to be his puppet, Kagura can manipulate the dead.

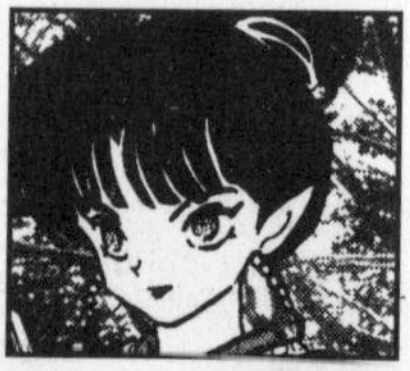

KANNA
Another of Naraku's "offspring," Kanna uses a magic mirror to trap souls.

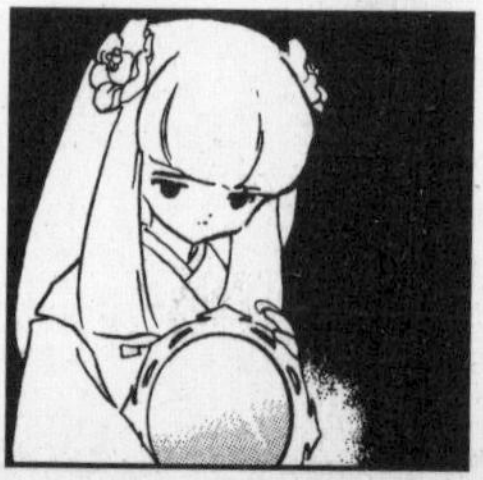

SCROLL ONE

THE ENEMY IN THE EARTH

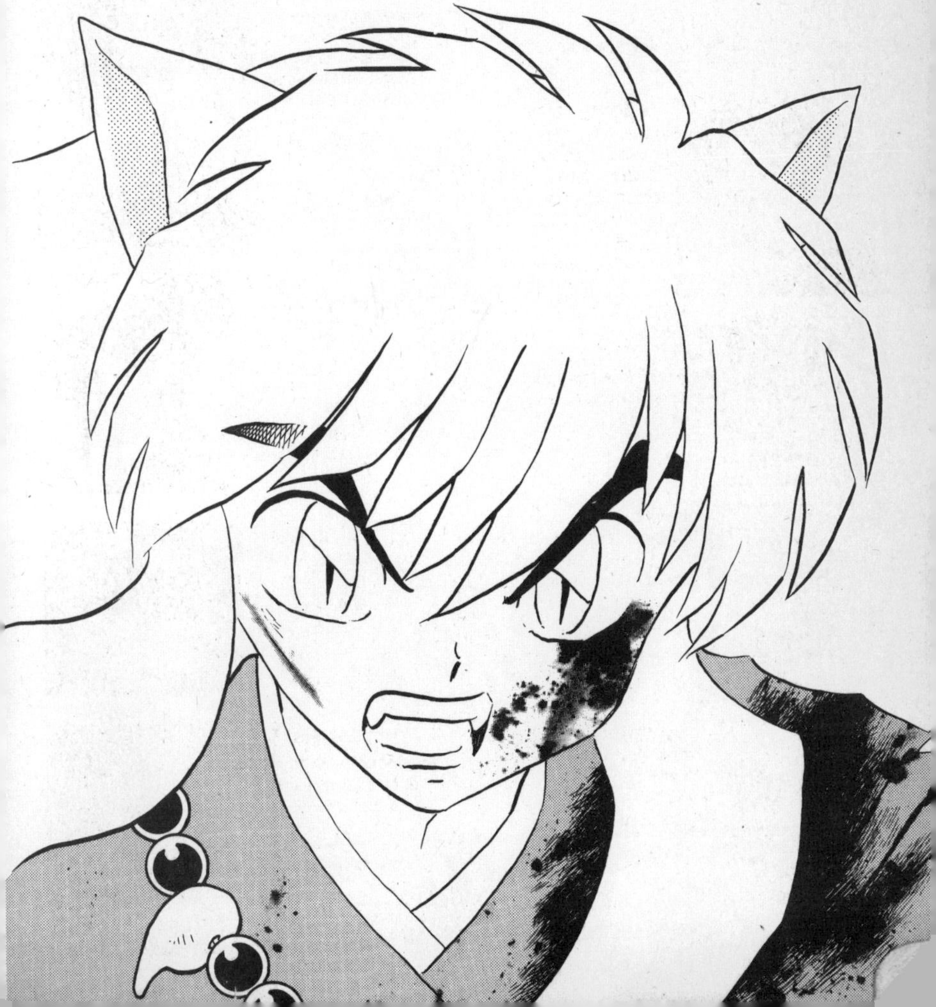

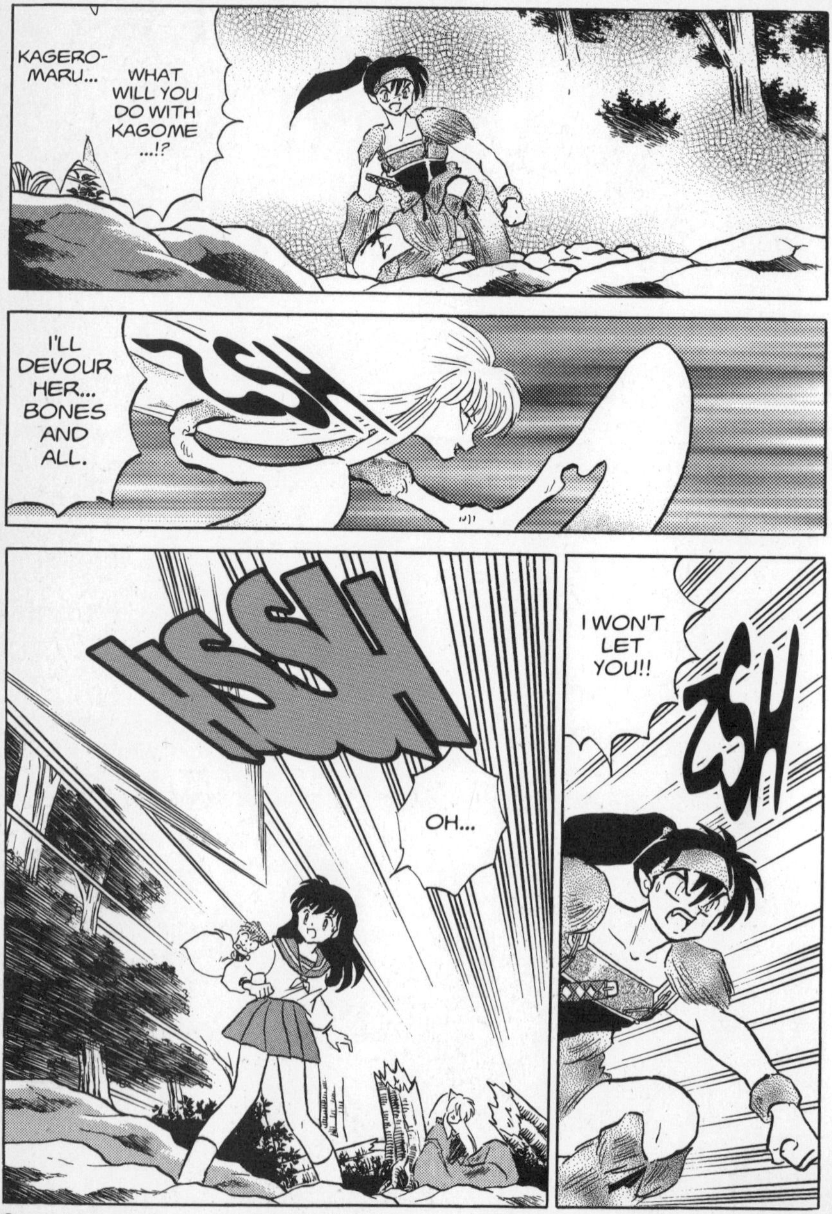
KAGERO-MARU... WHAT WILL YOU DO WITH KAGOME ...!?
I'LL DEVOUR HER... BONES AND ALL.
ZSH
WHSH
OH...
I WON'T LET YOU!!
ZSH

TH
GG
WAH!
HEH HEH HEH... YOU'LL NEVER BE IN TIME.

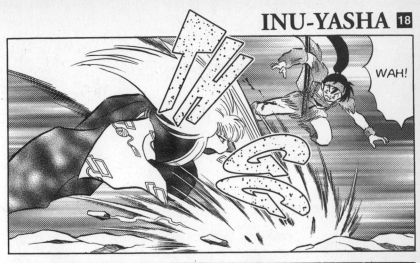

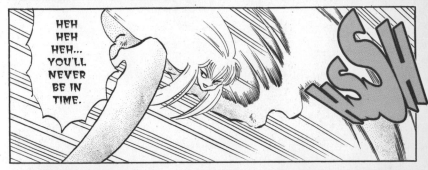

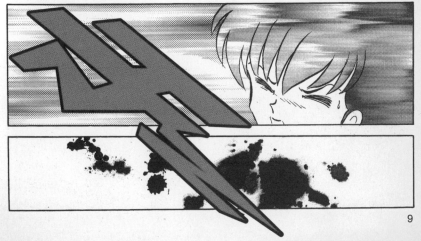

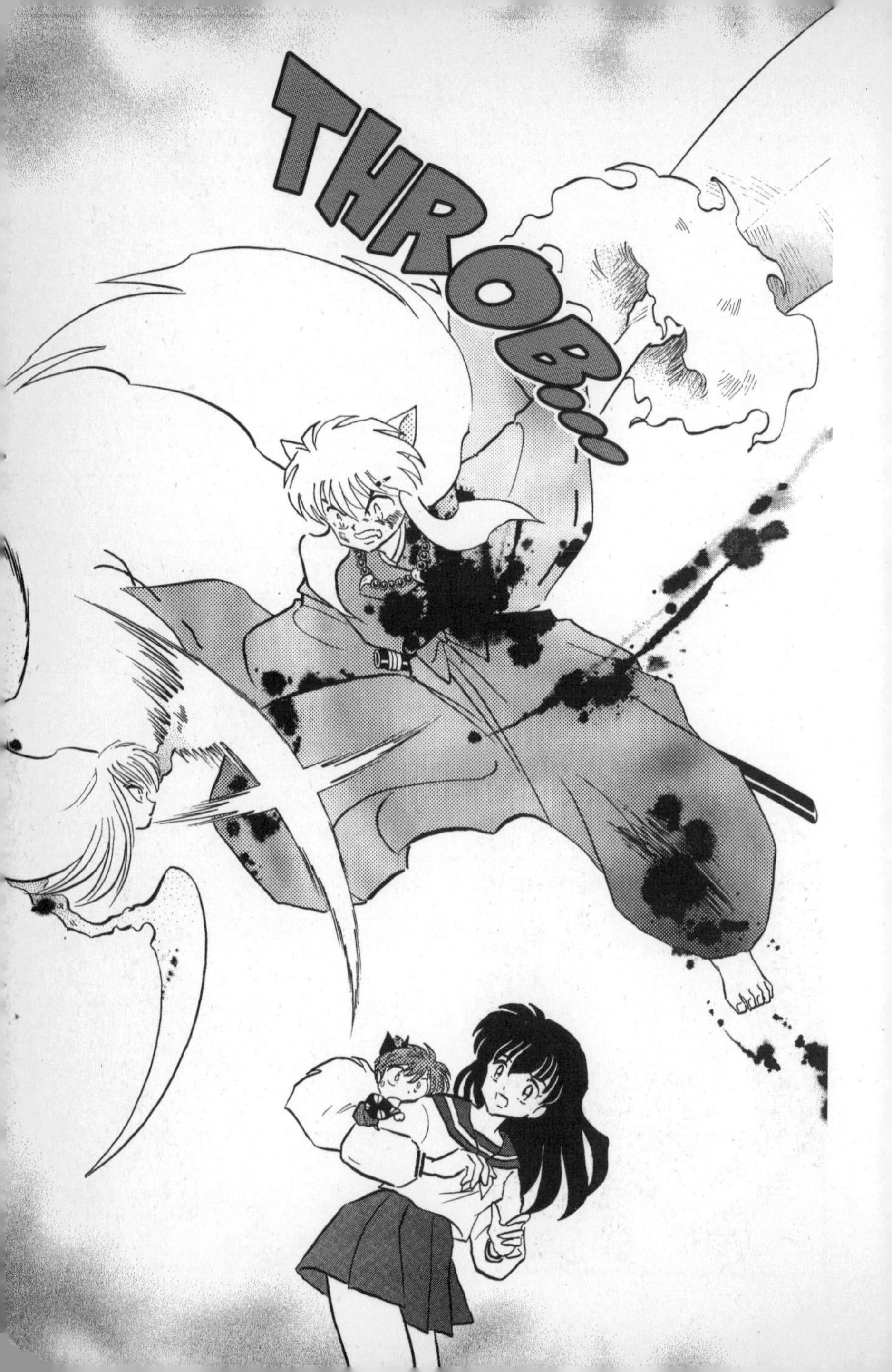
THROB...

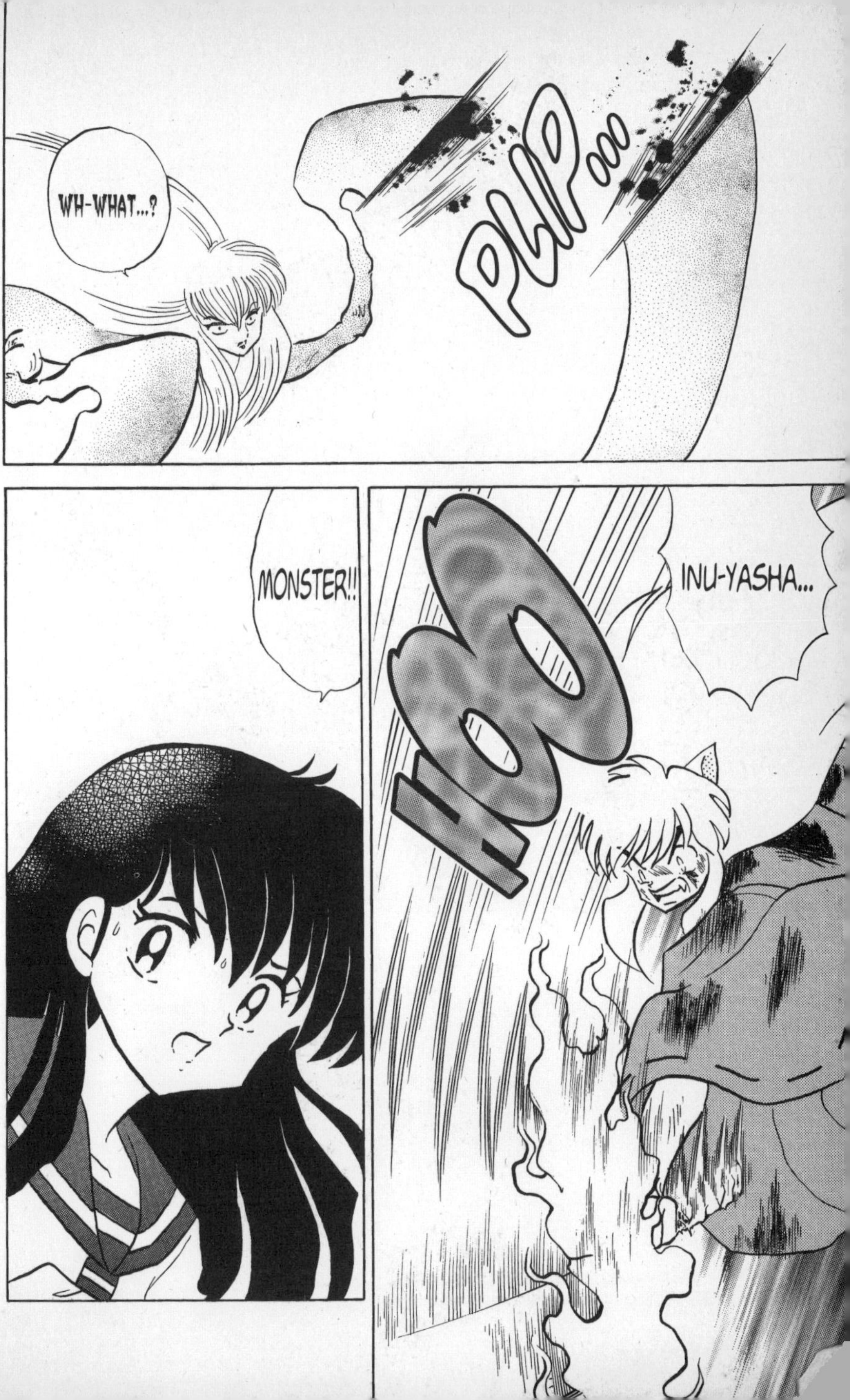
WH-WHAT...?
PLIP...
MONSTER!!
HOO
INU-YASHA...

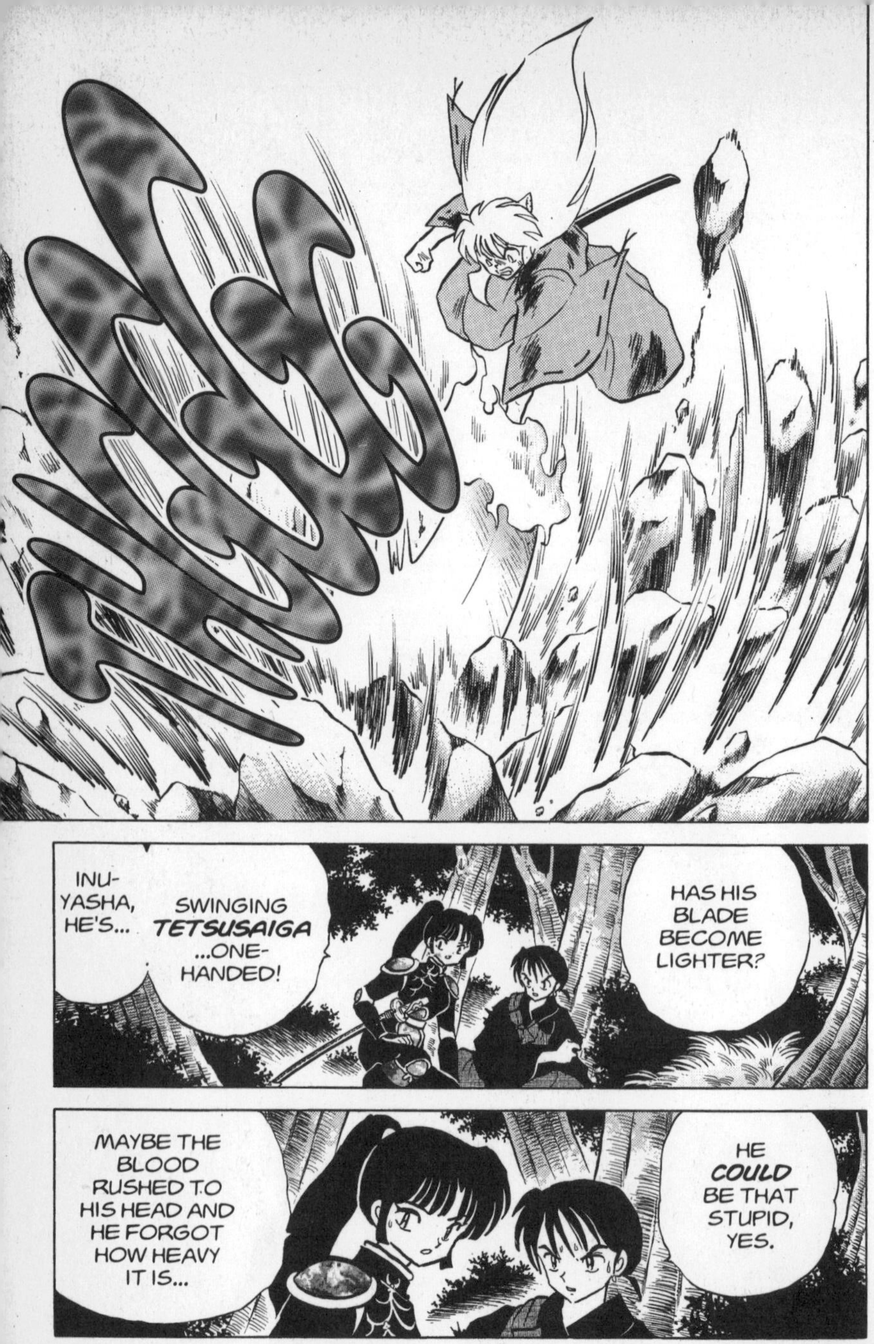
INU-YASHA, HE'S...
SWINGING TETSUSAIGA ...ONE-HANDED!
HAS HIS BLADE BECOME LIGHTER?
MAYBE THE BLOOD RUSHED TO HIS HEAD AND HE FORGOT HOW HEAVY IT IS...
HE COULD BE THAT STUPID, YES.

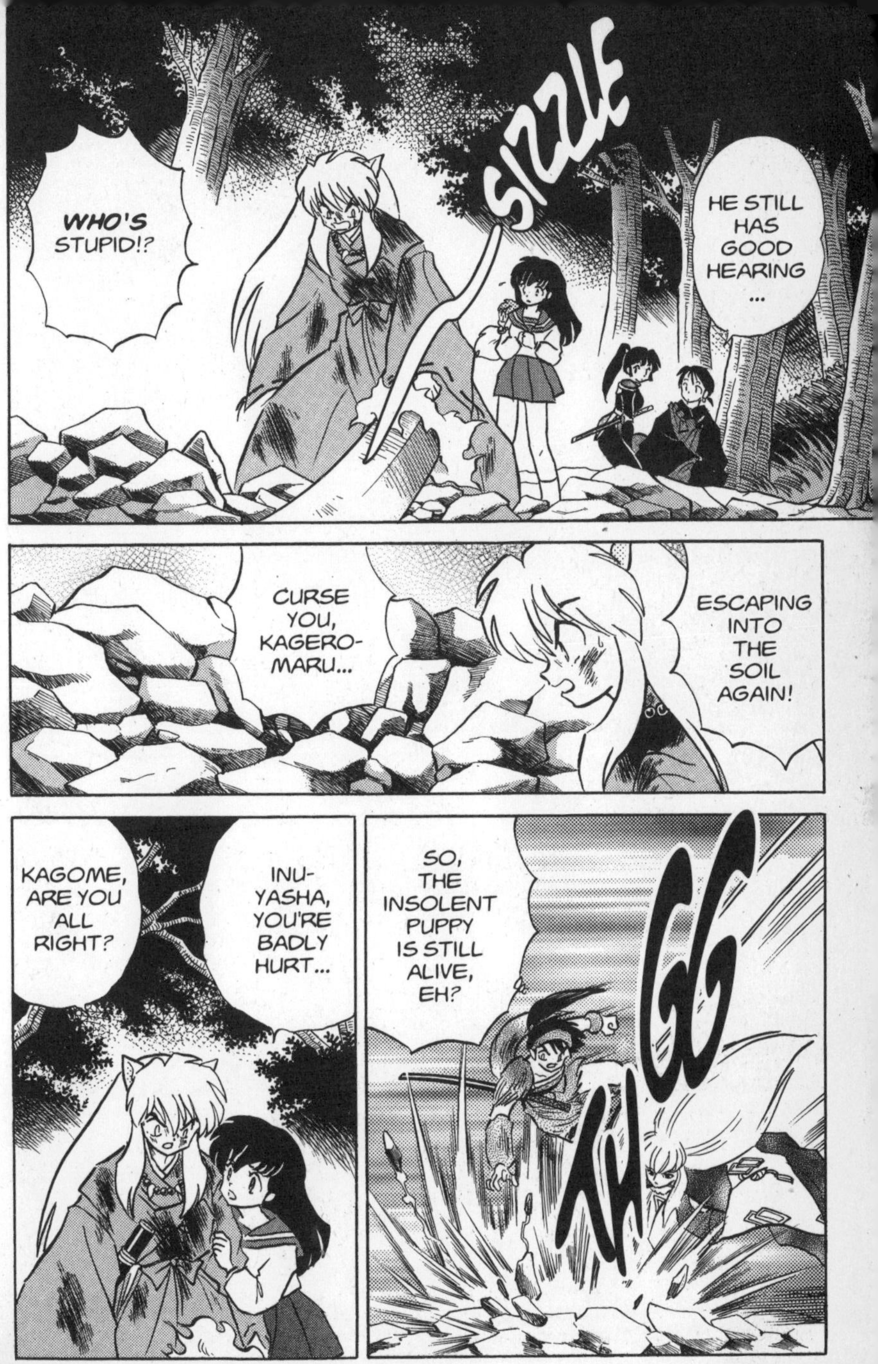
WHO'S STUPID!?
SIZZLE
HE STILL HAS GOOD HEARING ...
CURSE YOU, KAGERO-MARU...
ESCAPING INTO THE SOIL AGAIN!
KAGOME, ARE YOU ALL RIGHT?
INU-YASHA, YOU'RE BADLY HURT...
SO, THE INSOLENT PUPPY IS STILL ALIVE, EH?

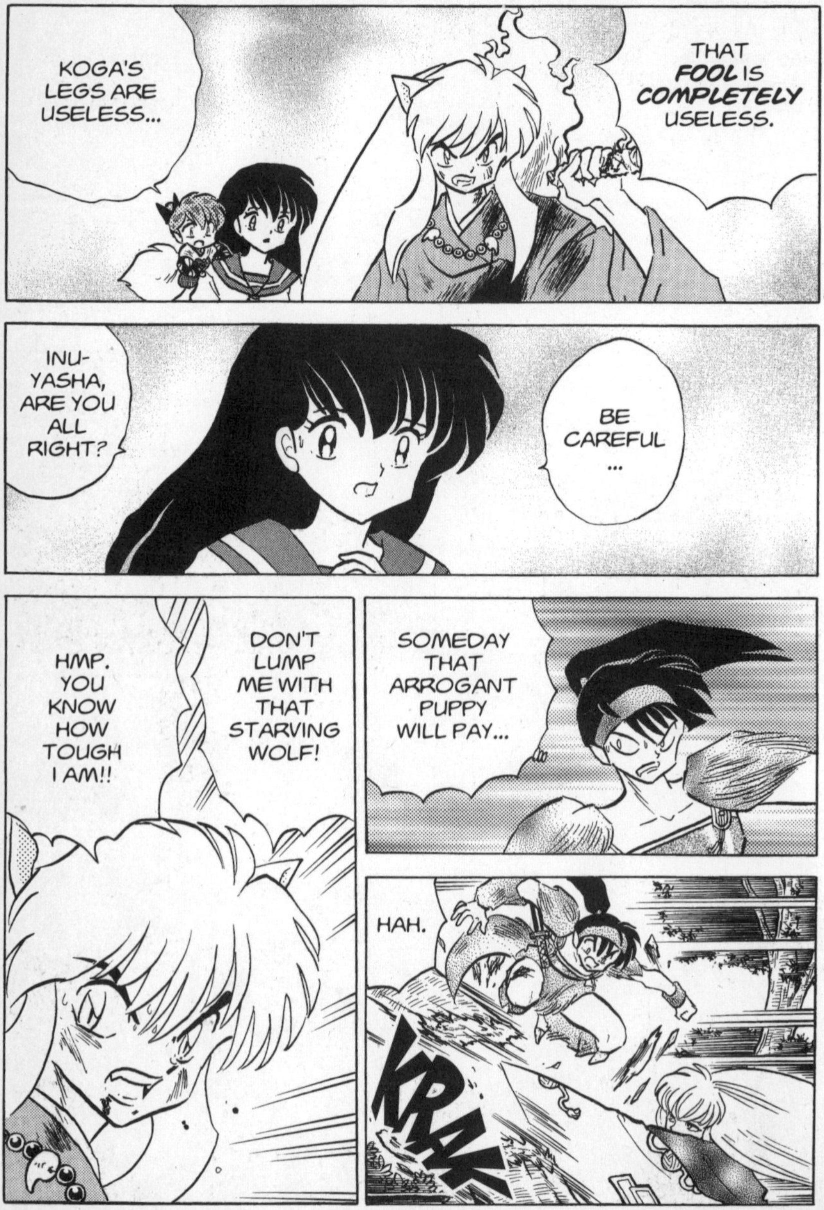
KOGA'S LEGS ARE USELESS...
THAT **FOOL** IS **COMPLETELY** USELESS.
INU-YASHA, ARE YOU ALL RIGHT?
BE CAREFUL ...
HMP. YOU KNOW HOW TOUGH I AM!!
DON'T LUMP ME WITH THAT STARVING WOLF!
SOMEDAY THAT ARROGANT PUPPY WILL PAY...
HAH.
KRAK

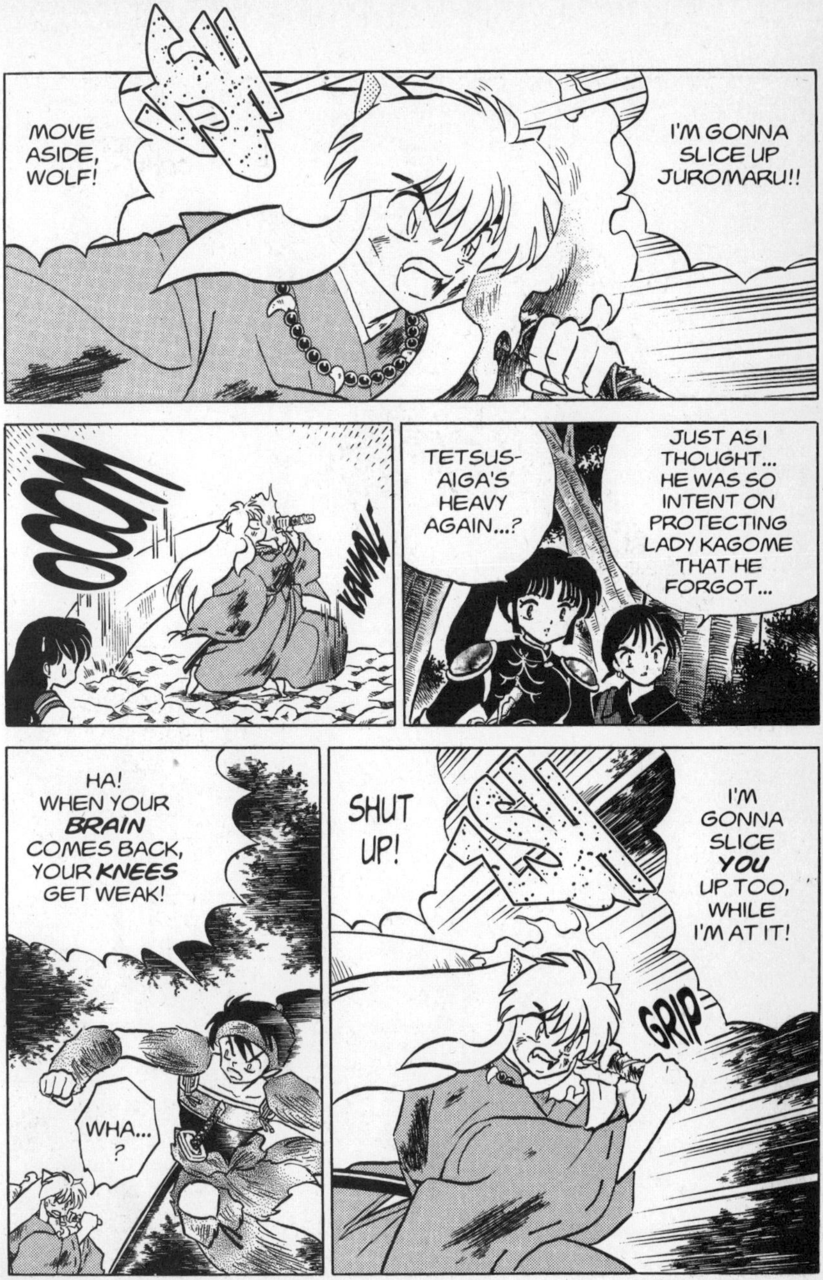
MOVE ASIDE, WOLF!
I'M GONNA SLICE UP JUROMARU!!
TETSUS-AIGA'S HEAVY AGAIN...?
JUST AS I THOUGHT... HE WAS SO INTENT ON PROTECTING LADY KAGOME THAT HE FORGOT...
HA! WHEN YOUR **BRAIN** COMES BACK, YOUR **KNEES** GET WEAK!
WHA... ?
SHUT UP!
I'M GONNA SLICE **YOU** UP TOO, WHILE I'M AT IT!
GRIP

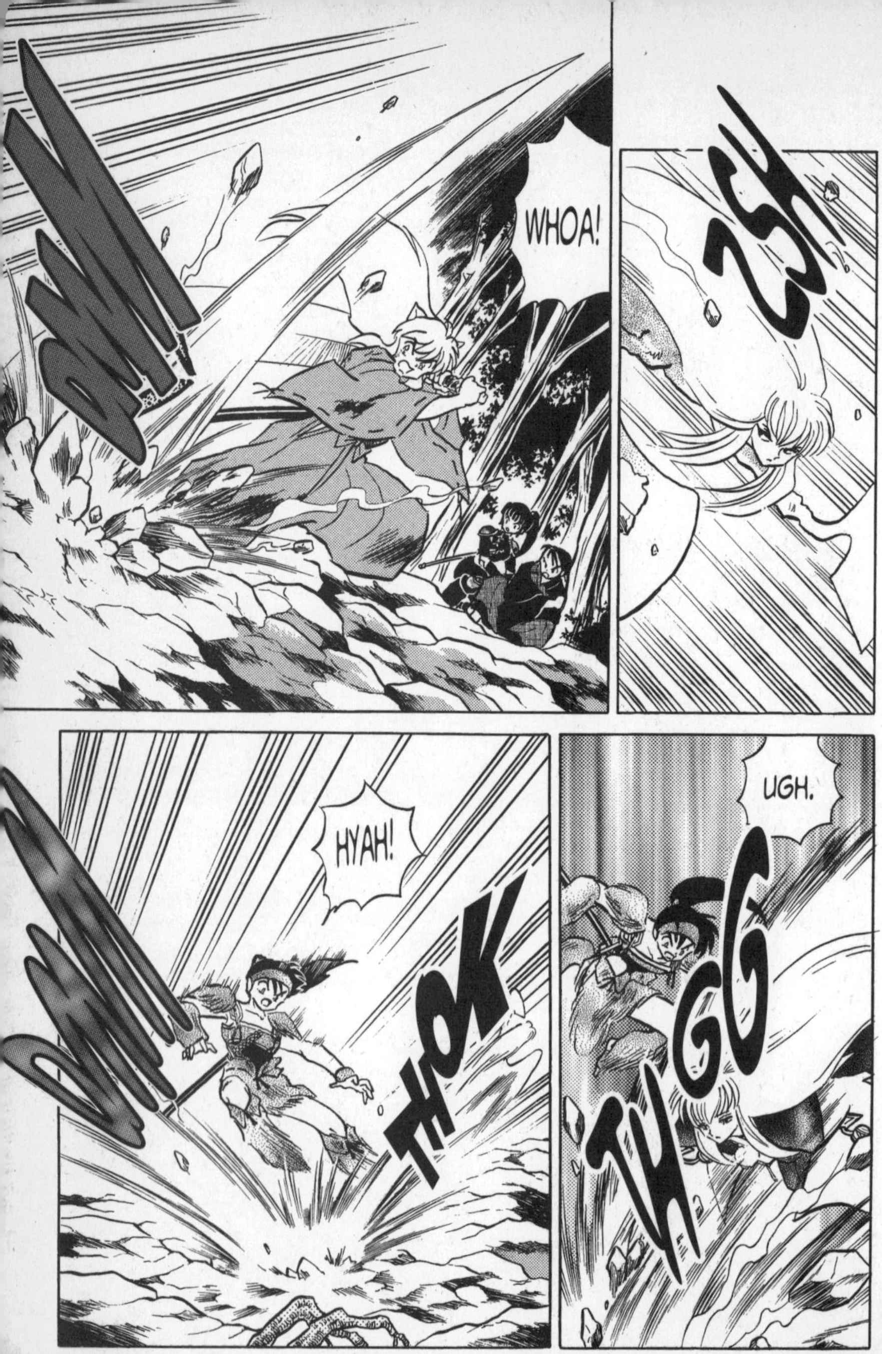
WHOA!
ZSH
HYAH!
THOK
UGH.
THGG

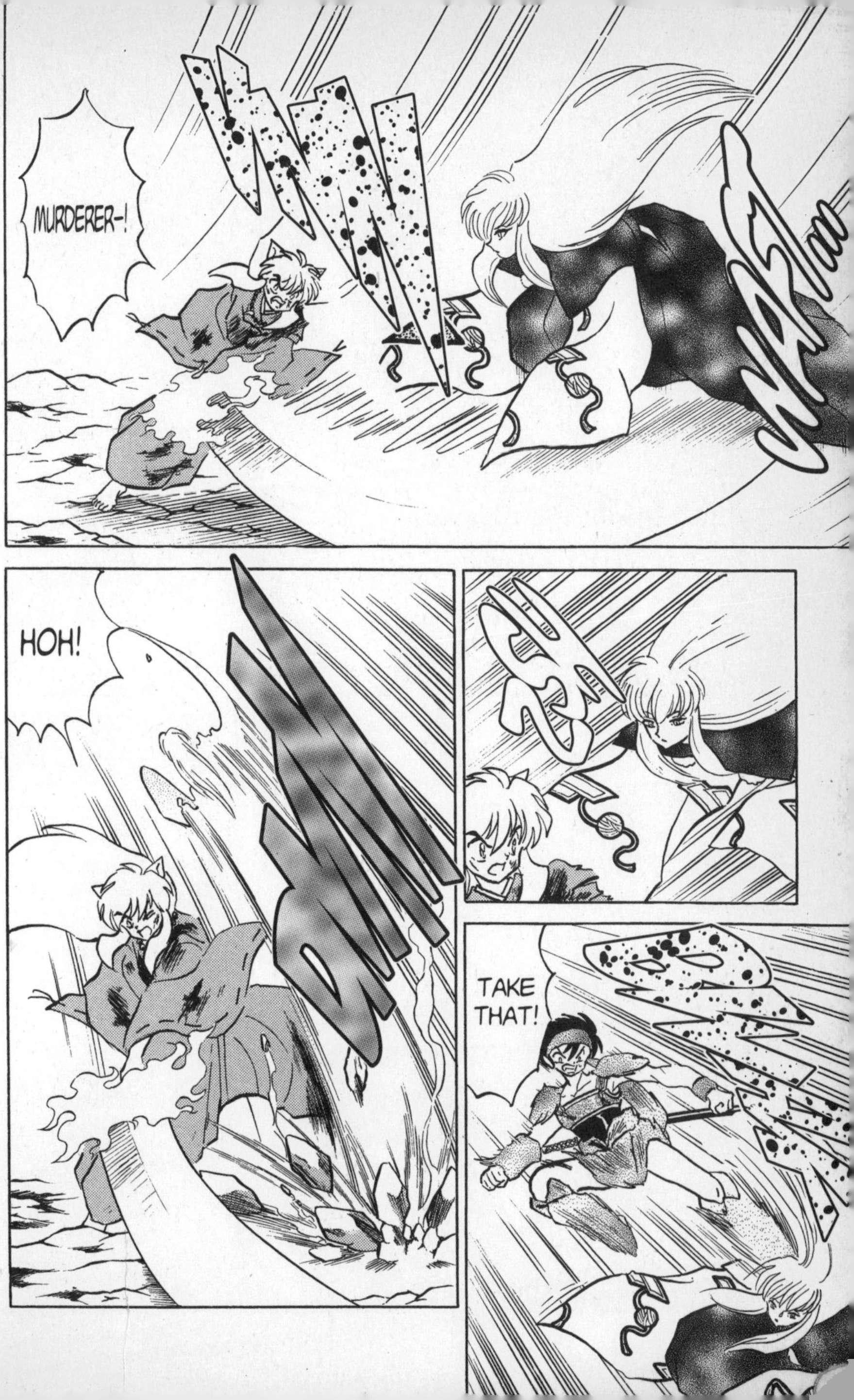
MURDERER-!
HOH!
TAKE THAT!

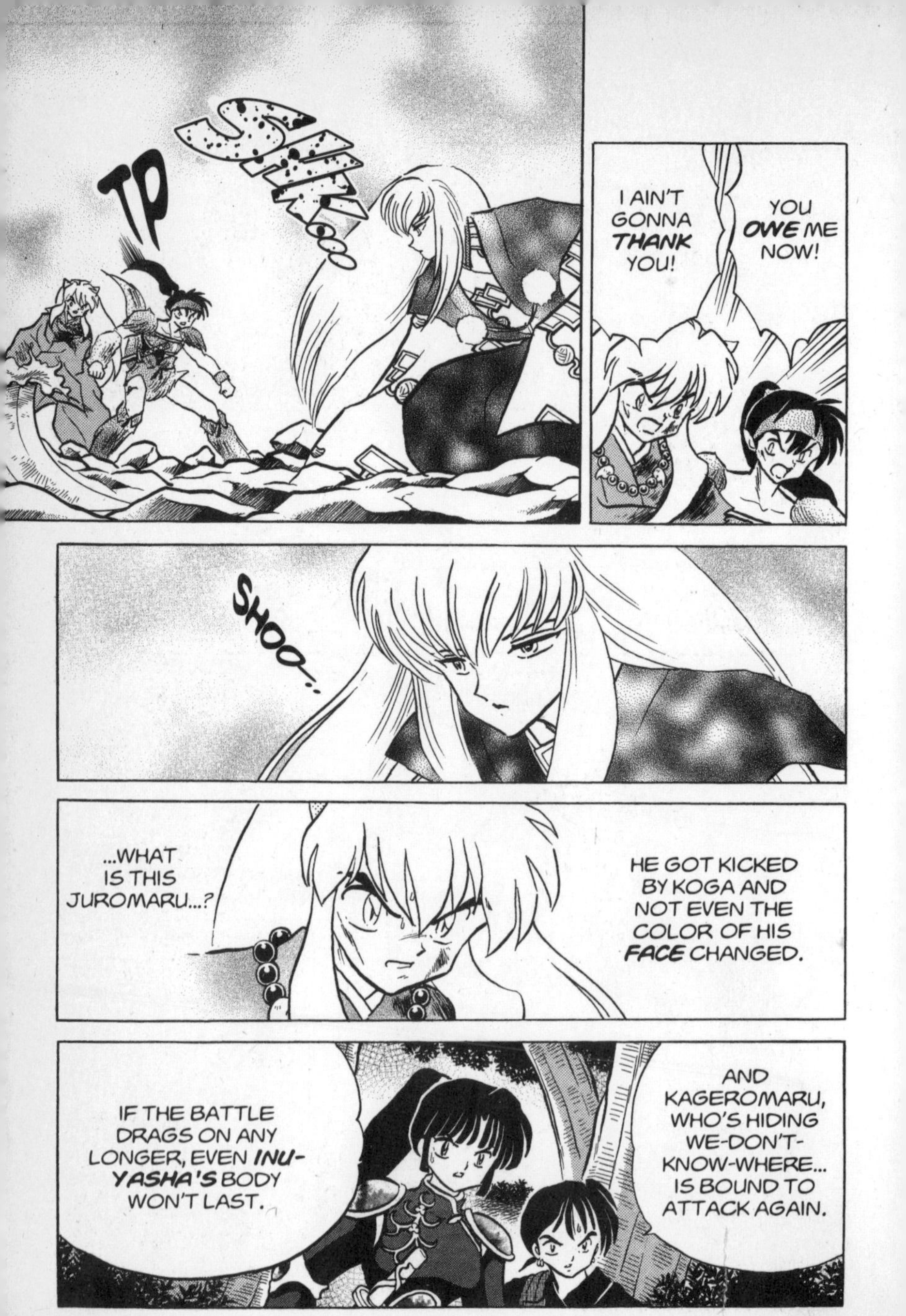
TP
SHK
SHOOO
I AIN'T GONNA THANK YOU!
YOU OWE ME NOW!
SHOO...
...WHAT IS THIS JUROMARU...?
HE GOT KICKED BY KOGA AND NOT EVEN THE COLOR OF HIS FACE CHANGED.
IF THE BATTLE DRAGS ON ANY LONGER, EVEN INU-YASHA'S BODY WON'T LAST.
AND KAGEROMARU, WHO'S HIDING WE-DON'T-KNOW-WHERE... IS BOUND TO ATTACK AGAIN.

THAT'S IT!

IF I COULD JUST NULLIFY KAGEROMARU ALONE...

MONK, LEND ME YOUR STAFF!

YOU HAVE AN IDEA...?

KWIP

RATTLE

THIS POISON... IT DOESN'T LAST TOO LONG, BUT...

IT PROBABLY CAN CHASE KAGEROMARU OUT INTO THE OPEN!

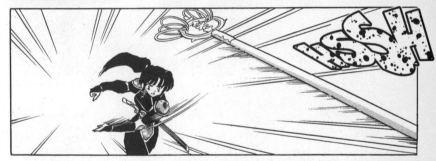

HISSH!!

RATTLE

THKK

SHH
SIZZLE
SHHH

THE SOIL'S TURNING *RED*...

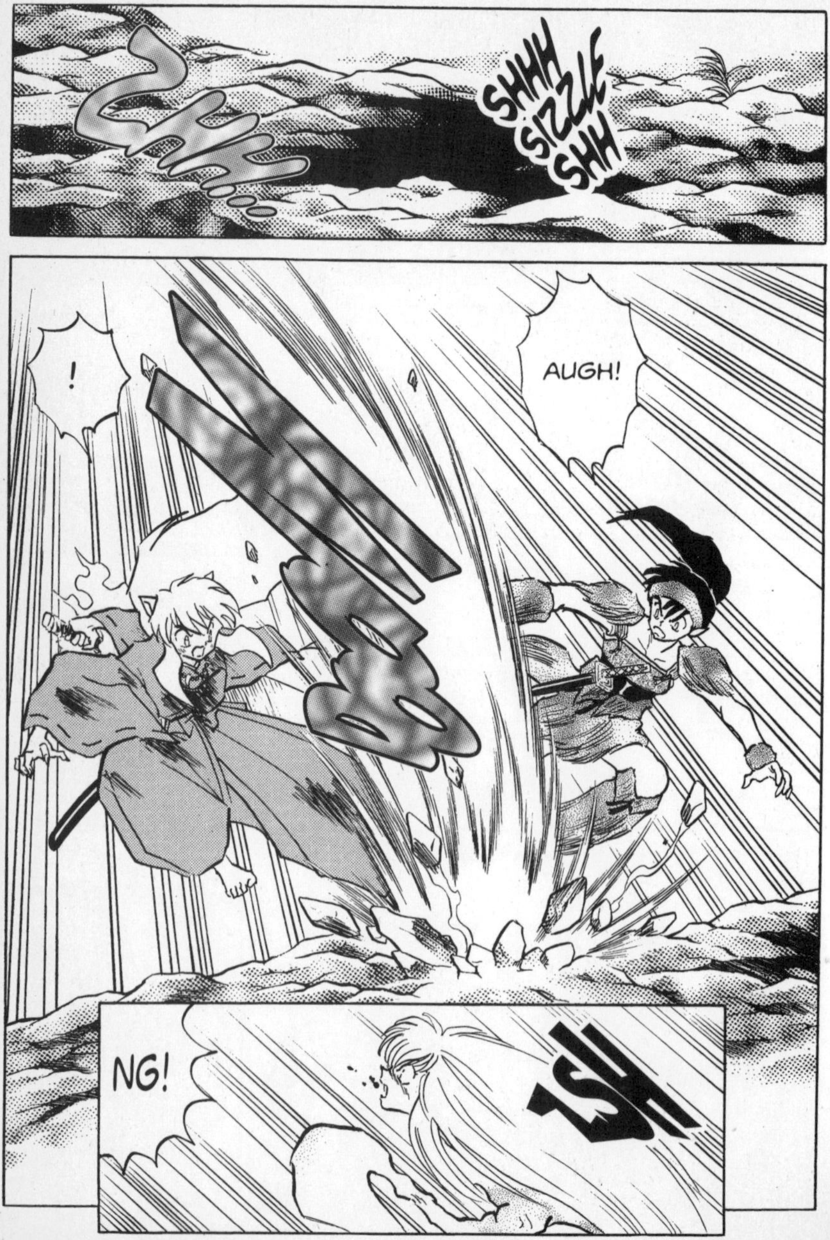
SHHH SIZZLE SHH
!
AUGH!
NG!

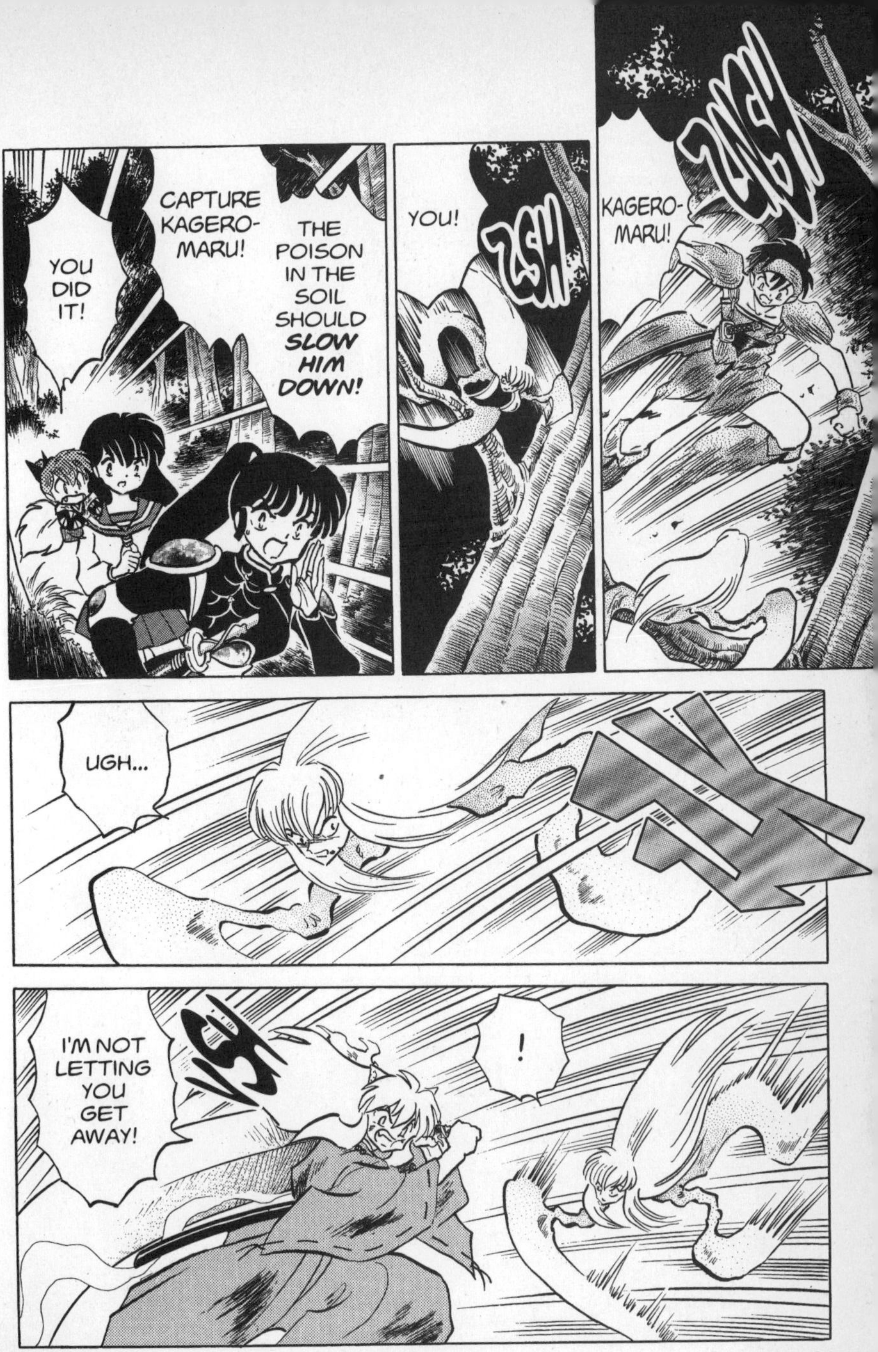
YOU DID IT!
CAPTURE KAGERO-MARU!
THE POISON IN THE SOIL SHOULD SLOW HIM DOWN!
YOU!
ZSH
KAGERO-MARU!
UGH...
I'M NOT LETTING YOU GET AWAY!
!

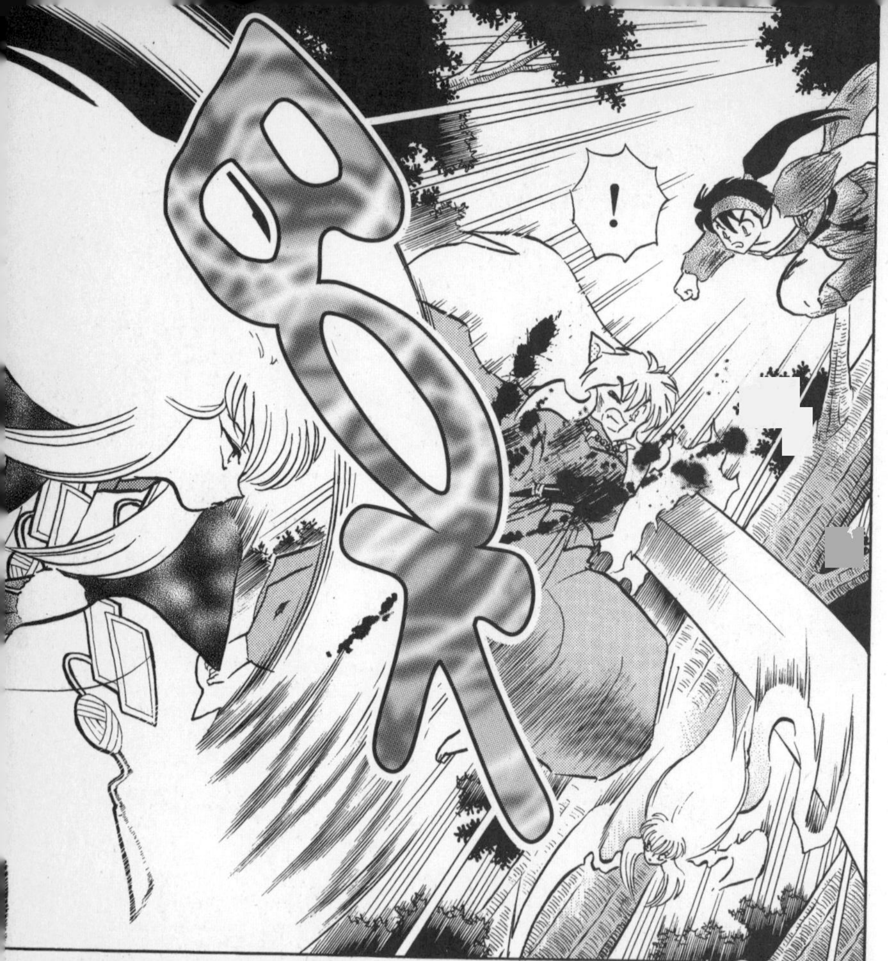
BOF
!

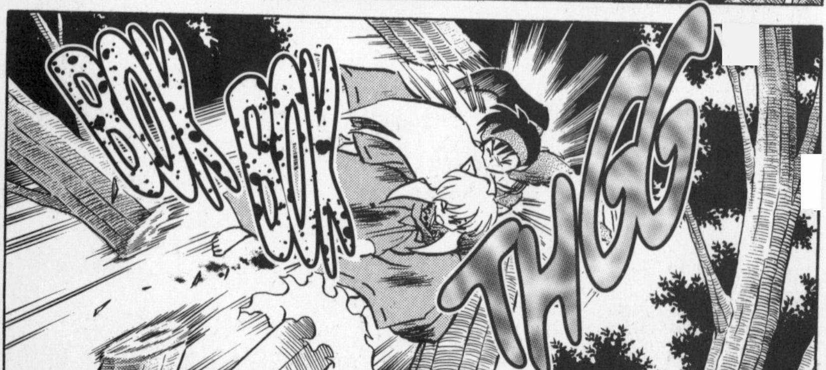
BOK BOK

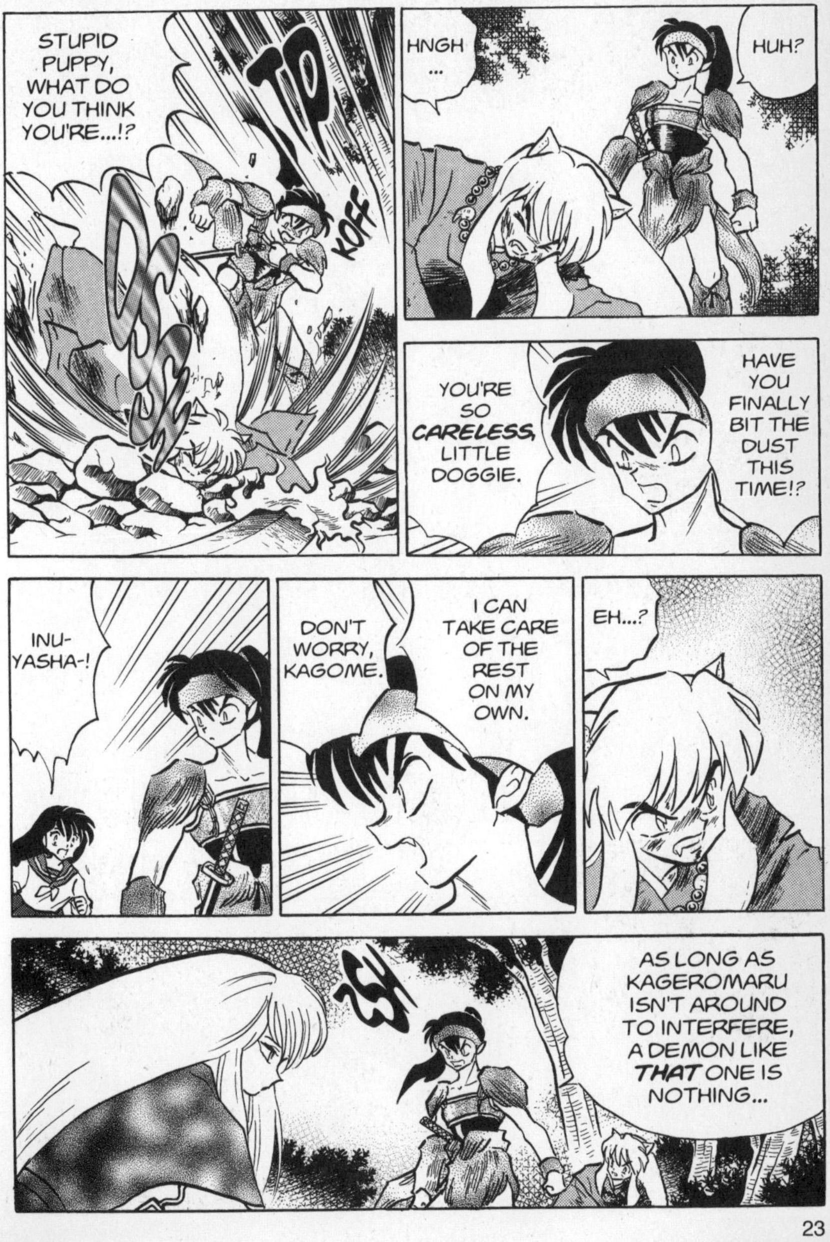
STUPID PUPPY, WHAT DO YOU THINK YOU'RE...!?
TIP
KOFF
HNGH ...
HUH?
YOU'RE SO ***CARELESS***, LITTLE DOGGIE.
HAVE YOU FINALLY BIT THE DUST THIS TIME!?
INU-YASHA-!
DON'T WORRY, KAGOME.
I CAN TAKE CARE OF THE REST ON MY OWN.
EH...?
ZSH
AS LONG AS KAGEROMARU ISN'T AROUND TO INTERFERE, A DEMON LIKE ***THAT*** ONE IS NOTHING...

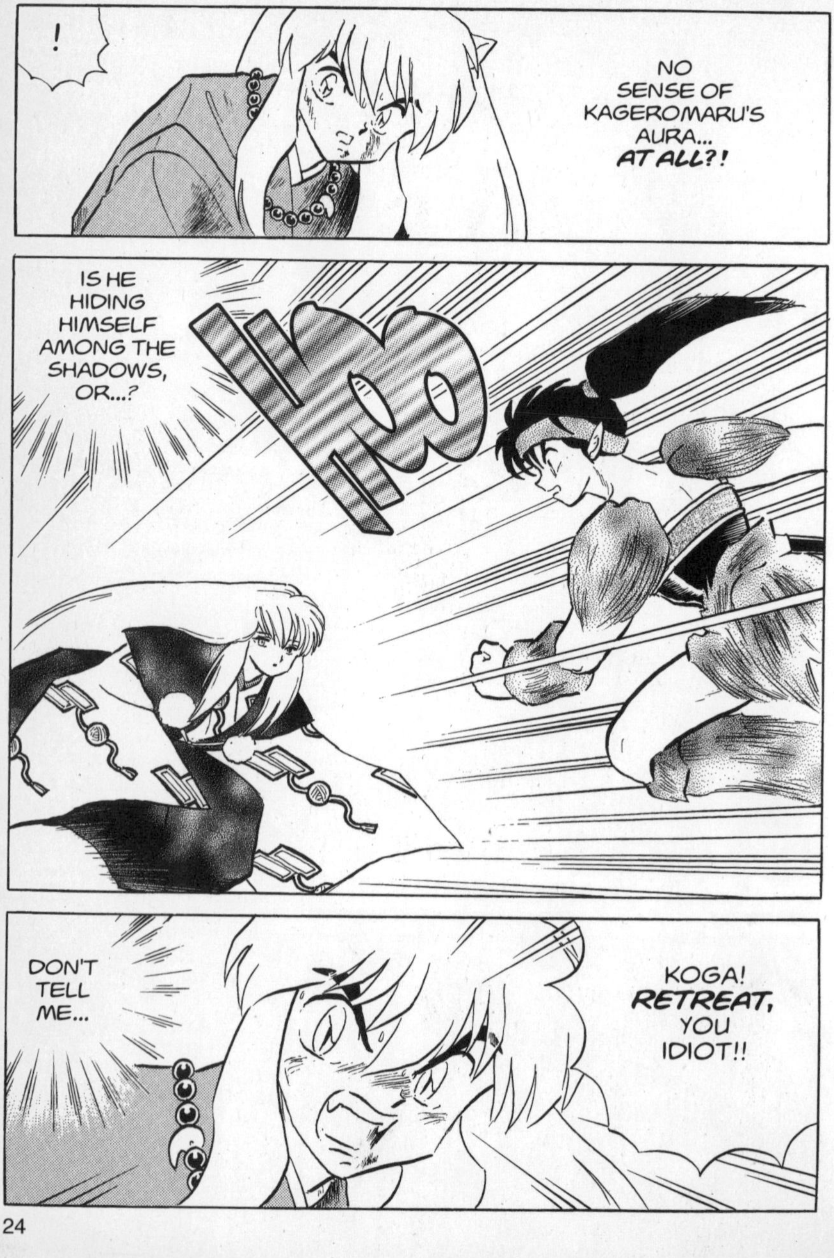
!
NO SENSE OF KAGEROMARU'S AURA... AT ALL?!
IS HE HIDING HIMSELF AMONG THE SHADOWS, OR...?
DON'T TELL ME...
KOGA! RETREAT, YOU IDIOT!!

SCROLL TWO
PULVERIZED

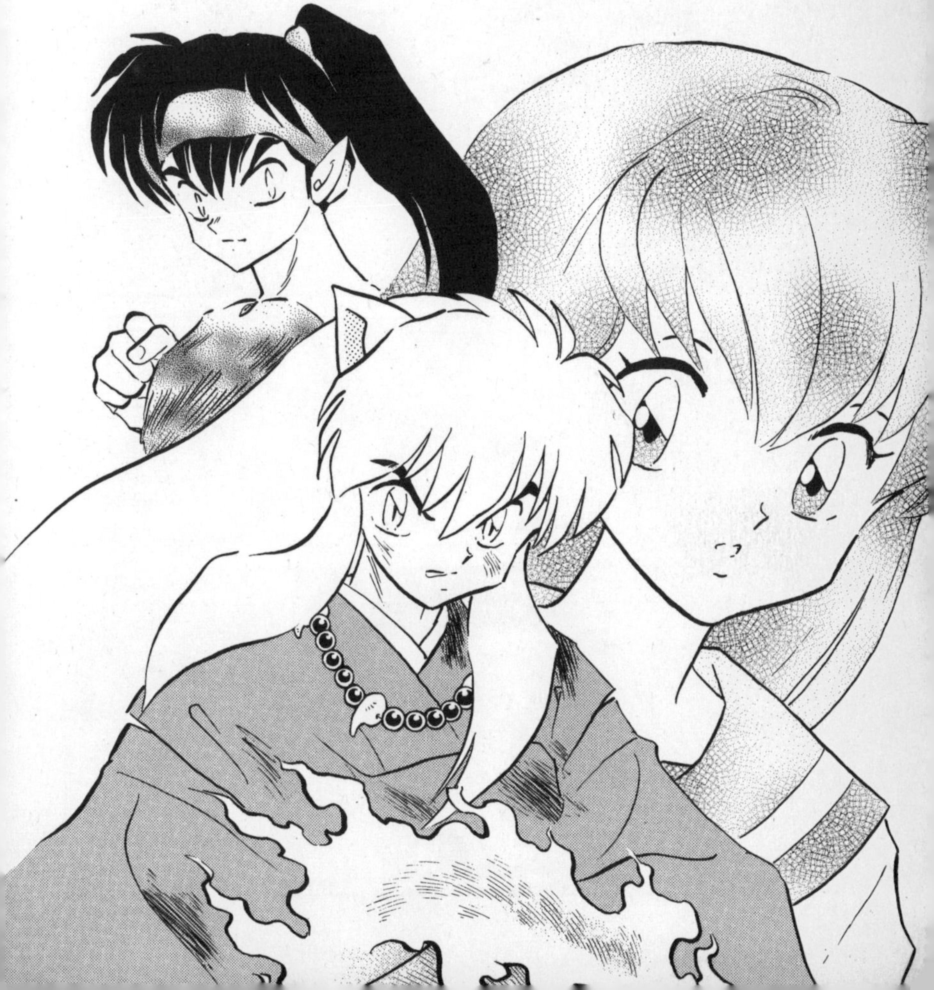

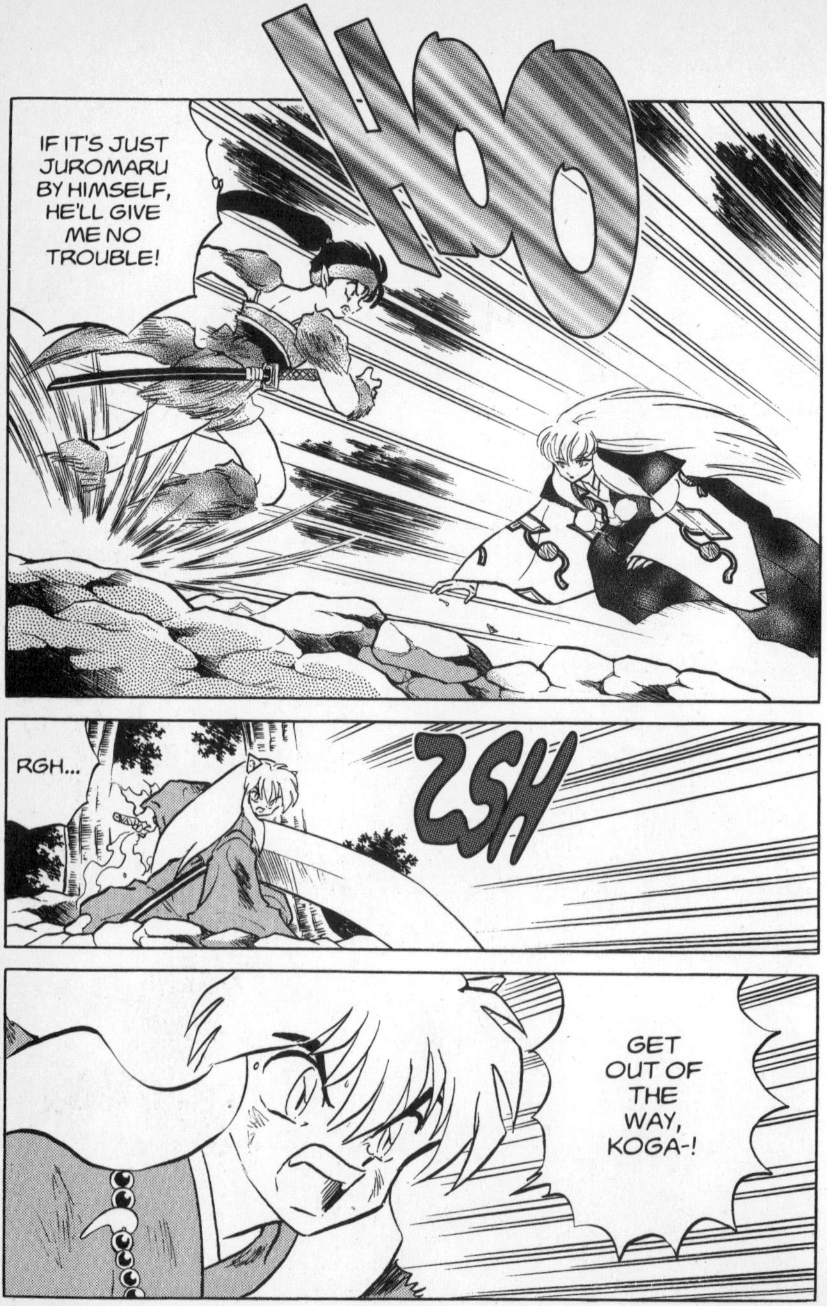
HOO
IF IT'S JUST JUROMARU BY HIMSELF, HE'LL GIVE ME NO TROUBLE!
RGH...
ZSH
GET OUT OF THE WAY, KOGA-!

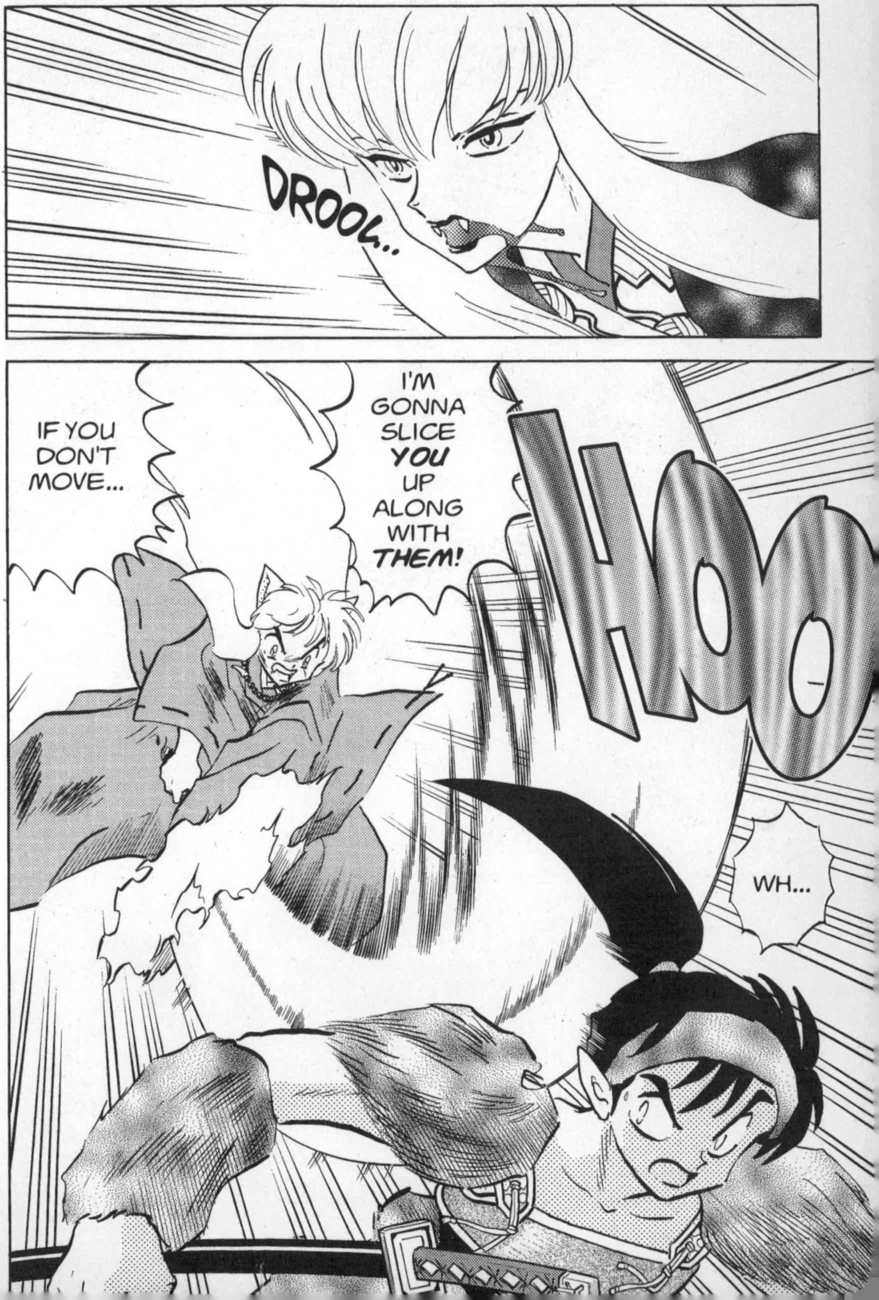

DROOL...
IF YOU DON'T MOVE...
I'M GONNA SLICE *YOU* UP ALONG WITH *THEM!*
WHOO
WH...

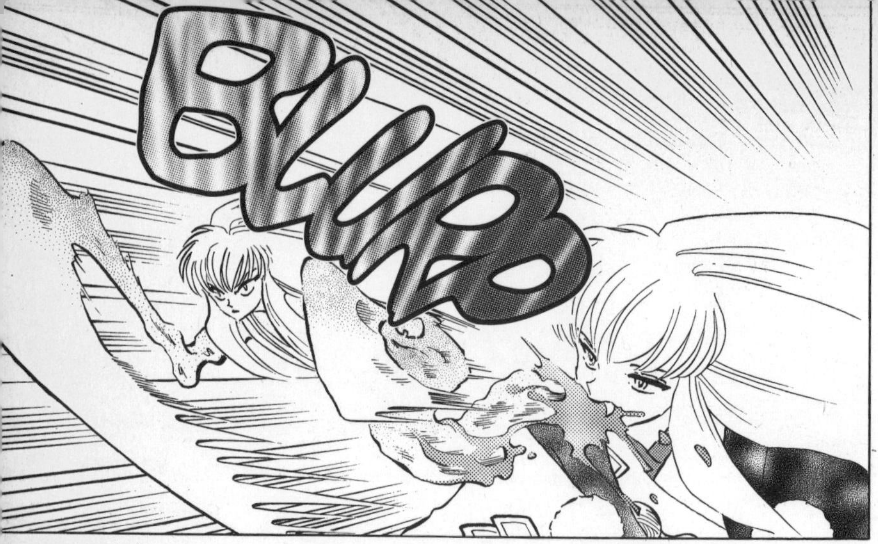

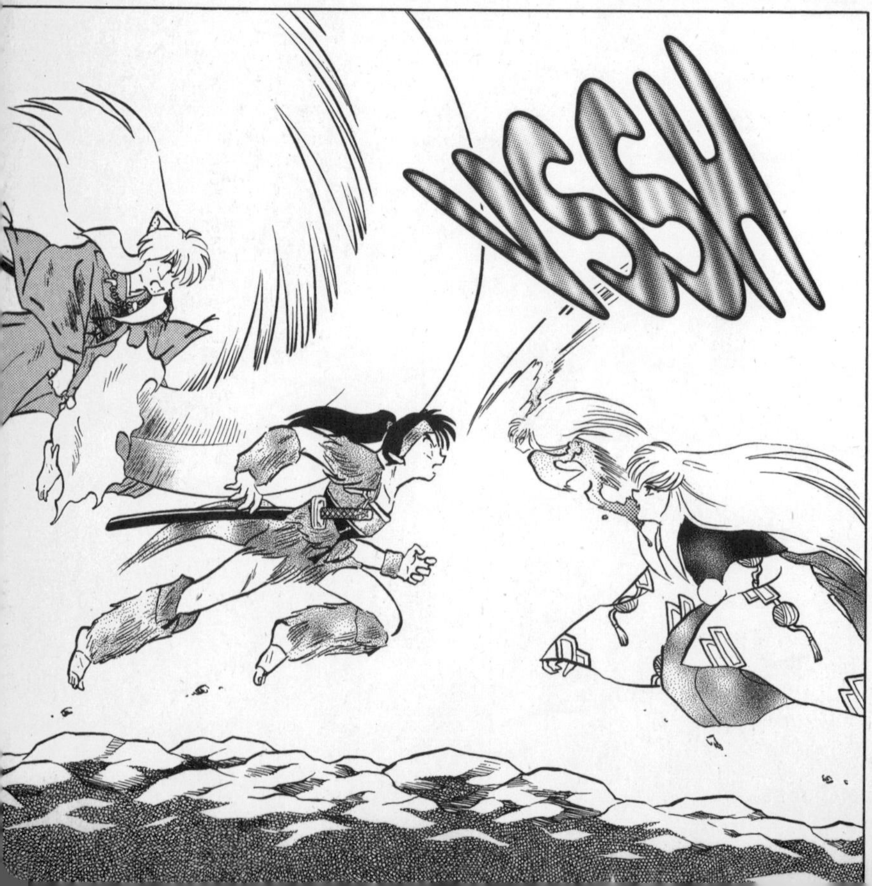
VSSH

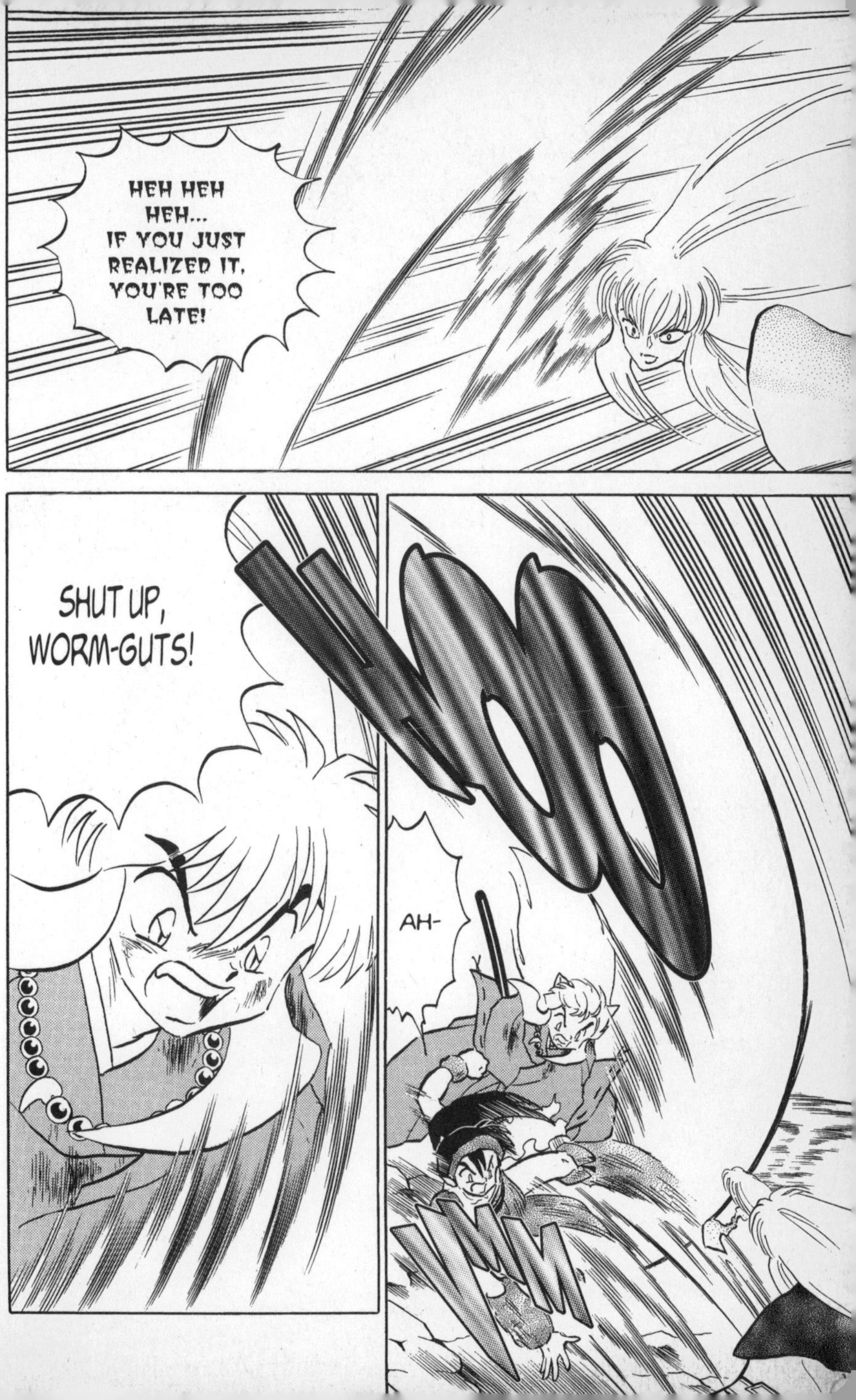
HEH HEH HEH... IF YOU JUST REALIZED IT, YOU'RE TOO LATE!
SHUT UP, WORM-GUTS!
AH-

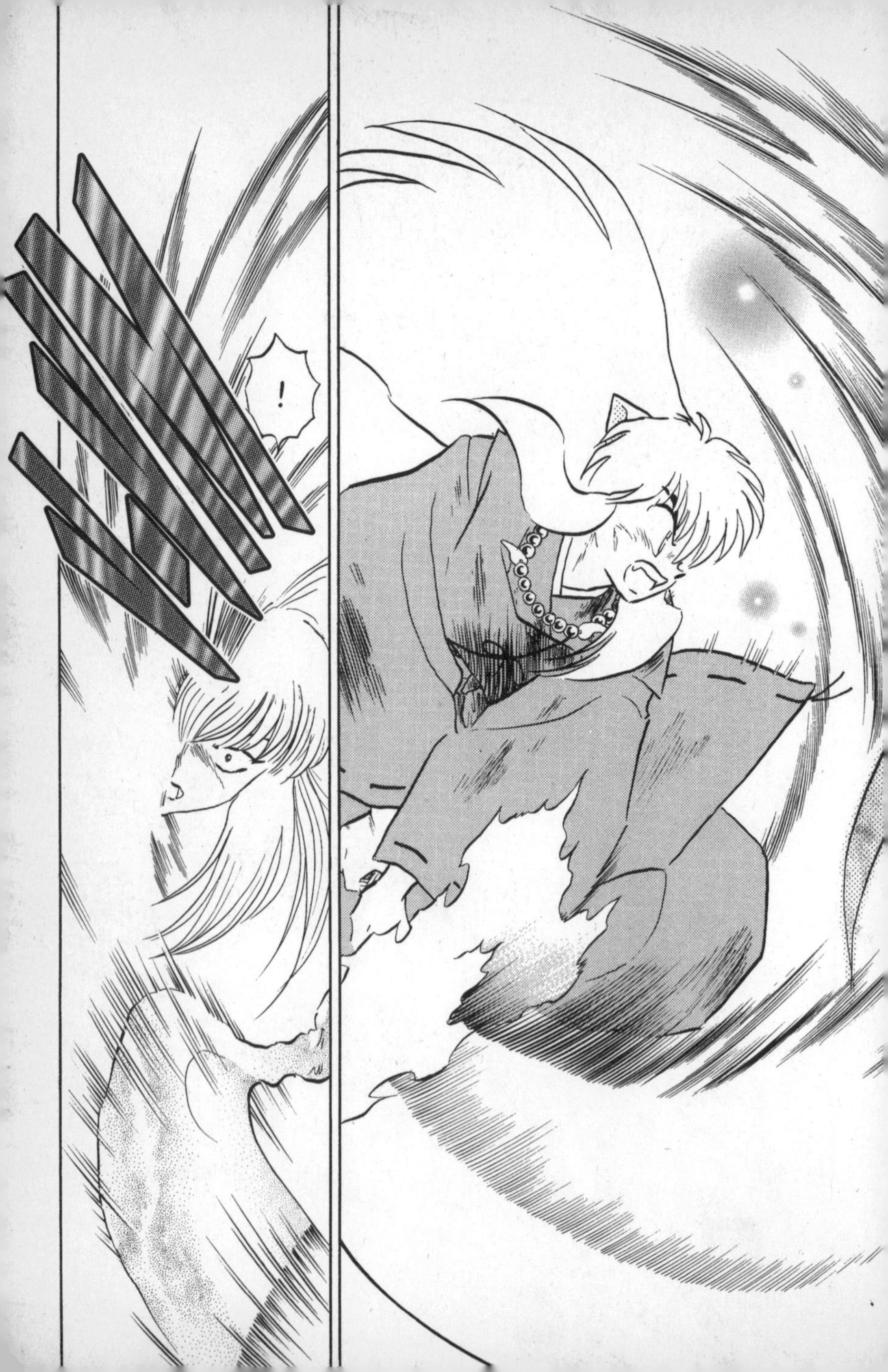
!

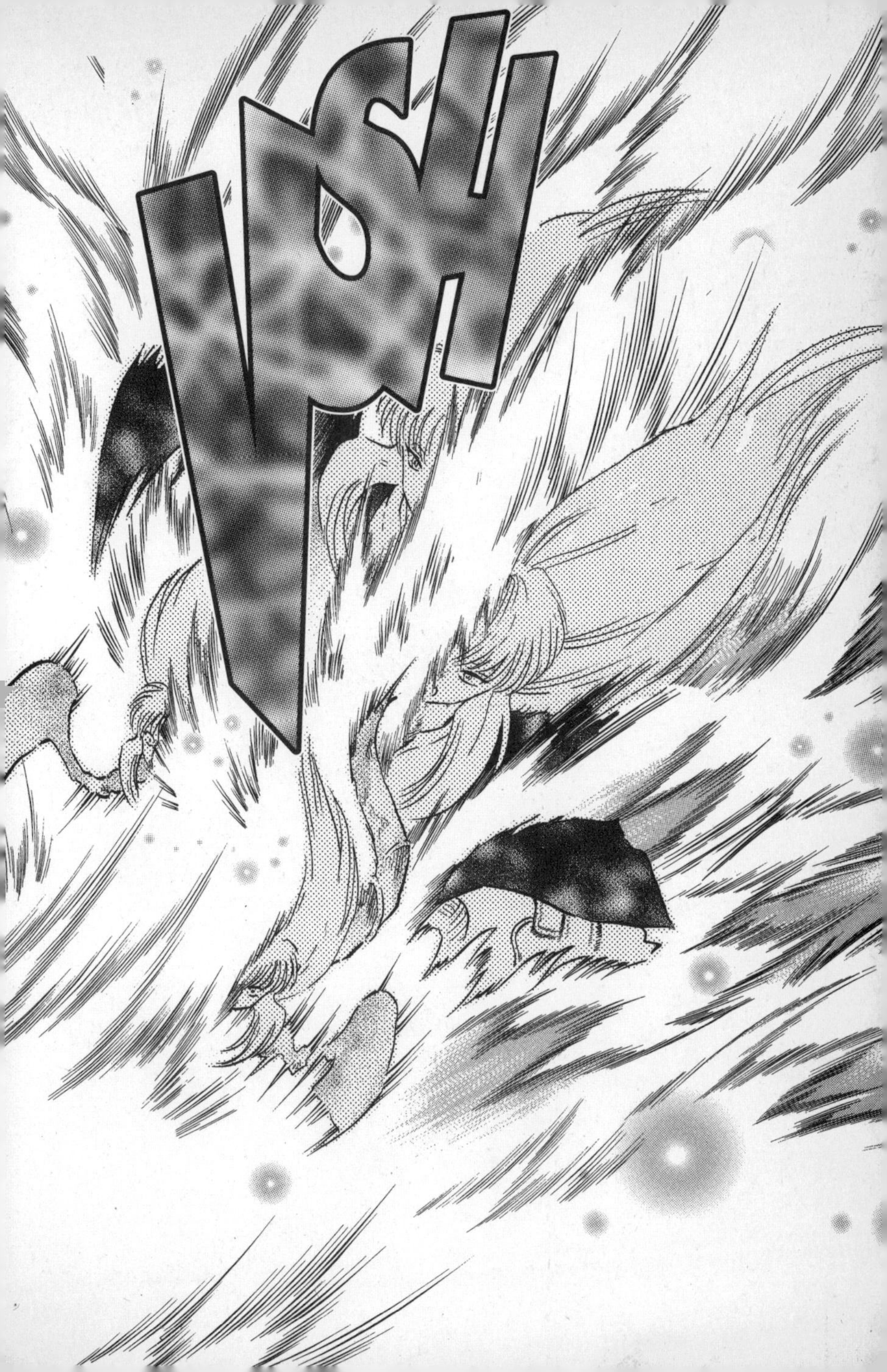
VSH

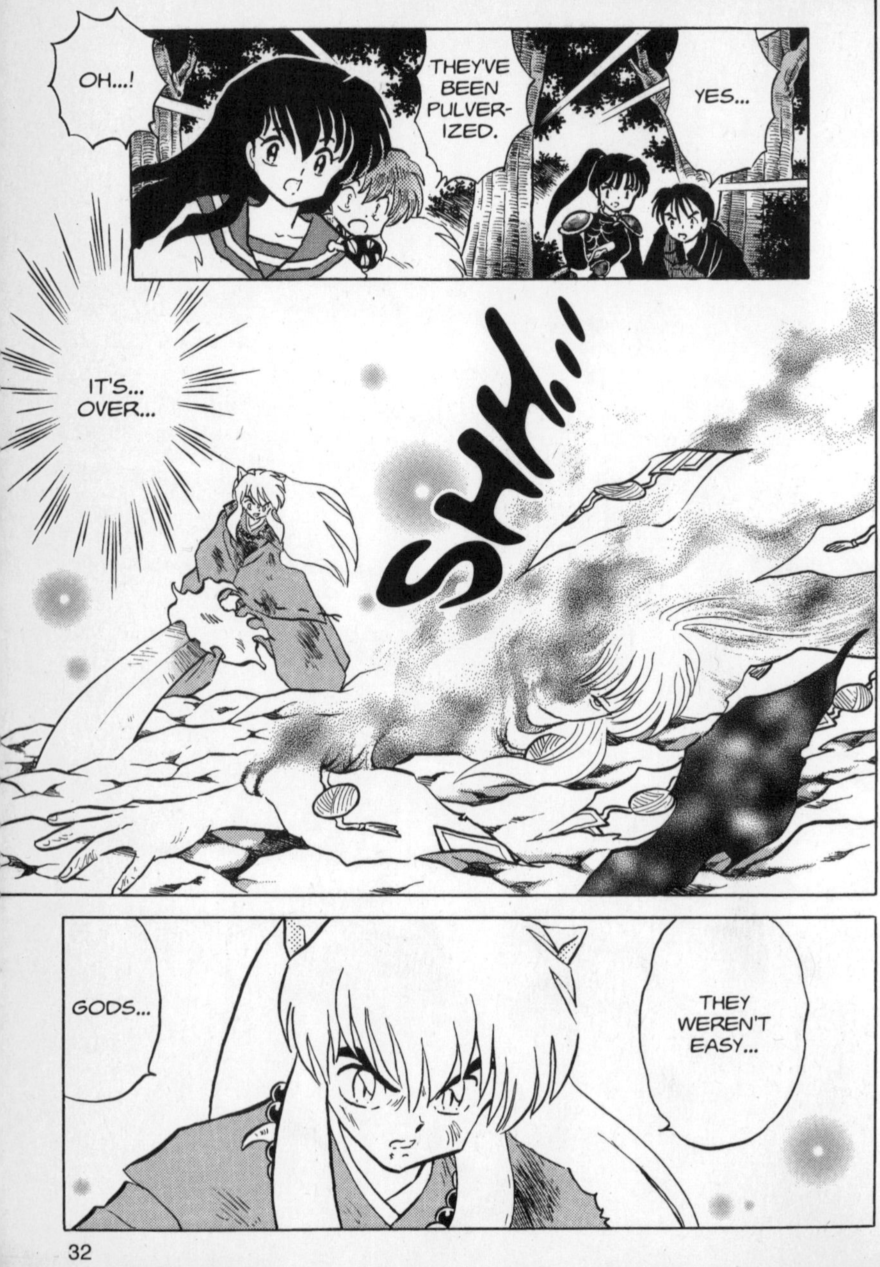
OH...!
THEY'VE BEEN PULVER-IZED.
YES...
IT'S... OVER...
SHH...
GODS...
THEY WEREN'T EASY...

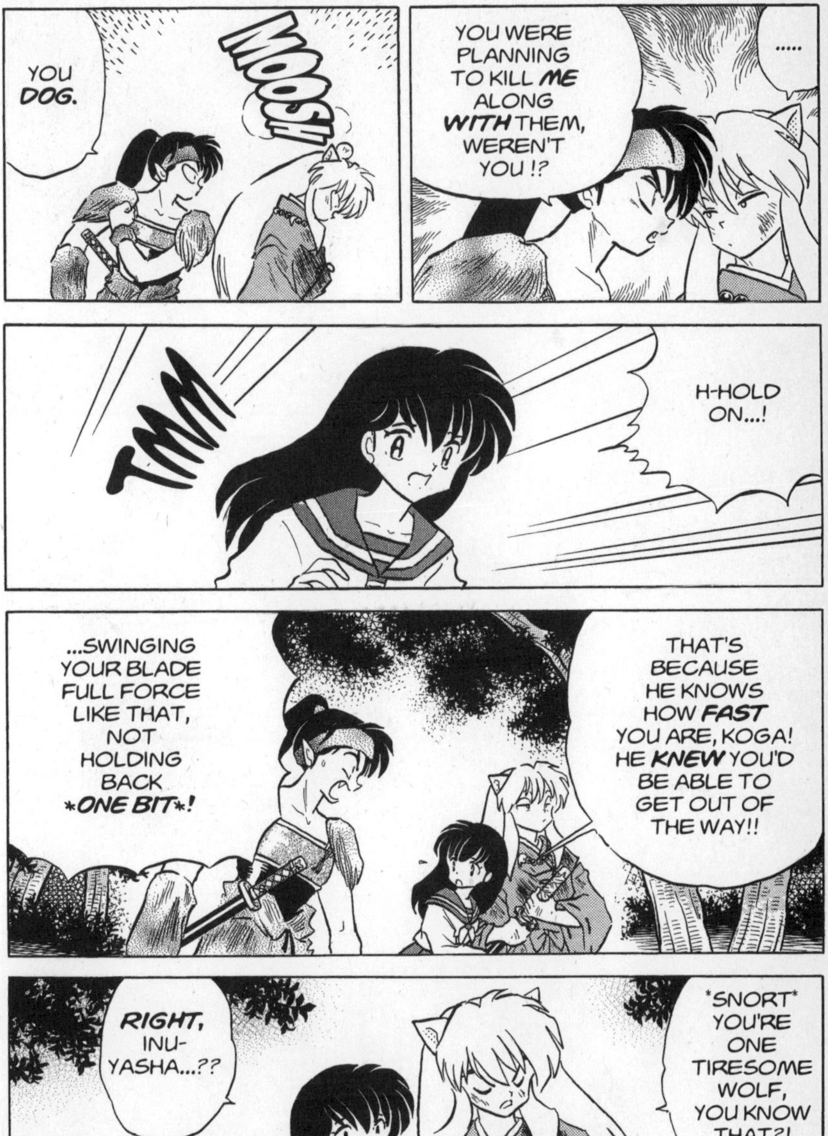

YOU DOG.
WOOSH
YOU WERE PLANNING TO KILL ME ALONG WITH THEM, WEREN'T YOU !?
.....
TMM
H-HOLD ON...!
...SWINGING YOUR BLADE FULL FORCE LIKE THAT, NOT HOLDING BACK *ONE BIT*!
THAT'S BECAUSE HE KNOWS HOW FAST YOU ARE, KOGA! HE KNEW YOU'D BE ABLE TO GET OUT OF THE WAY!!
RIGHT, INU-YASHA...??
SNORT YOU'RE ONE TIRESOME WOLF, YOU KNOW THAT?!

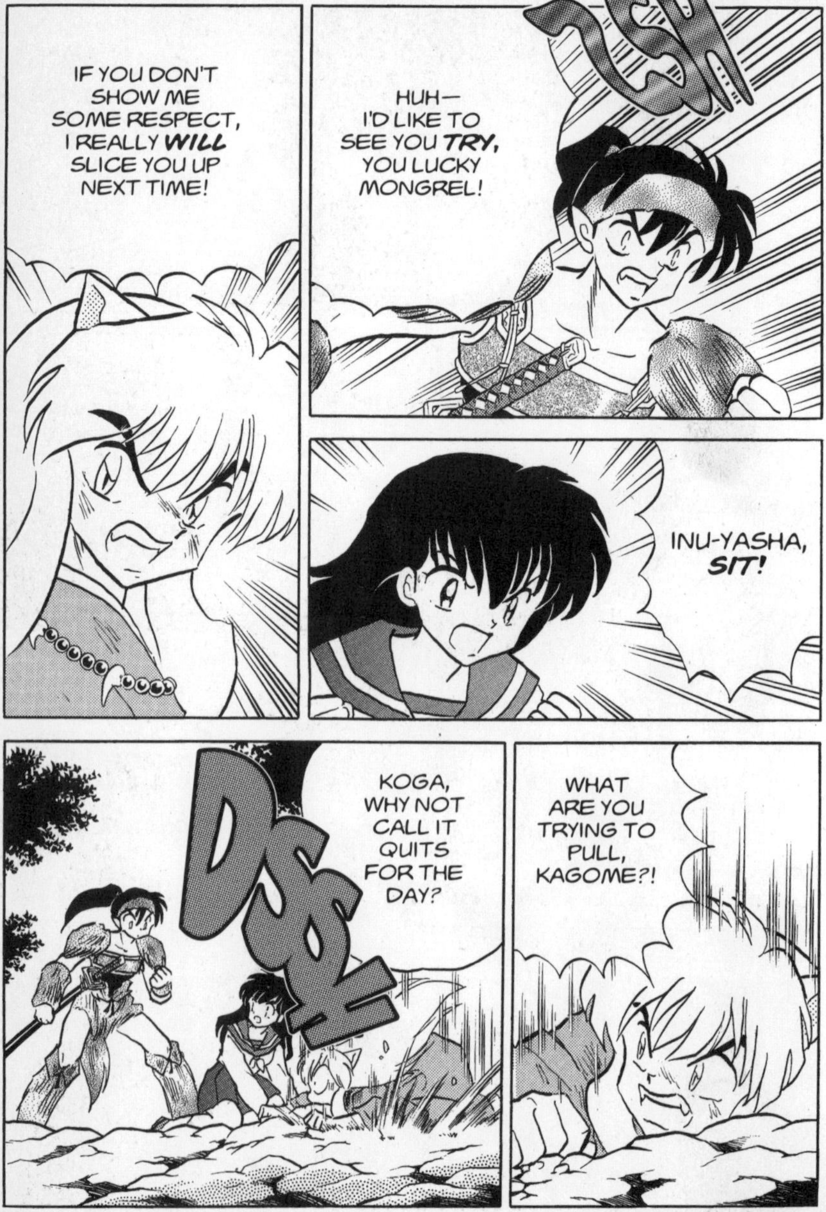
IF YOU DON'T SHOW ME SOME RESPECT, I REALLY **WILL** SLICE YOU UP NEXT TIME!
ZSH
HUH— I'D LIKE TO SEE YOU **TRY**, YOU LUCKY MONGREL!
INU-YASHA, **SIT!**
KOGA, WHY NOT CALL IT QUITS FOR THE DAY?
WHAT ARE YOU TRYING TO PULL, KAGOME?!

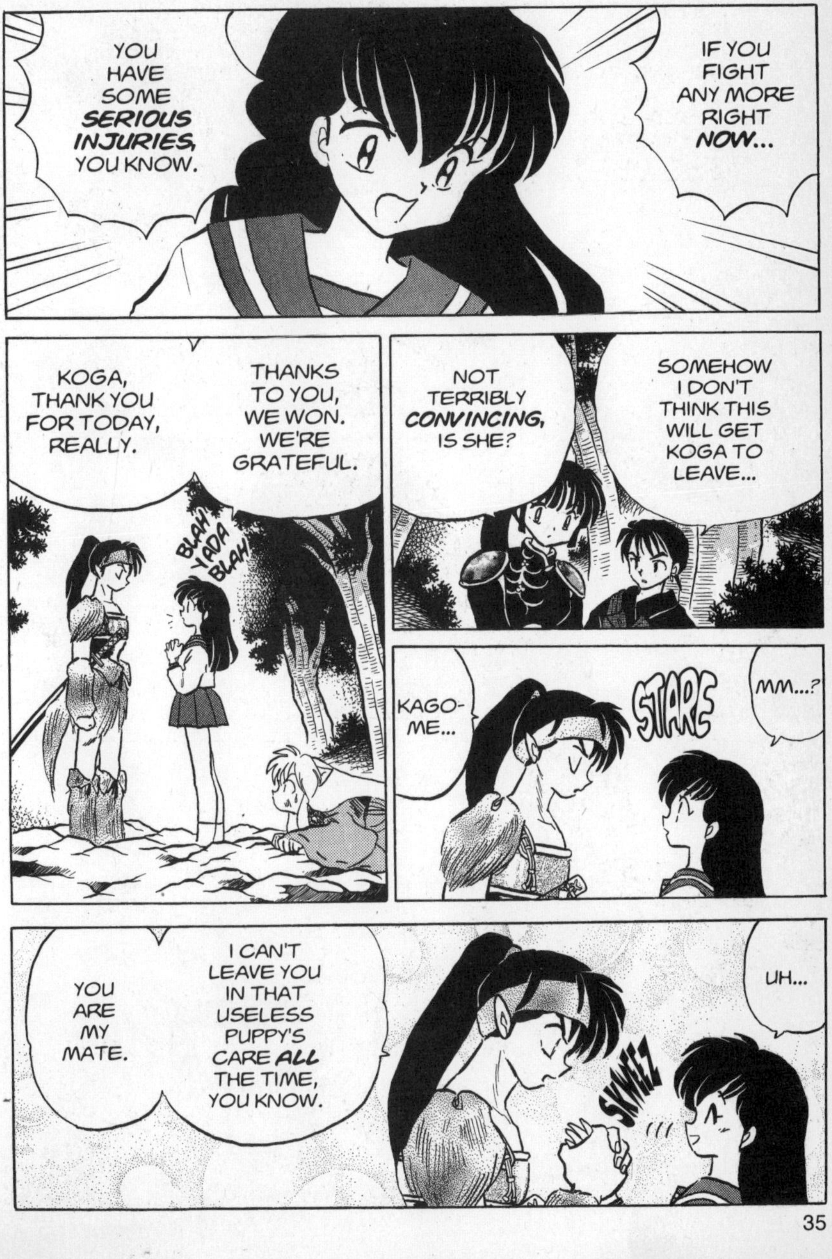
YOU HAVE SOME SERIOUS INJURIES, YOU KNOW.
IF YOU FIGHT ANY MORE RIGHT NOW...
KOGA, THANK YOU FOR TODAY, REALLY.
THANKS TO YOU, WE WON. WE'RE GRATEFUL.
BLAH YADA BLAH
NOT TERRIBLY CONVINCING, IS SHE?
SOMEHOW I DON'T THINK THIS WILL GET KOGA TO LEAVE...
KAGO-ME...
STARE
MM...?
YOU ARE MY MATE.
I CAN'T LEAVE YOU IN THAT USELESS PUPPY'S CARE ALL THE TIME, YOU KNOW.
UH...
SKWEEZ

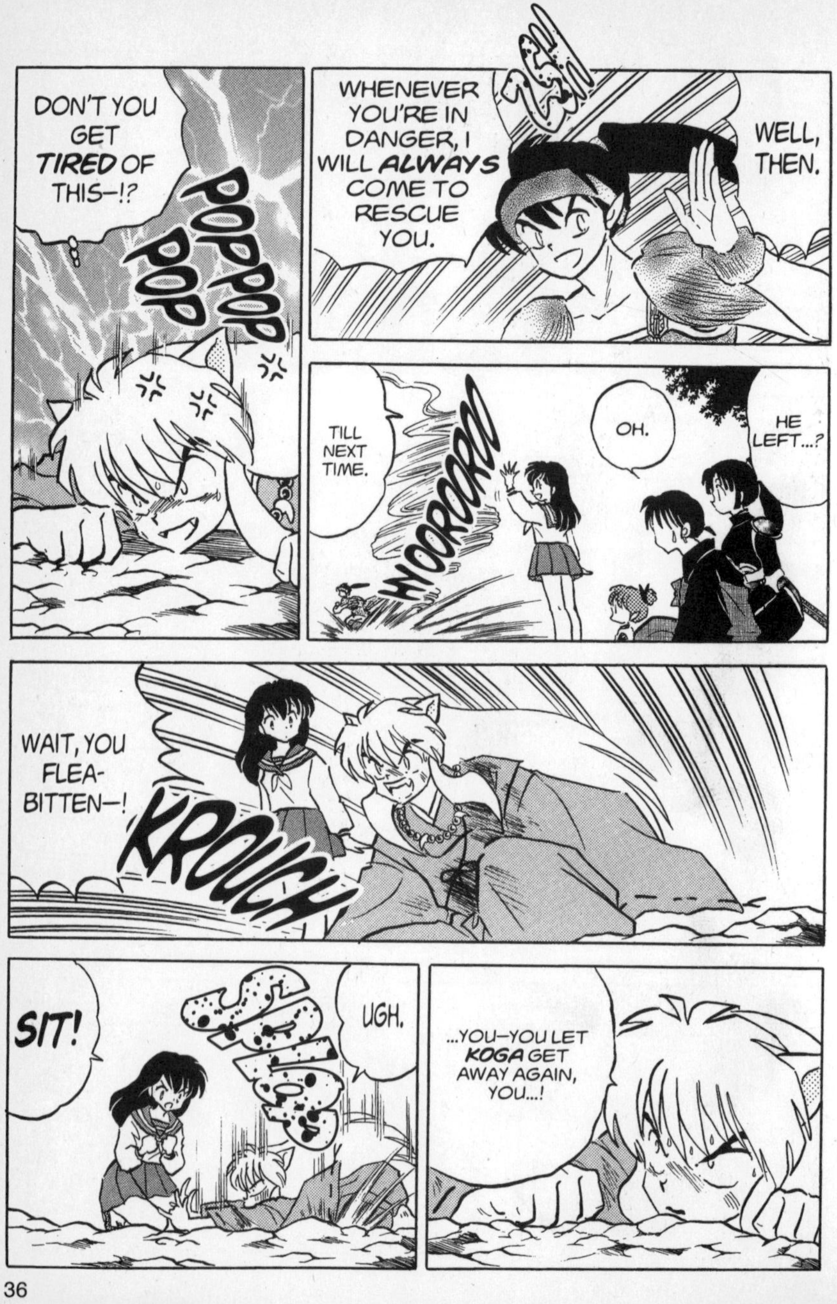

DON'T YOU GET TIRED OF THIS—!?
POP POP POP
WHENEVER YOU'RE IN DANGER, I WILL ALWAYS COME TO RESCUE YOU.
WELL, THEN.
TILL NEXT TIME.
HYOOROORO
OH.
HE LEFT...?
WAIT, YOU FLEA-BITTEN—!
KROUCH
SIT!
UGH.
...YOU—YOU LET KOGA GET AWAY AGAIN, YOU...!

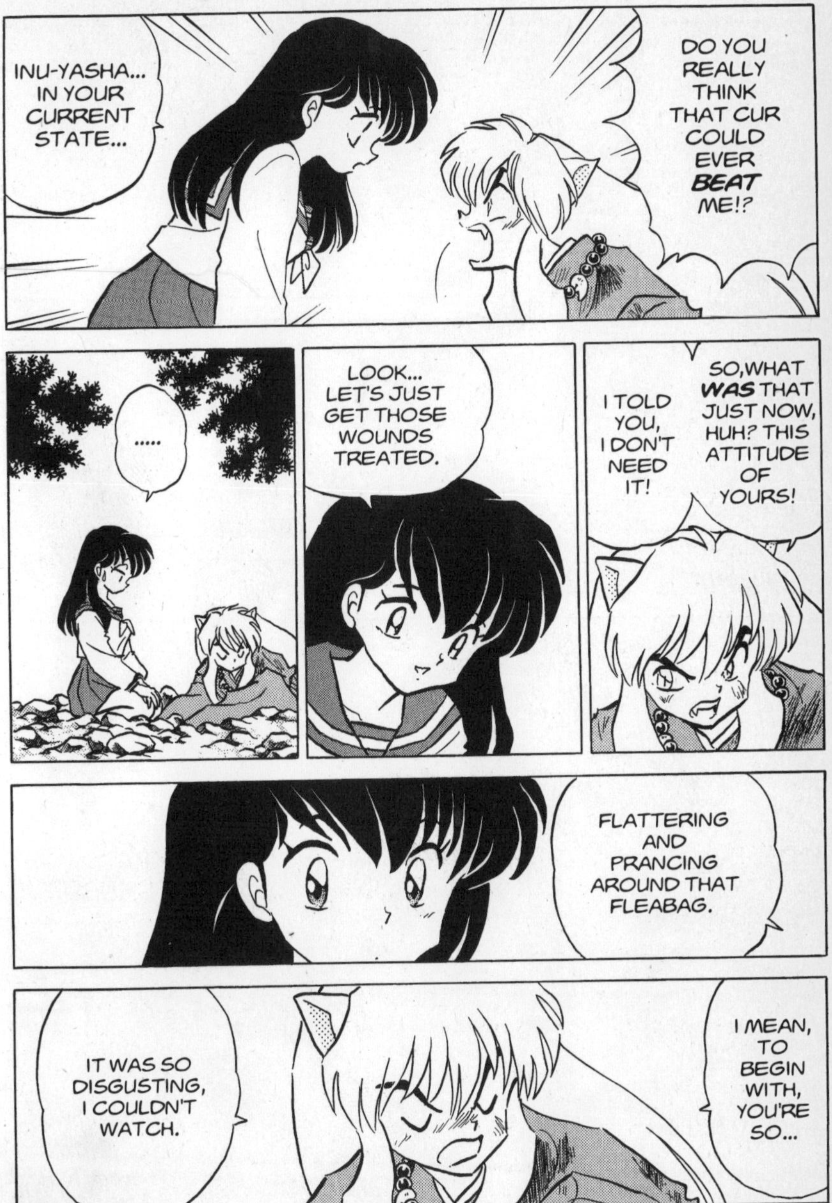
INU-YASHA... IN YOUR CURRENT STATE...
DO YOU REALLY THINK THAT CUR COULD EVER **BEAT** ME!?
.....
LOOK... LET'S JUST GET THOSE WOUNDS TREATED.
I TOLD YOU, I DON'T NEED IT!
SO,WHAT **WAS** THAT JUST NOW, HUH? THIS ATTITUDE OF YOURS!
FLATTERING AND PRANCING AROUND THAT FLEABAG.
IT WAS SO DISGUSTING, I COULDN'T WATCH.
I MEAN, TO BEGIN WITH, YOU'RE SO...

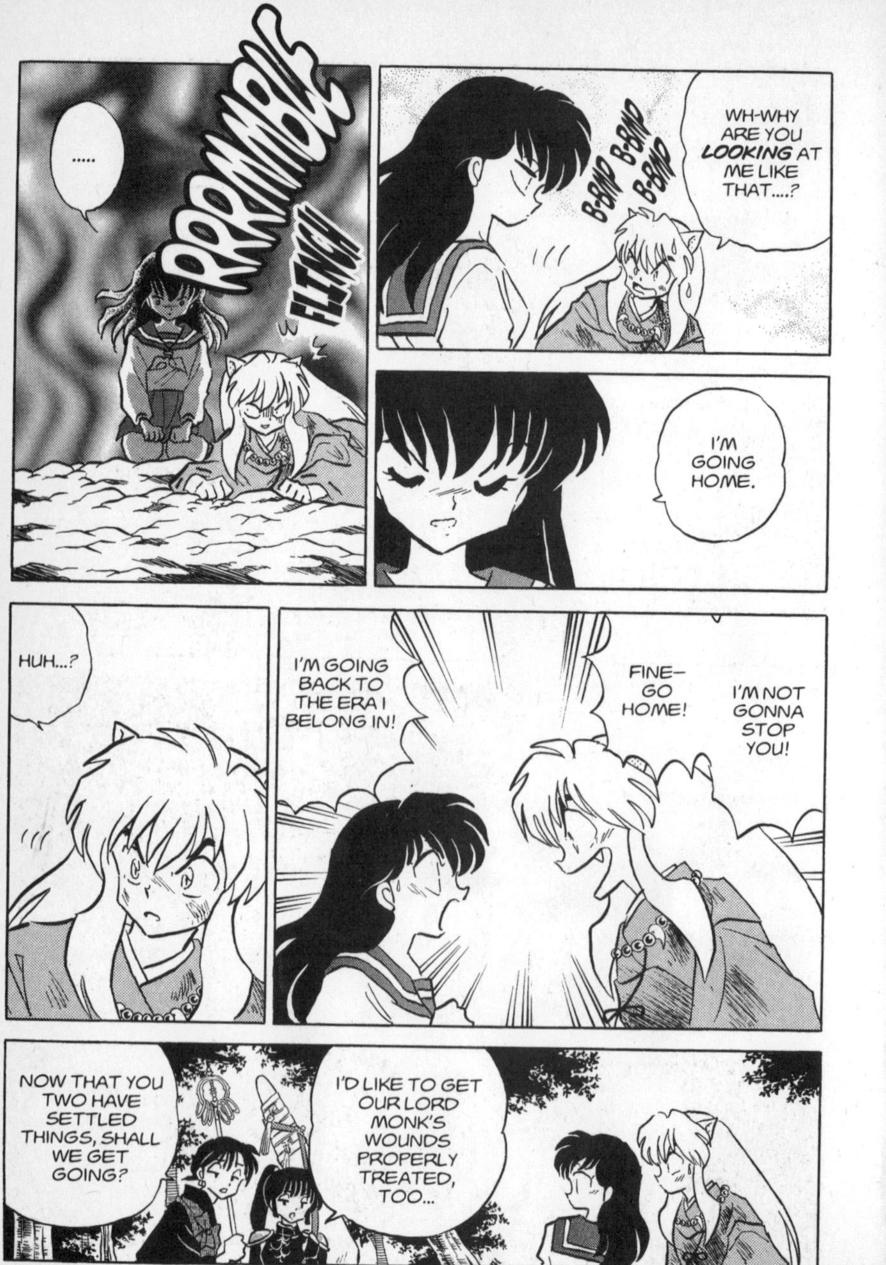
.....
RRRMMBLE
FLINCH
B-BMP B-BMP B-BMP
WH-WHY ARE YOU **LOOKING** AT ME LIKE THAT....?
I'M GOING HOME.
HUH...?
I'M GOING BACK TO THE ERA I BELONG IN!
FINE— GO HOME!
I'M NOT GONNA STOP YOU!
NOW THAT YOU TWO HAVE SETTLED THINGS, SHALL WE GET GOING?
I'D LIKE TO GET OUR LORD MONK'S WOUNDS PROPERLY TREATED, TOO...

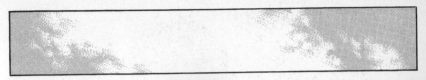

FLUTTER
FLUTTER

HSSH...

NARAKU,
EH...?

NOW
WHAT.

...HO.

HSSH...

YOUR
INSTINCTS
ARE RAZOR-
SHARP AS
USUAL,
KIKYO.

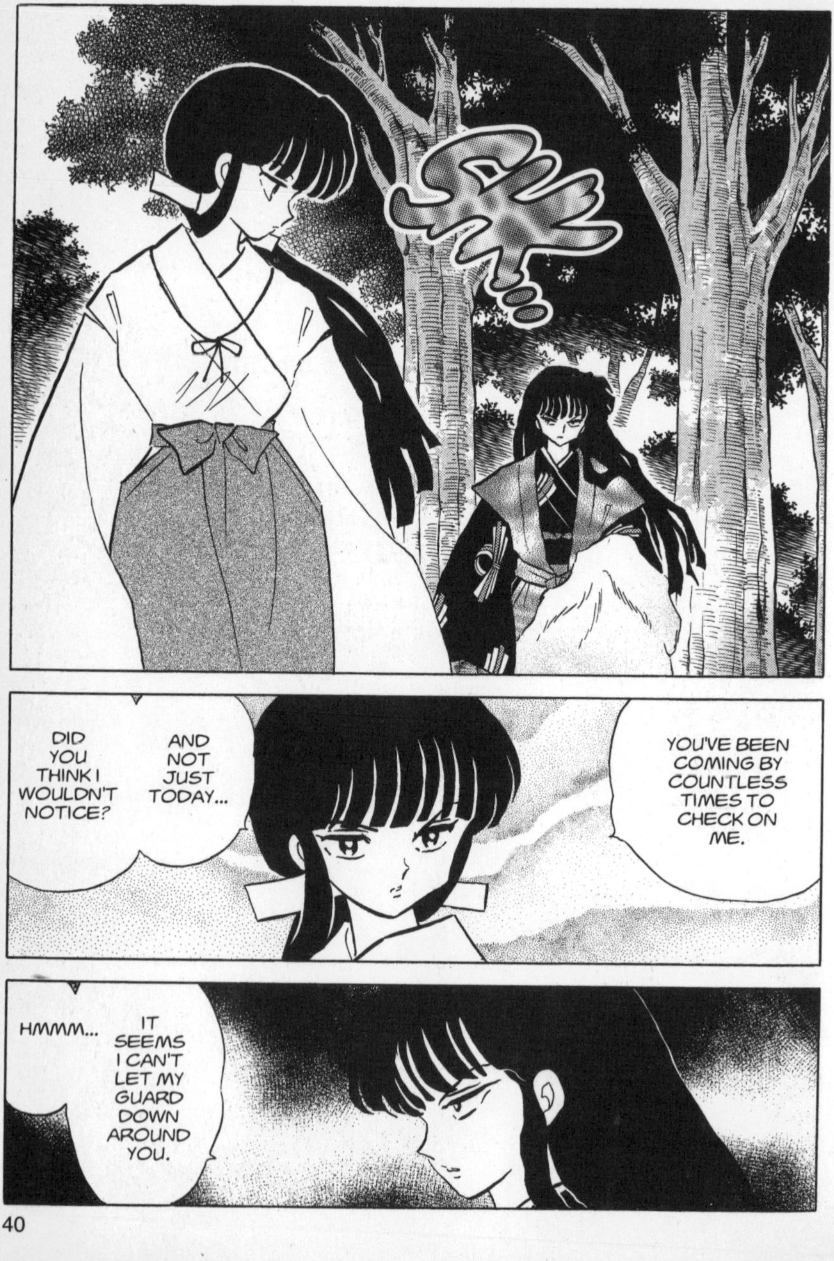
DID YOU THINK I WOULDN'T NOTICE?
AND NOT JUST TODAY...
YOU'VE BEEN COMING BY COUNTLESS TIMES TO CHECK ON ME.
HMMM...
IT SEEMS I CAN'T LET MY GUARD DOWN AROUND YOU.

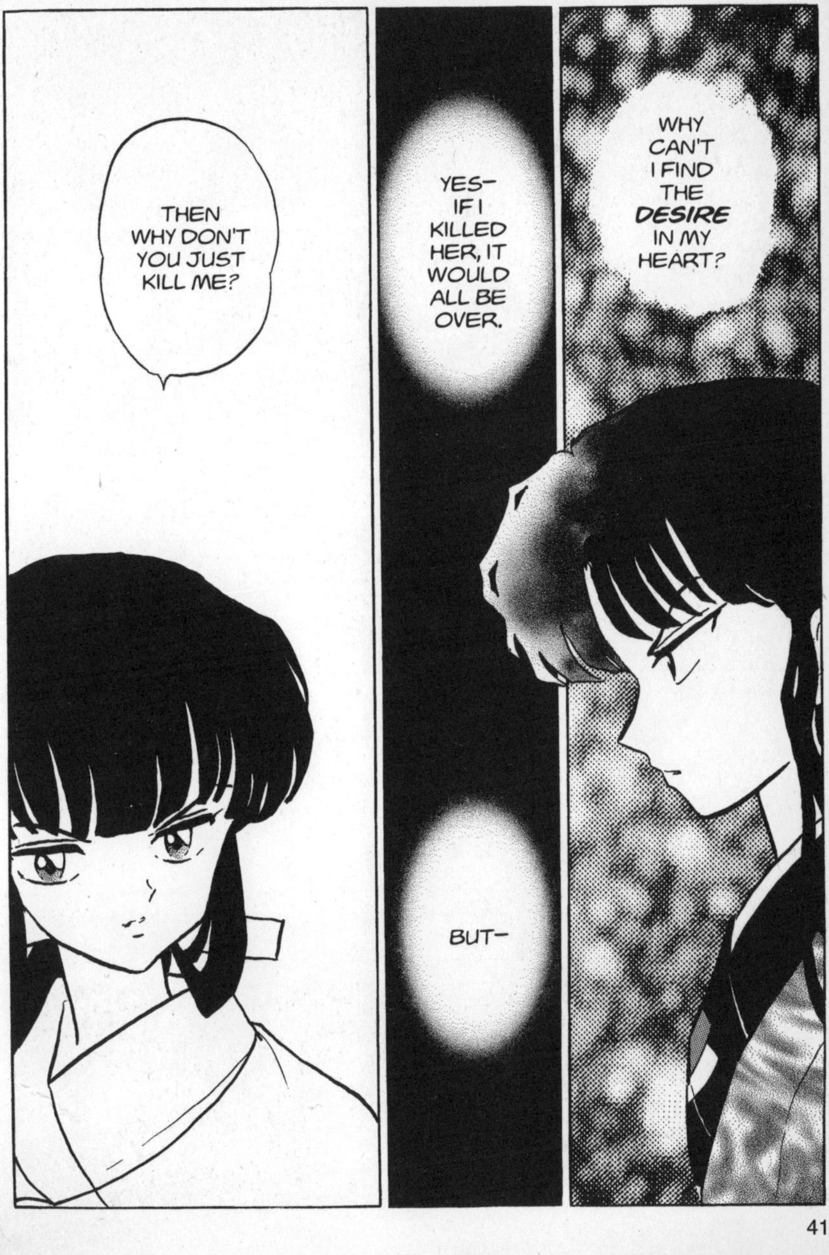
THEN WHY DON'T YOU JUST KILL ME?
YES- IF I KILLED HER, IT WOULD ALL BE OVER.
BUT-
WHY CAN'T I FIND THE **DESIRE** IN MY HEART?

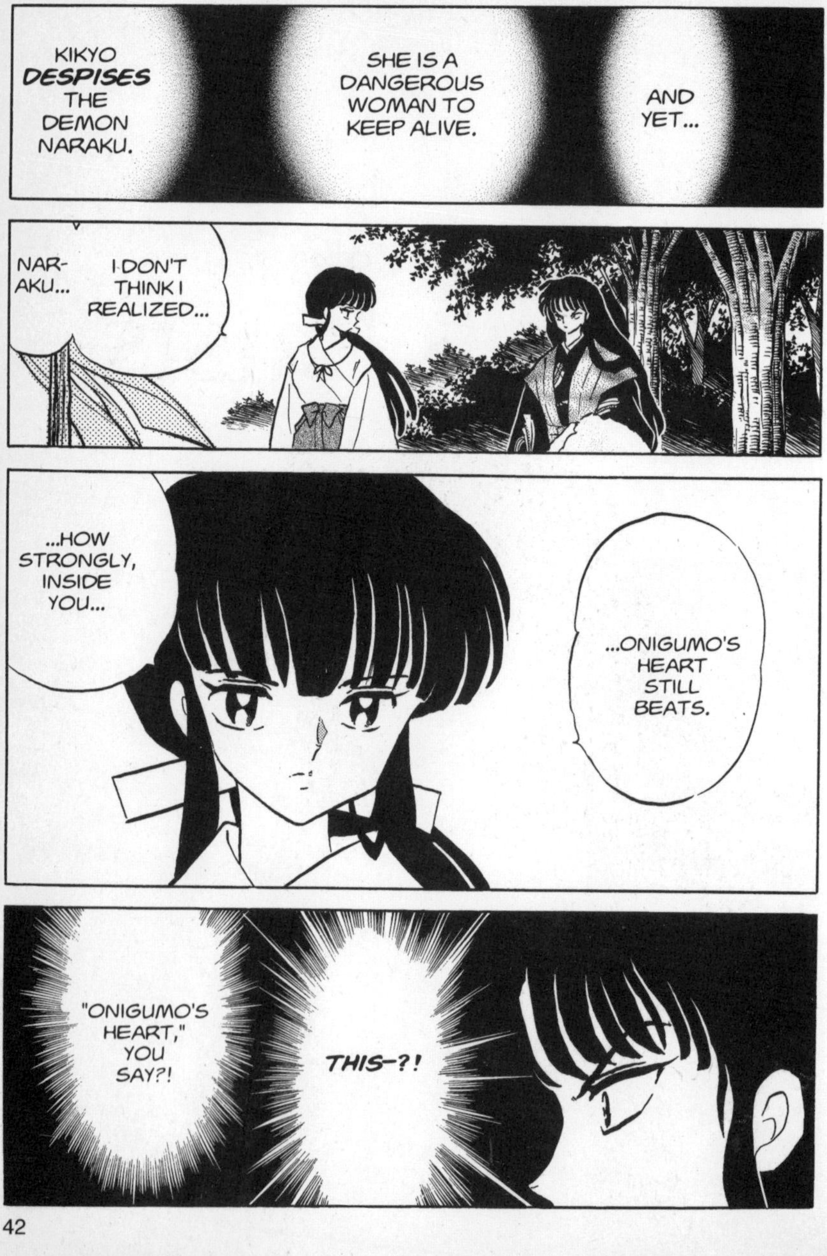
KIKYO DESPISES THE DEMON NARAKU.
SHE IS A DANGEROUS WOMAN TO KEEP ALIVE.
AND YET...
NAR-AKU...
I DON'T THINK I REALIZED...
...HOW STRONGLY, INSIDE YOU...
...ONIGUMO'S HEART STILL BEATS.
"ONIGUMO'S HEART," YOU SAY?!
THIS-?!

SCROLL THREE
KIKYO'S CRISIS

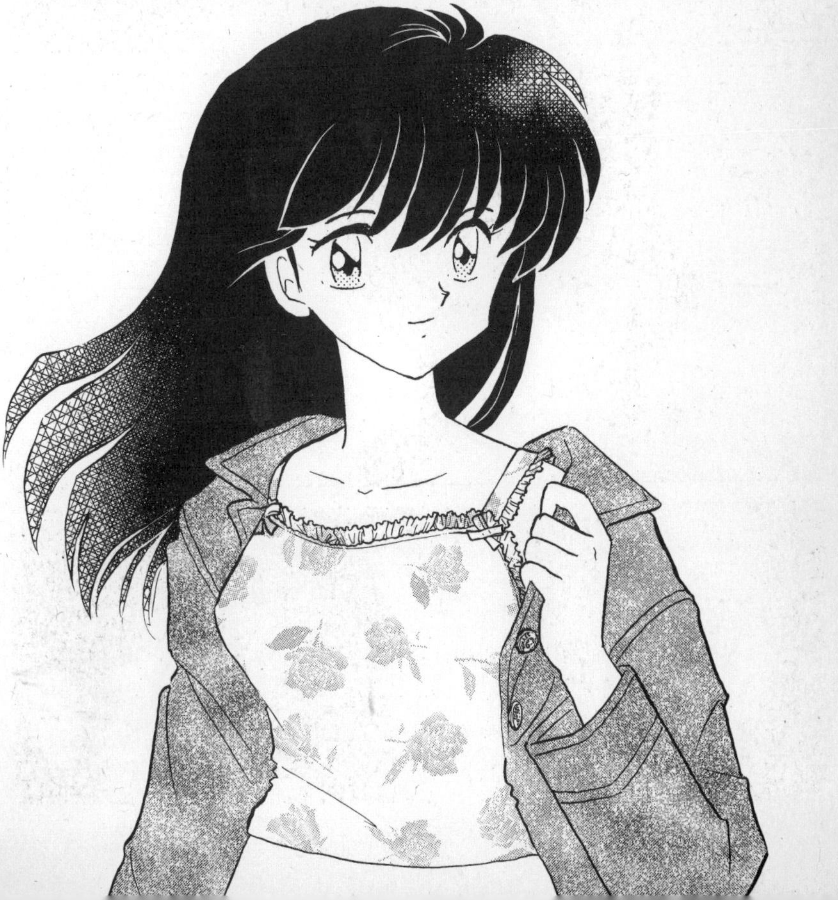

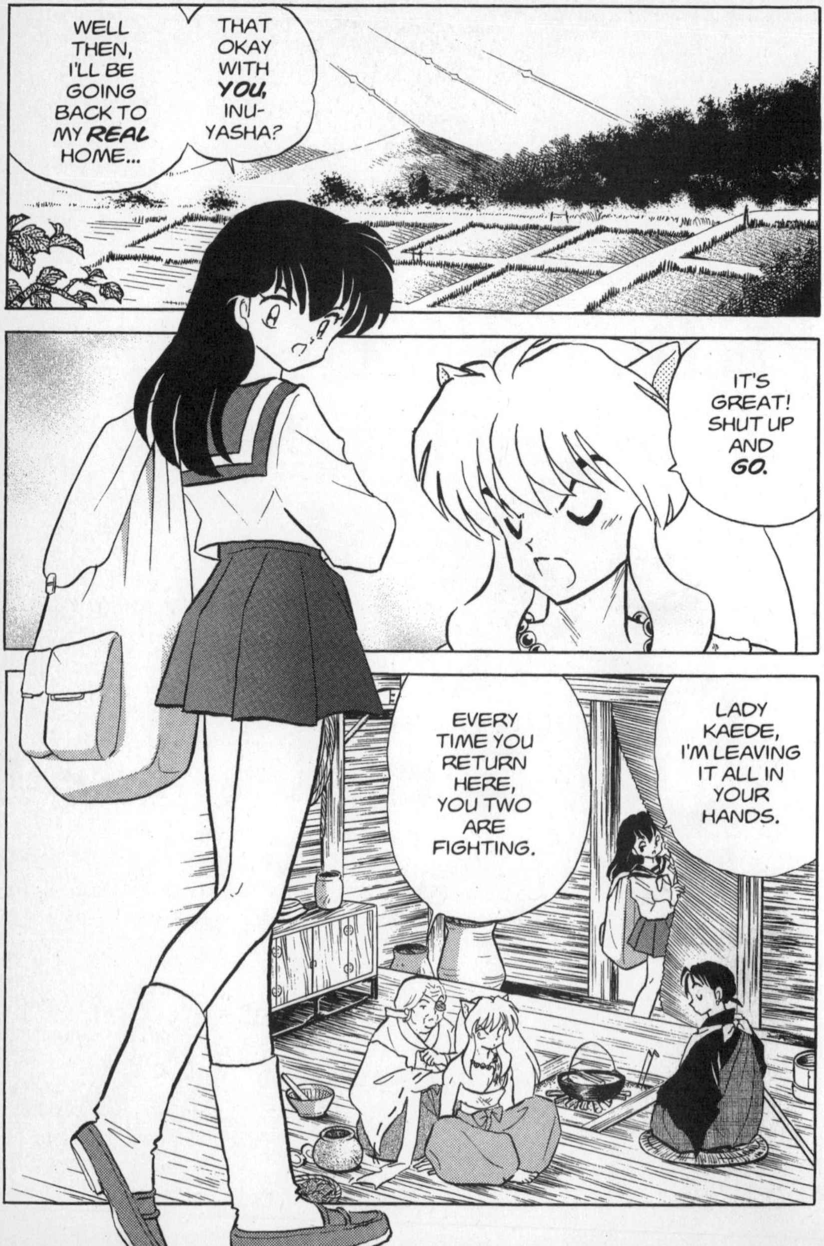
WELL THEN, I'LL BE GOING BACK TO MY **REAL** HOME...
THAT OKAY WITH **YOU,** INU-YASHA?
IT'S GREAT! SHUT UP AND **GO.**
EVERY TIME YOU RETURN HERE, YOU TWO ARE FIGHTING.
LADY KAEDE, I'M LEAVING IT ALL IN YOUR HANDS.

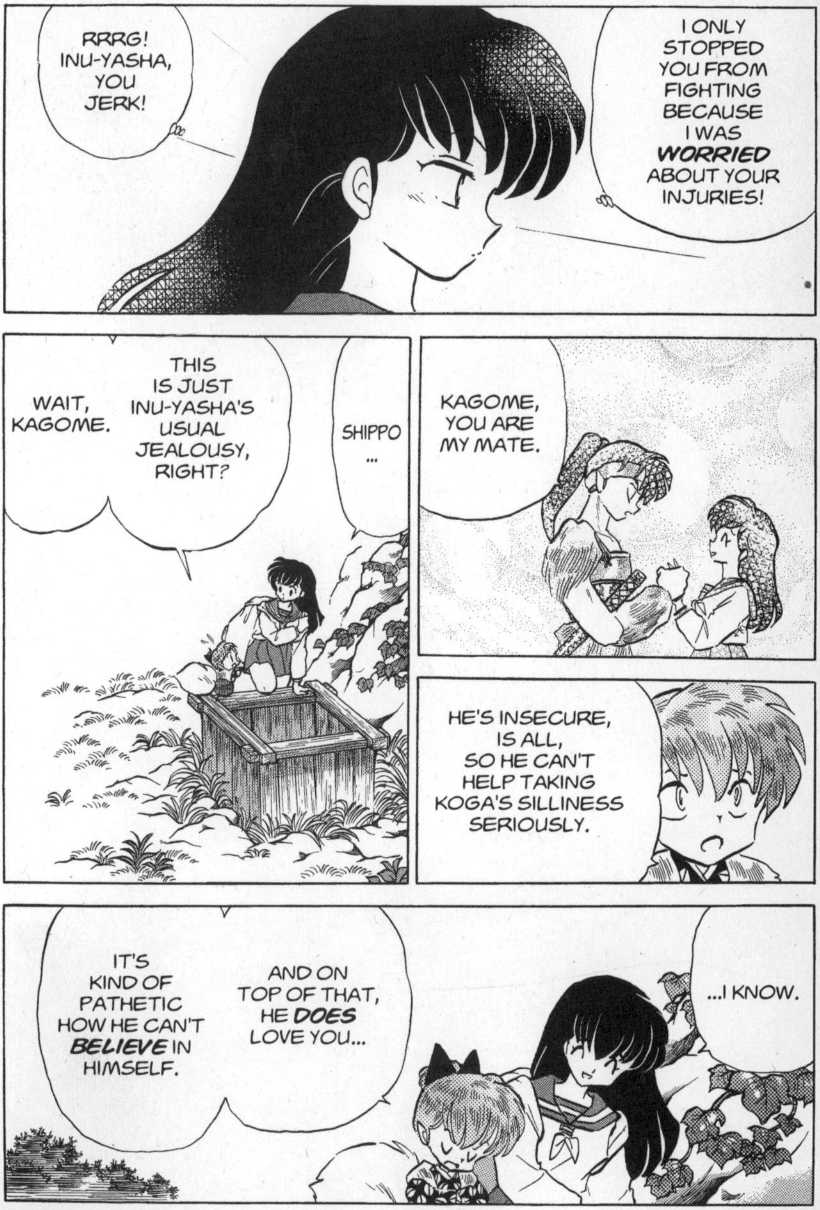
RRRG! INU-YASHA, YOU JERK!
I ONLY STOPPED YOU FROM FIGHTING BECAUSE I WAS **WORRIED** ABOUT YOUR INJURIES!
WAIT, KAGOME.
THIS IS JUST INU-YASHA'S USUAL JEALOUSY, RIGHT?
SHIPPO ...
KAGOME, YOU ARE MY MATE.
HE'S INSECURE, IS ALL, SO HE CAN'T HELP TAKING KOGA'S SILLINESS SERIOUSLY.
IT'S KIND OF PATHETIC HOW HE CAN'T **BELIEVE** IN HIMSELF.
AND ON TOP OF THAT, HE **DOES** LOVE YOU...
...I KNOW.

DON'T WORRY, I'LL BE RIGHT BACK.

I'M JUST GOING TO PICK UP SOME MODERN MEDICINE AND BRING IT HERE.

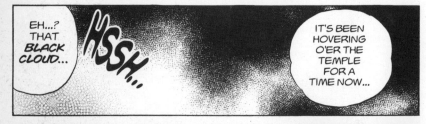

EH...? THAT *BLACK CLOUD...*

HSSH...

IT'S BEEN HOVERING O'ER THE TEMPLE FOR A TIME NOW...

.....

IT'S AN *OMEN,* IT IS...

FLICKER

FLICKER

THOSE LIGHTS... THE **SOULS** OF THE **DEAD.**

IS THAT "THING"...

...**DEVOURING** THOSE SOULS?!

FWOOO

HAH ...!?

WHAT **IS** THAT THING!?

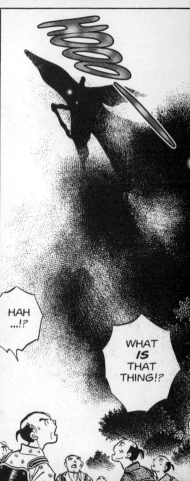

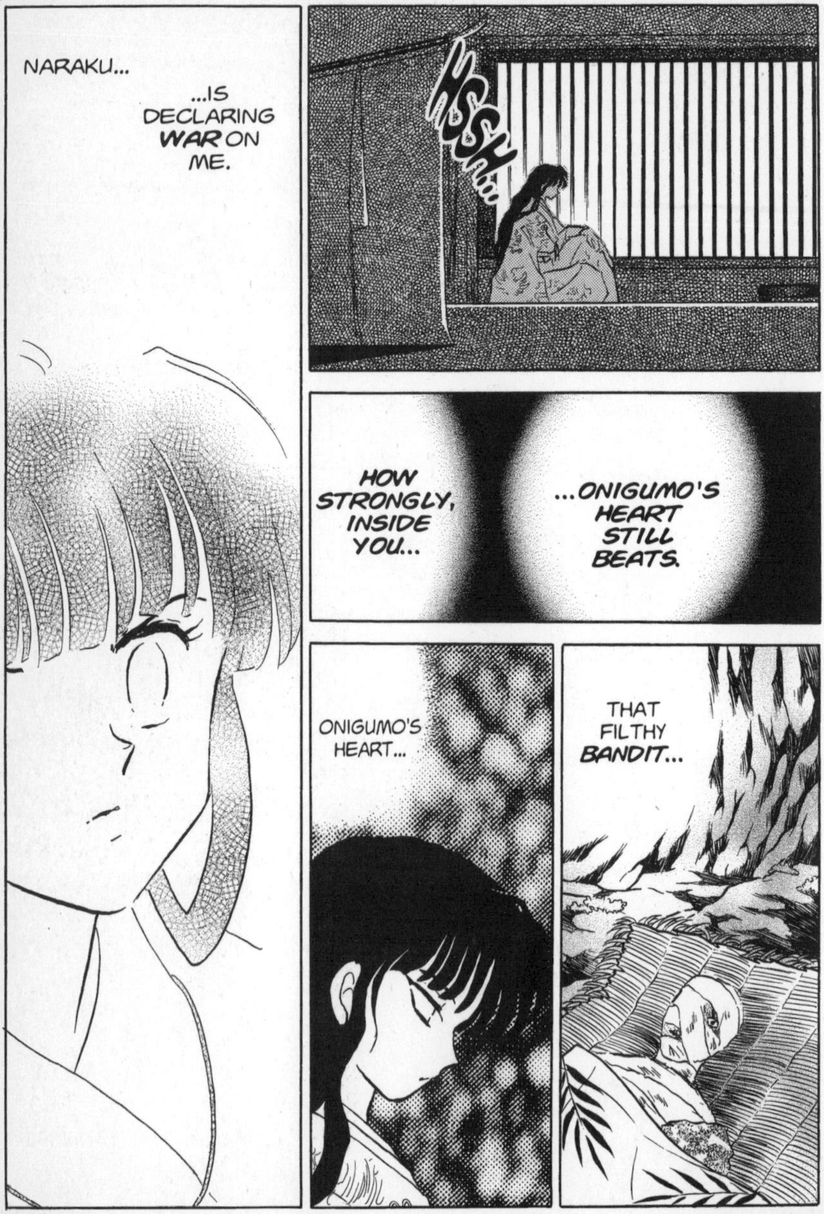

NARAKU...
...IS DECLARING WAR ON ME.
HSSH...
HOW STRONGLY, INSIDE YOU...
...ONIGUMO'S HEART STILL BEATS.
ONIGUMO'S HEART...
THAT FILTHY BANDIT...

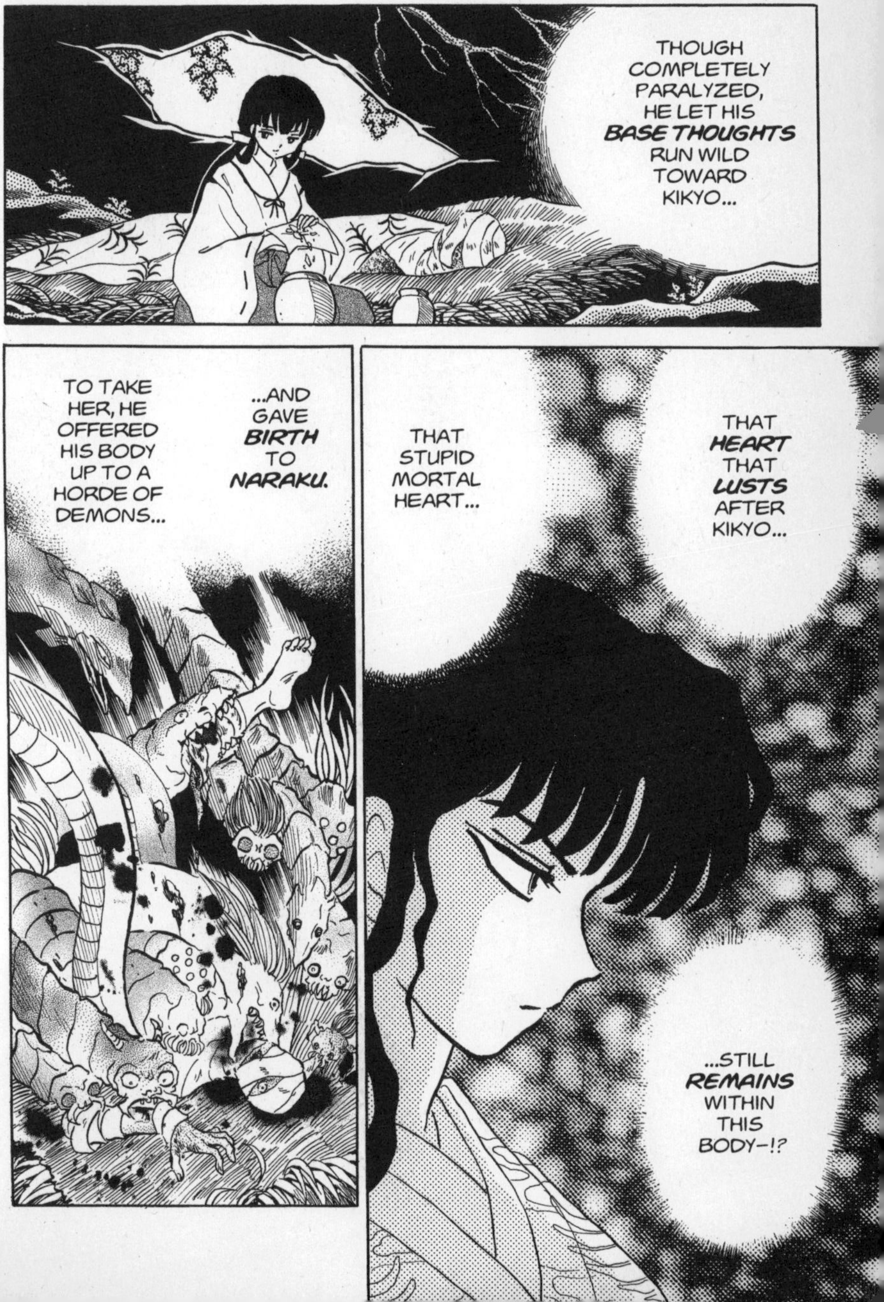

THOUGH COMPLETELY PARALYZED, HE LET HIS BASE THOUGHTS RUN WILD TOWARD KIKYO...
TO TAKE HER, HE OFFERED HIS BODY UP TO A HORDE OF DEMONS...
...AND GAVE BIRTH TO NARAKU.
THAT STUPID MORTAL HEART...
THAT HEART THAT LUSTS AFTER KIKYO...
...STILL REMAINS WITHIN THIS BODY-!?

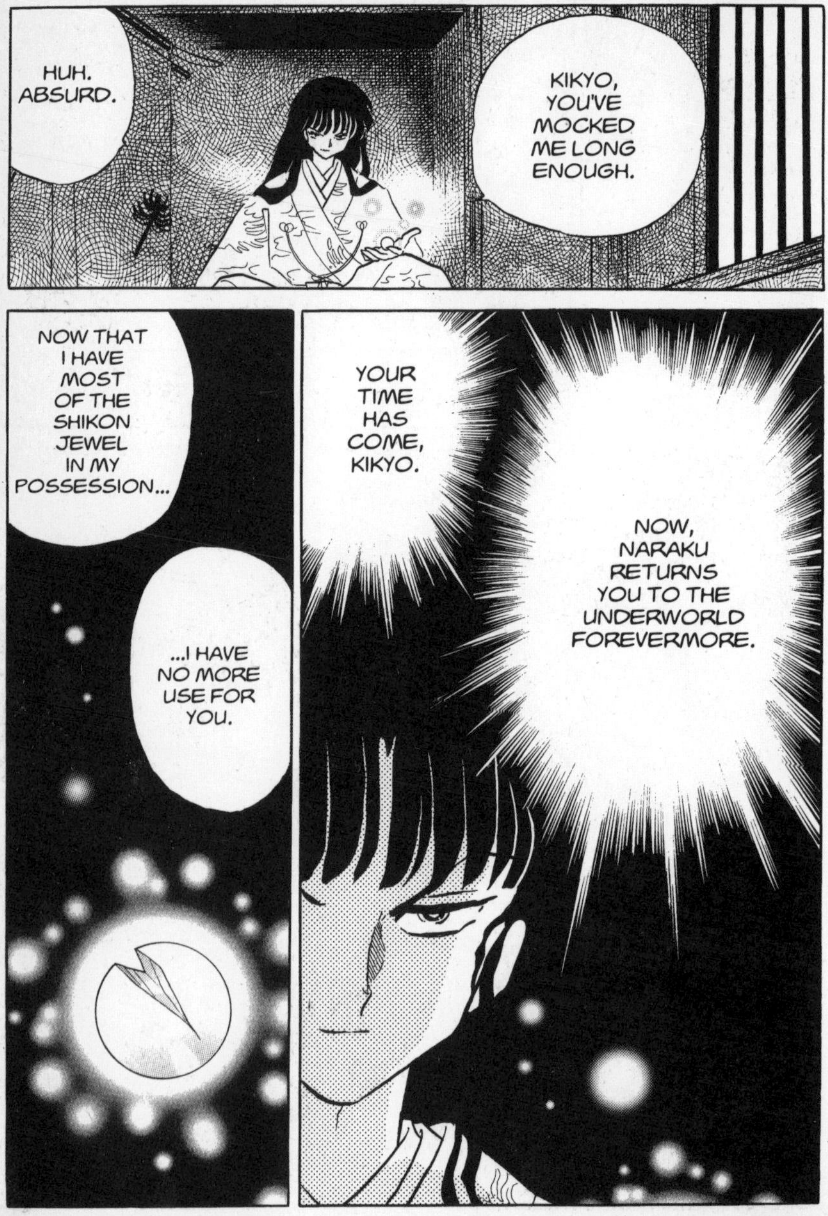
HUH. ABSURD.
KIKYO, YOU'VE MOCKED ME LONG ENOUGH.
NOW THAT I HAVE MOST OF THE SHIKON JEWEL IN MY POSSESSION...
...I HAVE NO MORE USE FOR YOU.
YOUR TIME HAS COME, KIKYO.
NOW, NARAKU RETURNS YOU TO THE UNDERWORLD FOREVERMORE.

UHHH...

THAT DEMON...

PLANNING TO *DEVOUR* ALL THE SOULS IN THIS LAND.

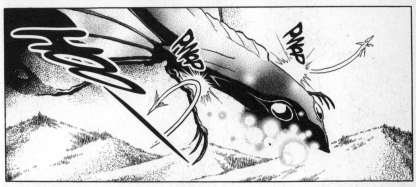

AND IF ALL THE DEAD SOULS ARE GONE... MY BODY WILL MOVE NO LONGER.

I MUST *DESTROY* HIM WHILE I STILL HAVE THE STRENGTH TO DRAW MY BOW...

KREE...

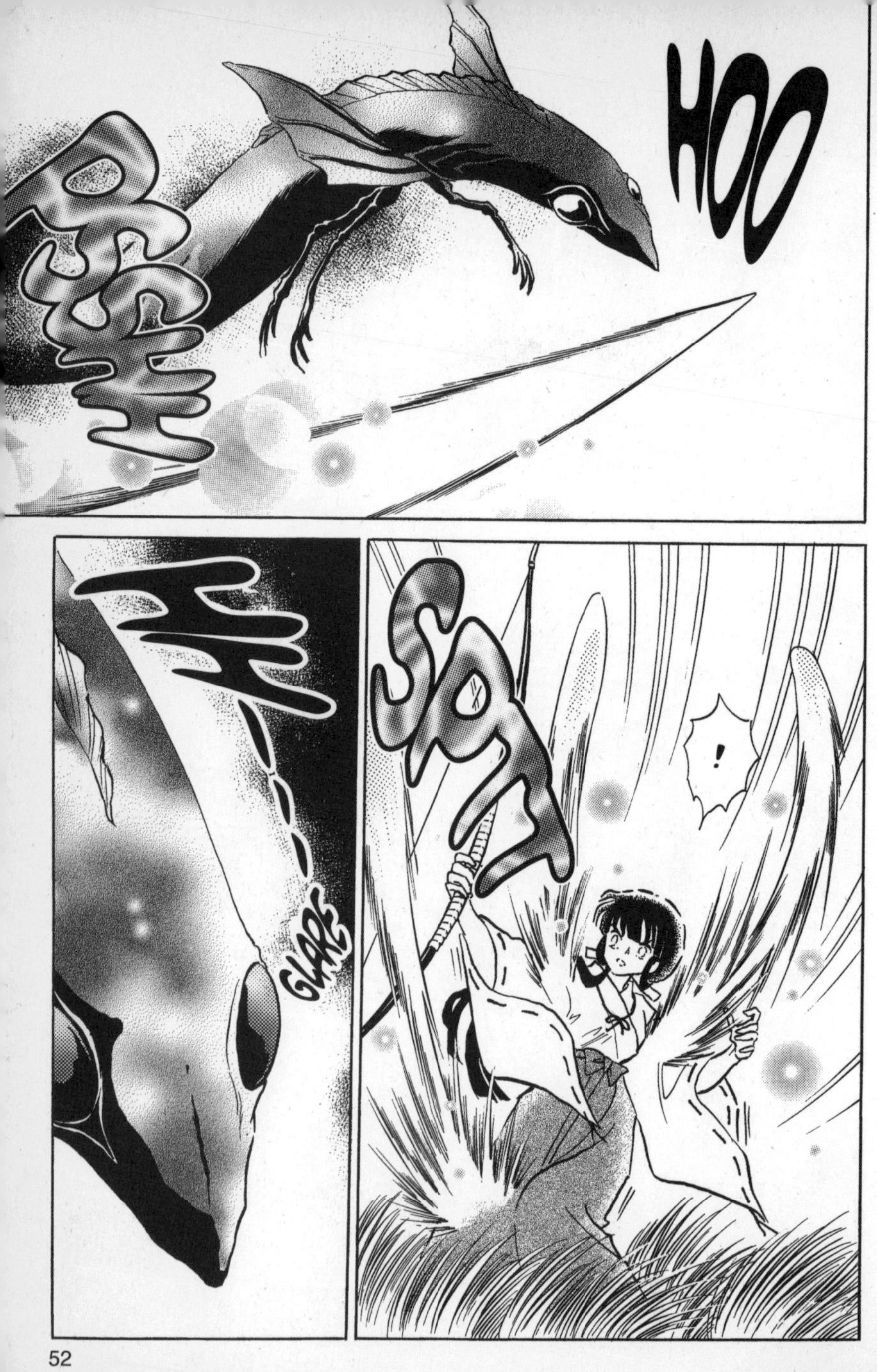
HOO
FWH----
GLARE
SPAT
!

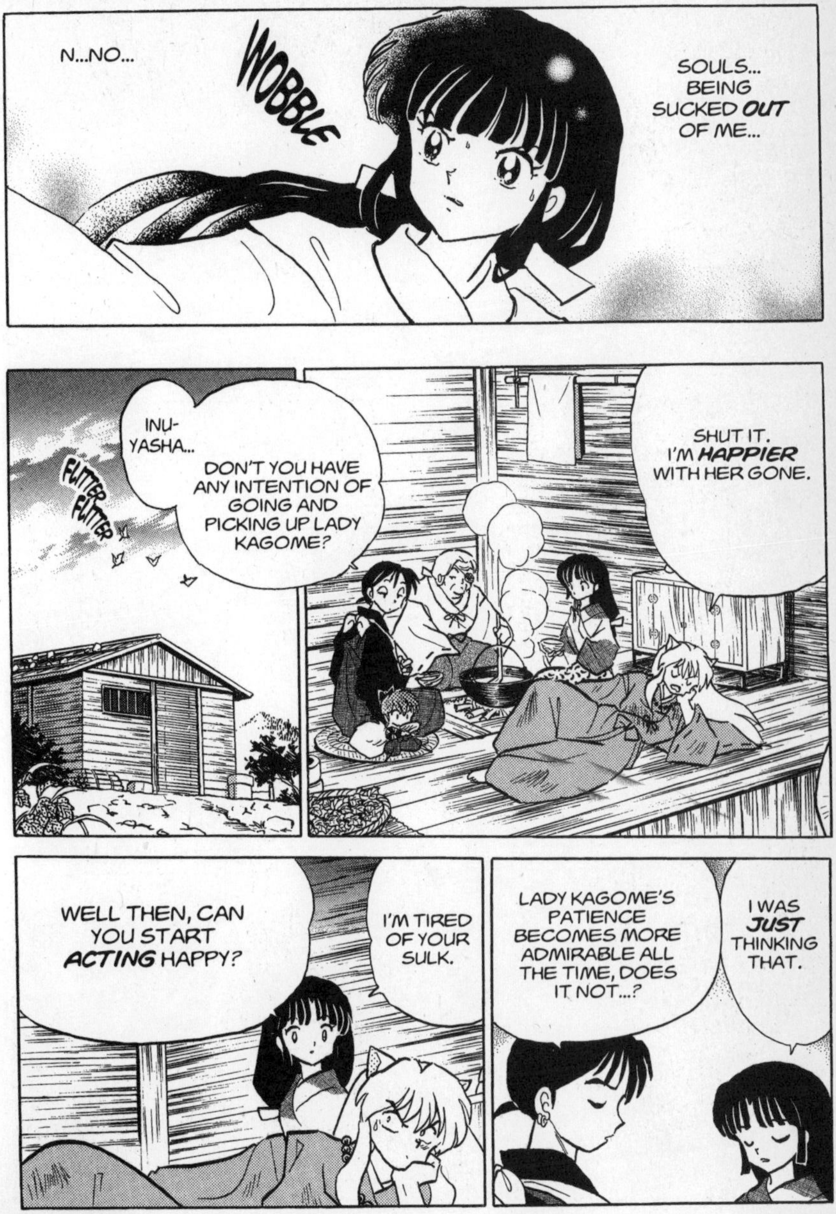
N...NO...
WOBBLE
SOULS... BEING SUCKED OUT OF ME...
FLITTER FLITTER
INU-YASHA...
DON'T YOU HAVE ANY INTENTION OF GOING AND PICKING UP LADY KAGOME?
SHUT IT. I'M HAPPIER WITH HER GONE.
WELL THEN, CAN YOU START ACTING HAPPY?
I'M TIRED OF YOUR SULK.
LADY KAGOME'S PATIENCE BECOMES MORE ADMIRABLE ALL THE TIME, DOES IT NOT...?
I WAS JUST THINKING THAT.

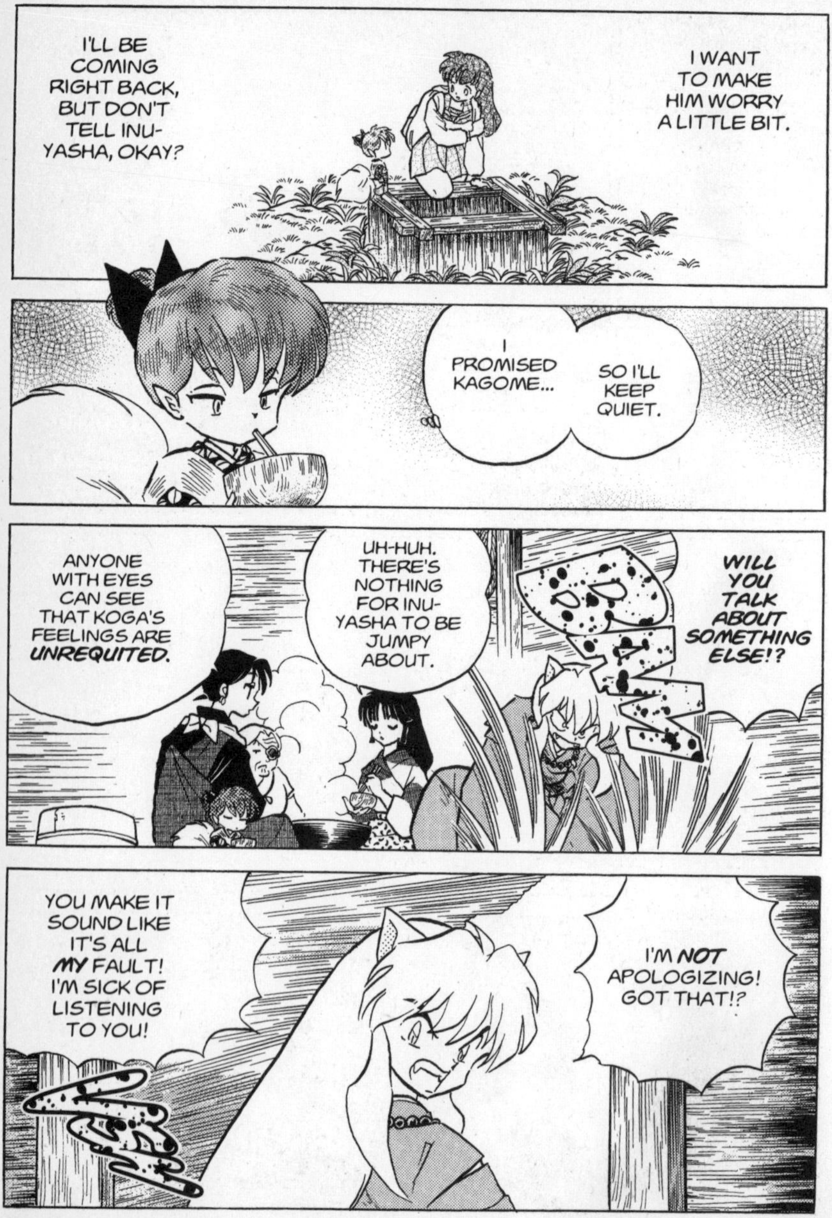
I'LL BE COMING RIGHT BACK, BUT DON'T TELL INU-YASHA, OKAY?
I WANT TO MAKE HIM WORRY A LITTLE BIT.
I PROMISED KAGOME...
SO I'LL KEEP QUIET.
ANYONE WITH EYES CAN SEE THAT KOGA'S FEELINGS ARE *UNREQUITED.*
UH-HUH. THERE'S NOTHING FOR INU-YASHA TO BE JUMPY ABOUT.
WILL YOU TALK ABOUT SOMETHING ELSE!?
YOU MAKE IT SOUND LIKE IT'S ALL *MY* FAULT! I'M SICK OF LISTENING TO YOU!
I'M *NOT* APOLOGIZING! GOT THAT!?

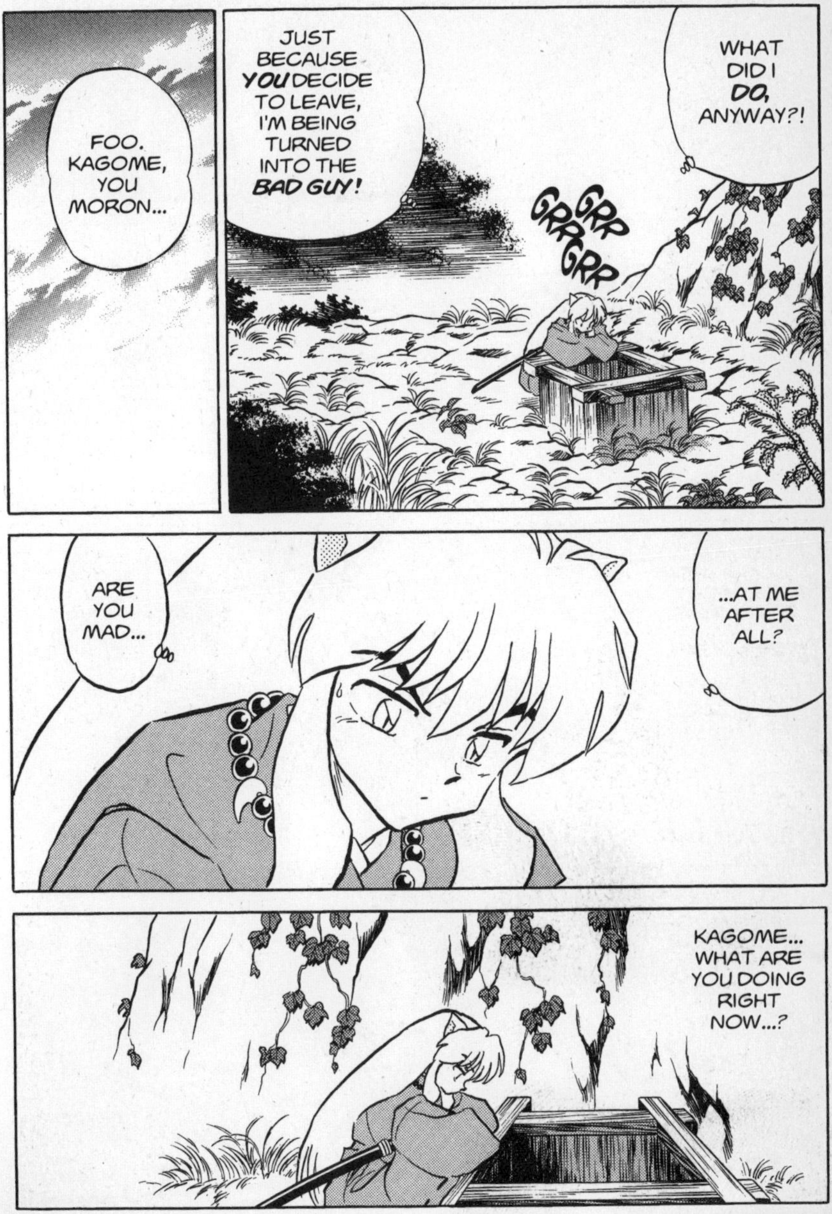
FOO. KAGOME, YOU MORON...
JUST BECAUSE YOU DECIDE TO LEAVE, I'M BEING TURNED INTO THE BAD GUY!
GRR GRR GRR
WHAT DID I DO, ANYWAY?!
ARE YOU MAD...
...AT ME AFTER ALL?
KAGOME... WHAT ARE YOU DOING RIGHT NOW...?

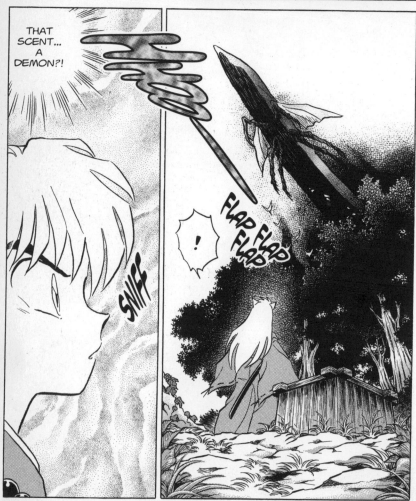

THAT
SCENT...
A
DEMON?!

SNIFF

FLAP FLAP
FLAP

!

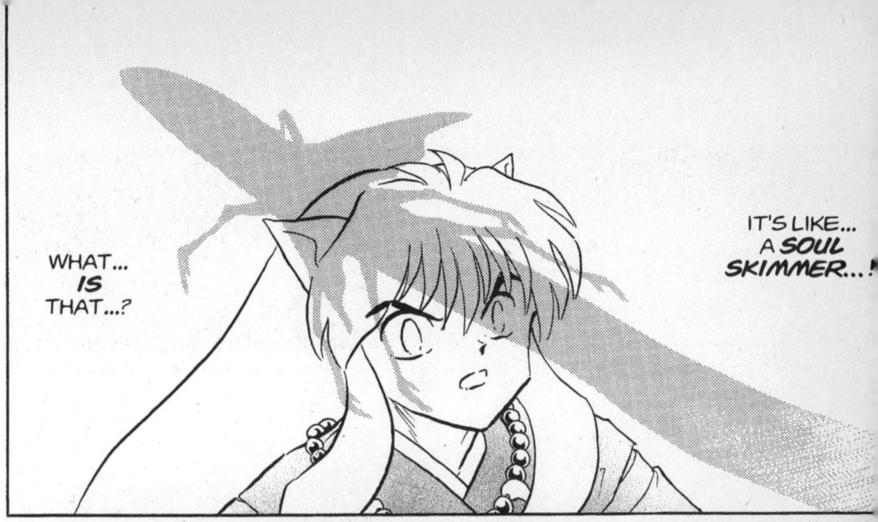
WHAT... IS THAT...?
IT'S LIKE... A SOUL SKIMMER...!
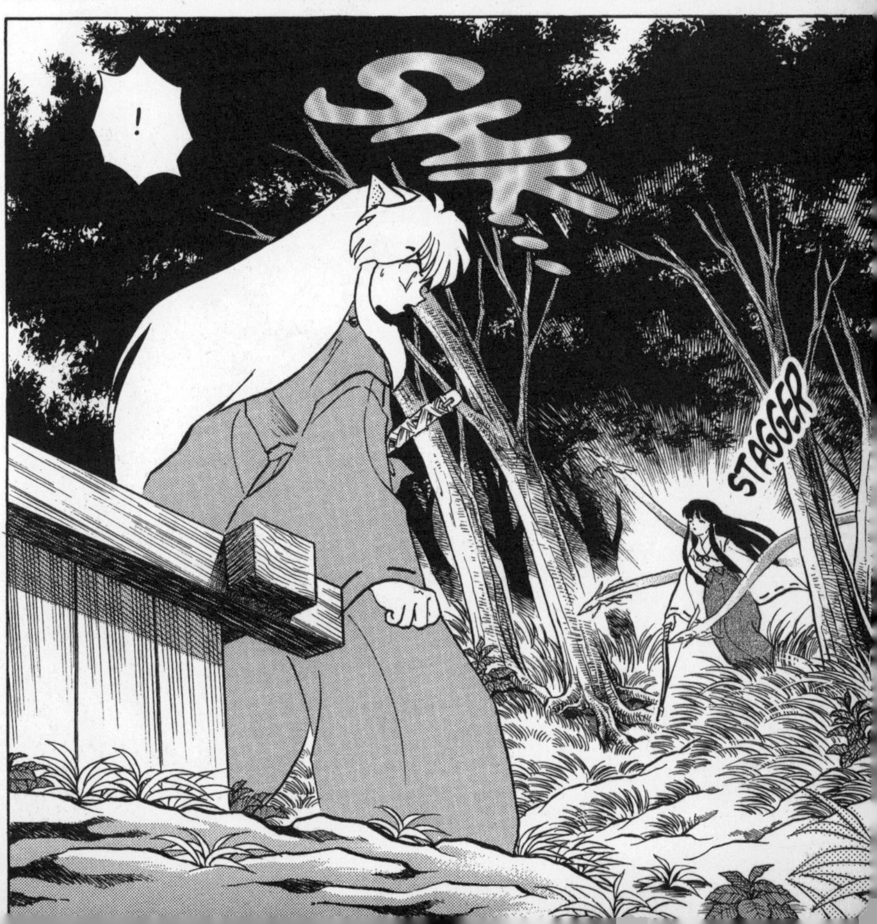
!
STAGGER

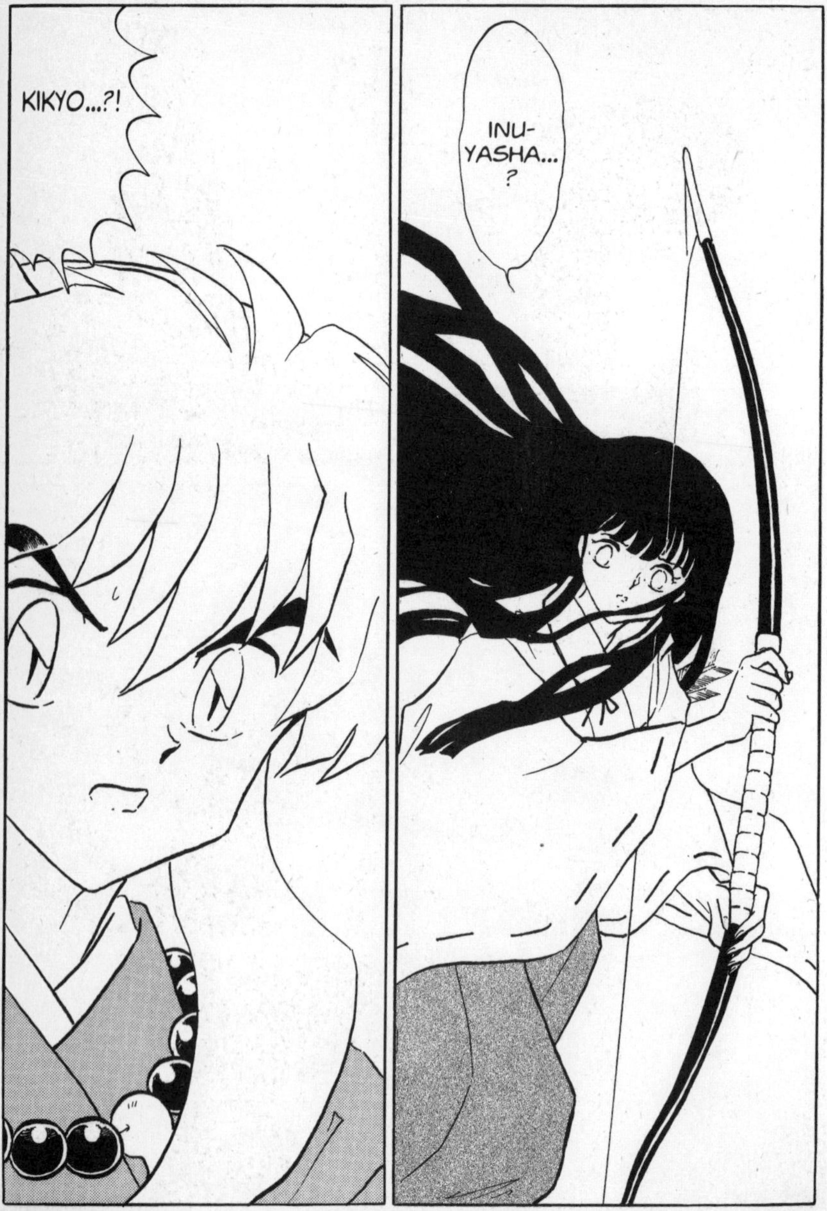
KIKYO...?!
INU-YASHA...?

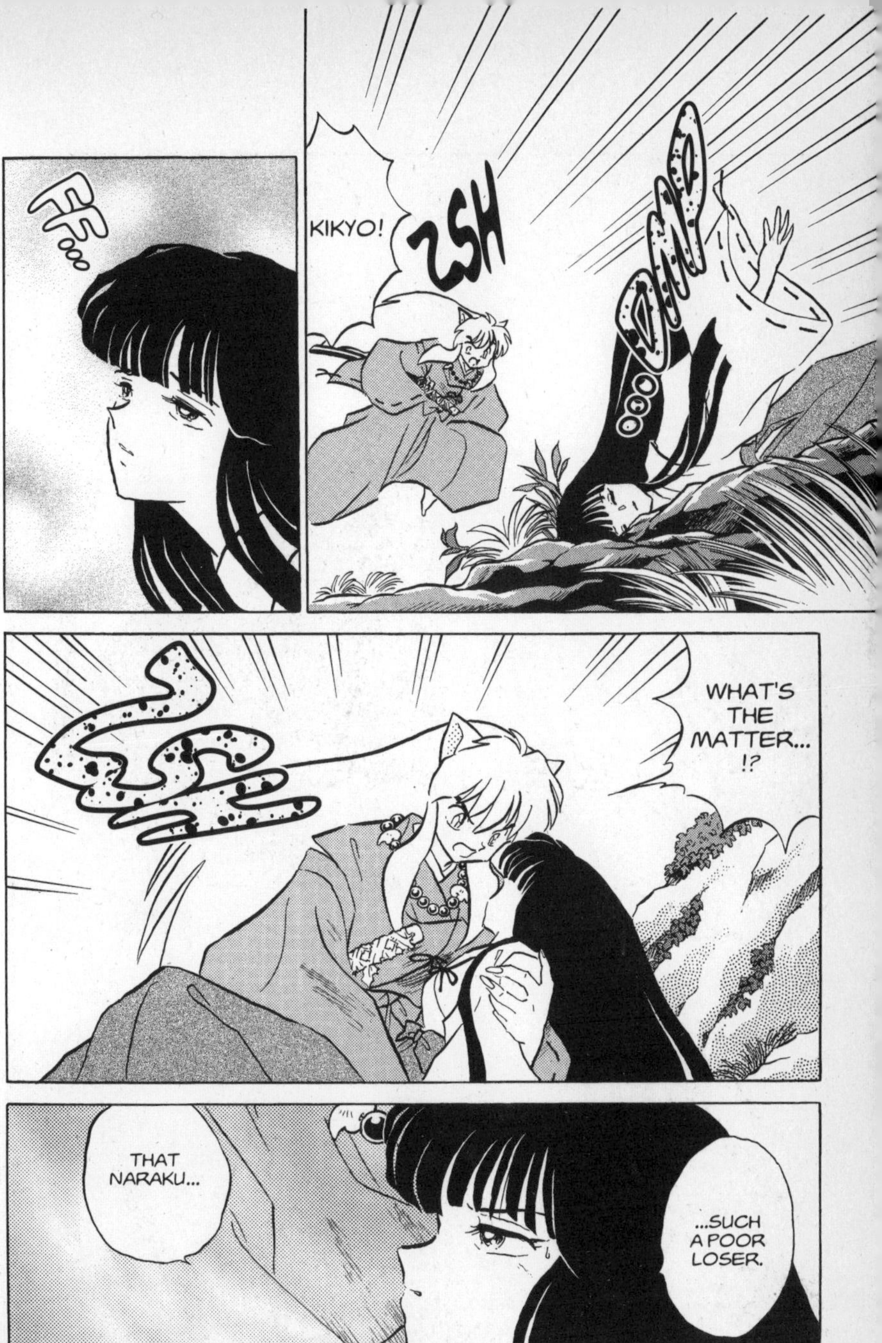
FFooo
KIKYO!
ZSH
WHAT'S THE MATTER... !?
THAT NARAKU...
...SUCH A POOR LOSER.

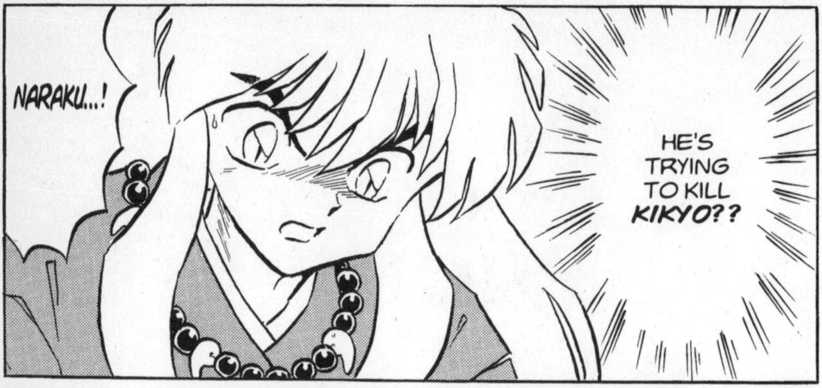
NARAKU...!
HE'S TRYING TO KILL KIKYO??
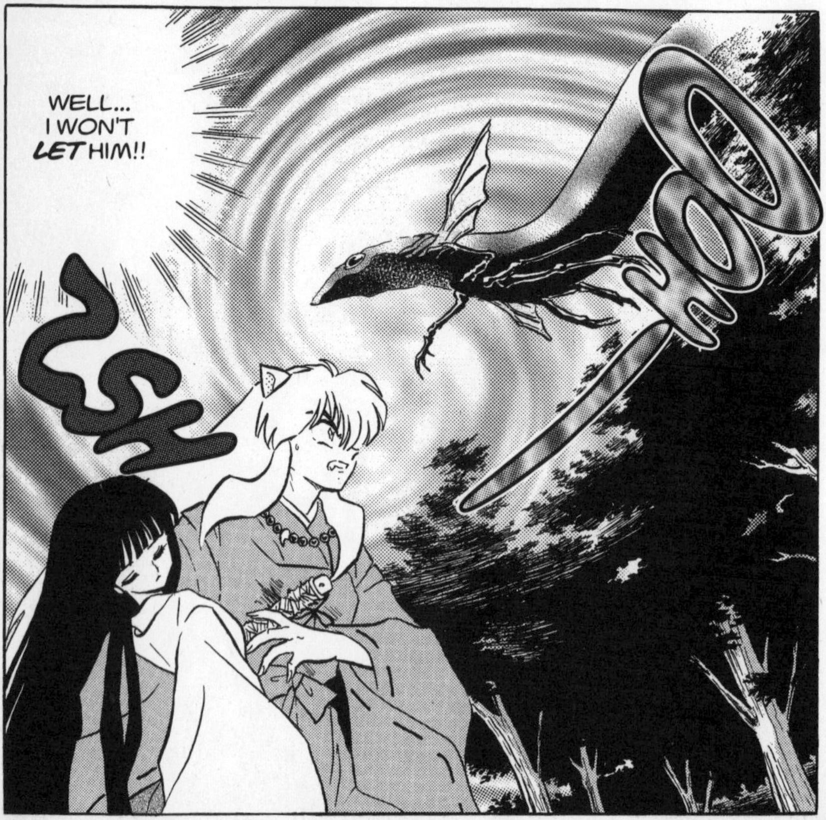
WELL... I WON'T LET HIM!!
ZSH
WHOOO

SCROLL FOUR
ONIGUMO'S HEART

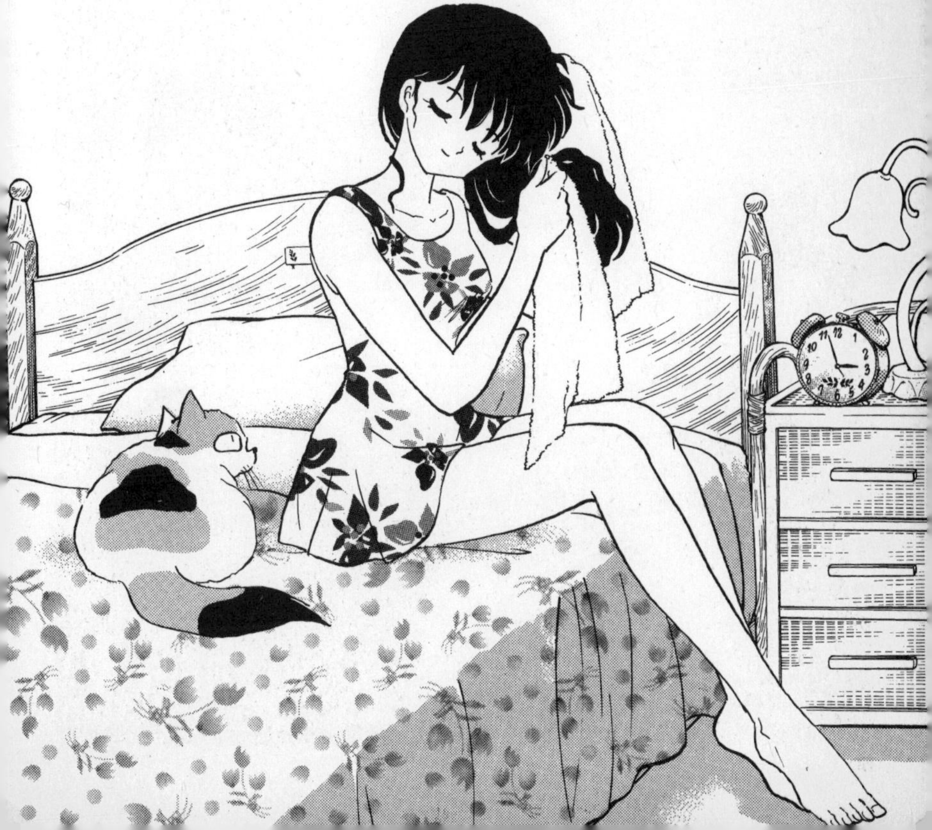

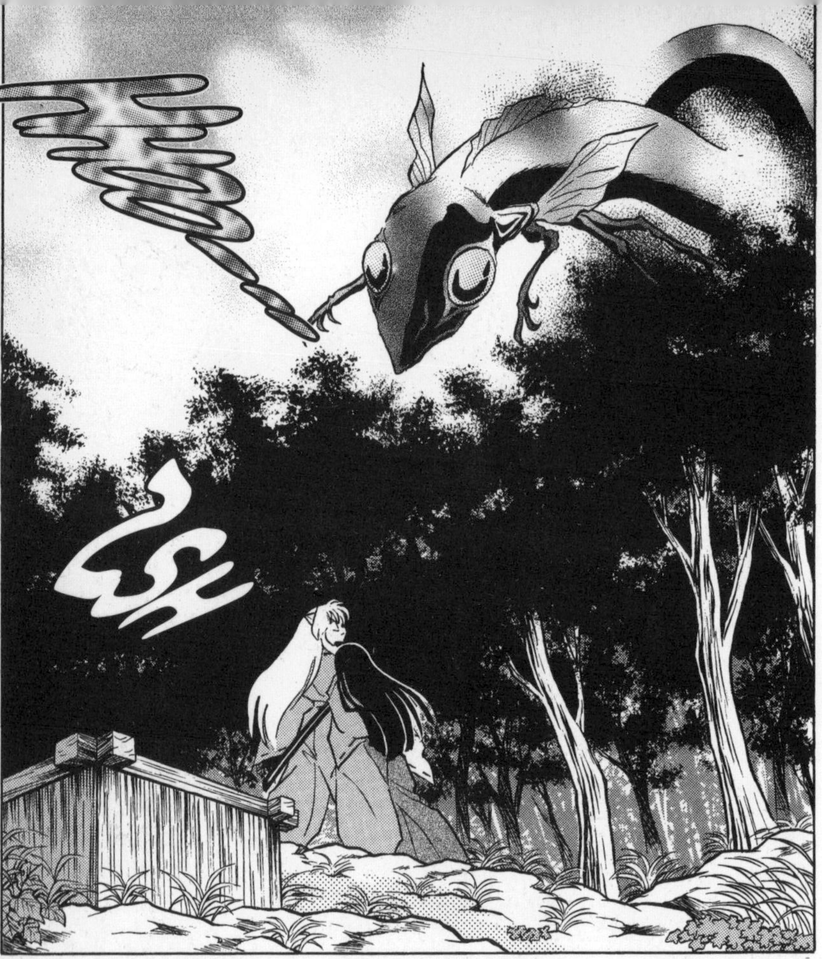

VSH

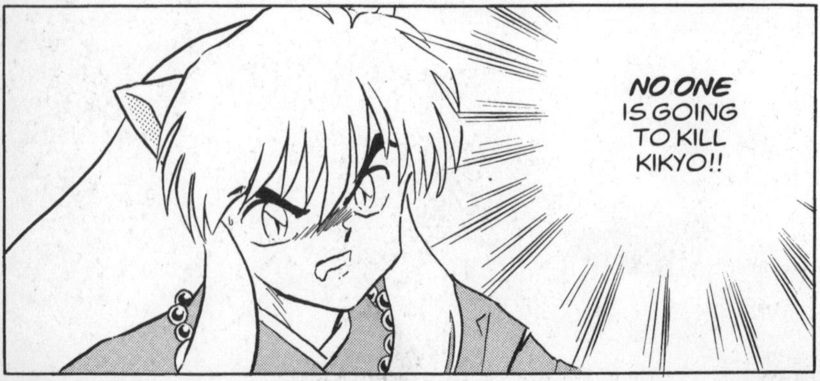

NO ONE IS GOING TO KILL KIKYO!!

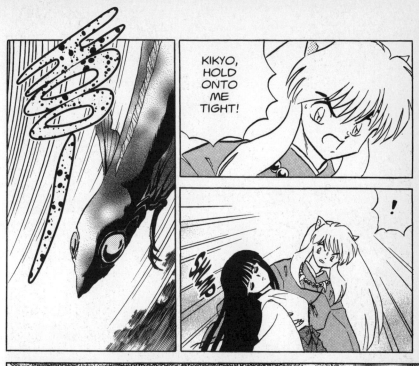

KIKYO, HOLD ONTO ME TIGHT!

SHUMP

!

WHOA!

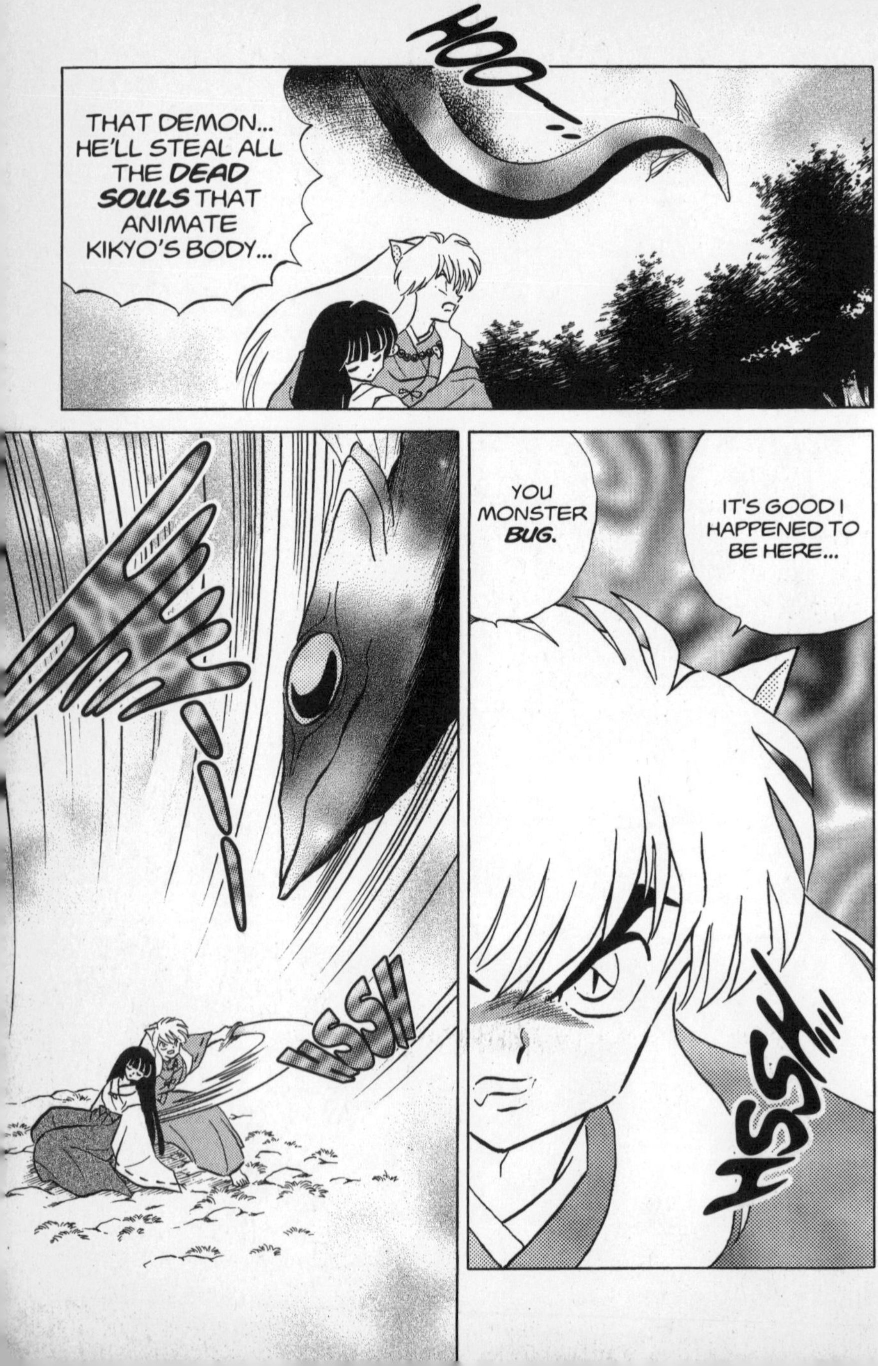
HOO...!!
THAT DEMON... HE'LL STEAL ALL THE **DEAD SOULS** THAT ANIMATE KIKYO'S BODY...
HSSH
YOU MONSTER **BUG**.
IT'S GOOD I HAPPENED TO BE HERE...
HSSH...!!

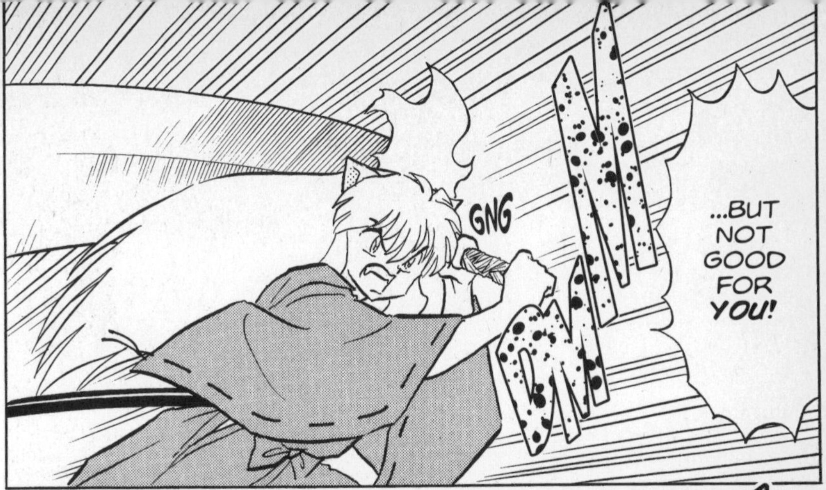
GNG
...BUT NOT GOOD FOR YOU!
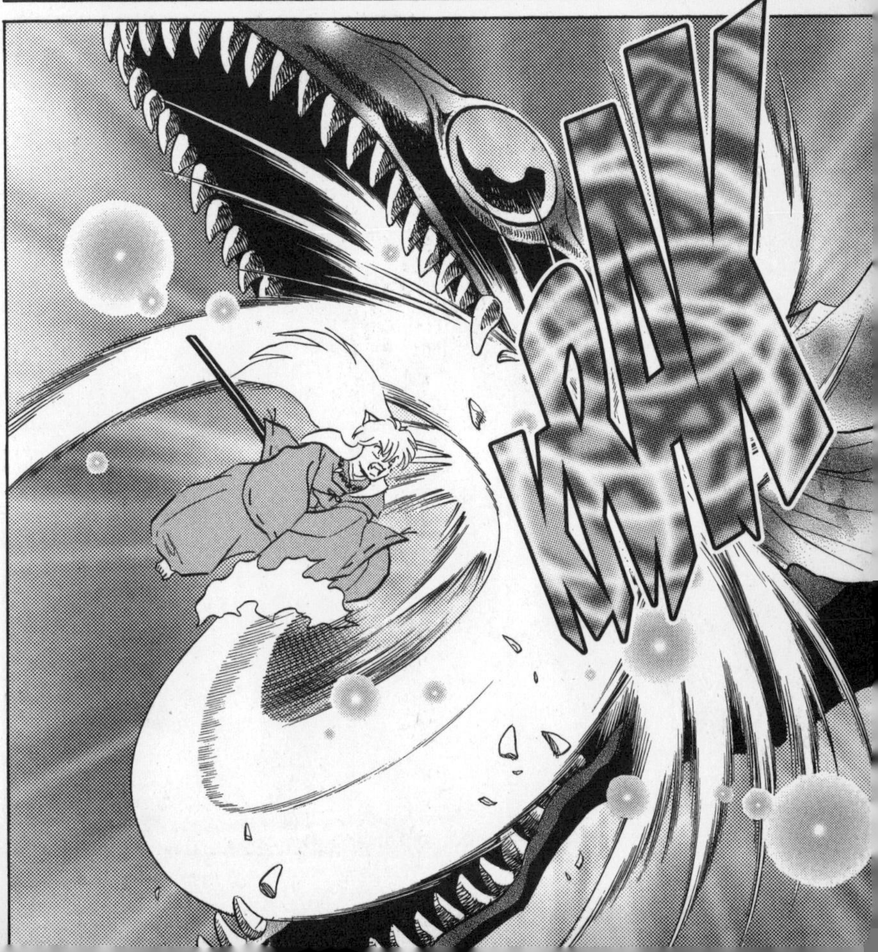

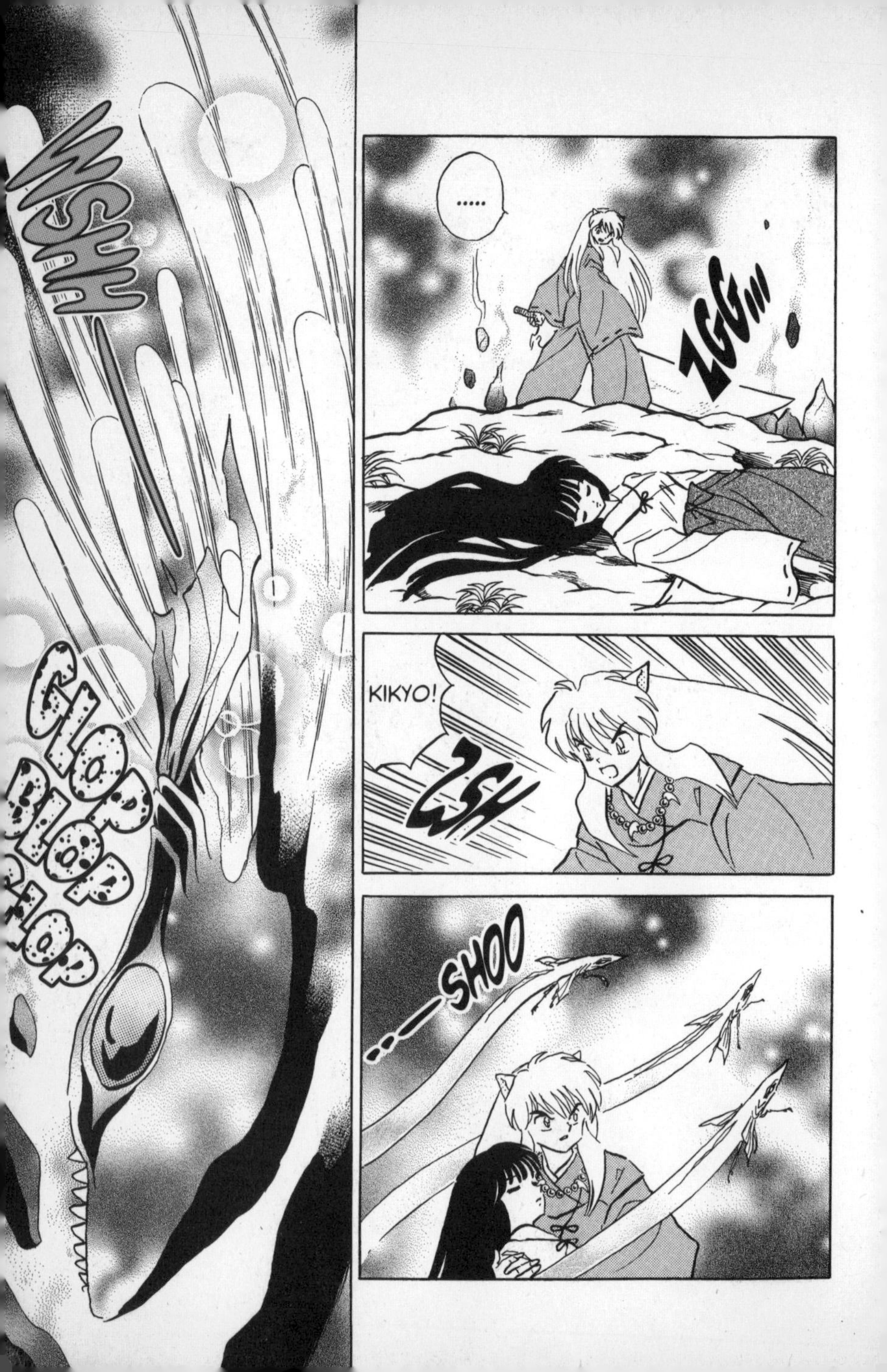
WSHH
GLOP BLOP PLOP
......
ZGG...
KIKYO!
ZSH
...SHOO

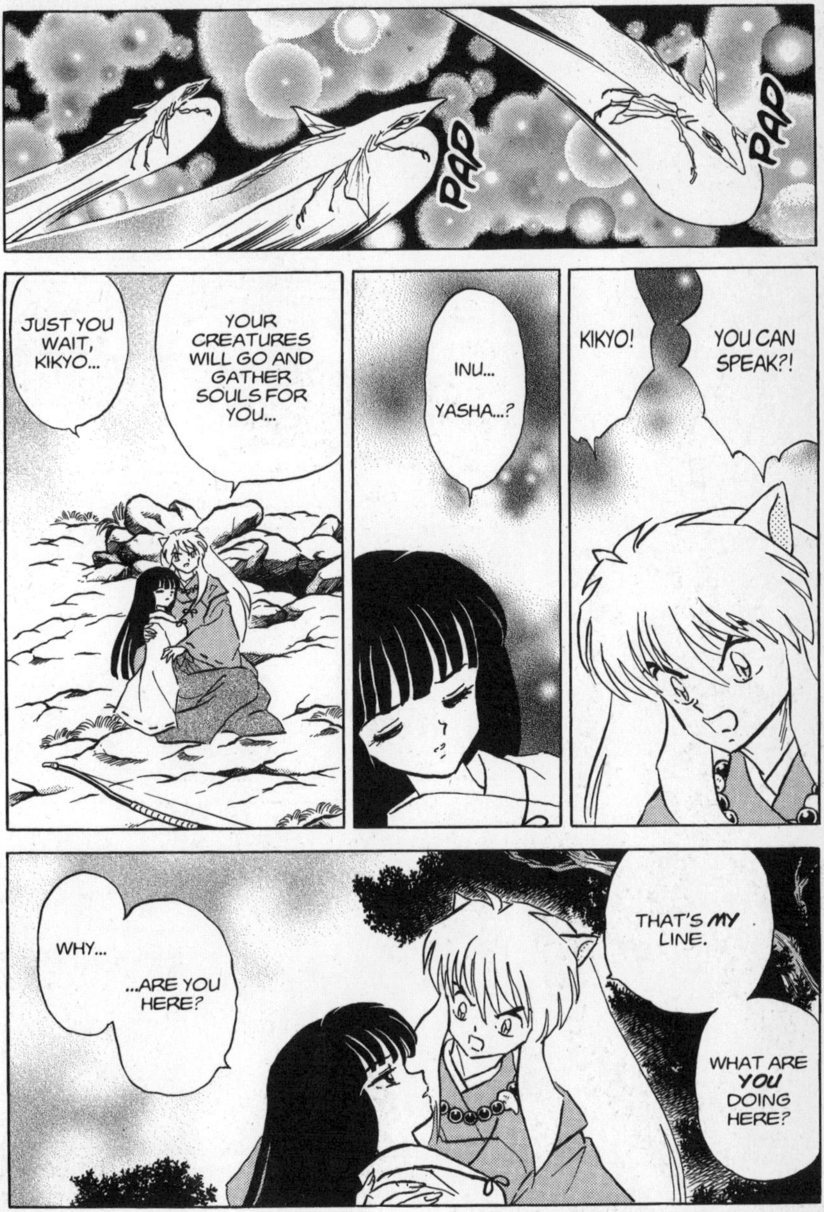
PAP
PAP
JUST YOU WAIT, KIKYO...
YOUR CREATURES WILL GO AND GATHER SOULS FOR YOU...
INU...
YASHA...?
KIKYO!
YOU CAN SPEAK?!
WHY...
...ARE YOU HERE?
THAT'S *MY* LINE.
WHAT ARE *YOU* DOING HERE?

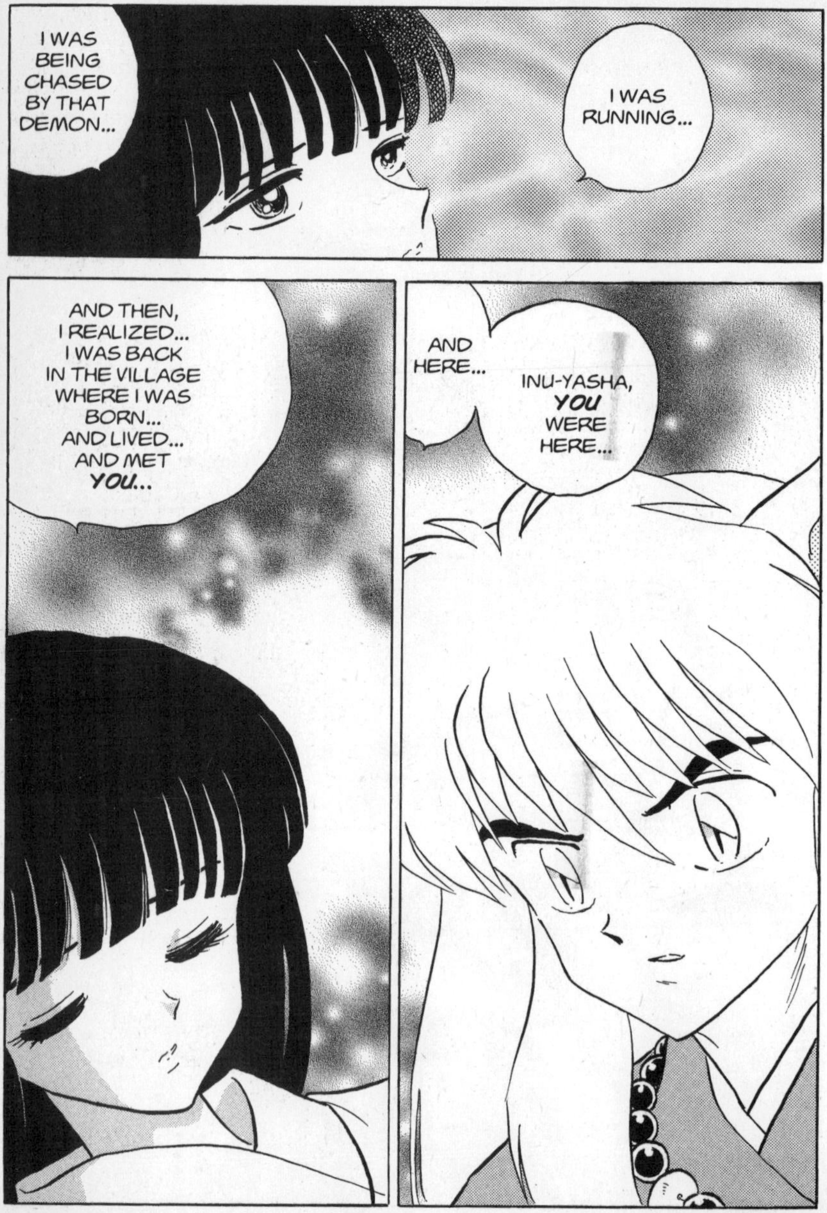
I WAS BEING CHASED BY THAT DEMON...
I WAS RUNNING...
AND THEN, I REALIZED... I WAS BACK IN THE VILLAGE WHERE I WAS BORN... AND LIVED... AND MET *YOU*...
AND HERE...
INU-YASHA, *YOU* WERE HERE...

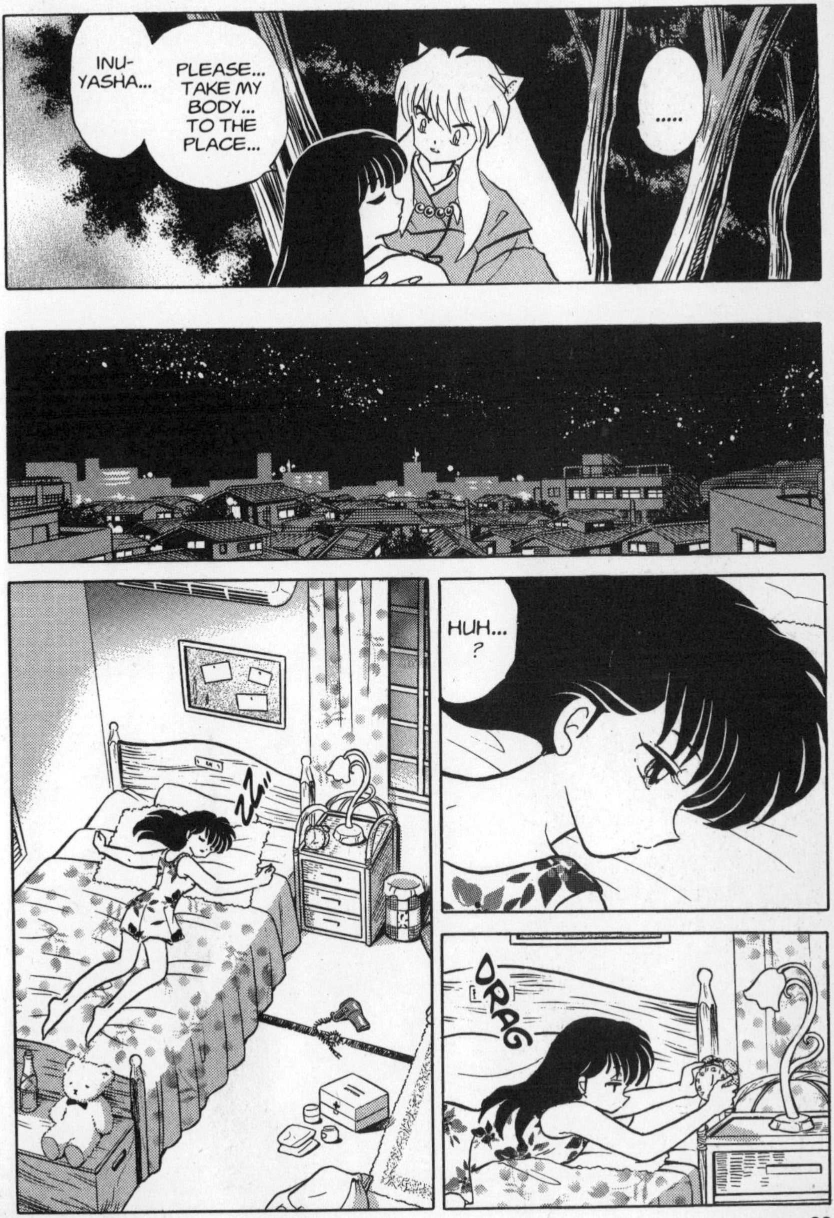
INU-YASHA...
PLEASE... TAKE MY BODY... TO THE PLACE...
......
ZZZ
HUH... ?
DRAG

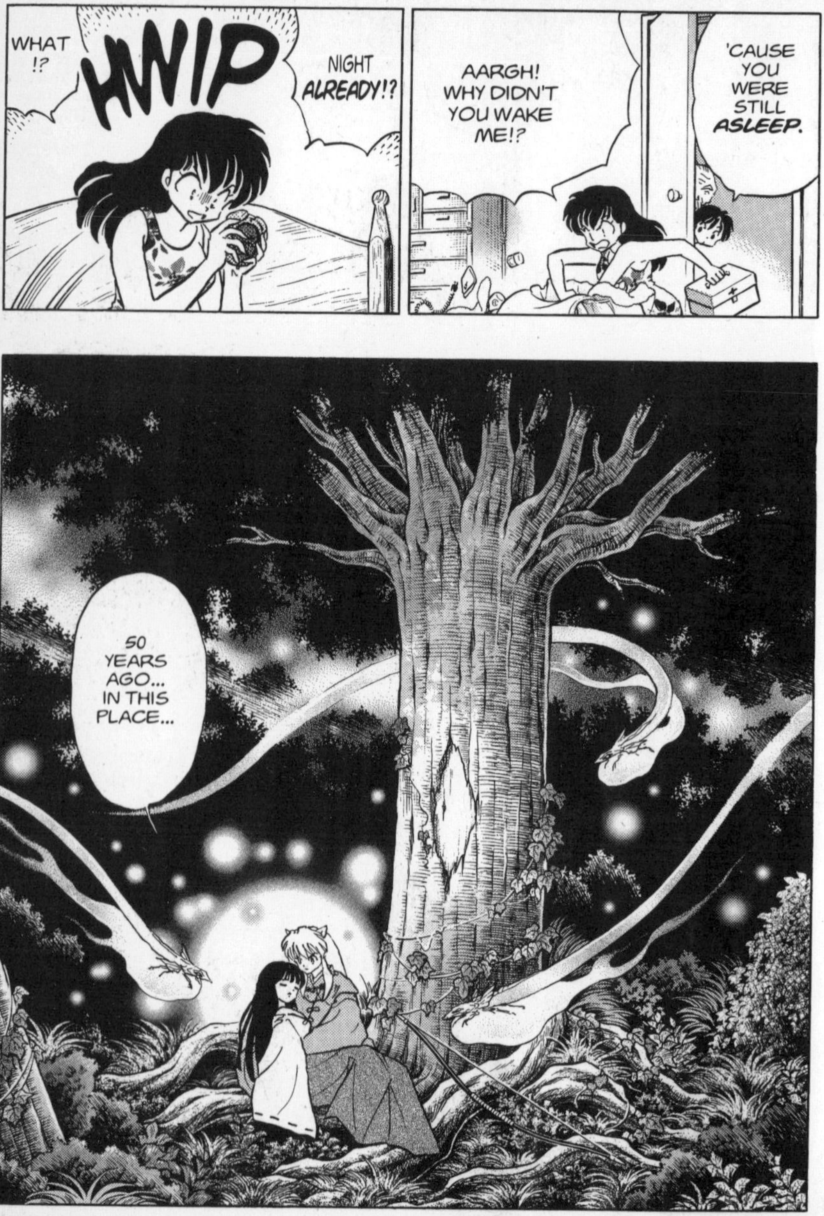
WHAT !?
HWIP
NIGHT ALREADY!?
AARGH! WHY DIDN'T YOU WAKE ME!?
'CAUSE YOU WERE STILL ASLEEP.
50 YEARS AGO... IN THIS PLACE...

I SHOT YOU IN THE CHEST WITH AN ARROW...

AND THEN *MY* LIFE ENDED, TOO.

YEAH...

KIKYO...WHY ARE YOU BRINGING THIS UP NOW...?

INU-YASHA...

WHY DO YOU THINK NARAKU ENSNARED BOTH OF US IN HIS TRAPS... AND MADE US *HATE* EACH OTHER...?

IT WAS...

...TO CORRUPT THE *SHIKON JEWEL.*

TO STAIN YOUR *"HEART"*- WHICH COULD *"CLEANSE"* THE JEWEL, WITH *"HATRED"*...

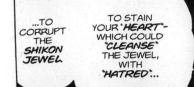

HMPH...

BUT... HE DIDN'T HAVE TO.

EVEN *WITHOUT* CORRUPTING MY HEART...

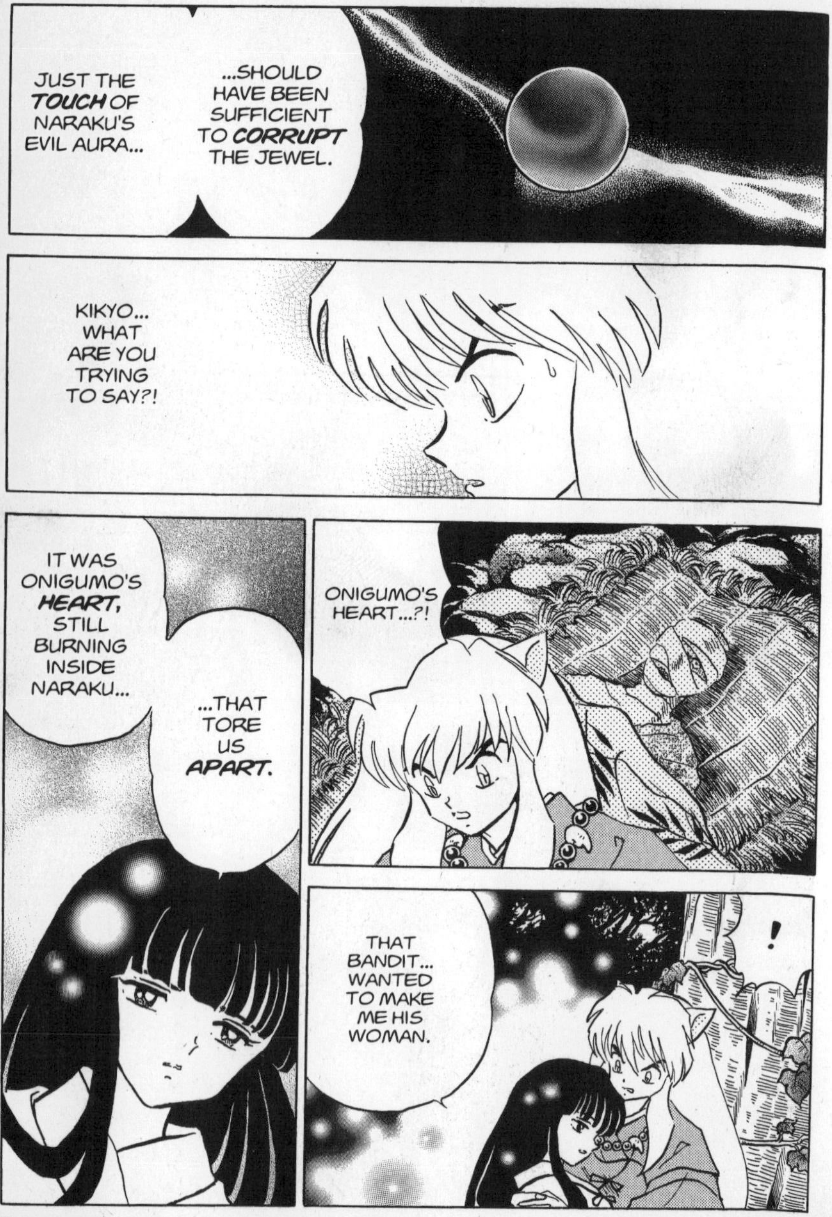

JUST THE TOUCH OF NARAKU'S EVIL AURA...
...SHOULD HAVE BEEN SUFFICIENT TO CORRUPT THE JEWEL.
KIKYO... WHAT ARE YOU TRYING TO SAY?!
IT WAS ONIGUMO'S HEART, STILL BURNING INSIDE NARAKU...
...THAT TORE US APART.
ONIGUMO'S HEART...?!
THAT BANDIT... WANTED TO MAKE ME HIS WOMAN.
!

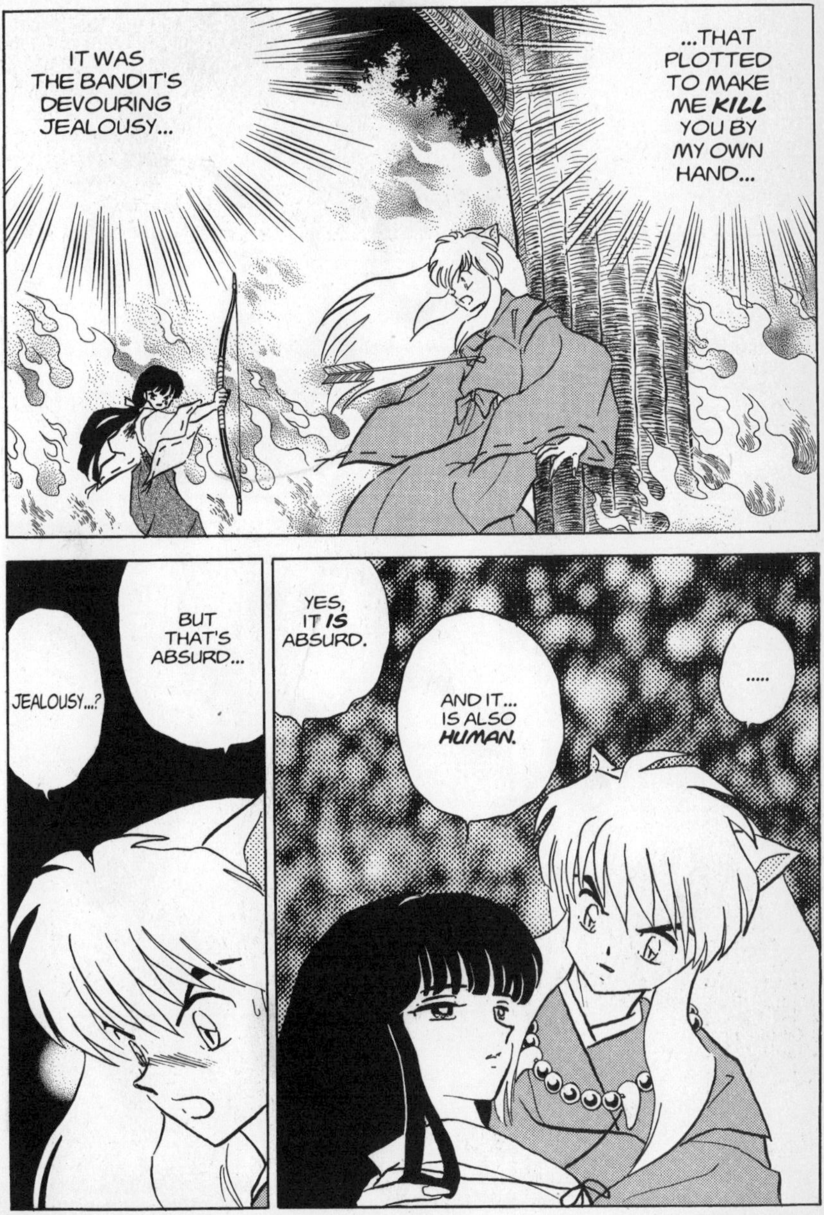
IT WAS THE BANDIT'S DEVOURING JEALOUSY...
...THAT PLOTTED TO MAKE ME **KILL** YOU BY MY OWN HAND...
JEALOUSY...?
BUT THAT'S ABSURD...
YES, IT ***IS*** ABSURD.
AND IT... IS ALSO ***HUMAN***.
.....

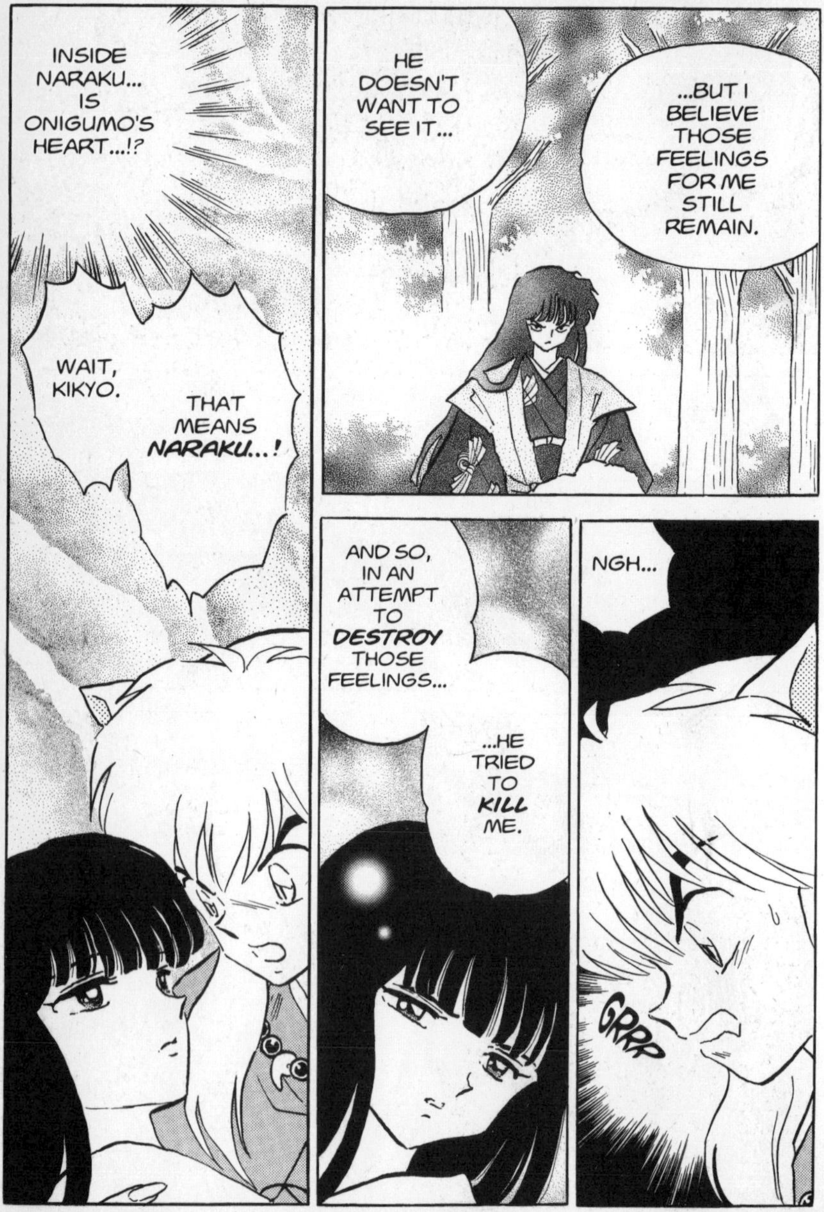
INSIDE NARAKU... IS ONIGUMO'S HEART...!?
WAIT, KIKYO.
THAT MEANS NARAKU...!
HE DOESN'T WANT TO SEE IT...
...BUT I BELIEVE THOSE FEELINGS FOR ME STILL REMAIN.
AND SO, IN AN ATTEMPT TO DESTROY THOSE FEELINGS...
...HE TRIED TO KILL ME.
NGH...
GRRR

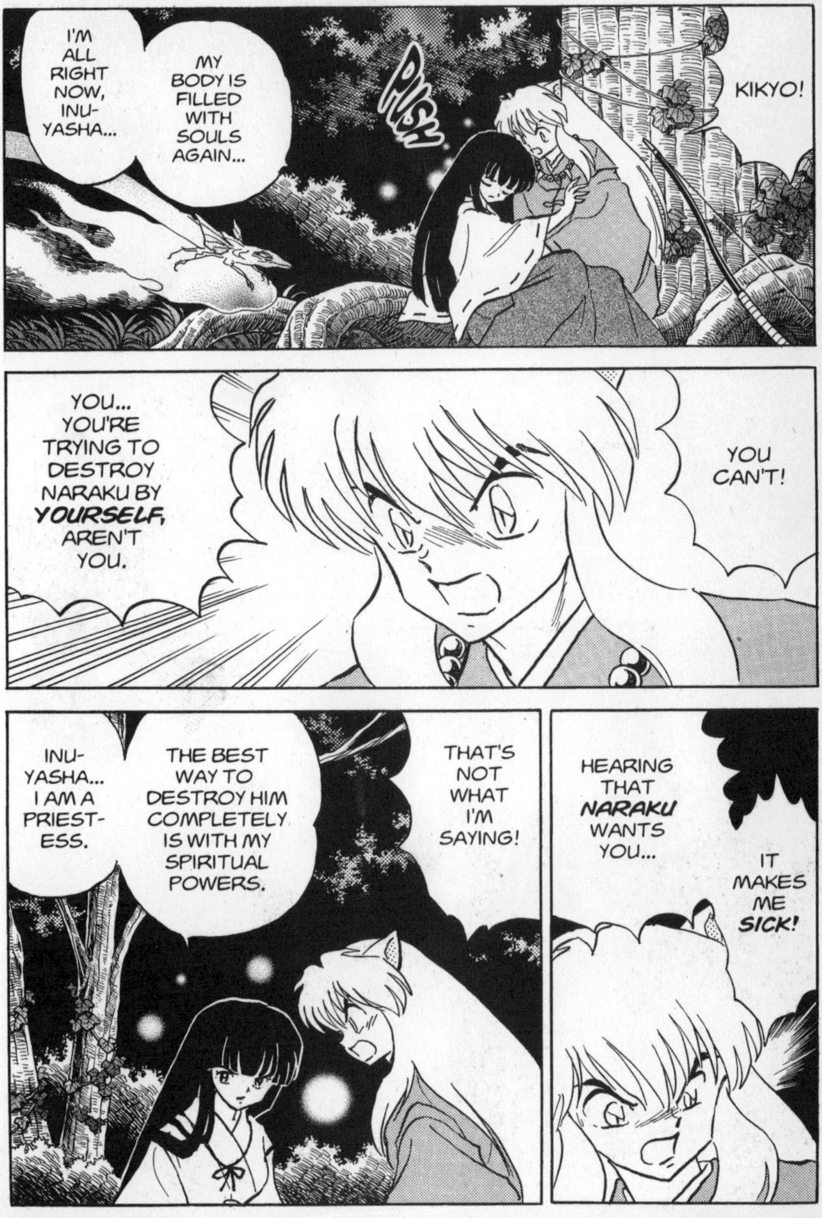
I'M ALL RIGHT NOW, INU-YASHA...
MY BODY IS FILLED WITH SOULS AGAIN...
PUSH
KIKYO!
YOU... YOU'RE TRYING TO DESTROY NARAKU BY *YOURSELF*, AREN'T YOU.
YOU CAN'T!
INU-YASHA... I AM A PRIEST-ESS.
THE BEST WAY TO DESTROY HIM COMPLETELY IS WITH MY SPIRITUAL POWERS.
THAT'S NOT WHAT I'M SAYING!
HEARING THAT *NARAKU* WANTS YOU...
IT MAKES ME *SICK!*

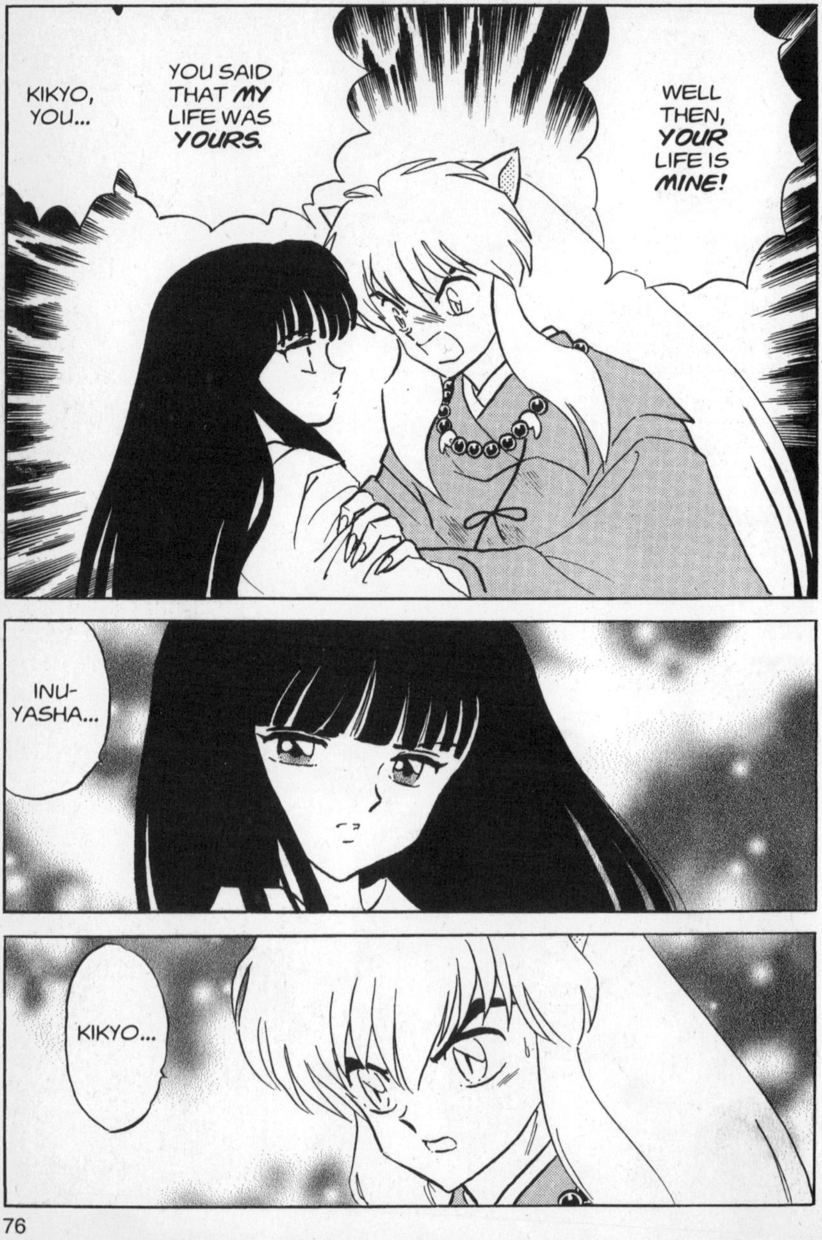
KIKYO, YOU...
YOU SAID THAT **MY** LIFE WAS **YOURS.**
WELL THEN, **YOUR** LIFE IS **MINE!**
INU-YASHA...
KIKYO...

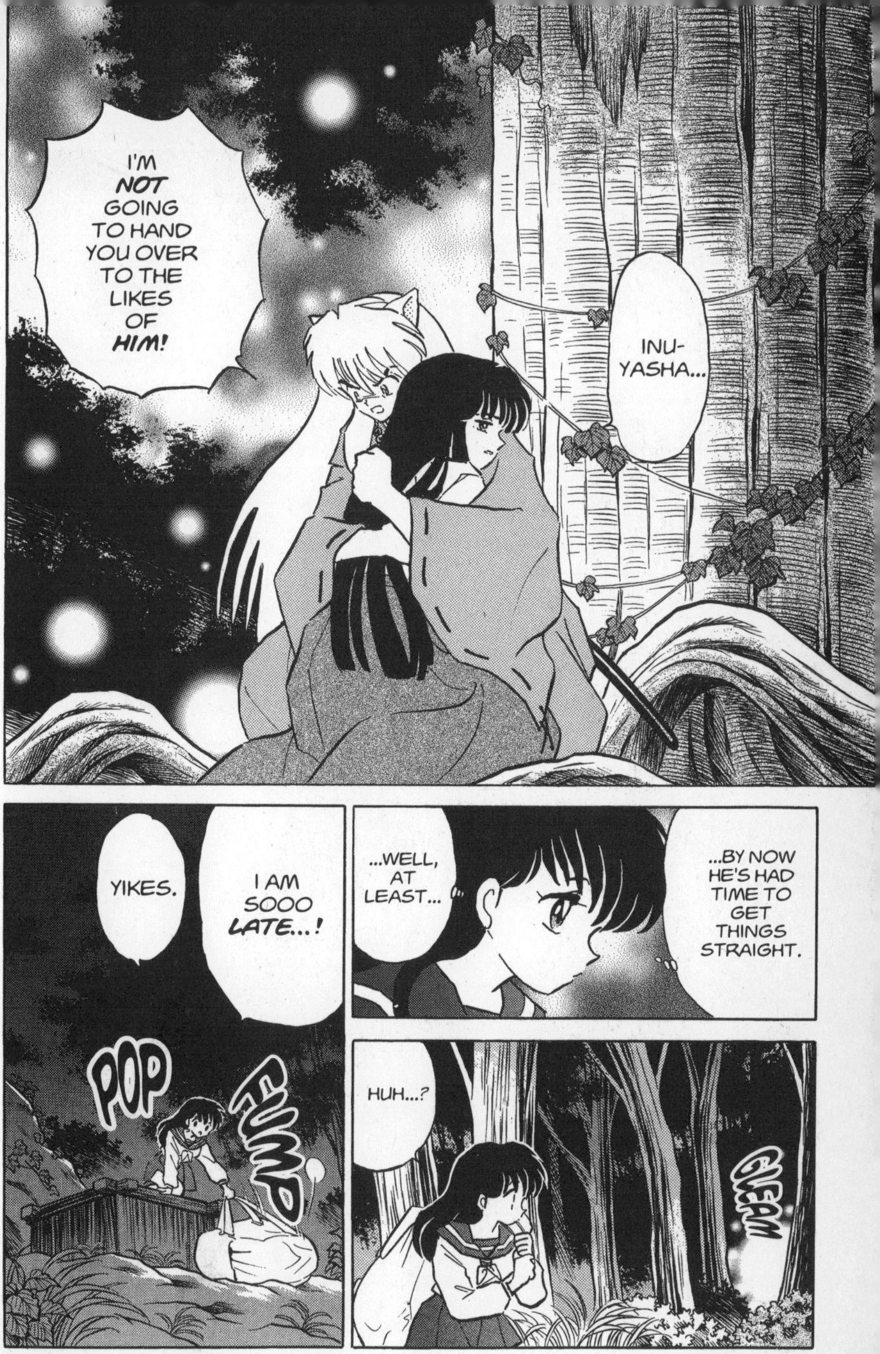
I'M NOT GOING TO HAND YOU OVER TO THE LIKES OF HIM!
INU-YASHA...
YIKES.
I AM SOOO LATE...!
POP
FUMP
...WELL, AT LEAST...
...BY NOW HE'S HAD TIME TO GET THINGS STRAIGHT.
HUH...?
GLEAM

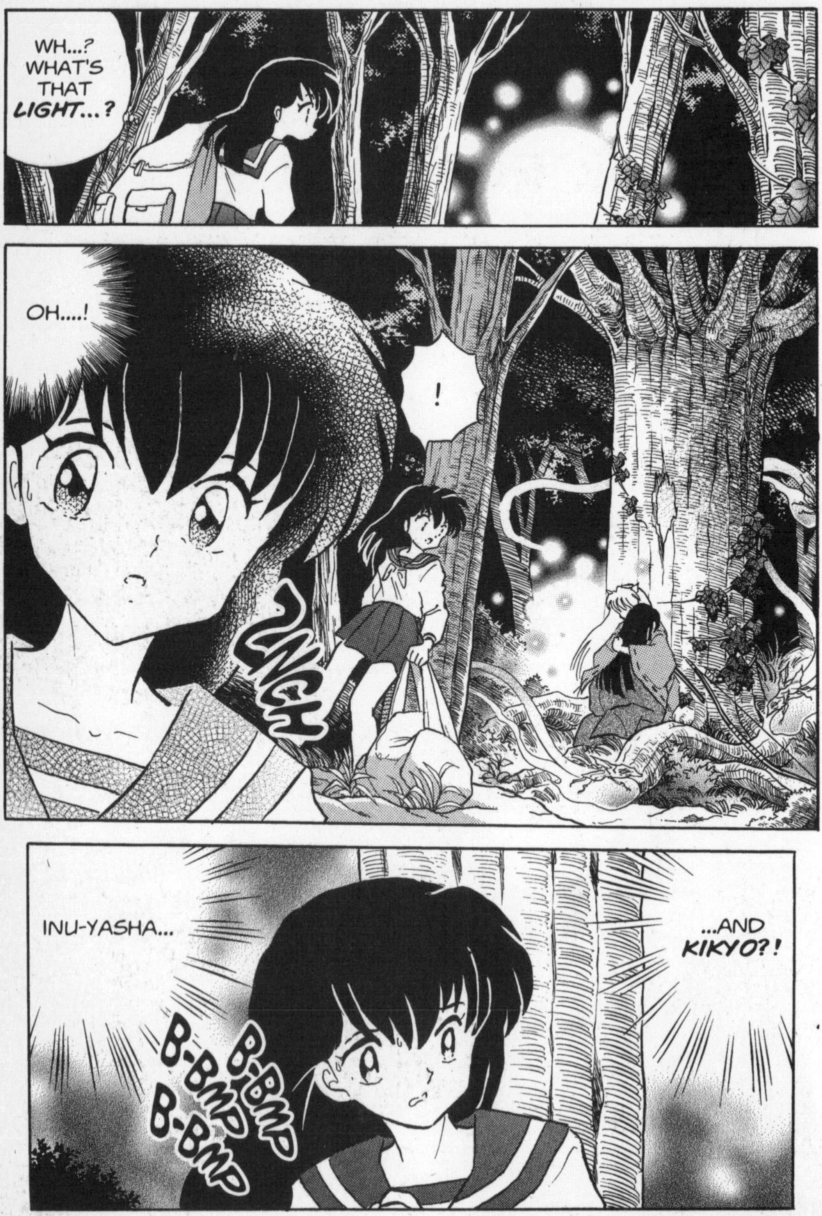
WH...? WHAT'S THAT LIGHT...?
OH....!
!
INU-YASHA...
...AND KIKYO?!
B-BMP B-BMP B-BMP

SCROLL FIVE
JEALOUSY

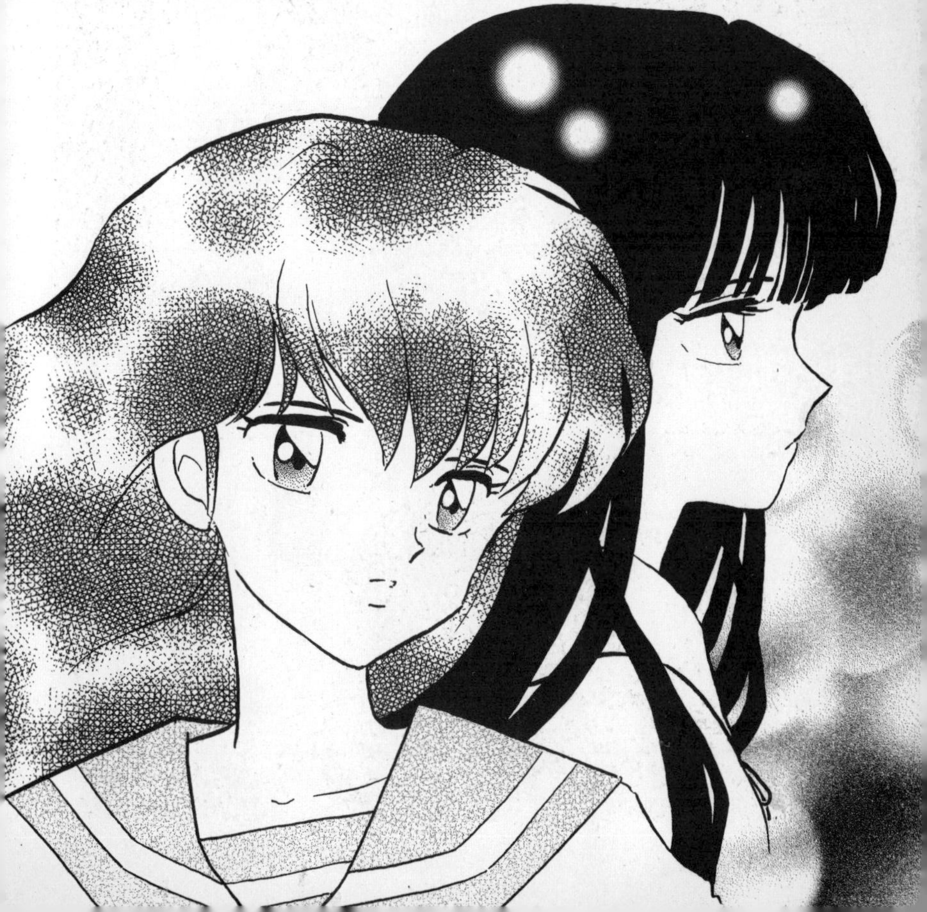

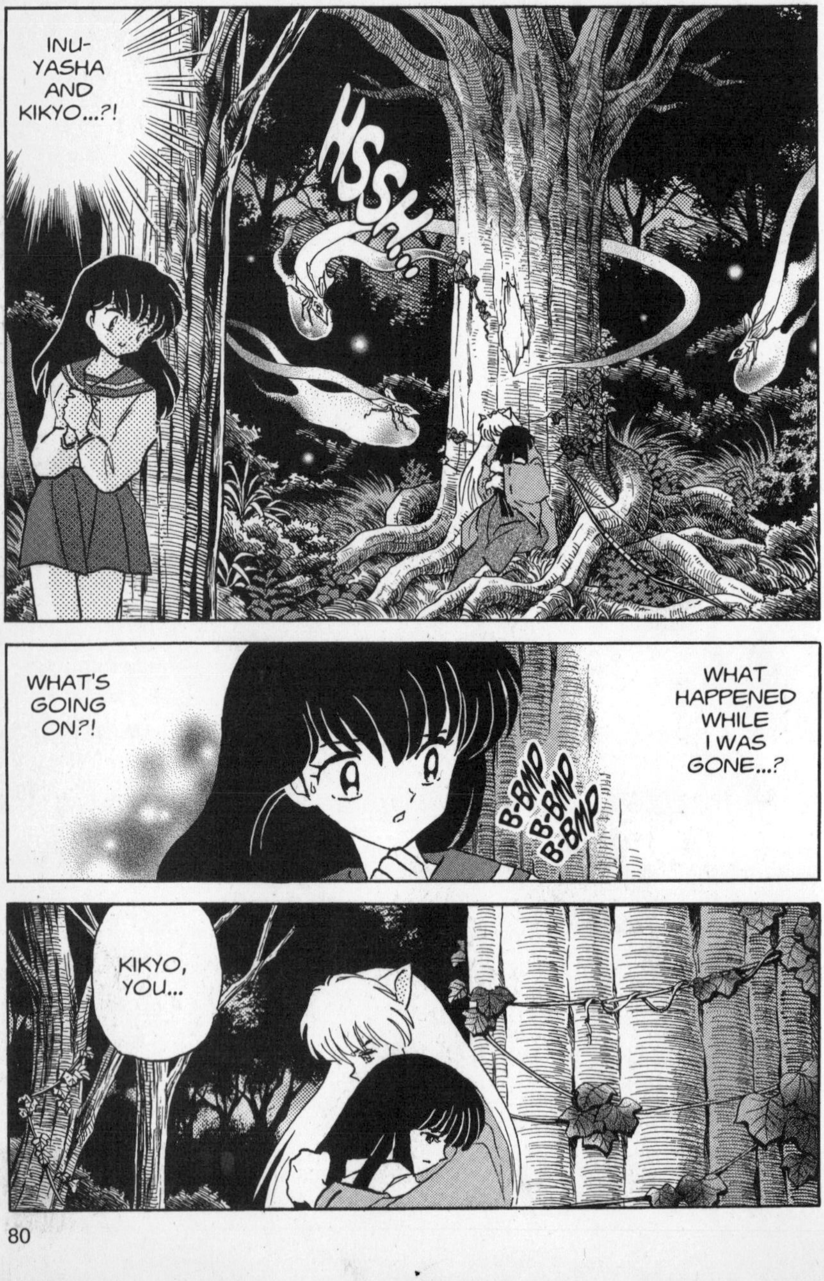
INU-YASHA AND KIKYO...?!
HSSH...
WHAT'S GOING ON?!
B-BMP B-BMP B-BMP
WHAT HAPPENED WHILE I WAS GONE...?
KIKYO, YOU...

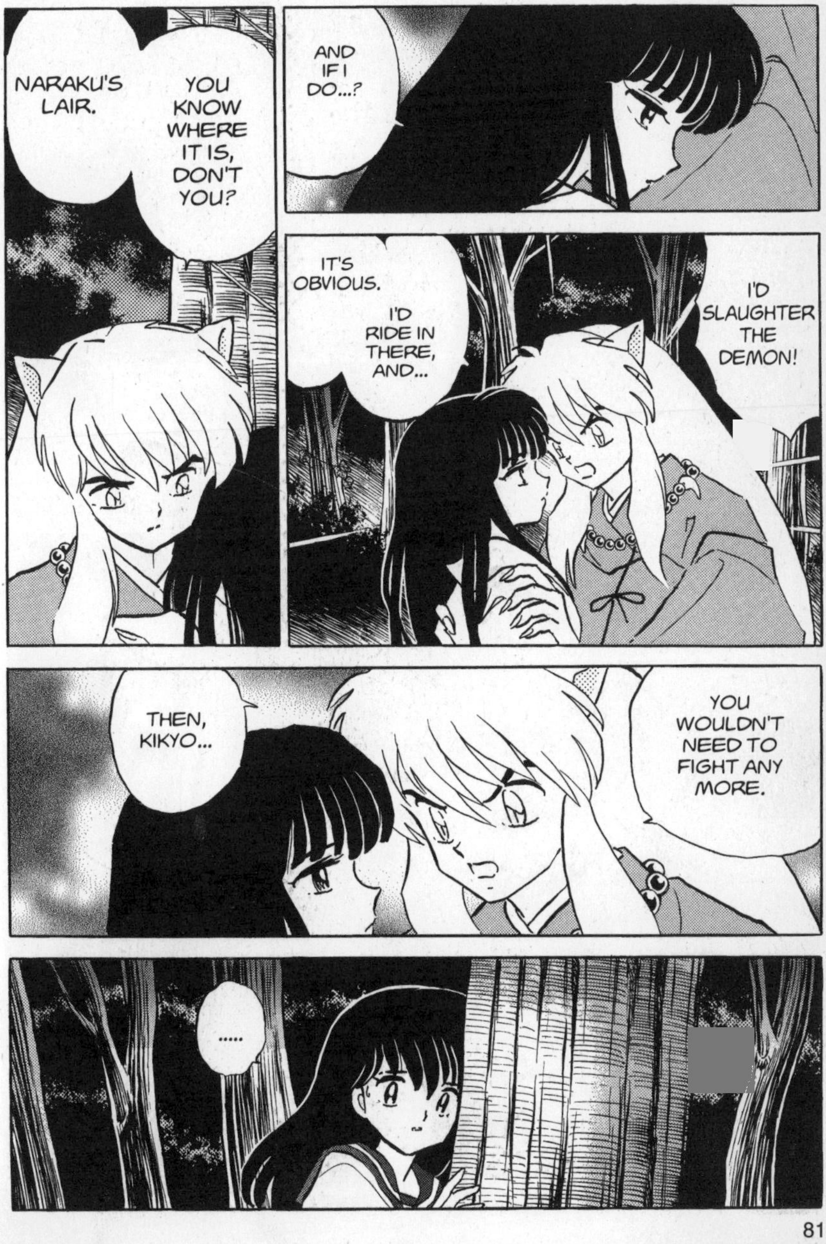
NARAKU'S LAIR.
YOU KNOW WHERE IT IS, DON'T YOU?
AND IF I DO...?
IT'S OBVIOUS.
I'D RIDE IN THERE, AND...
I'D SLAUGHTER THE DEMON!
THEN, KIKYO...
YOU WOULDN'T NEED TO FIGHT ANY MORE.
......

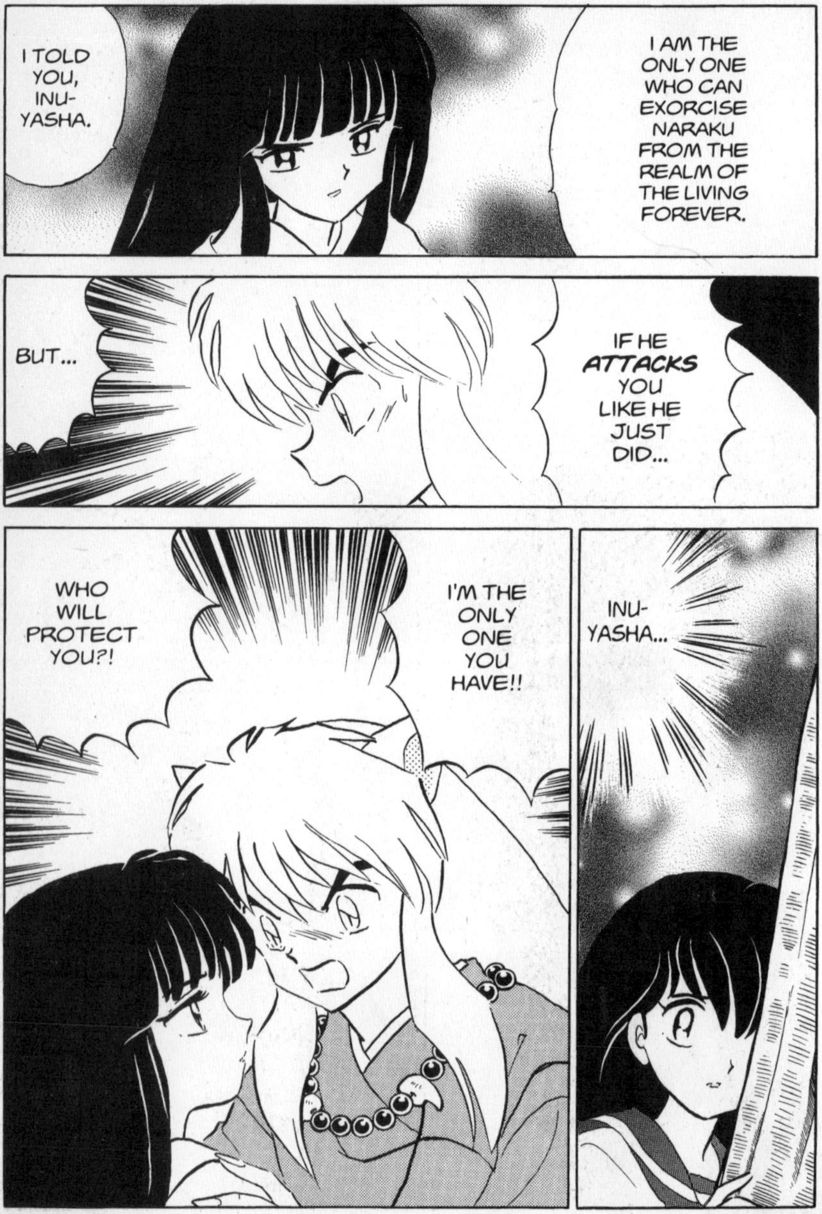
I TOLD YOU, INU-YASHA.
I AM THE ONLY ONE WHO CAN EXORCISE NARAKU FROM THE REALM OF THE LIVING FOREVER.
BUT...
IF HE ATTACKS YOU LIKE HE JUST DID...
WHO WILL PROTECT YOU?!
I'M THE ONLY ONE YOU HAVE!!
INU-YASHA...

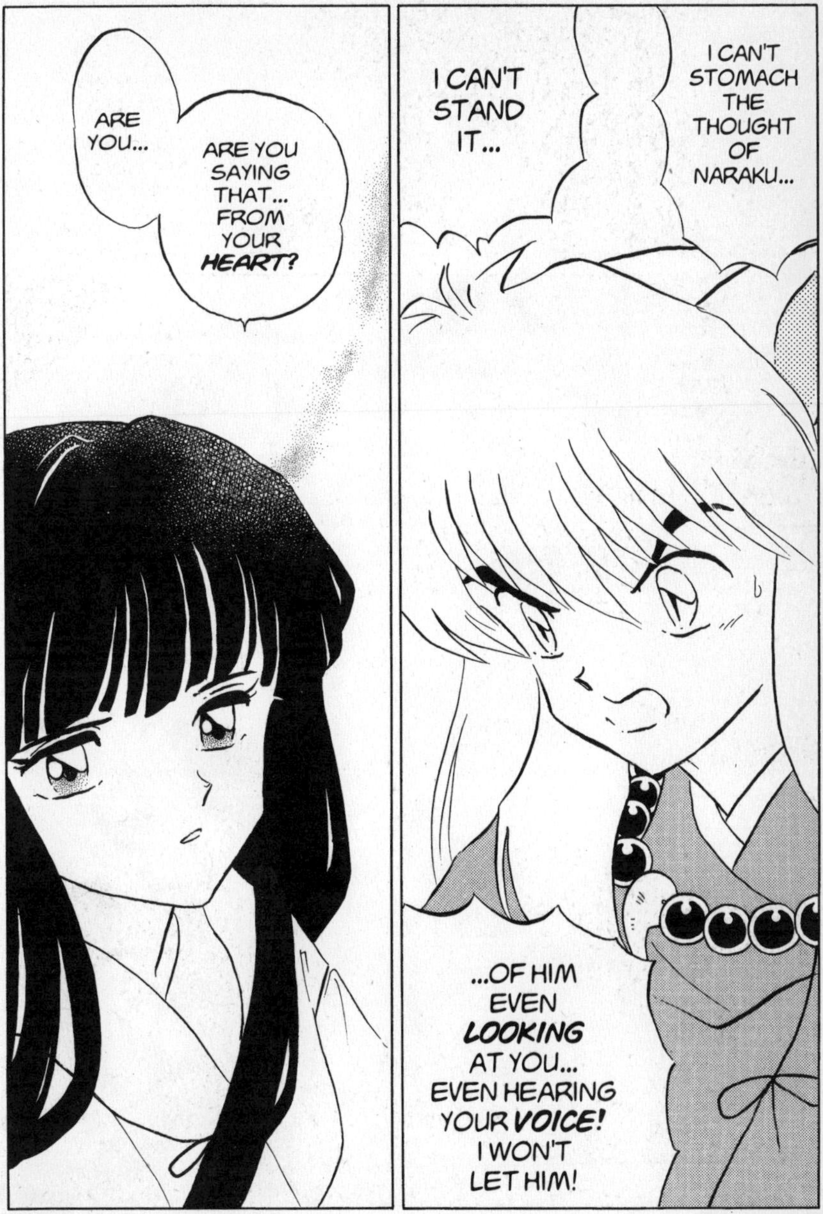
ARE YOU...
ARE YOU SAYING THAT... FROM YOUR HEART?
I CAN'T STAND IT...
I CAN'T STOMACH THE THOUGHT OF NARAKU...
...OF HIM EVEN LOOKING AT YOU... EVEN HEARING YOUR VOICE! I WON'T LET HIM!

I WON'T LET YOU HAND YOUR LIFE OVER TO HIM AGAIN!

INU-YASHA, PLEASE...

I WON'T LEAVE MYSELF VULNERABLE LIKE THIS EVER AGAIN.

BESIDES, NARAKU CAN'T KILL ME.

NOT SO LONG AS *ONIGUMO'S HEART* IS STILL IN HIM... AND STILL YEARNS FOR ME.

WHAT?

ONIGUMO'S HEART... IN NARAKU...?

THAT MEANS...

NARAKU LOVES *KIKYO*?!

SO *THAT'S* WHAT INU-YASHA IS SO WORKED UP ABOUT...

B-BMP B-BMP B-BMP

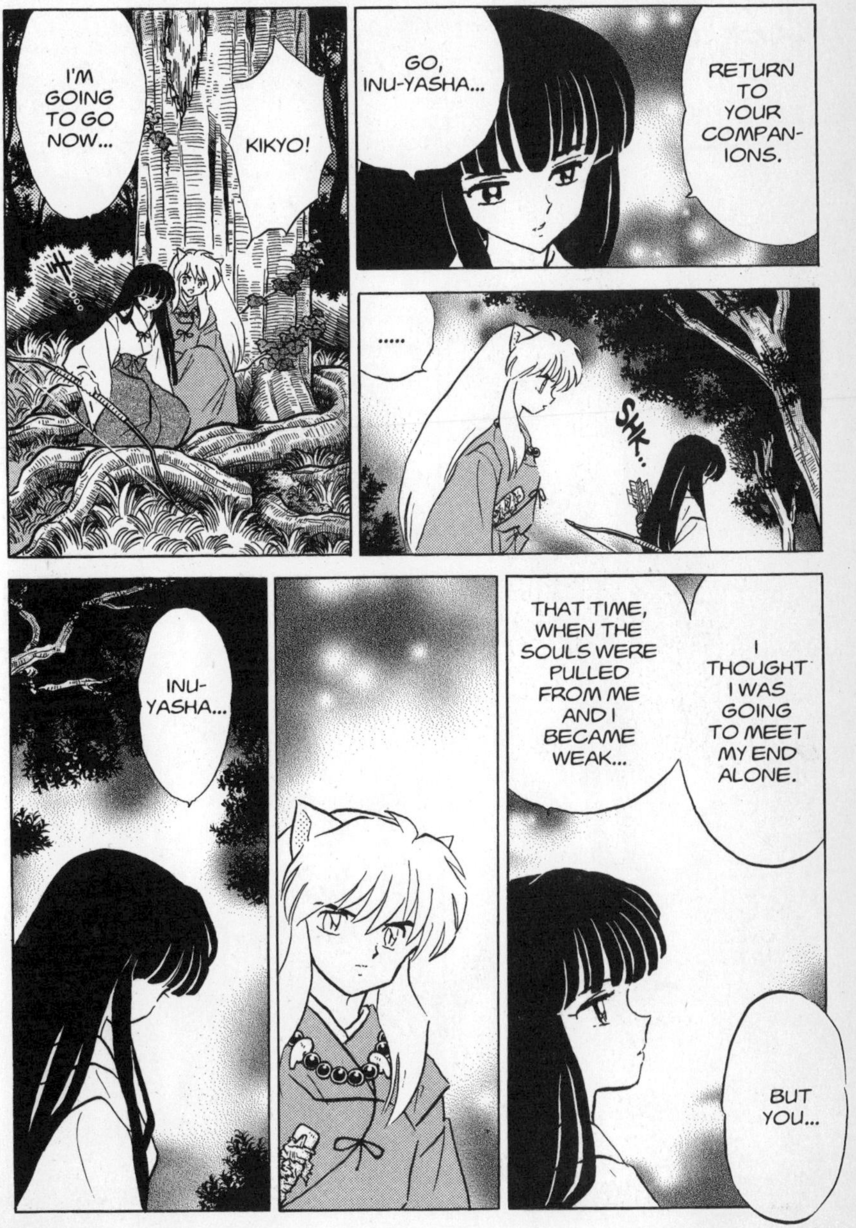
I'M GOING TO GO NOW...
KIKYO!
GO, INU-YASHA...
RETURN TO YOUR COMPAN-IONS.
.....
SHK...
INU-YASHA...
THAT TIME, WHEN THE SOULS WERE PULLED FROM ME AND I BECAME WEAK...
I THOUGHT I WAS GOING TO MEET MY END ALONE.
BUT YOU...

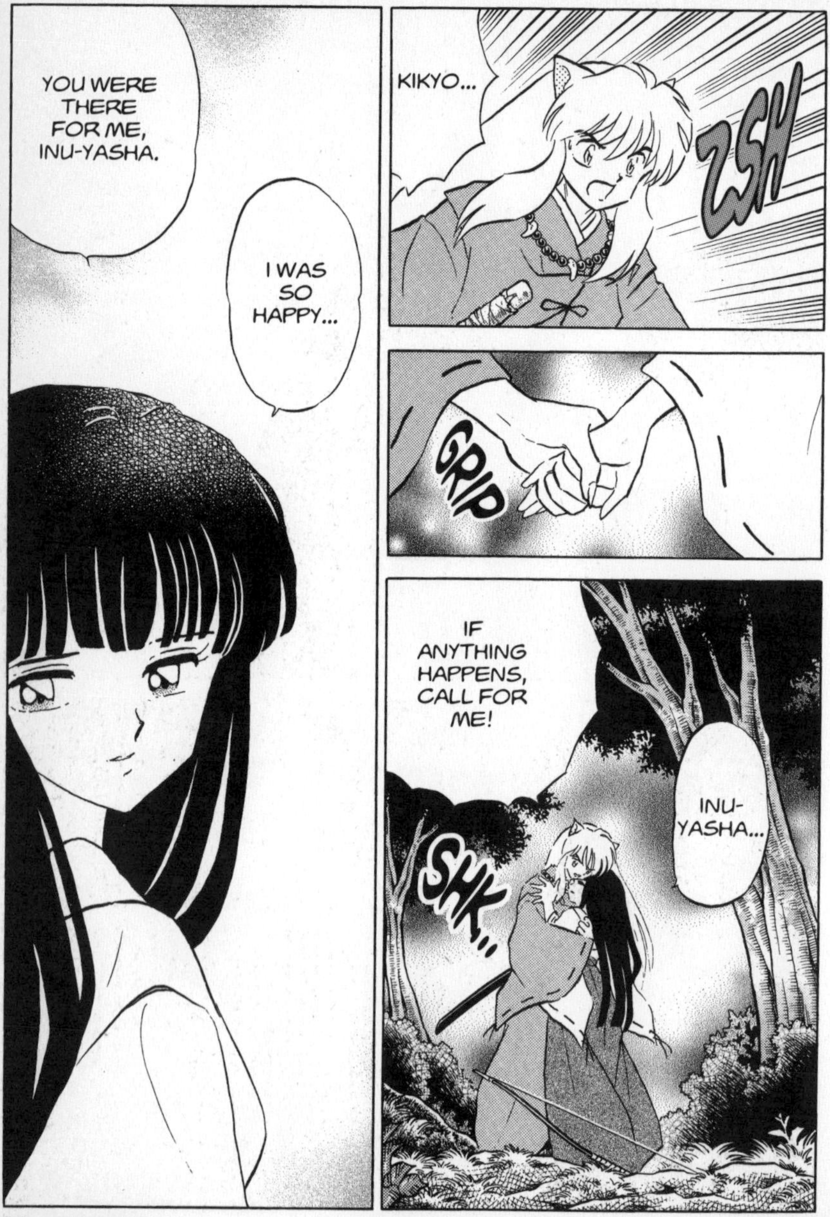
YOU WERE THERE FOR ME, INU-YASHA.
I WAS SO HAPPY...
KIKYO...
ZSH
GRIP
IF ANYTHING HAPPENS, CALL FOR ME!
INU-YASHA...
SHK...

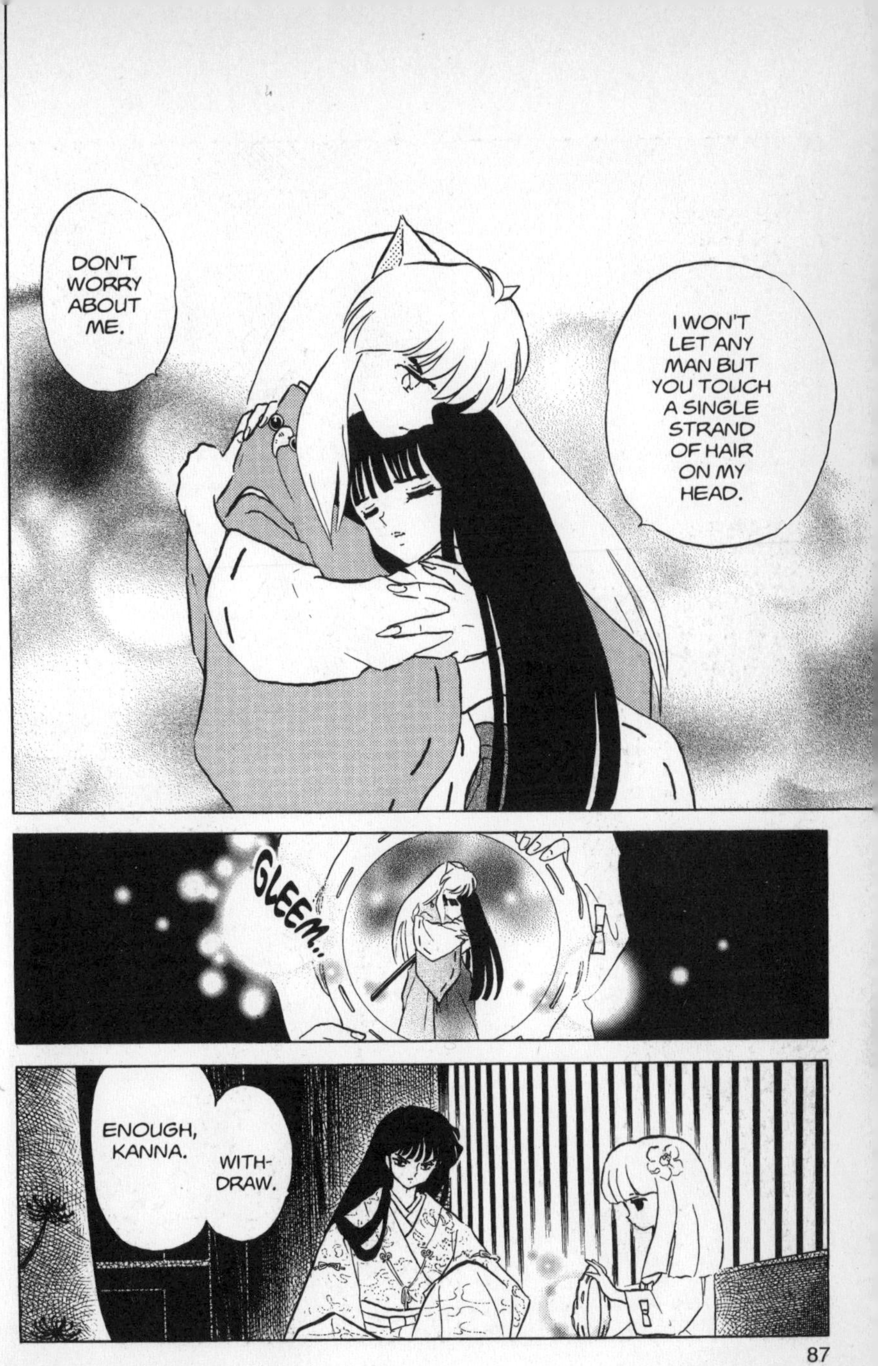
DON'T WORRY ABOUT ME.
I WON'T LET ANY MAN BUT YOU TOUCH A SINGLE STRAND OF HAIR ON MY HEAD.
GLEEM...
ENOUGH, KANNA.
WITH-DRAW.

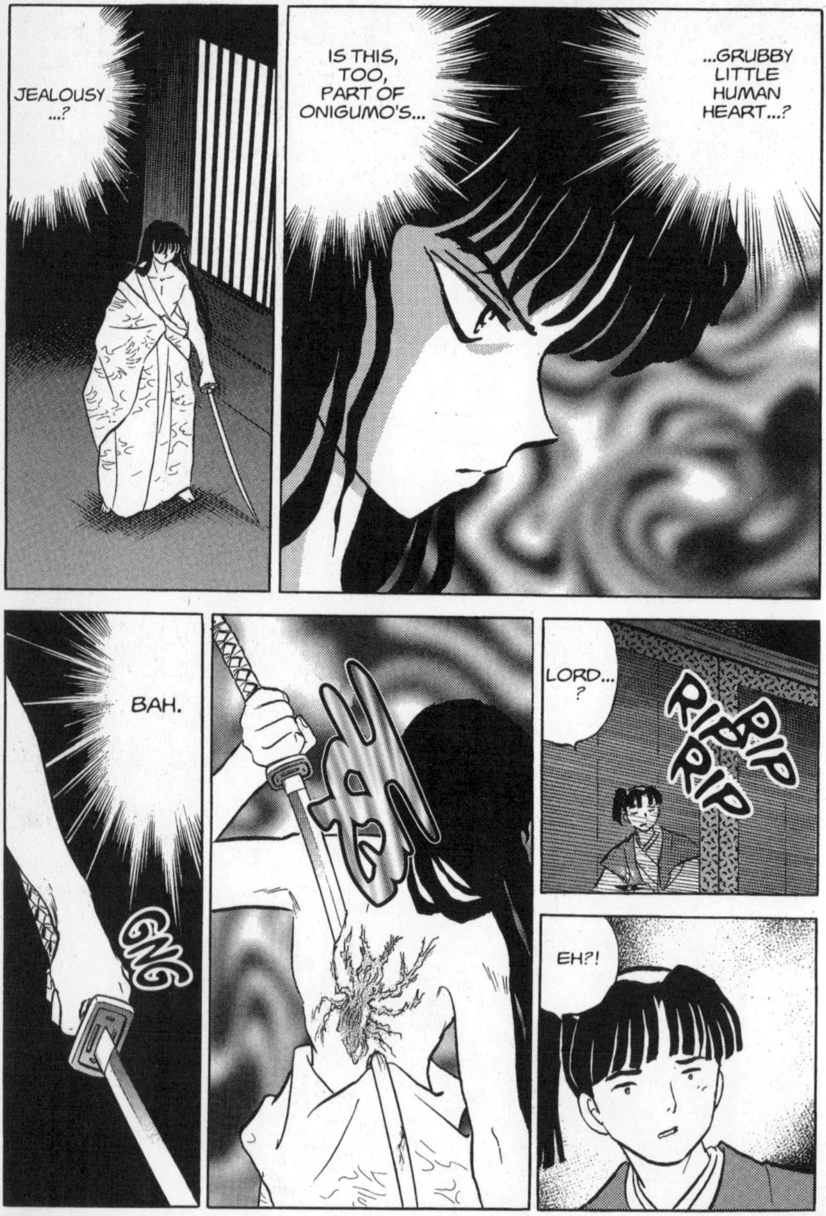
JEALOUSY ...?
IS THIS, TOO, PART OF ONIGUMO'S...
...GRUBBY LITTLE HUMAN HEART...?
BAH.
GNG
LORD... ?
RIP RIP RIP RIP
EH?!

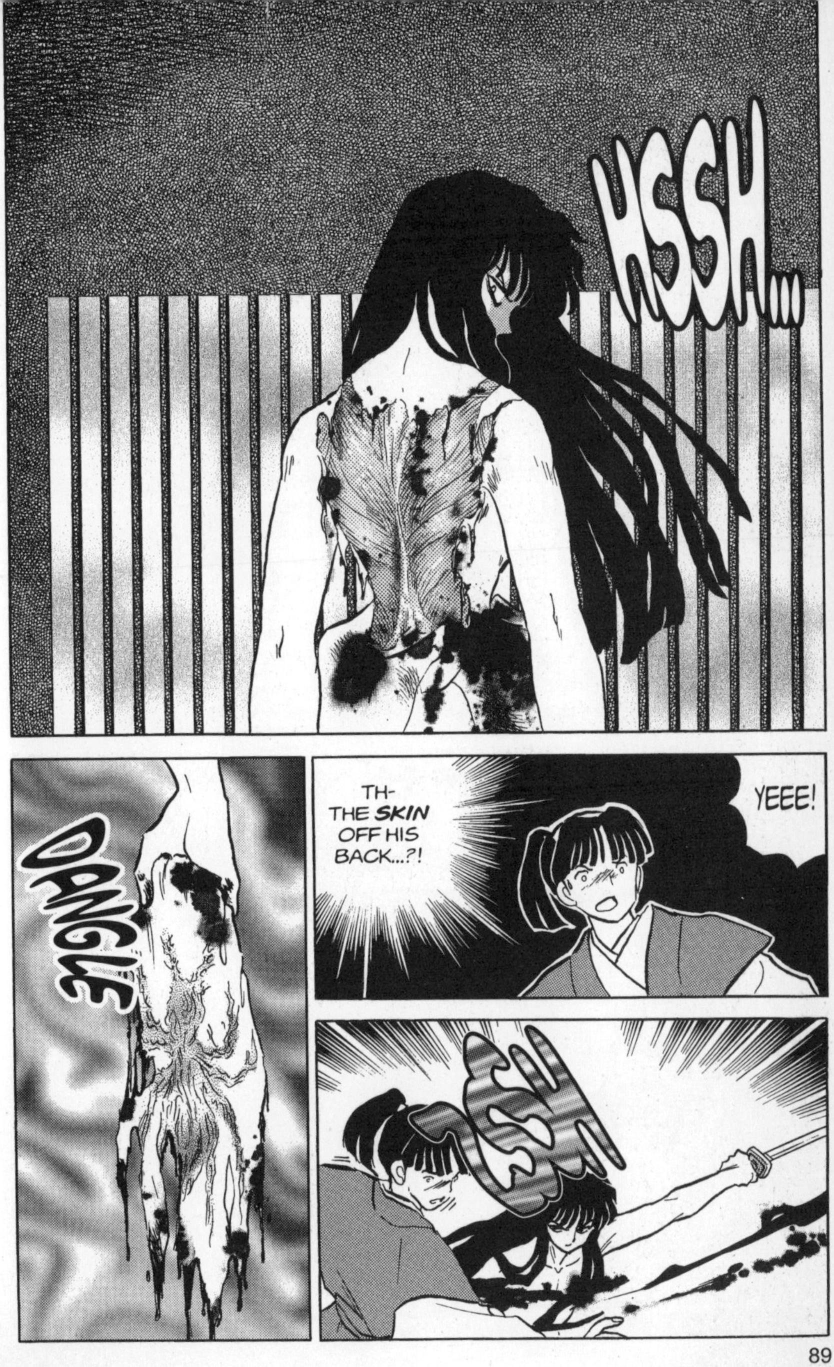
HSSH...
DANGLE
TH- THE SKIN OFF HIS BACK...?!
YEEE!
FSSH

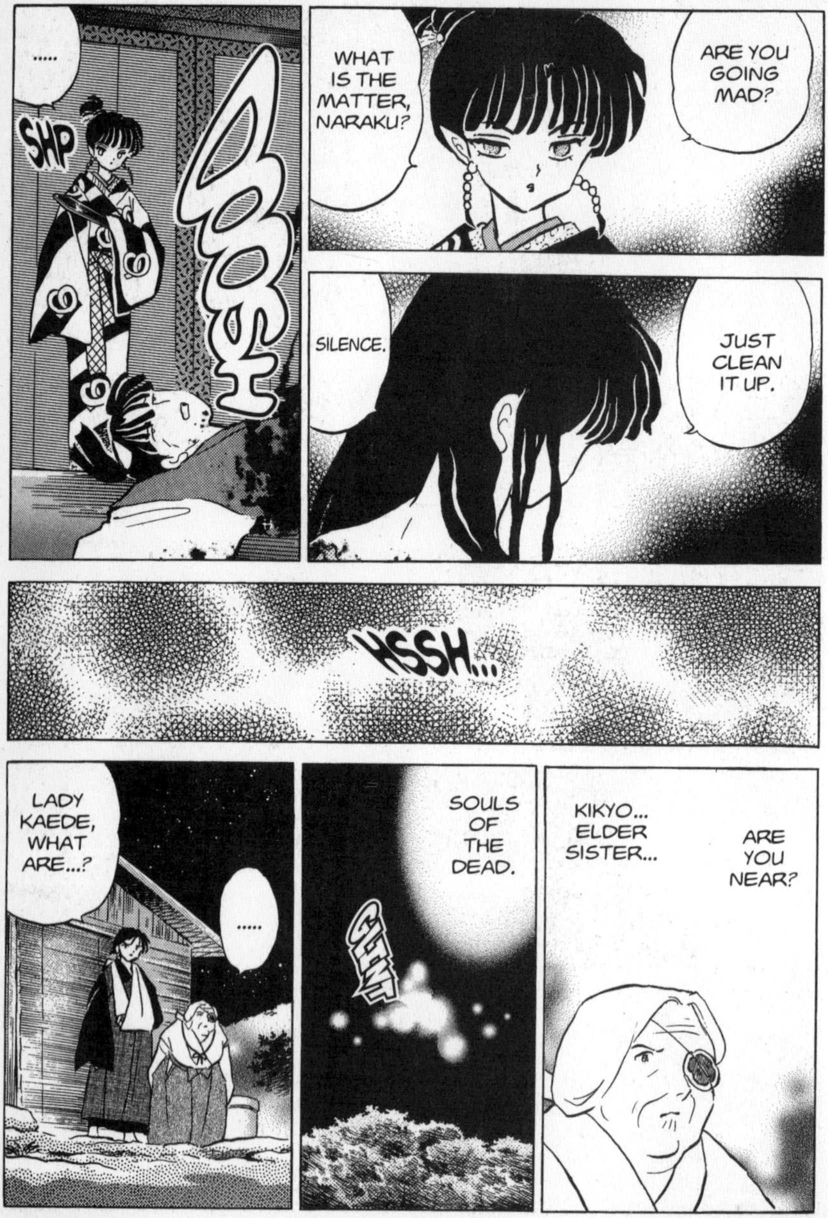
.....
SHP
WHAT IS THE MATTER, NARAKU?
ARE YOU GOING MAD?
SILENCE.
JUST CLEAN IT UP.
HSSH...
LADY KAEDE, WHAT ARE...?
.....
SOULS OF THE DEAD.
KIKYO... ELDER SISTER...
ARE YOU NEAR?

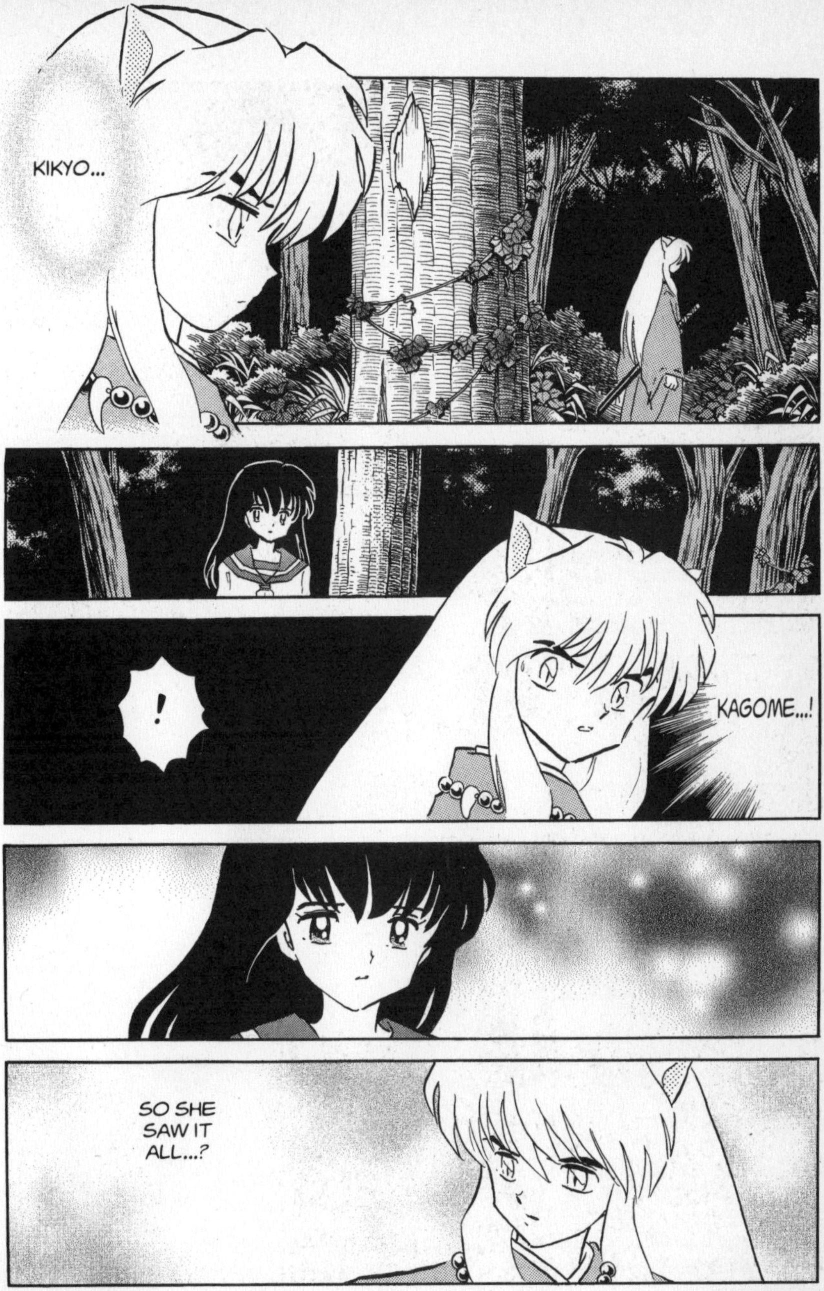
KIKYO...
!
KAGOME...!
SO SHE SAW IT ALL...?

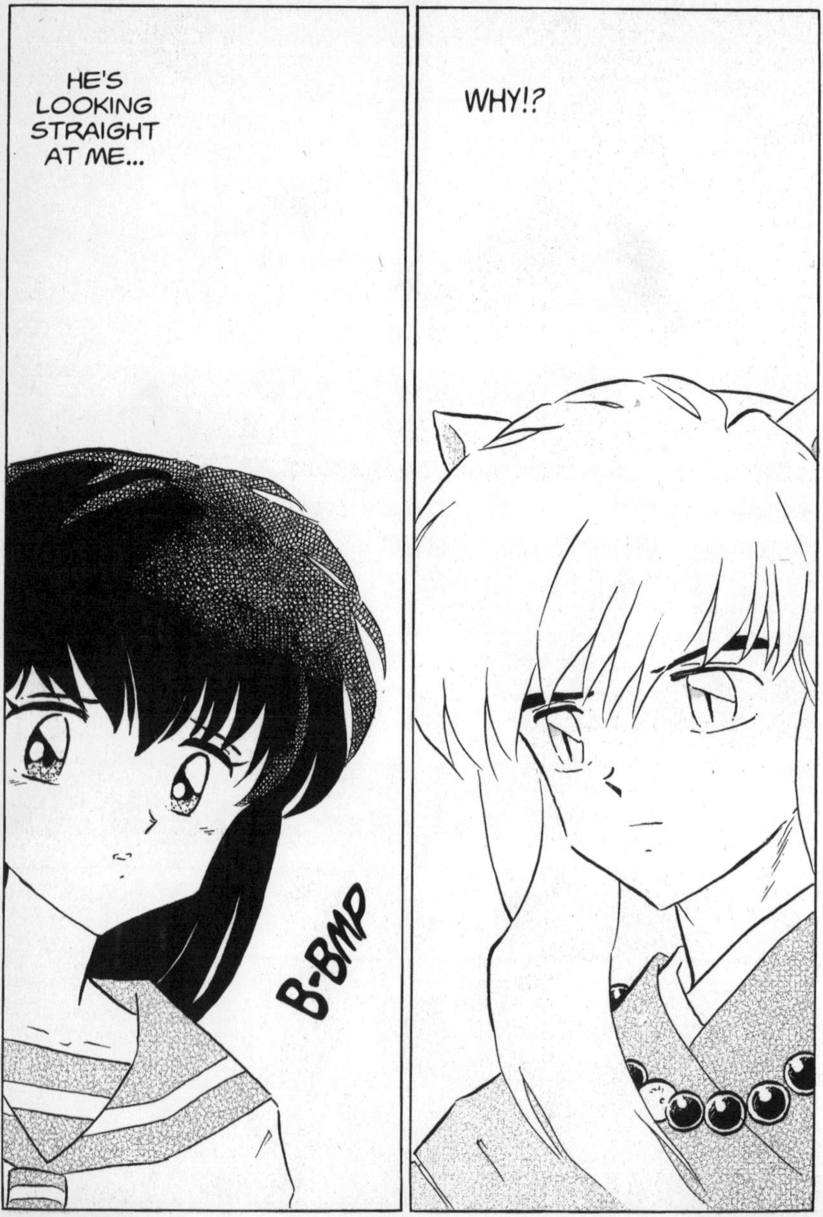
WHY!?
HE'S LOOKING STRAIGHT AT ME...
B-BMP

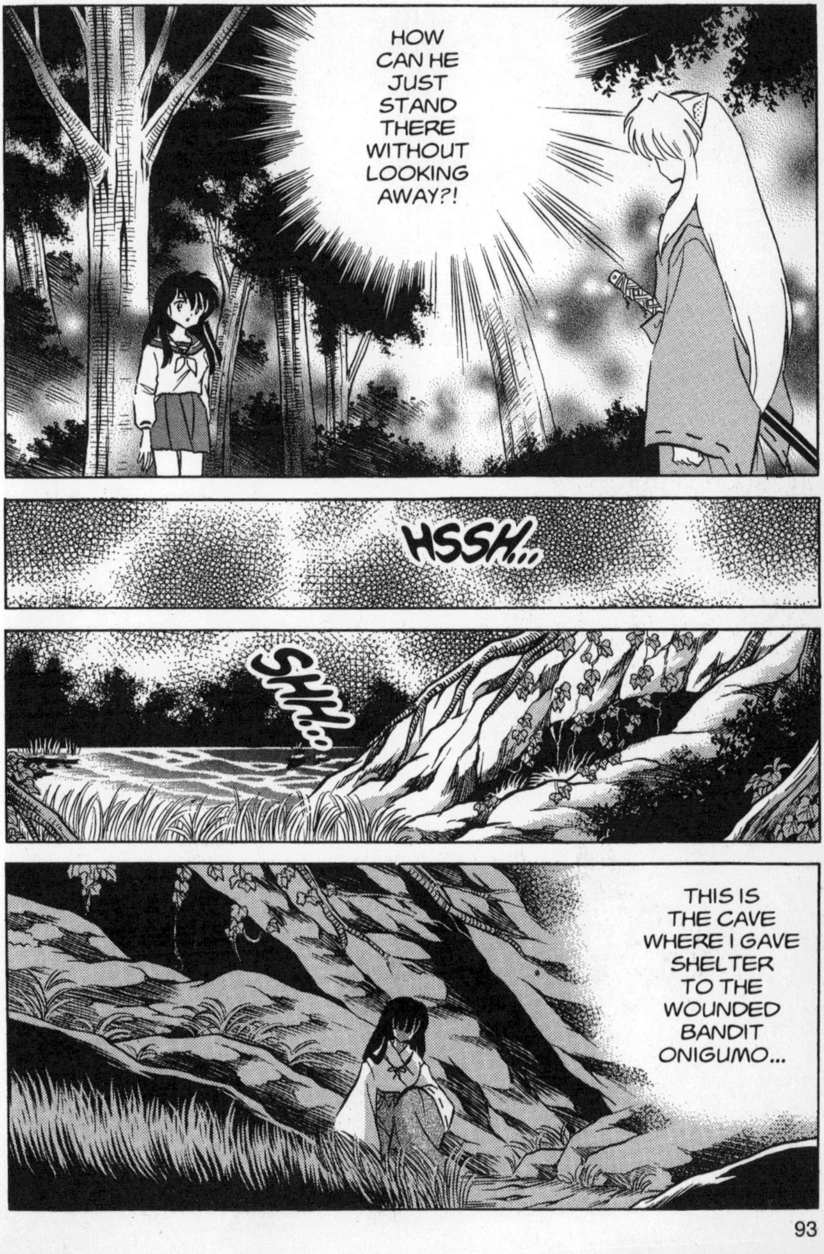
HOW CAN HE JUST STAND THERE WITHOUT LOOKING AWAY?!
HSSH...
SHH...
THIS IS THE CAVE WHERE I GAVE SHELTER TO THE WOUNDED BANDIT ONIGUMO...

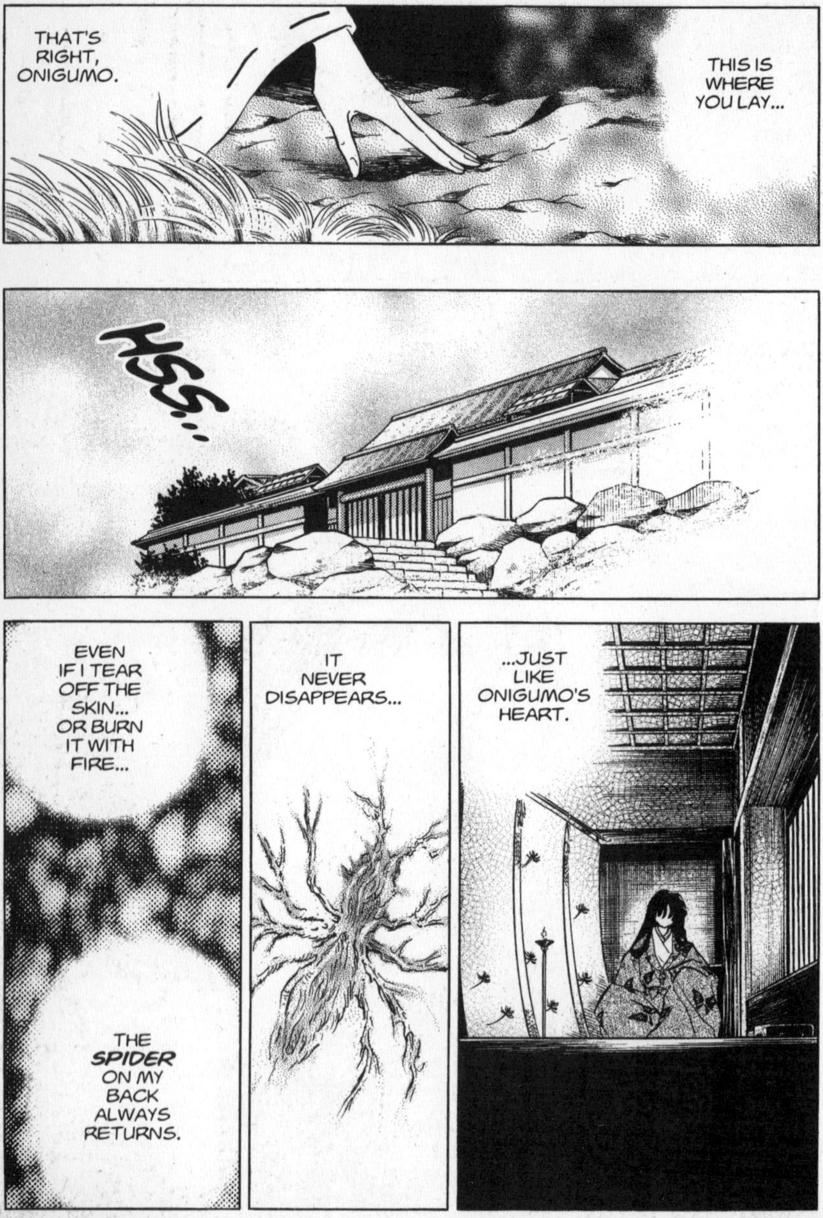
THAT'S RIGHT, ONIGUMO.
THIS IS WHERE YOU LAY...
HSS...
EVEN IF I TEAR OFF THE SKIN... OR BURN IT WITH FIRE...
THE **SPIDER** ON MY BACK ALWAYS RETURNS.
IT NEVER DISAPPEARS...
...JUST LIKE ONIGUMO'S HEART.

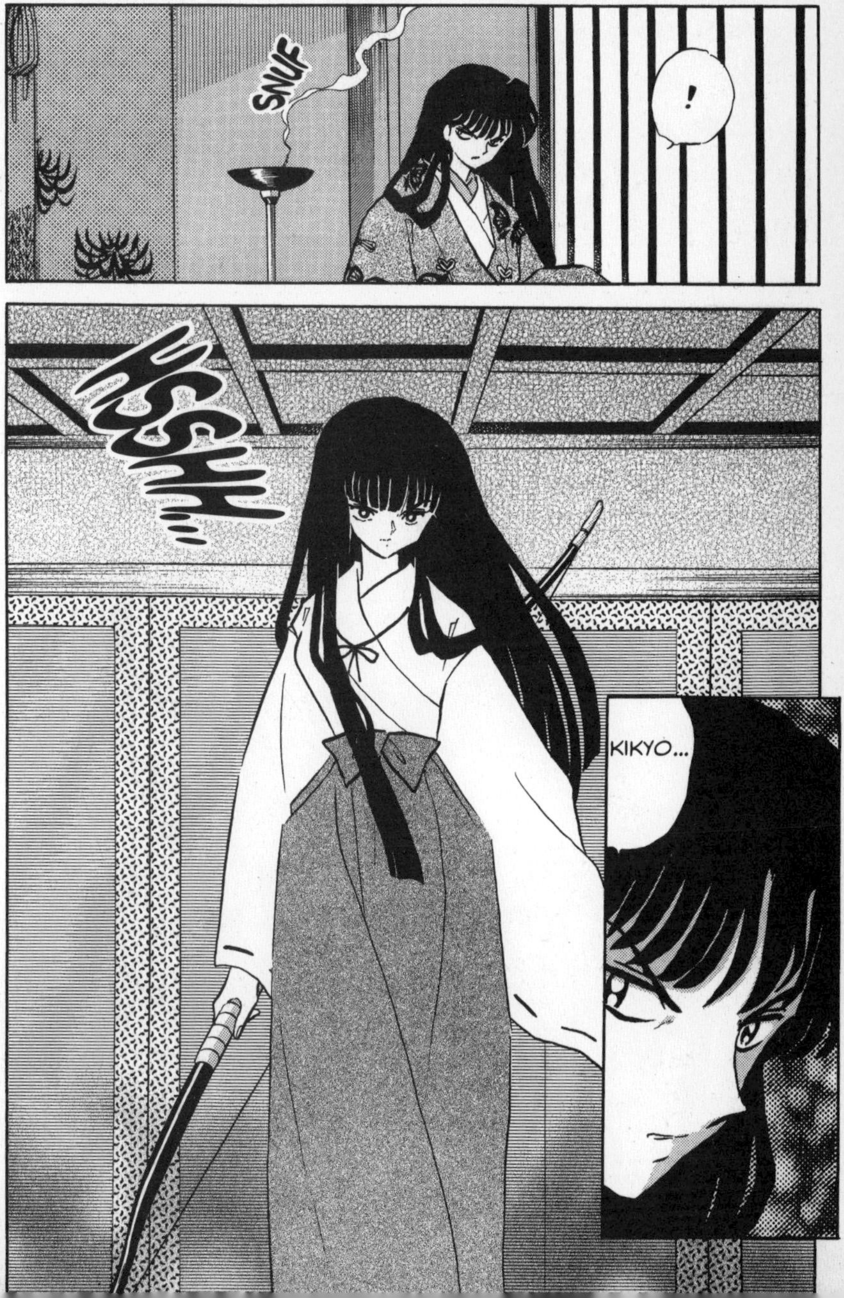
SNUF
!
HSSHH...
KIKYO...

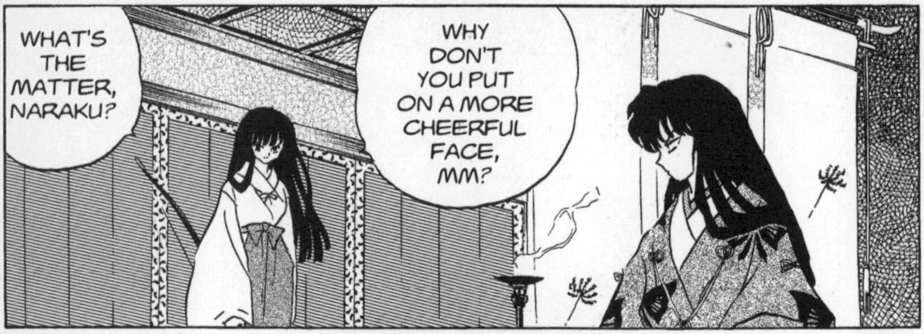
WHAT'S THE MATTER, NARAKU?
WHY DON'T YOU PUT ON A MORE CHEERFUL FACE, MM?

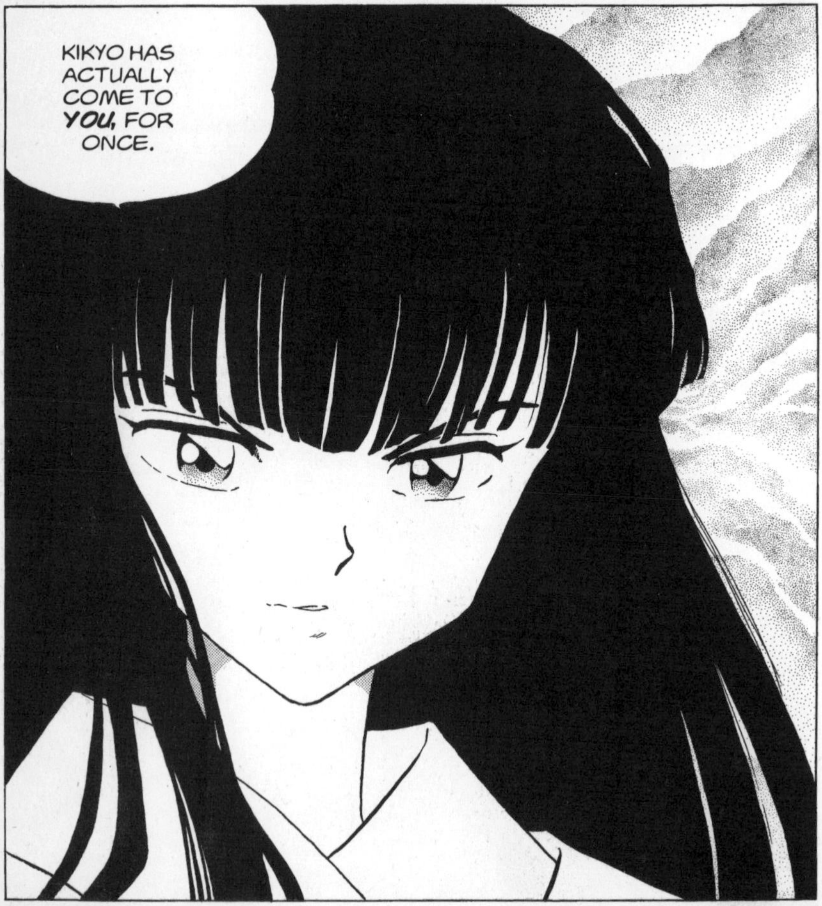
KIKYO HAS ACTUALLY COME TO ***YOU***, FOR ONCE.

SCROLL SIX

THE SOIL SHIELD

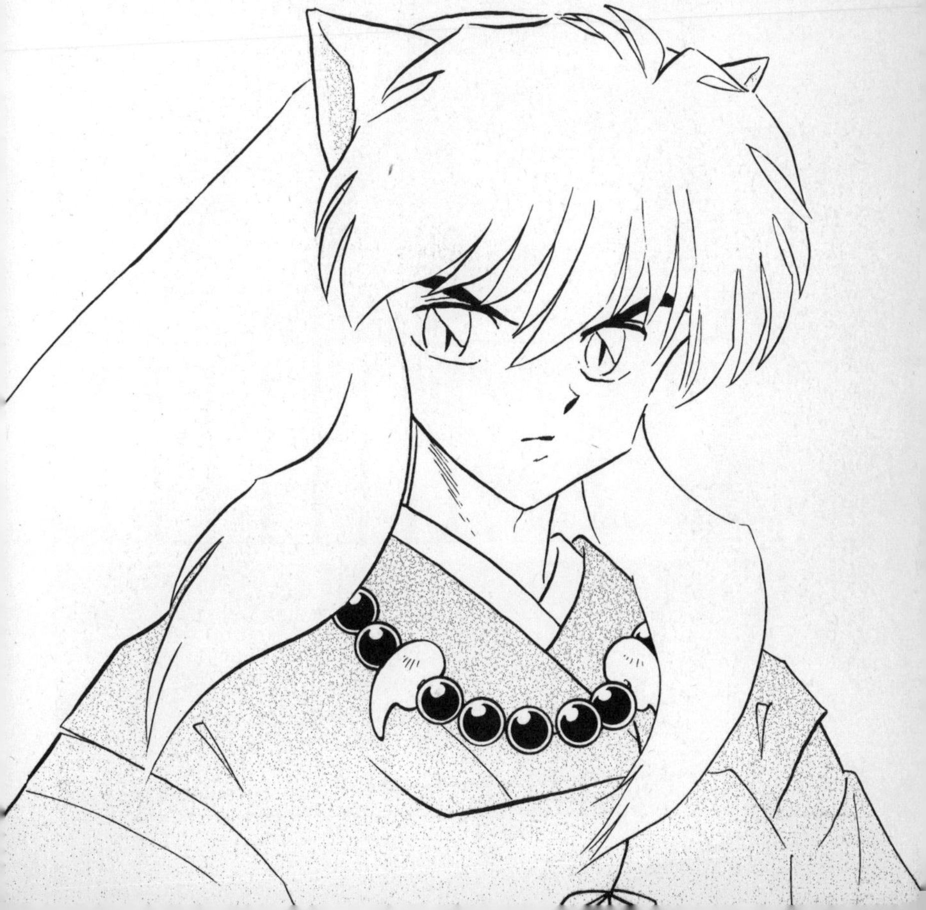

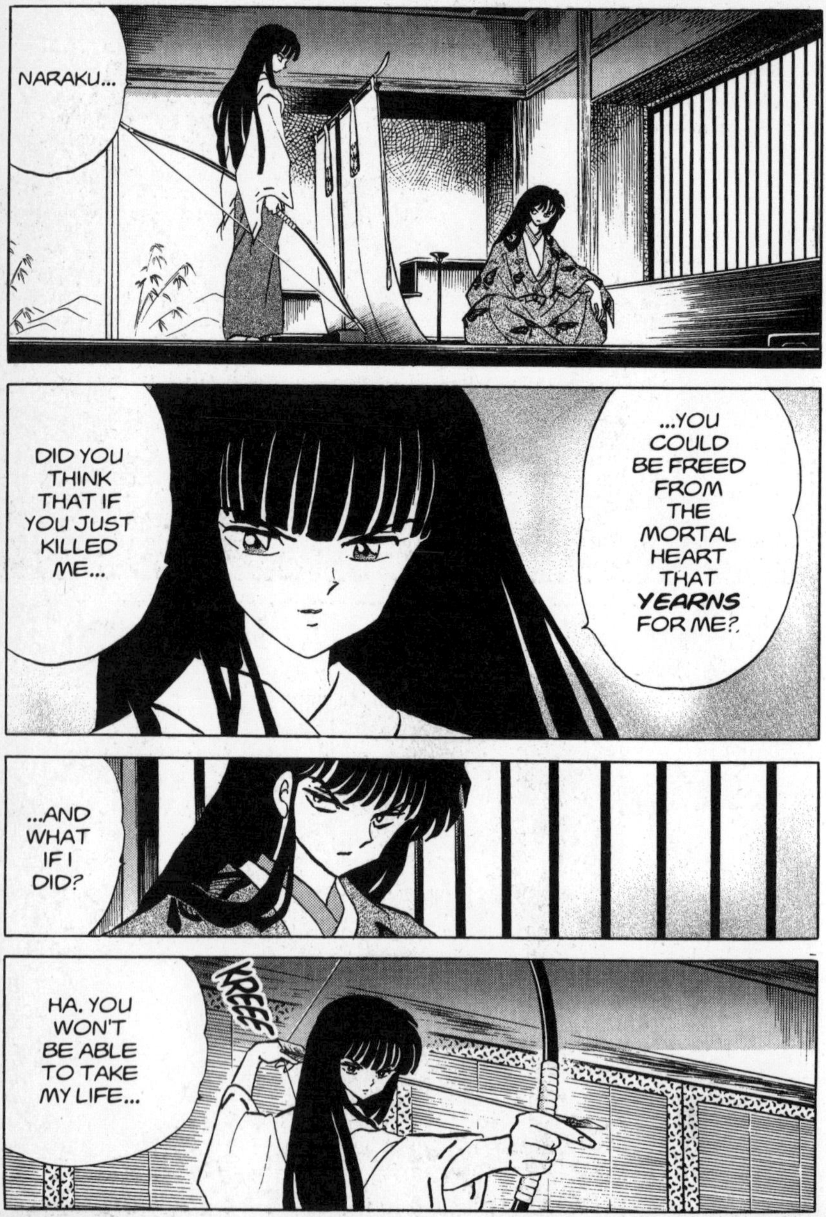

NARAKU...
DID YOU THINK THAT IF YOU JUST KILLED ME...
...YOU COULD BE FREED FROM THE MORTAL HEART THAT YEARNS FOR ME?
...AND WHAT IF I DID?
HA. YOU WON'T BE ABLE TO TAKE MY LIFE...
KREEE

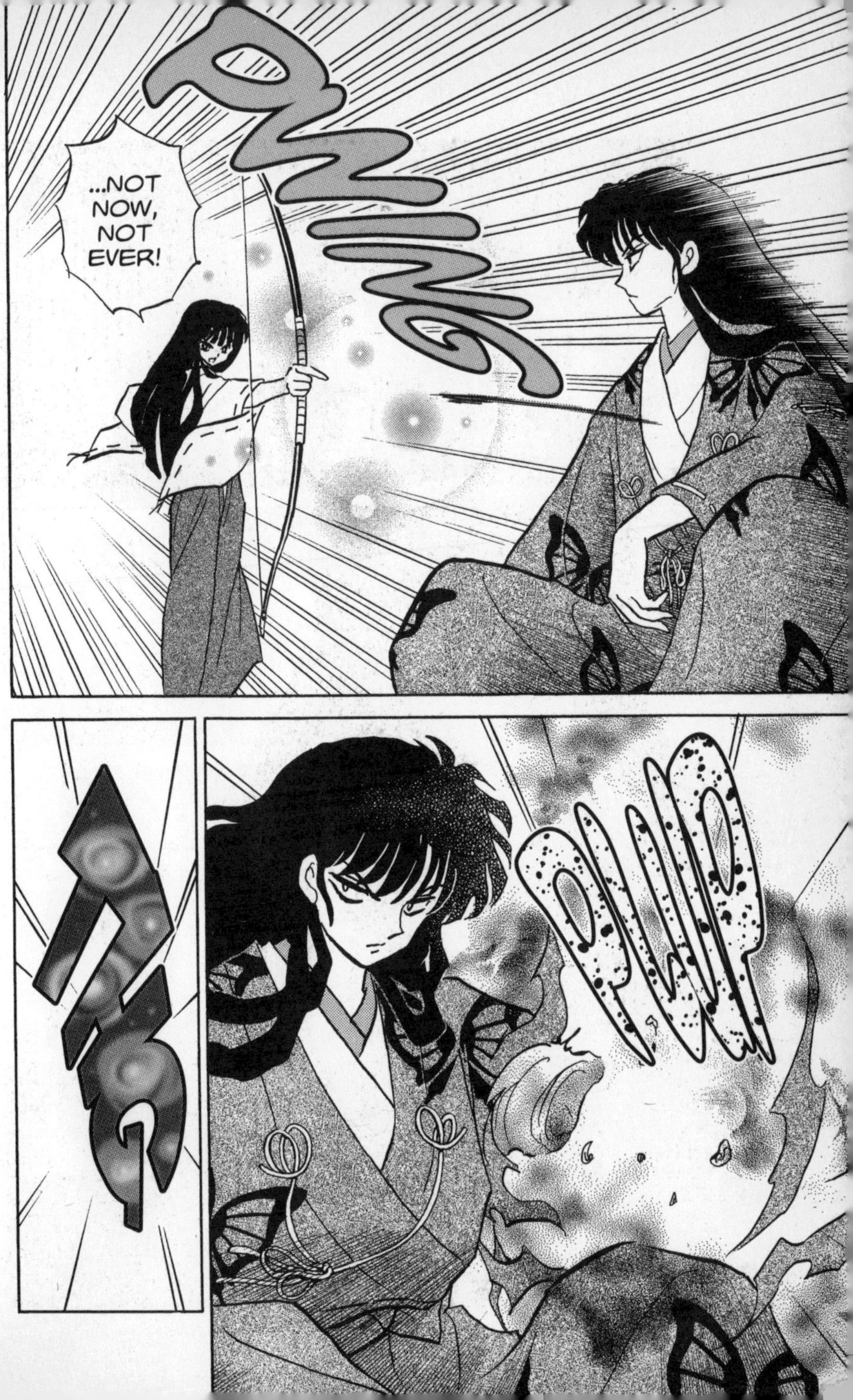
...NOT NOW, NOT EVER!
PWING
ZING

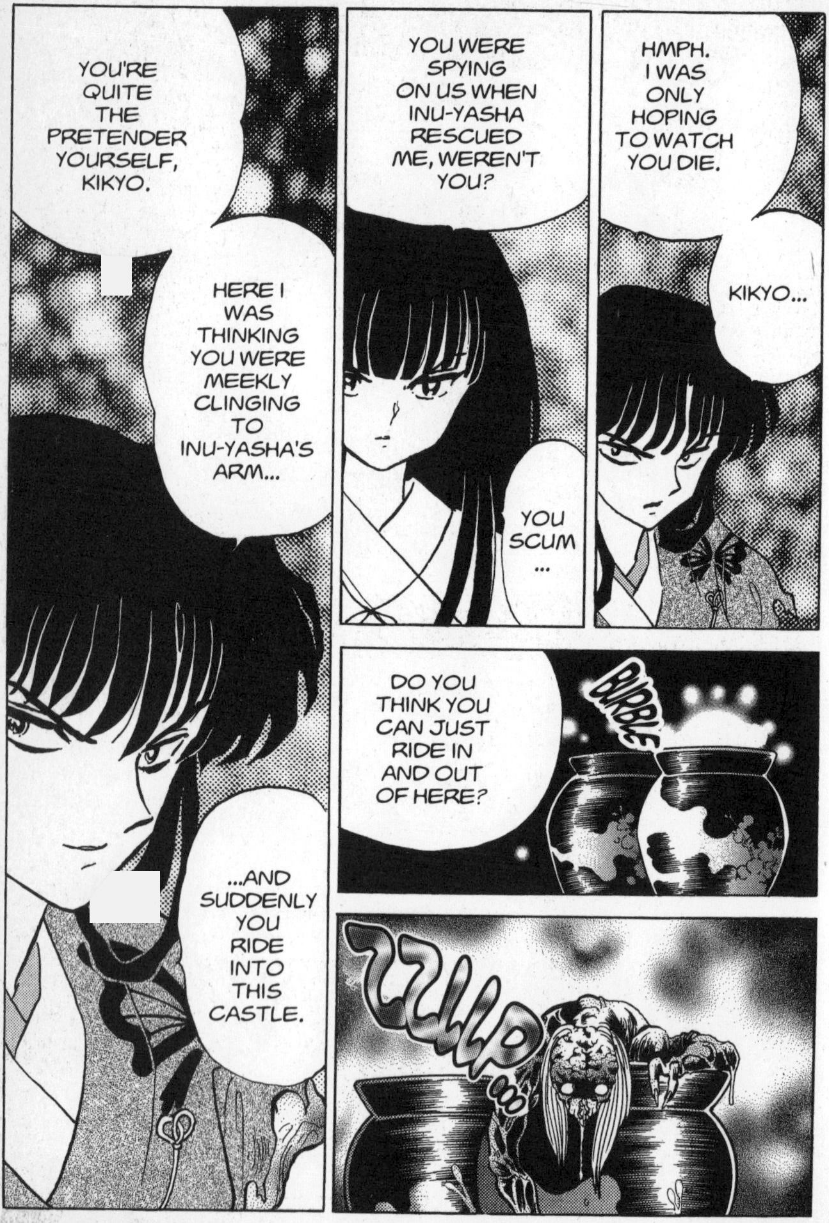
YOU'RE QUITE THE PRETENDER YOURSELF, KIKYO.
HERE I WAS THINKING YOU WERE MEEKLY CLINGING TO INU-YASHA'S ARM...
...AND SUDDENLY YOU RIDE INTO THIS CASTLE.
YOU WERE SPYING ON US WHEN INU-YASHA RESCUED ME, WEREN'T YOU?
YOU SCUM ...
HMPH. I WAS ONLY HOPING TO WATCH YOU DIE.
KIKYO...
DO YOU THINK YOU CAN JUST RIDE IN AND OUT OF HERE?
BURBLE
ZZLLP...

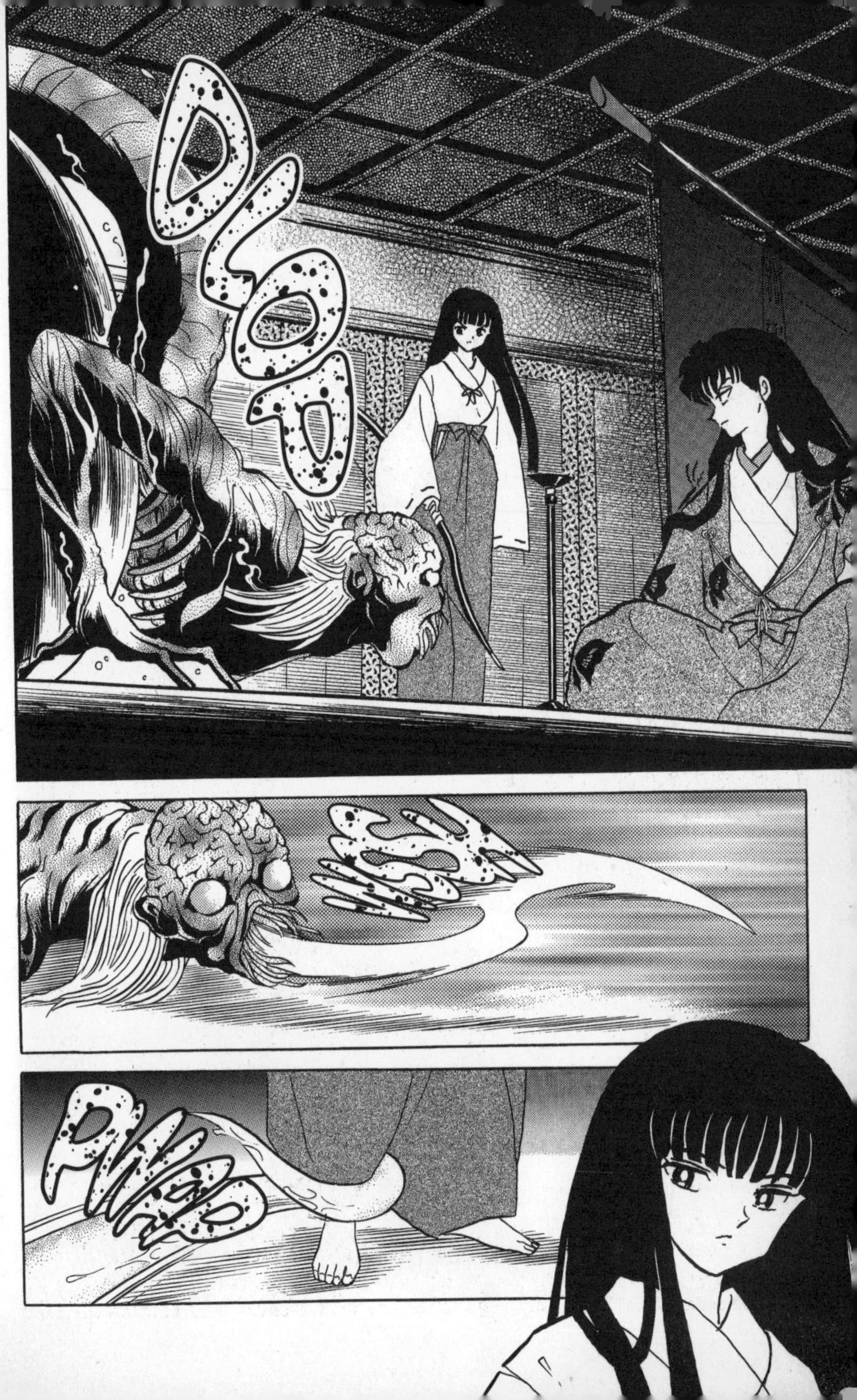
DLOOP

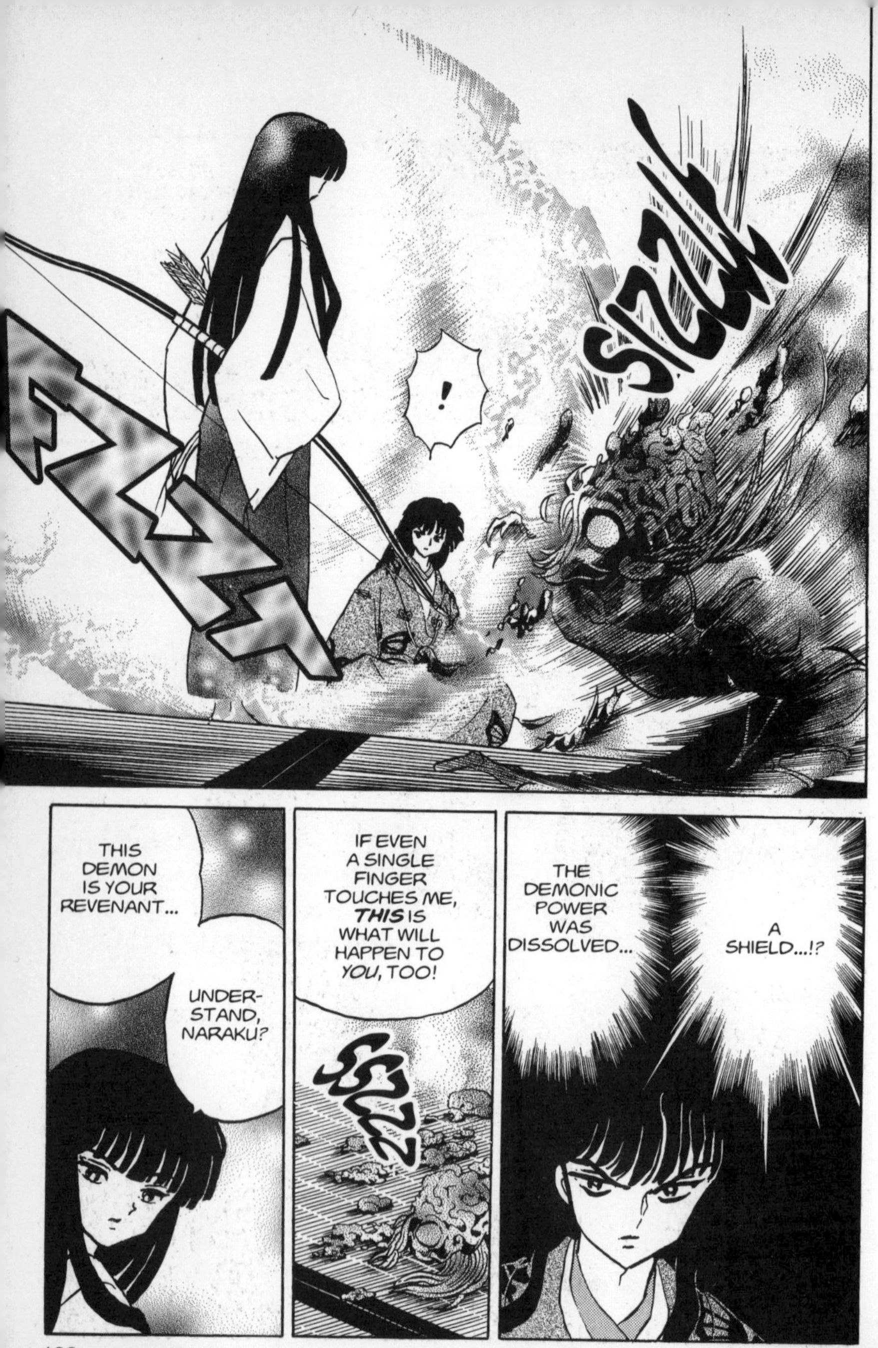
!
THIS DEMON IS YOUR REVENANT...
UNDER-STAND, NARAKU?
IF EVEN A SINGLE FINGER TOUCHES ME, **THIS** IS WHAT WILL HAPPEN TO *YOU*, TOO!
THE DEMONIC POWER WAS DISSOLVED...
A SHIELD...!?

NARAKU... THE SOIL FROM THE CAVE WHERE YOU LAY, WHEN YOU WERE THE BANDIT **ONIGUMO**...

IT IS STEEPED IN YOUR FOUL DESIRES.

SO YOU'VE ARMED YOURSELF WITH THE CAVE DIRT?

YES.

ONIGUMO DIDN'T WANT MY DEATH.

HIS DESIRE WILL PROTECT ME.

IF YOU TOUCH THE SOIL-SHIELD, ONIGUMO'S HEART WILL FLOW INTO YOU...

...AND IT WILL **STEAL AWAY** YOUR DEMONIC POWER.

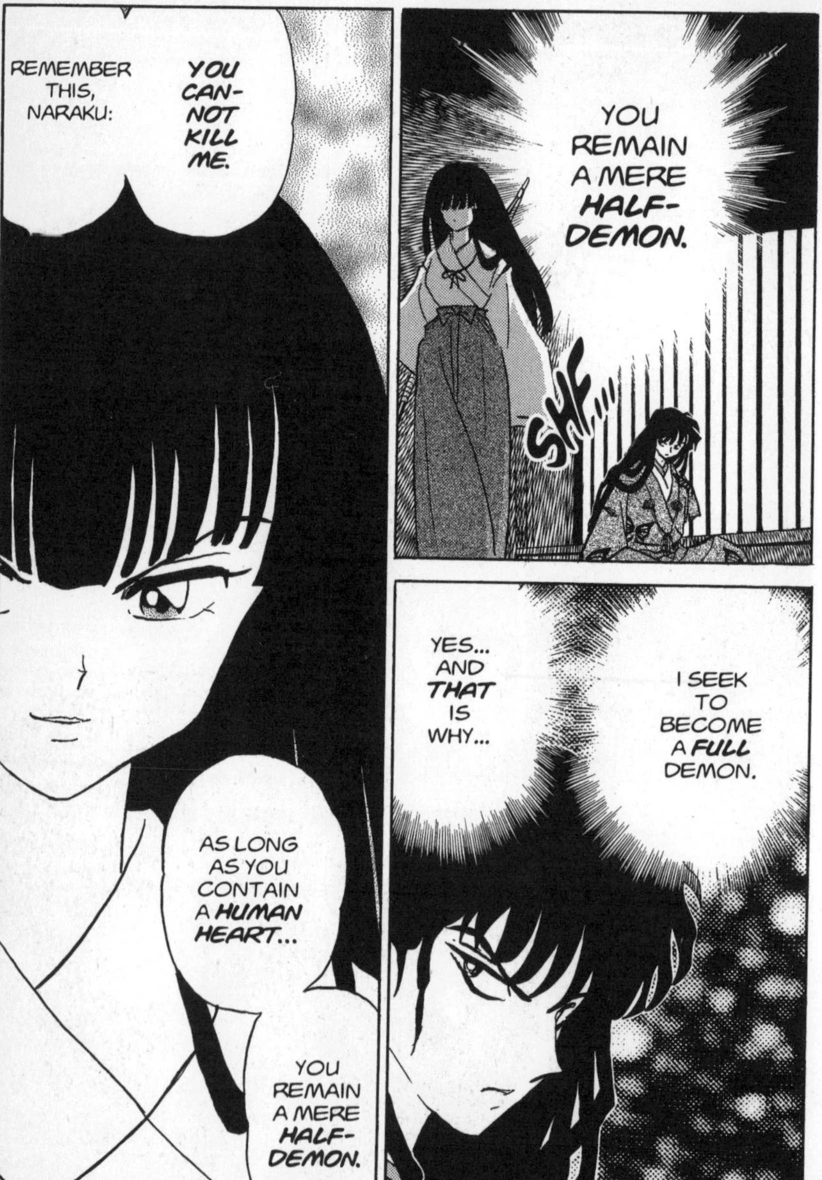
REMEMBER THIS, NARAKU:
YOU CANNOT KILL ME.
AS LONG AS YOU CONTAIN A HUMAN HEART...
YOU REMAIN A MERE HALF-DEMON.
YOU REMAIN A MERE HALF-DEMON.
SHF...
YES... AND THAT IS WHY...
I SEEK TO BECOME A FULL DEMON.

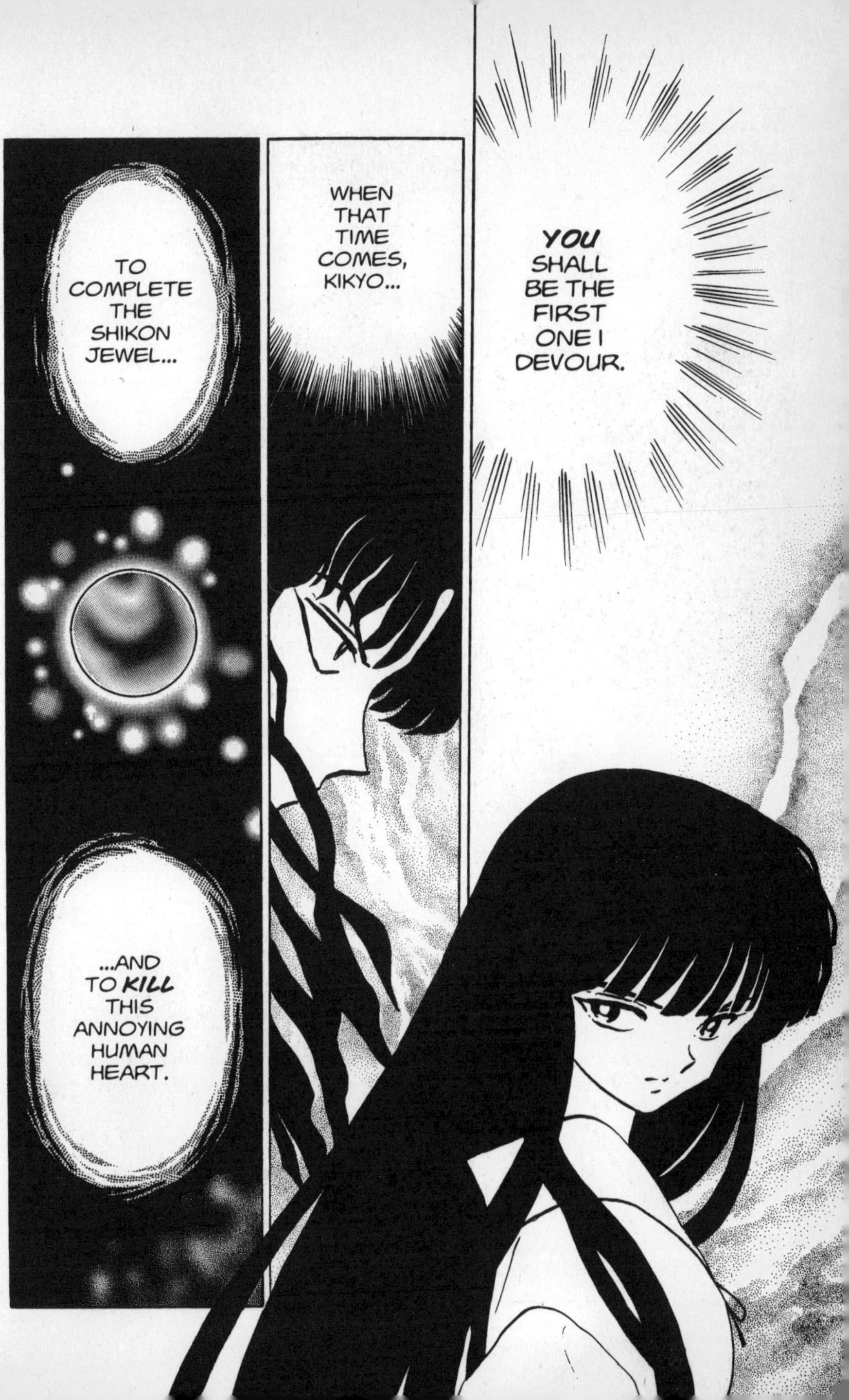
TO COMPLETE THE SHIKON JEWEL...
...AND TO KILL THIS ANNOYING HUMAN HEART.
WHEN THAT TIME COMES, KIKYO...
YOU SHALL BE THE FIRST ONE I DEVOUR.

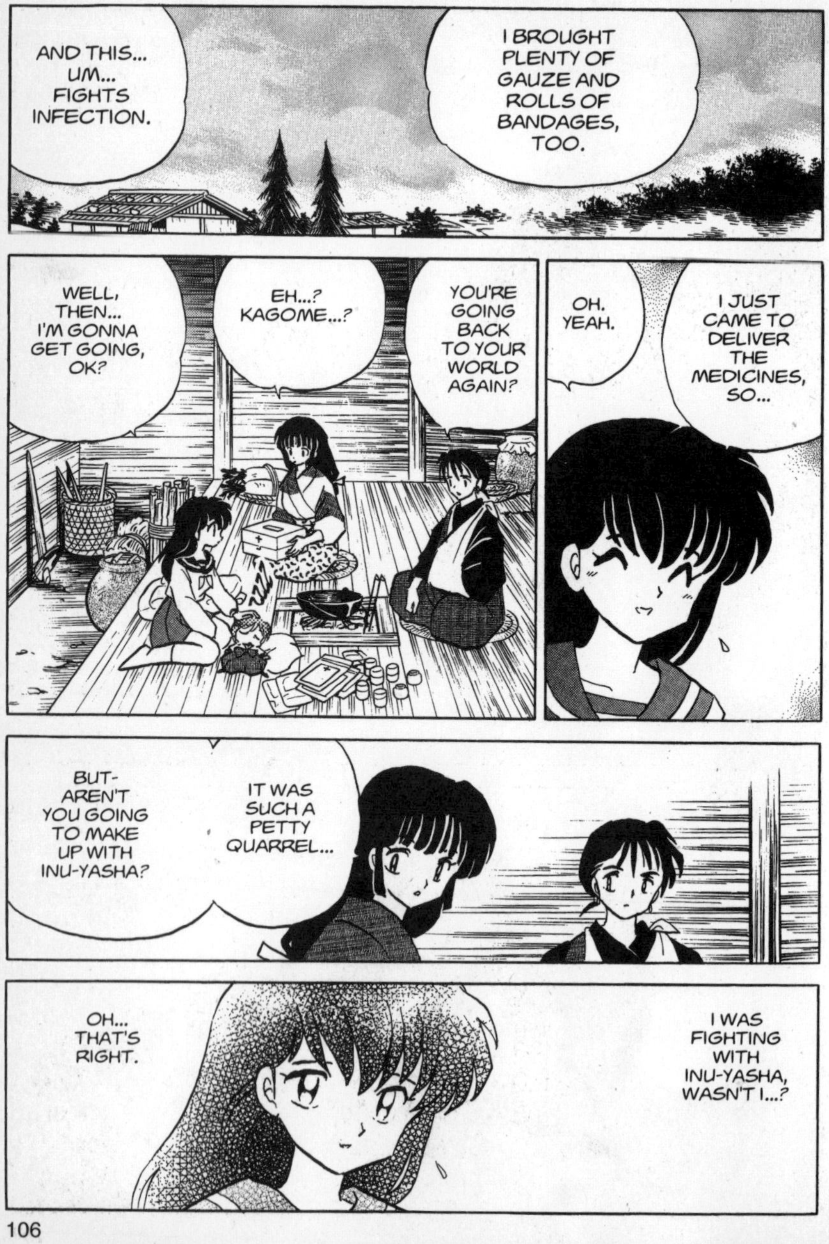
AND THIS... UM... FIGHTS INFECTION.
I BROUGHT PLENTY OF GAUZE AND ROLLS OF BANDAGES, TOO.
WELL, THEN... I'M GONNA GET GOING, OK?
EH...? KAGOME...?
YOU'RE GOING BACK TO YOUR WORLD AGAIN?
OH. YEAH.
I JUST CAME TO DELIVER THE MEDICINES, SO...
BUT- AREN'T YOU GOING TO MAKE UP WITH INU-YASHA?
IT WAS SUCH A PETTY QUARREL...
OH... THAT'S RIGHT.
I WAS FIGHTING WITH INU-YASHA, WASN'T I...?

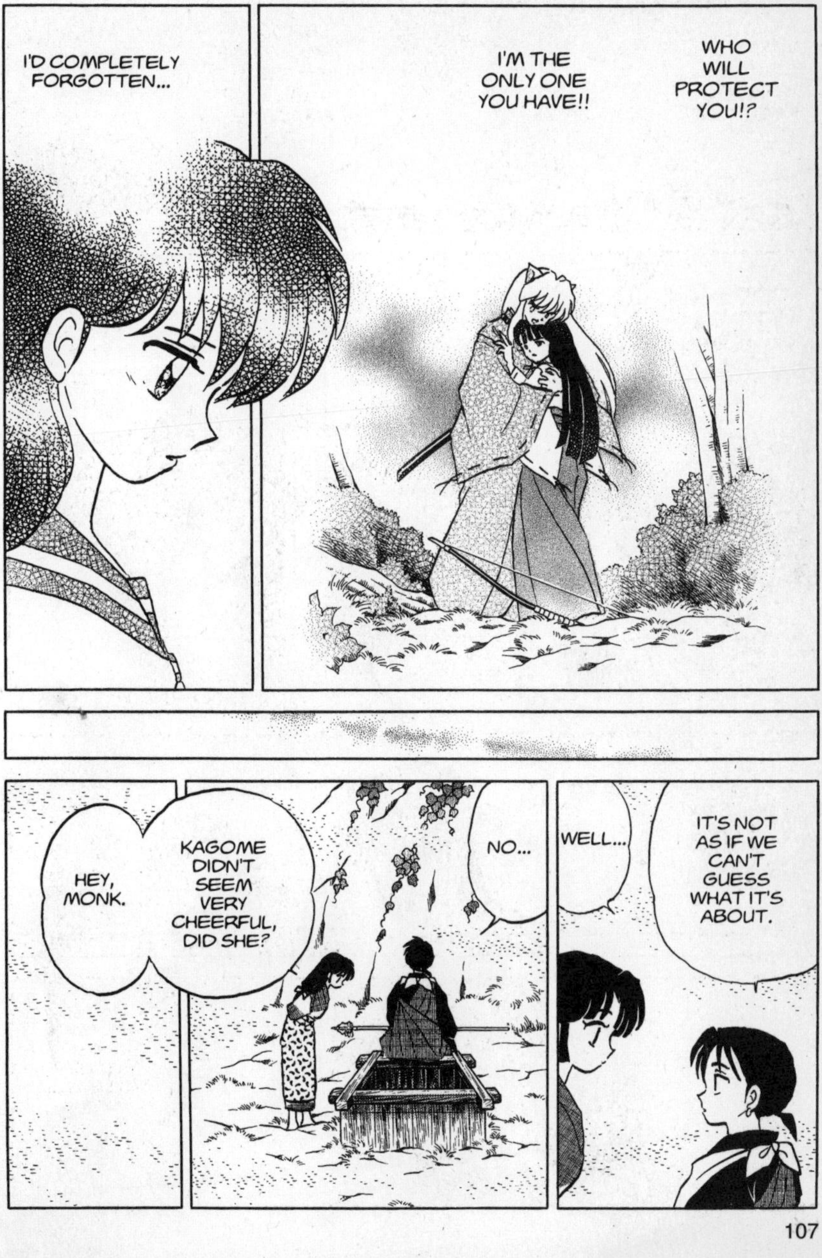

I'D COMPLETELY FORGOTTEN...
I'M THE ONLY ONE YOU HAVE!!
WHO WILL PROTECT YOU!?
HEY, MONK.
KAGOME DIDN'T SEEM VERY CHEERFUL, DID SHE?
NO...
WELL...
IT'S NOT AS IF WE CAN'T GUESS WHAT IT'S ABOUT.

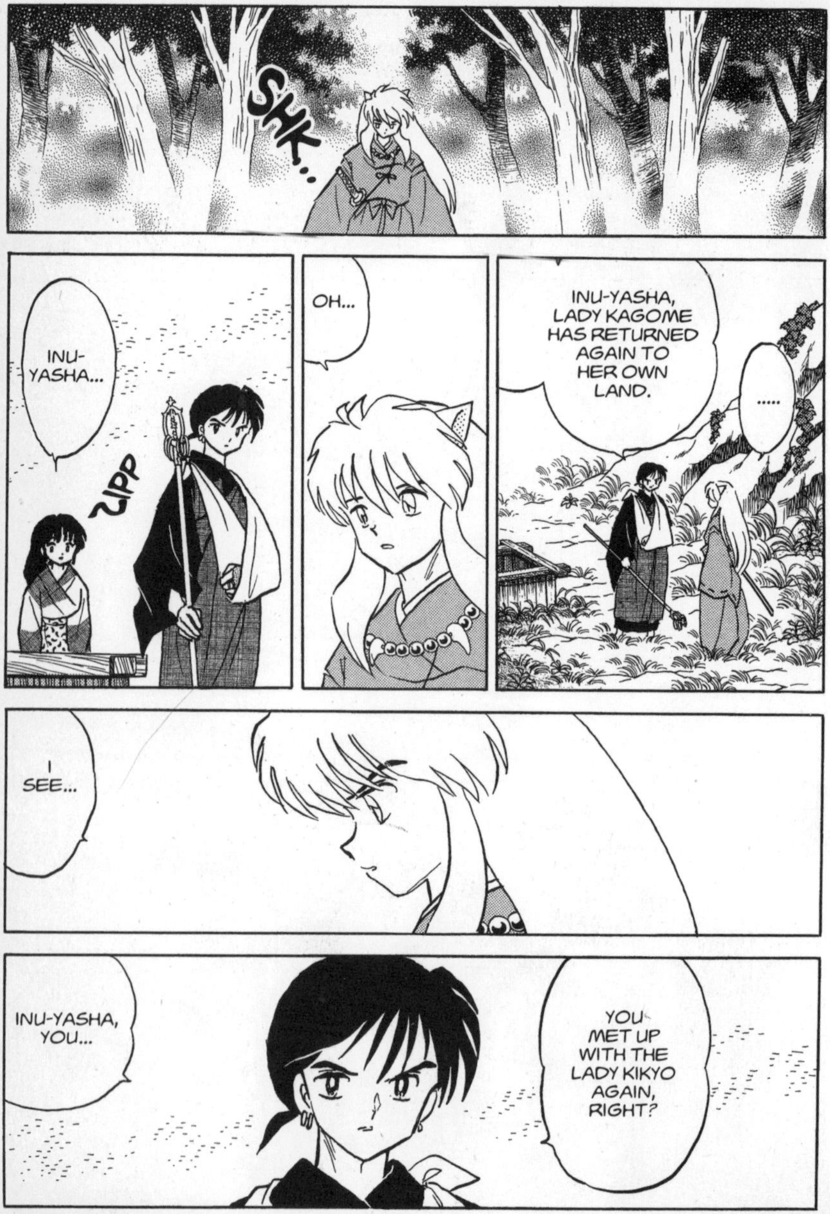
SHK...
INU-YASHA...
ZIPP
OH...
INU-YASHA, LADY KAGOME HAS RETURNED AGAIN TO HER OWN LAND.
.....
I SEE...
INU-YASHA, YOU...
YOU MET UP WITH THE LADY KIKYO AGAIN, RIGHT?

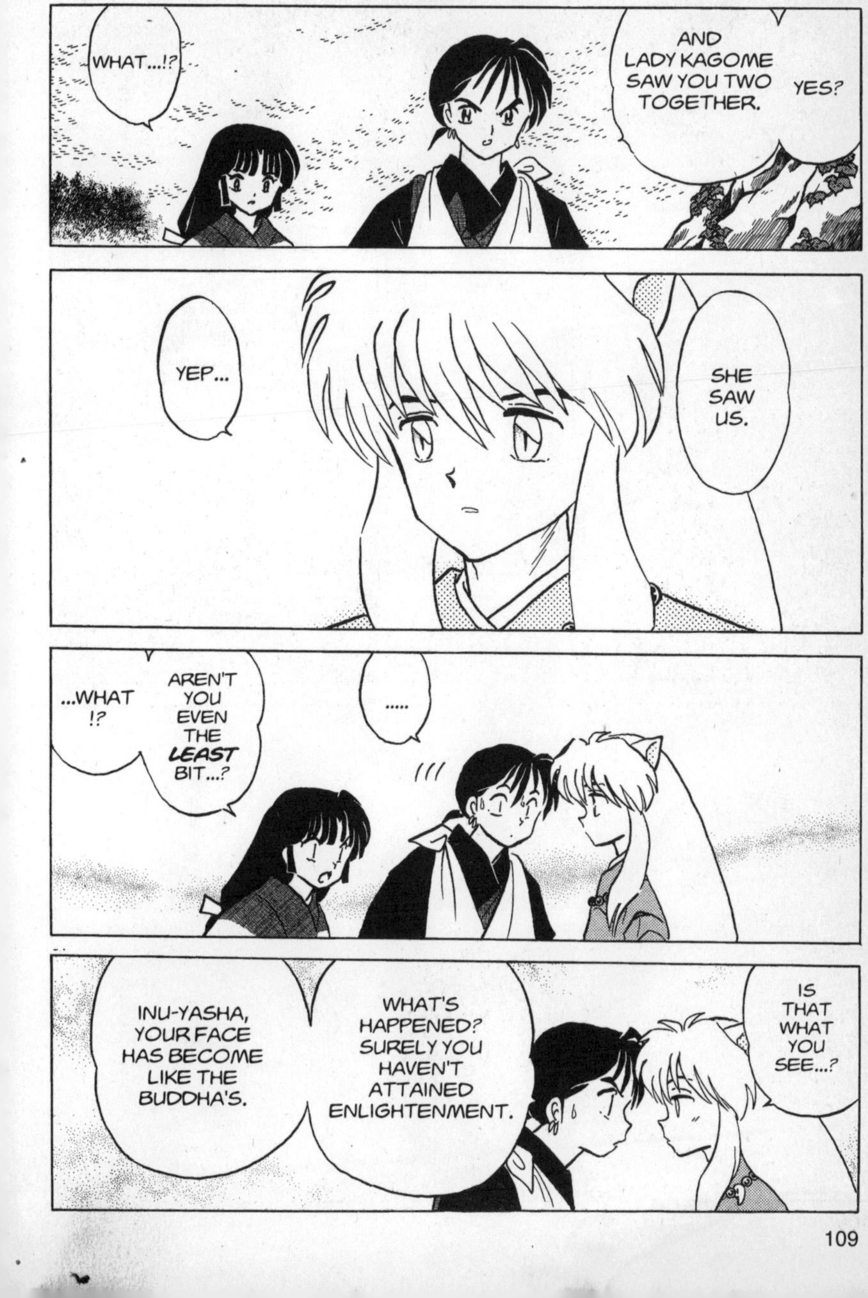
WHAT...!?
AND LADY KAGOME SAW YOU TWO TOGETHER.
YES?
YEP...
SHE SAW US.
...WHAT !?
AREN'T YOU EVEN THE LEAST BIT...?
.....
INU-YASHA, YOUR FACE HAS BECOME LIKE THE BUDDHA'S.
WHAT'S HAPPENED? SURELY YOU HAVEN'T ATTAINED ENLIGHTENMENT.
IS THAT WHAT YOU SEE...?

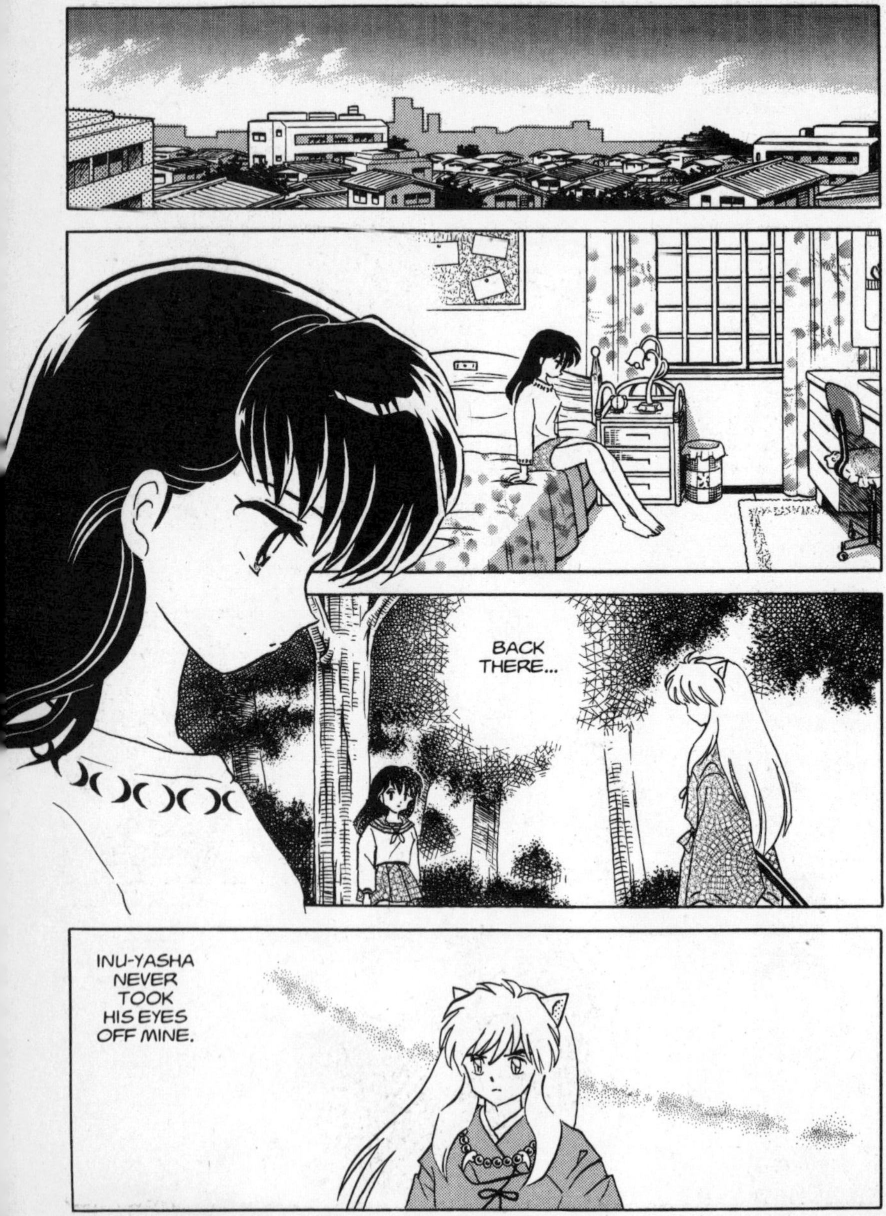
BACK THERE...
INU-YASHA NEVER TOOK HIS EYES OFF MINE.

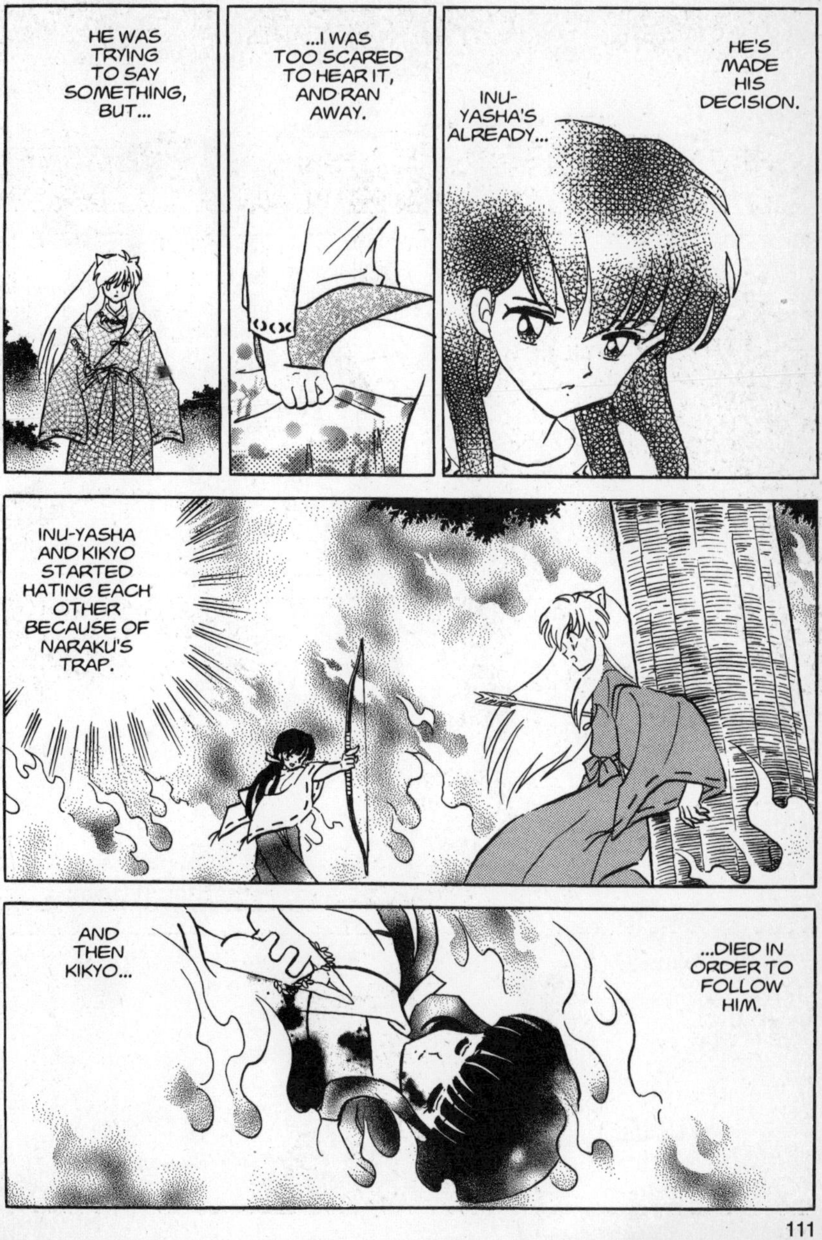
HE WAS TRYING TO SAY SOMETHING, BUT...
...I WAS TOO SCARED TO HEAR IT, AND RAN AWAY.
INU-YASHA'S ALREADY...
HE'S MADE HIS DECISION.
INU-YASHA AND KIKYO STARTED HATING EACH OTHER BECAUSE OF NARAKU'S TRAP.
AND THEN KIKYO...
...DIED IN ORDER TO FOLLOW HIM.

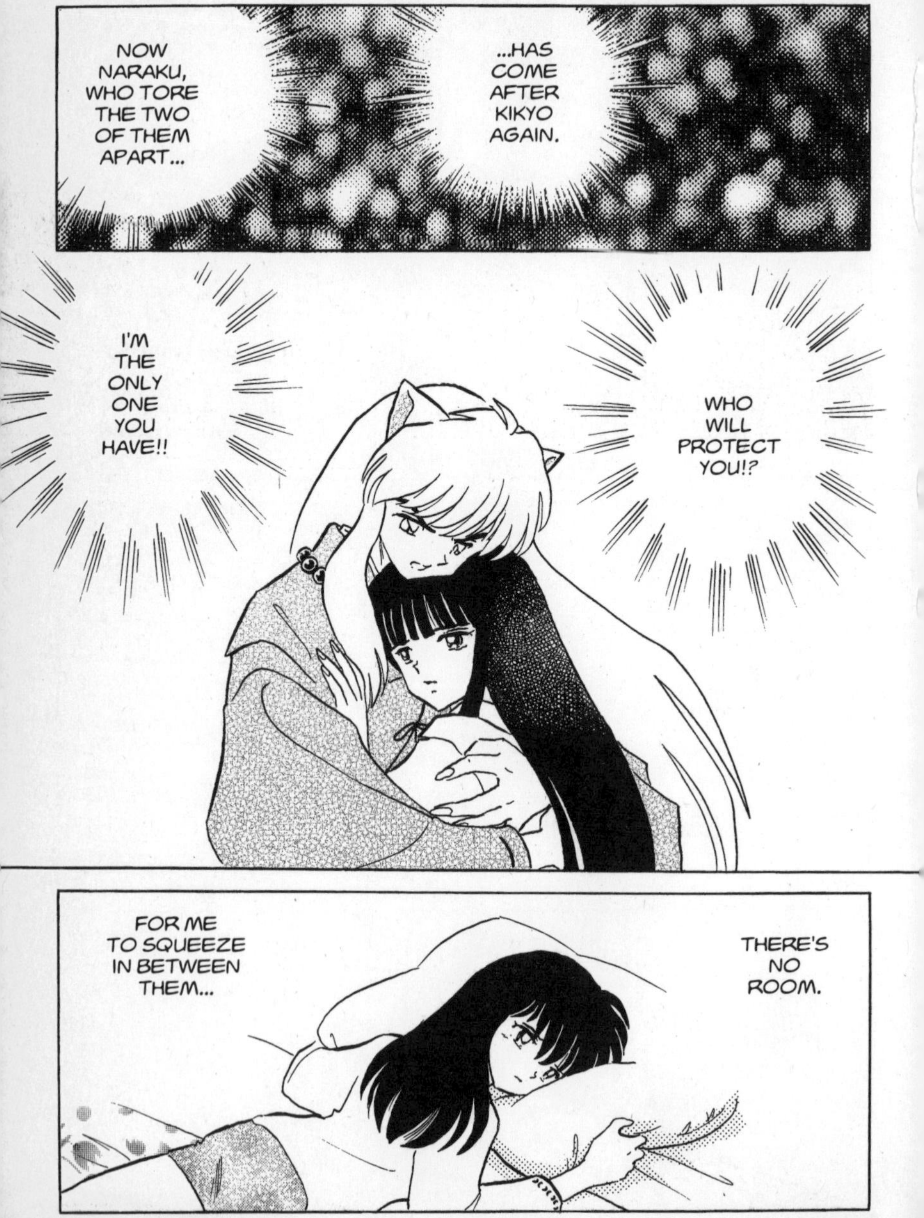
NOW NARAKU, WHO TORE THE TWO OF THEM APART...
...HAS COME AFTER KIKYO AGAIN.
I'M THE ONLY ONE YOU HAVE!!
WHO WILL PROTECT YOU!?
FOR ME TO SQUEEZE IN BETWEEN THEM...
THERE'S NO ROOM.

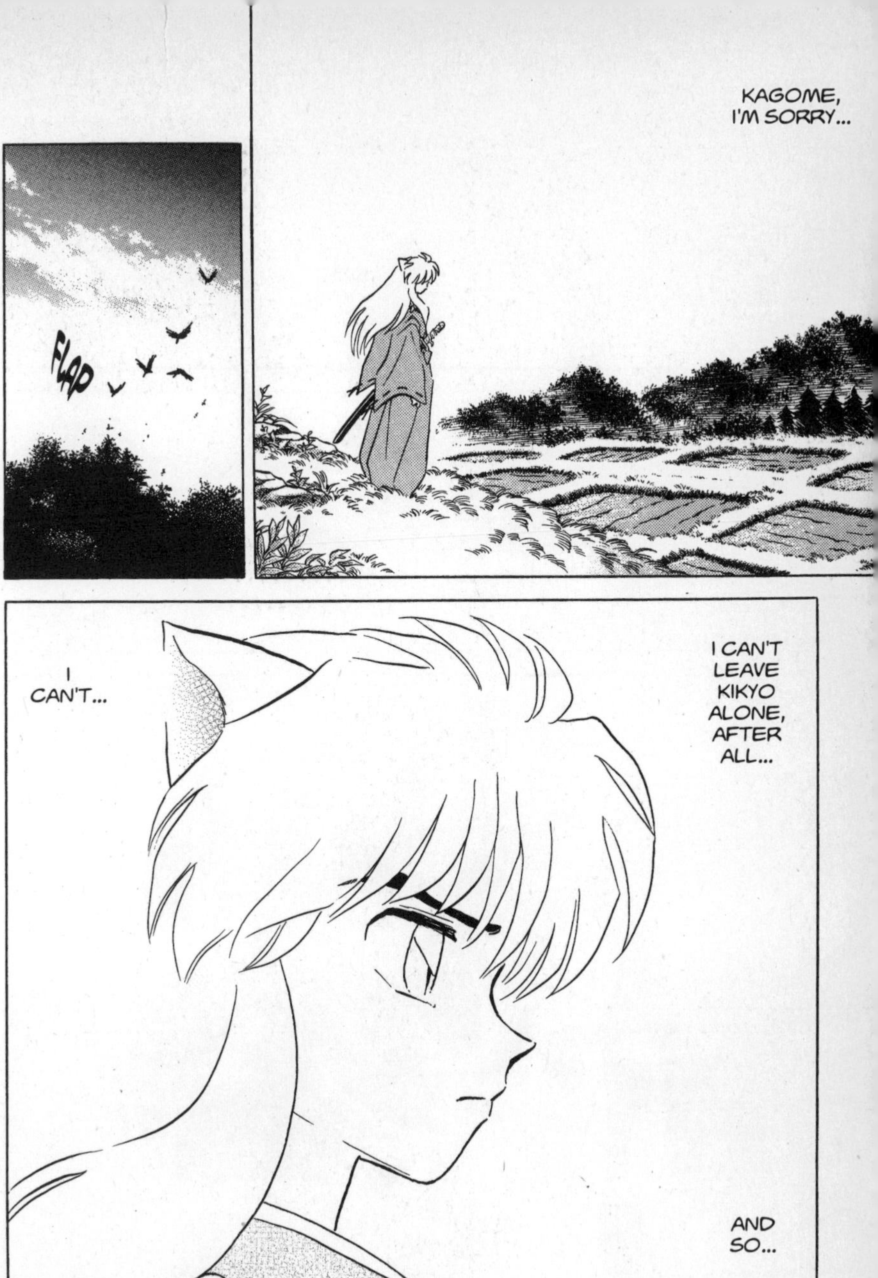
FLAP
KAGOME, I'M SORRY...
I CAN'T...
I CAN'T LEAVE KIKYO ALONE, AFTER ALL...
AND SO...

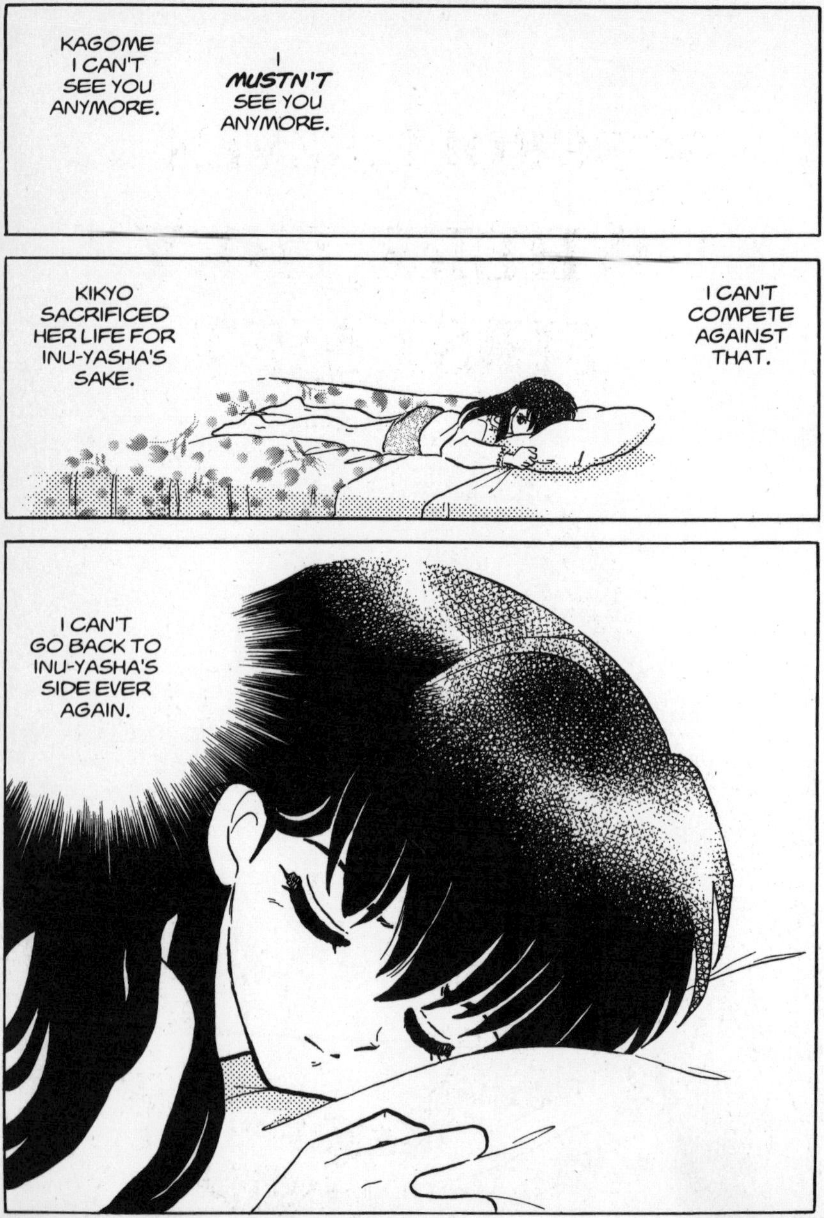
KAGOME I CAN'T SEE YOU ANYMORE.
I *MUSTN'T* SEE YOU ANYMORE.
KIKYO SACRIFICED HER LIFE FOR INU-YASHA'S SAKE.
I CAN'T COMPETE AGAINST THAT.
I CAN'T GO BACK TO INU-YASHA'S SIDE EVER AGAIN.

SCROLL SEVEN
WHERE THEY FIRST MET

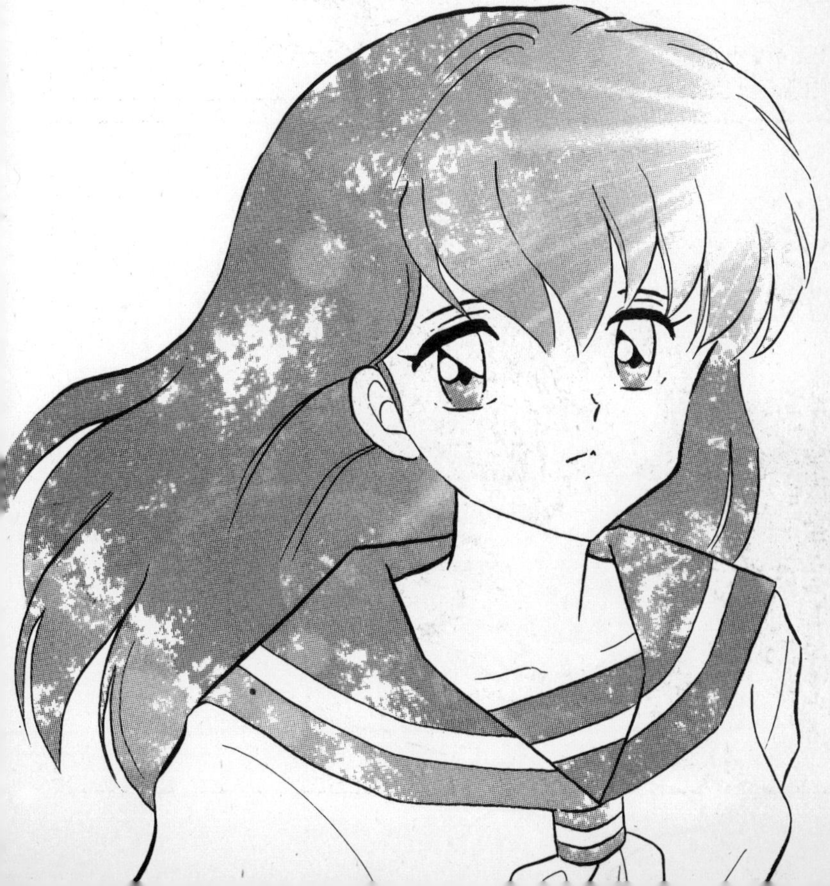

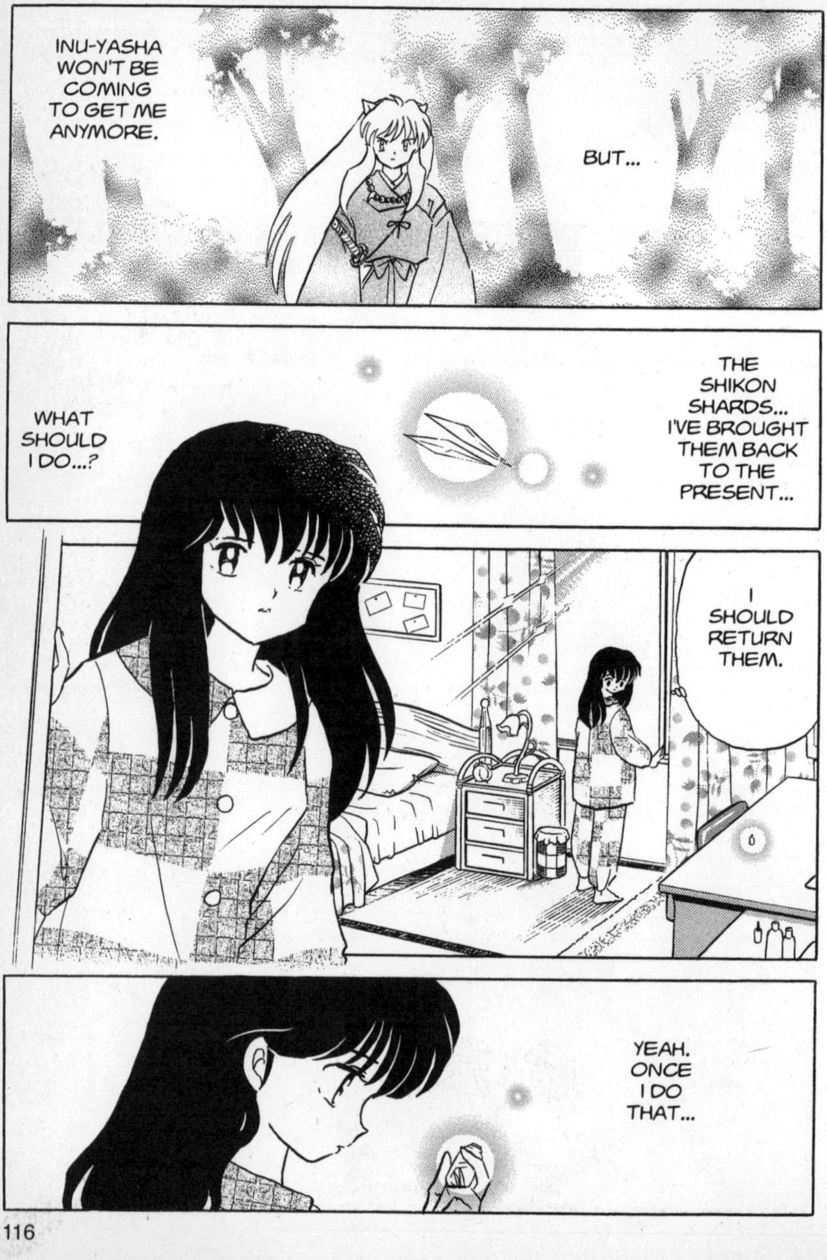
INU-YASHA WON'T BE COMING TO GET ME ANYMORE.
BUT...
WHAT SHOULD I DO...?
THE SHIKON SHARDS... I'VE BROUGHT THEM BACK TO THE PRESENT...
I SHOULD RETURN THEM.
YEAH. ONCE I DO THAT...

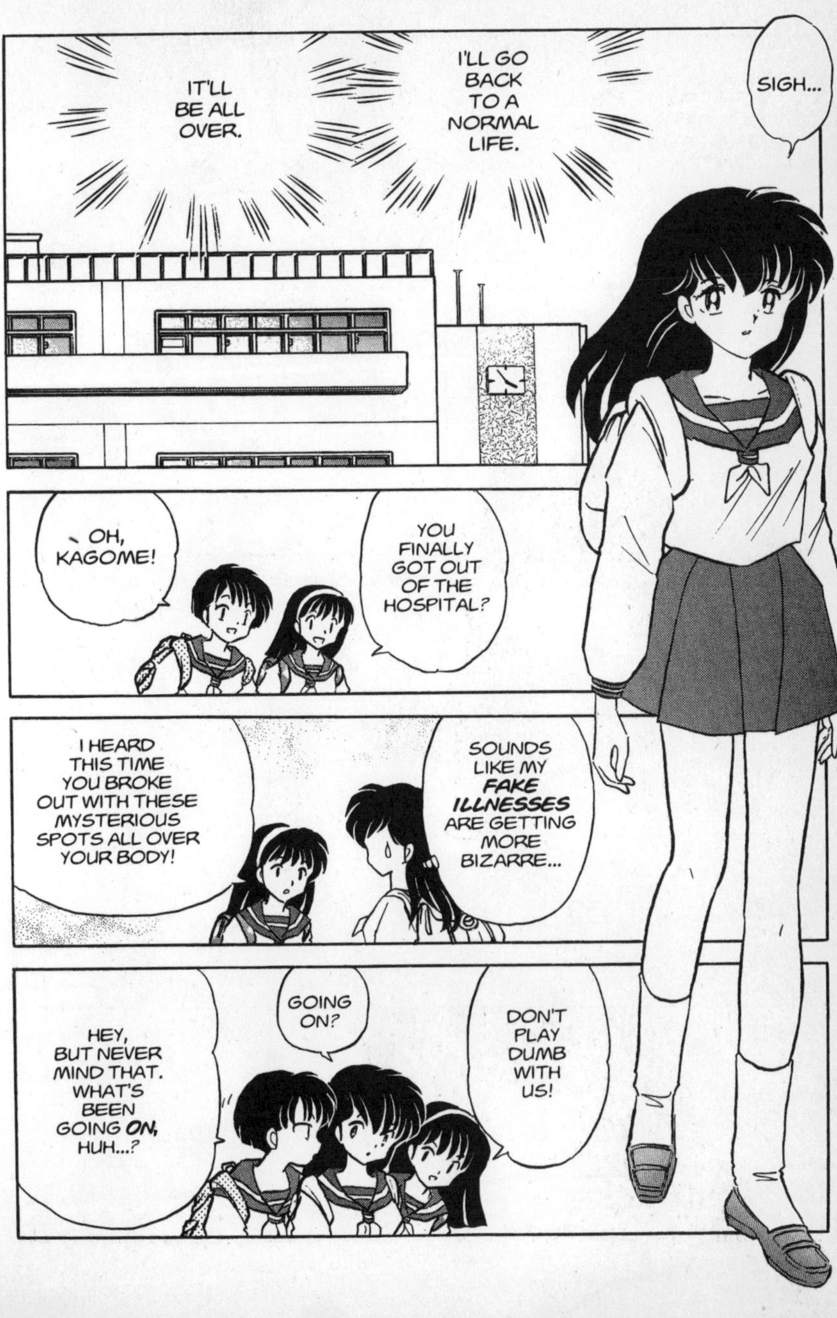

IT'LL BE ALL OVER.
I'LL GO BACK TO A NORMAL LIFE.
SIGH...
OH, KAGOME!
YOU FINALLY GOT OUT OF THE HOSPITAL?
I HEARD THIS TIME YOU BROKE OUT WITH THESE MYSTERIOUS SPOTS ALL OVER YOUR BODY!
SOUNDS LIKE MY *FAKE ILLNESSES* ARE GETTING MORE BIZARRE...
HEY, BUT NEVER MIND THAT. WHAT'S BEEN GOING *ON,* HUH...?
GOING ON?
DON'T PLAY DUMB WITH US!

YOU KNOW! THE RELATIONSHIP BETWEEN YOU AND THAT GUY WHO GETS VIOLENTLY JEALOUS EVEN WHILE HE'S DOUBLE-DIPPING ON YOU!

SO'D YOU *DUMP* HIM, OR...?

FLINCH

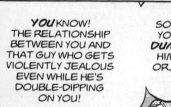

...HUH?

SH-HH

KAGO-ME?

DID I... SAY SOMETHING I SHOULDN'T HAVE?

ZZZZZIP

B-BMP B-BMP B-BMP

SIGH

I THINK *I* GOT DUMPED.

WHIRL

WHAT...?

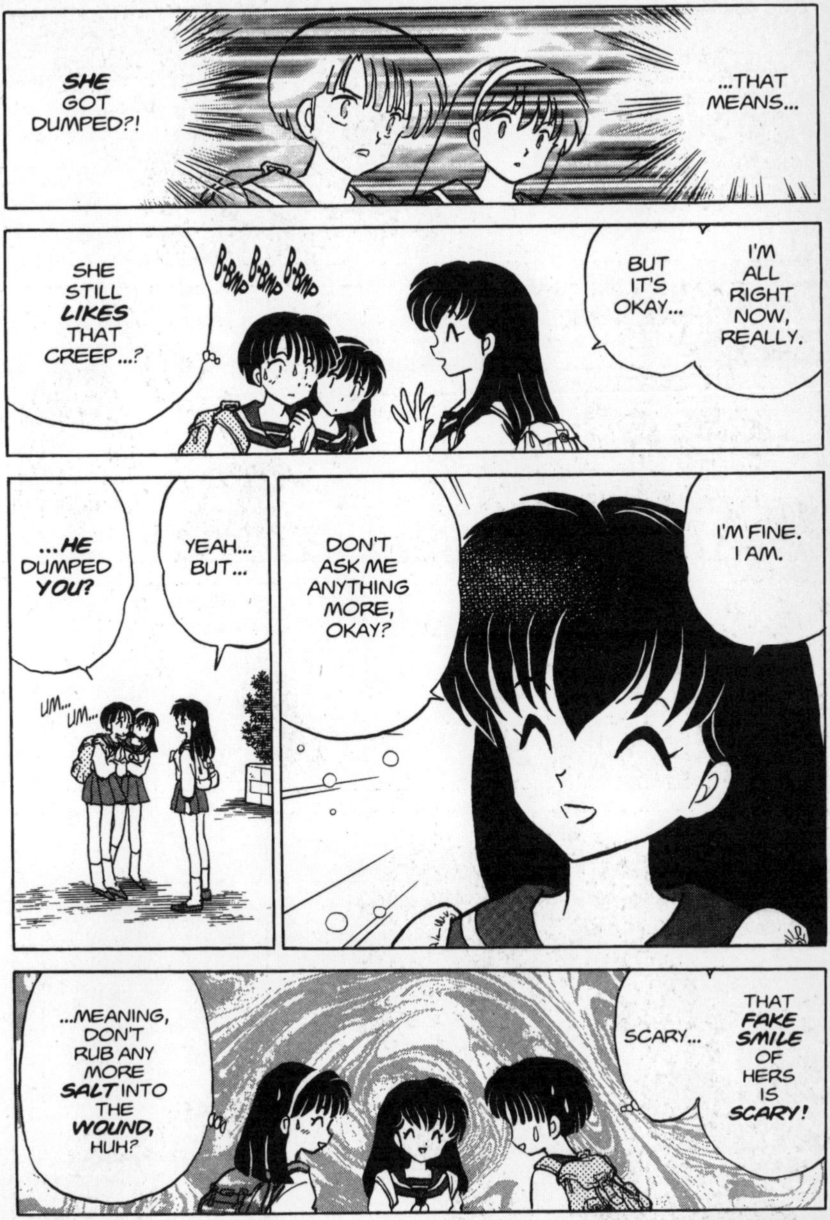
SHE GOT DUMPED?!
...THAT MEANS...
SHE STILL LIKES THAT CREEP...?
B-BMP B-BMP B-BMP
BUT IT'S OKAY...
I'M ALL RIGHT NOW, REALLY.
...HE DUMPED YOU?
YEAH... BUT...
UM... UM...
DON'T ASK ME ANYTHING MORE, OKAY?
I'M FINE. I AM.
...MEANING, DON'T RUB ANY MORE SALT INTO THE WOUND, HUH?
SCARY...
THAT FAKE SMILE OF HERS IS SCARY!

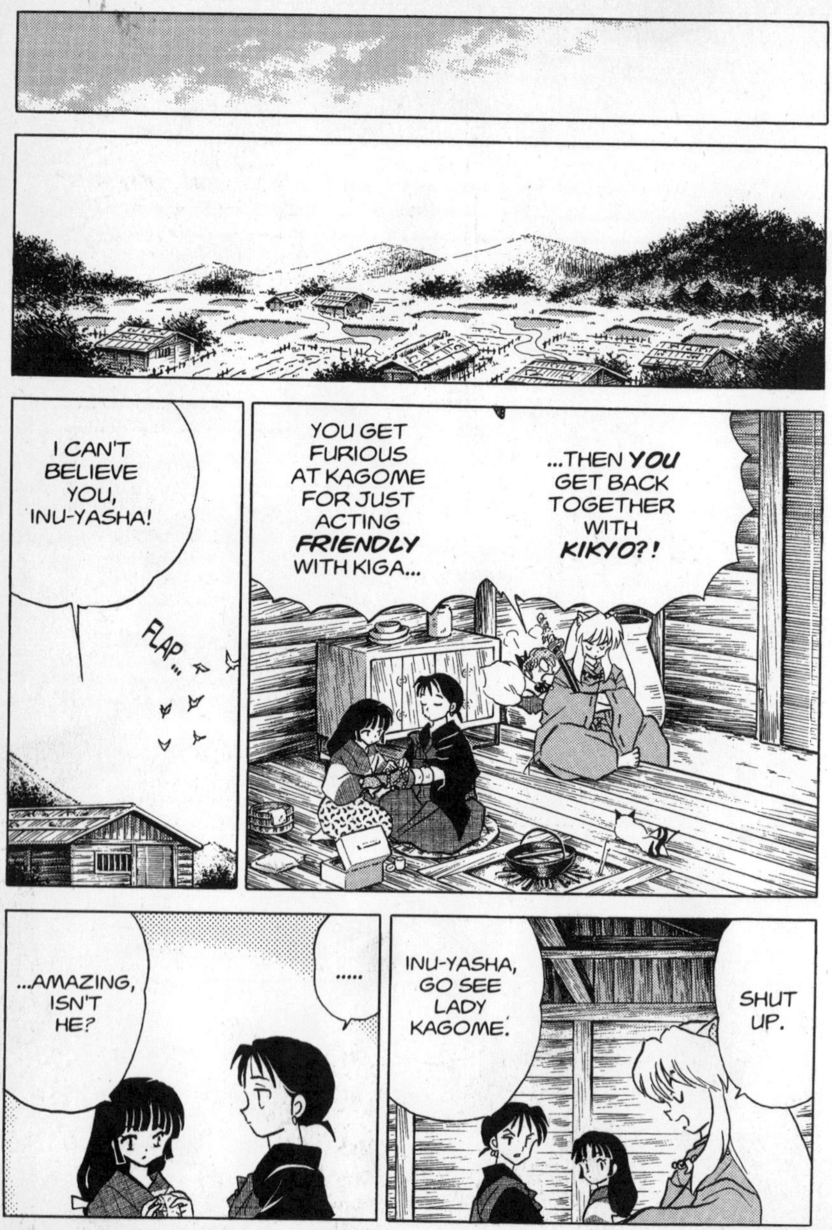
I CAN'T BELIEVE YOU, INU-YASHA!
FLAP...
YOU GET FURIOUS AT KAGOME FOR JUST ACTING FRIENDLY WITH KIGA...
...THEN YOU GET BACK TOGETHER WITH KIKYO?!
...AMAZING, ISN'T HE?
.....
INU-YASHA, GO SEE LADY KAGOME.
SHUT UP.

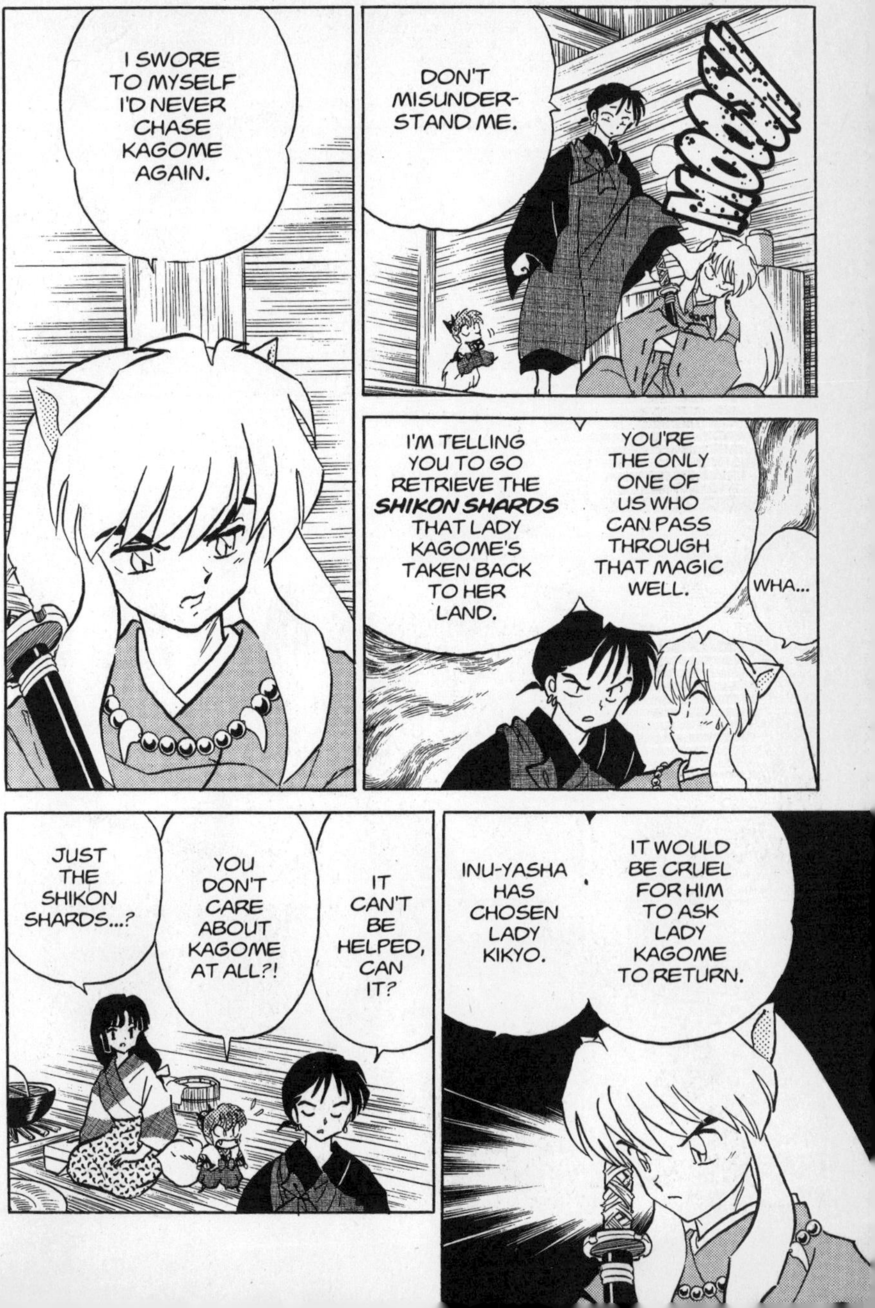
I SWORE TO MYSELF I'D NEVER CHASE KAGOME AGAIN.
DON'T MISUNDER-STAND ME.
I'M TELLING YOU TO GO RETRIEVE THE ***SHIKON SHARDS*** THAT LADY KAGOME'S TAKEN BACK TO HER LAND.
YOU'RE THE ONLY ONE OF US WHO CAN PASS THROUGH THAT MAGIC WELL.
WHA...
JUST THE SHIKON SHARDS...?
YOU DON'T CARE ABOUT KAGOME AT ALL?!
IT CAN'T BE HELPED, CAN IT?
INU-YASHA HAS CHOSEN LADY KIKYO.
IT WOULD BE CRUEL FOR HIM TO ASK LADY KAGOME TO RETURN.

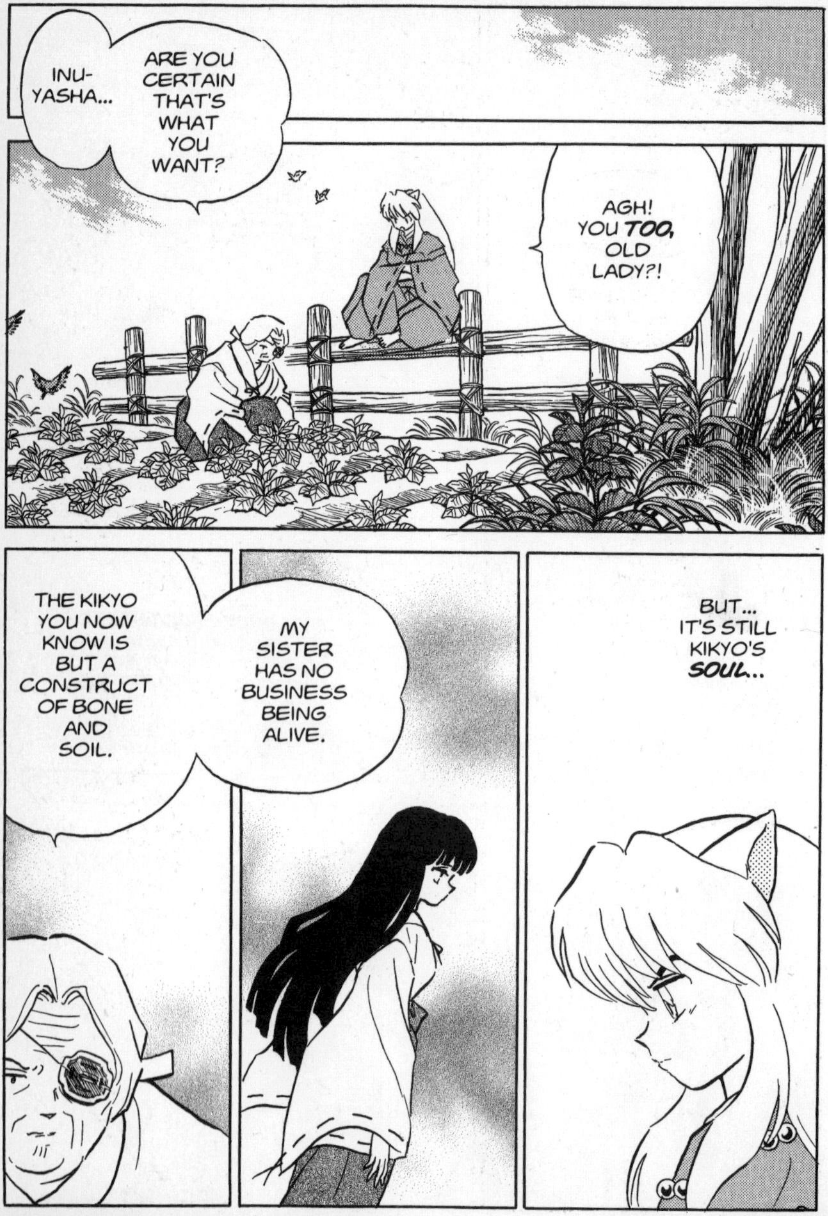
INU-YASHA...
ARE YOU CERTAIN THAT'S WHAT YOU WANT?
AGH! YOU TOO, OLD LADY?!
THE KIKYO YOU NOW KNOW IS BUT A CONSTRUCT OF BONE AND SOIL.
MY SISTER HAS NO BUSINESS BEING ALIVE.
BUT... IT'S STILL KIKYO'S SOUL...

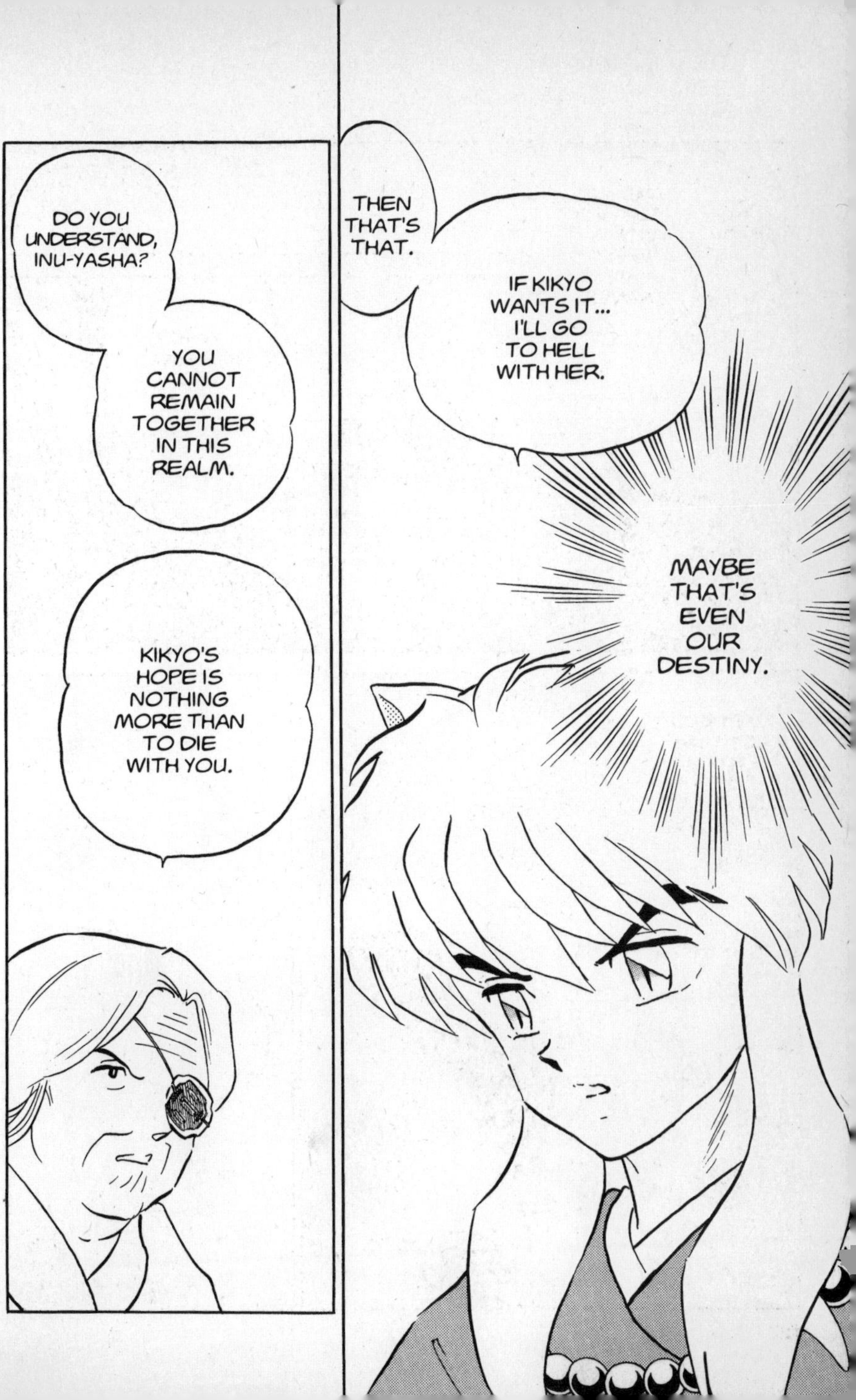
DO YOU UNDERSTAND, INU-YASHA?
YOU CANNOT REMAIN TOGETHER IN THIS REALM.
KIKYO'S HOPE IS NOTHING MORE THAN TO DIE WITH YOU.
THEN THAT'S THAT.
IF KIKYO WANTS IT... I'LL GO TO HELL WITH HER.
MAYBE THAT'S EVEN OUR DESTINY.

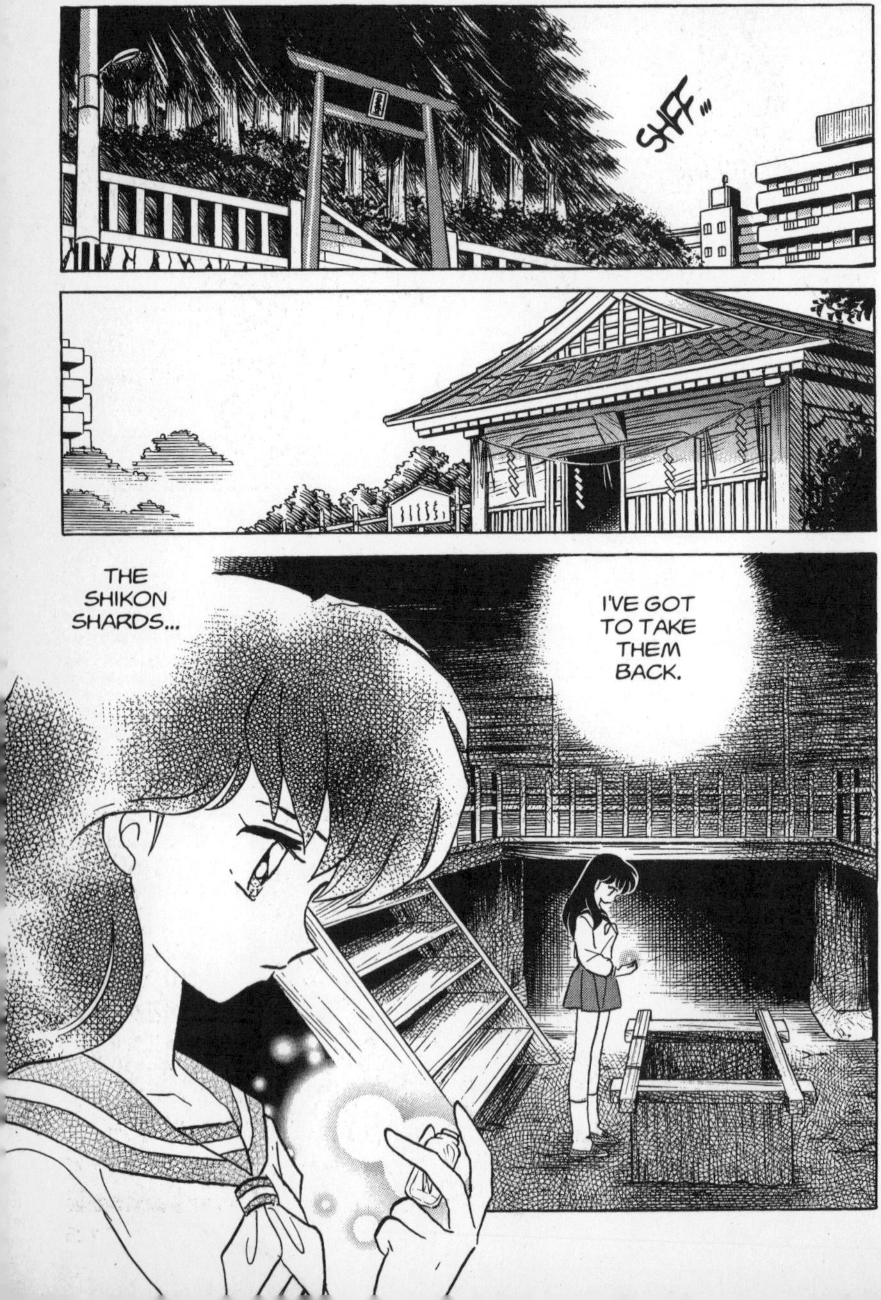
SHFF...
THE SHIKON SHARDS...
I'VE GOT TO TAKE THEM BACK.

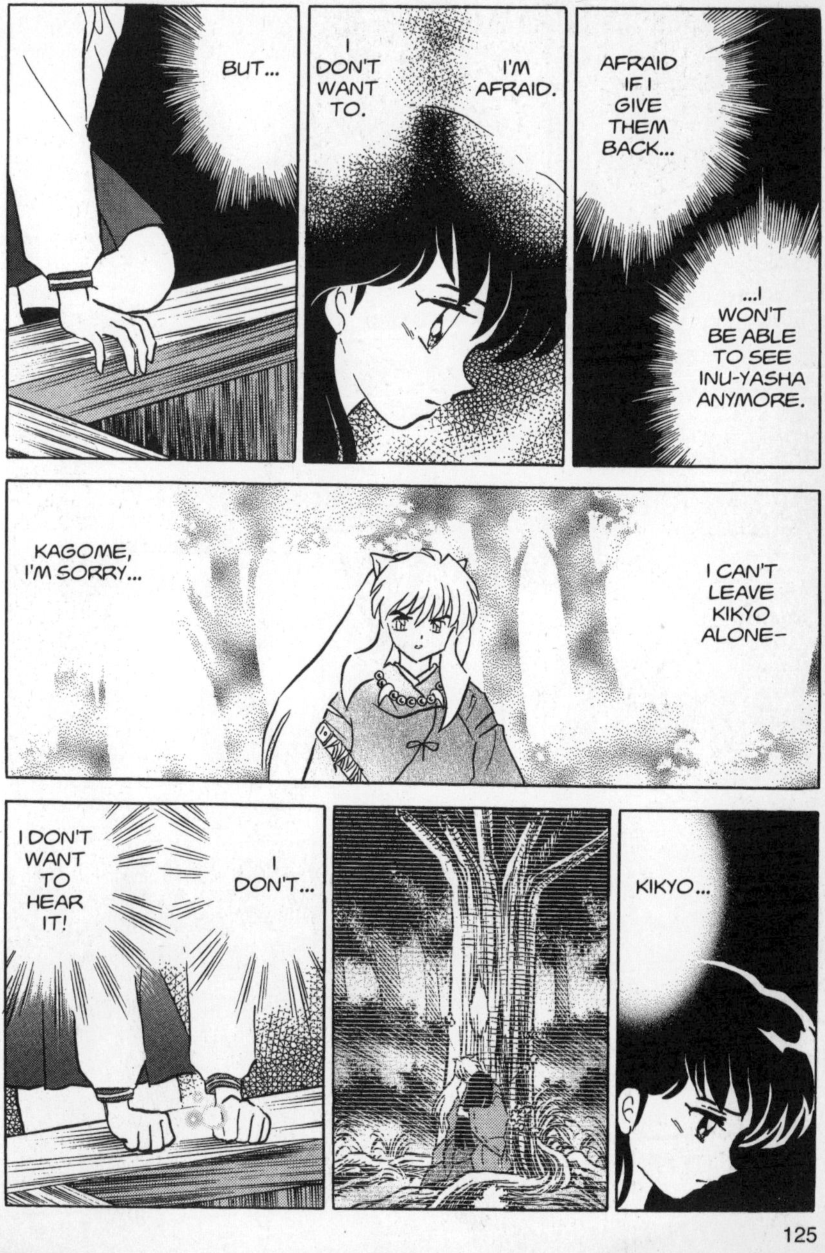
BUT...
I DON'T WANT TO.
I'M AFRAID.
AFRAID IF I GIVE THEM BACK...
...I WON'T BE ABLE TO SEE INU-YASHA ANYMORE.
KAGOME, I'M SORRY...
I CAN'T LEAVE KIKYO ALONE–
I DON'T WANT TO HEAR IT!
I DON'T...
KIKYO...

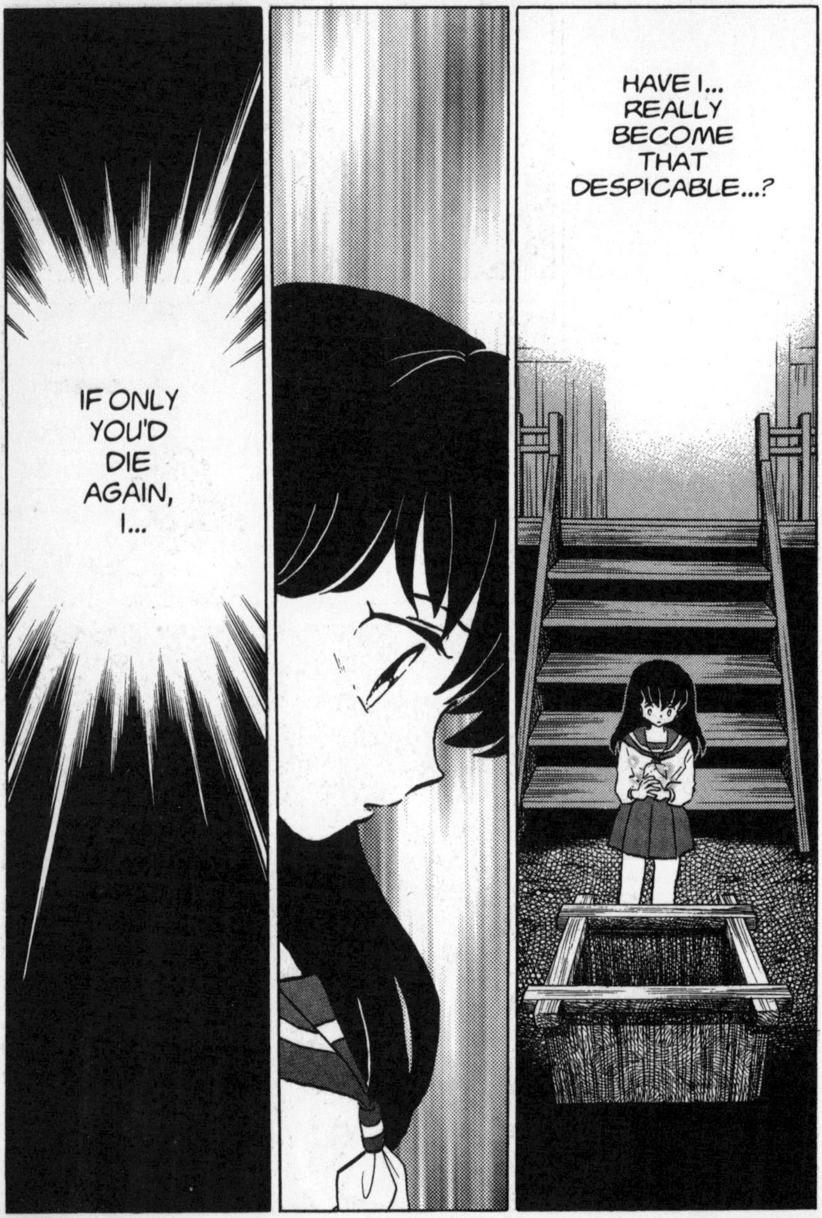
IF ONLY YOU'D DIE AGAIN, I...
HAVE I... REALLY BECOME THAT DESPICABLE...?

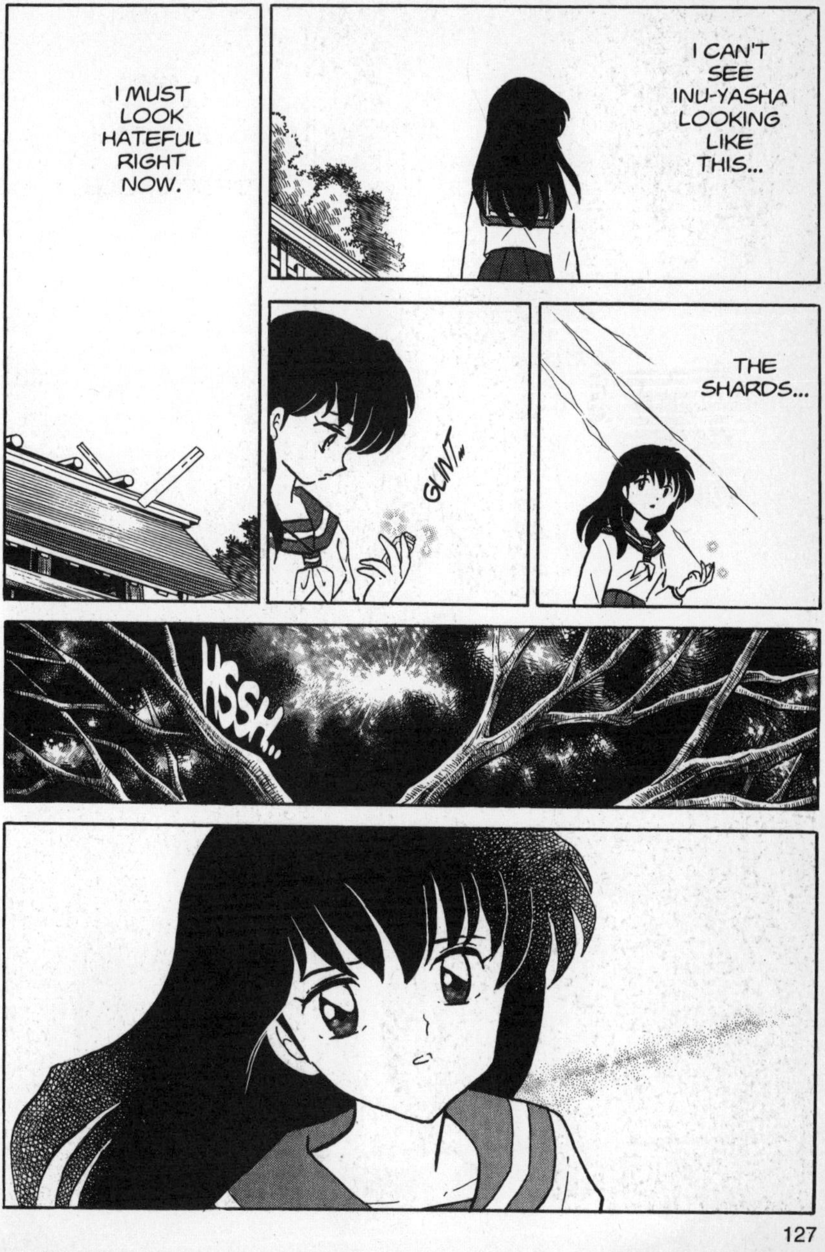
I MUST LOOK HATEFUL RIGHT NOW.
I CAN'T SEE INU-YASHA LOOKING LIKE THIS...
GLINT...
THE SHARDS...
HSSH...

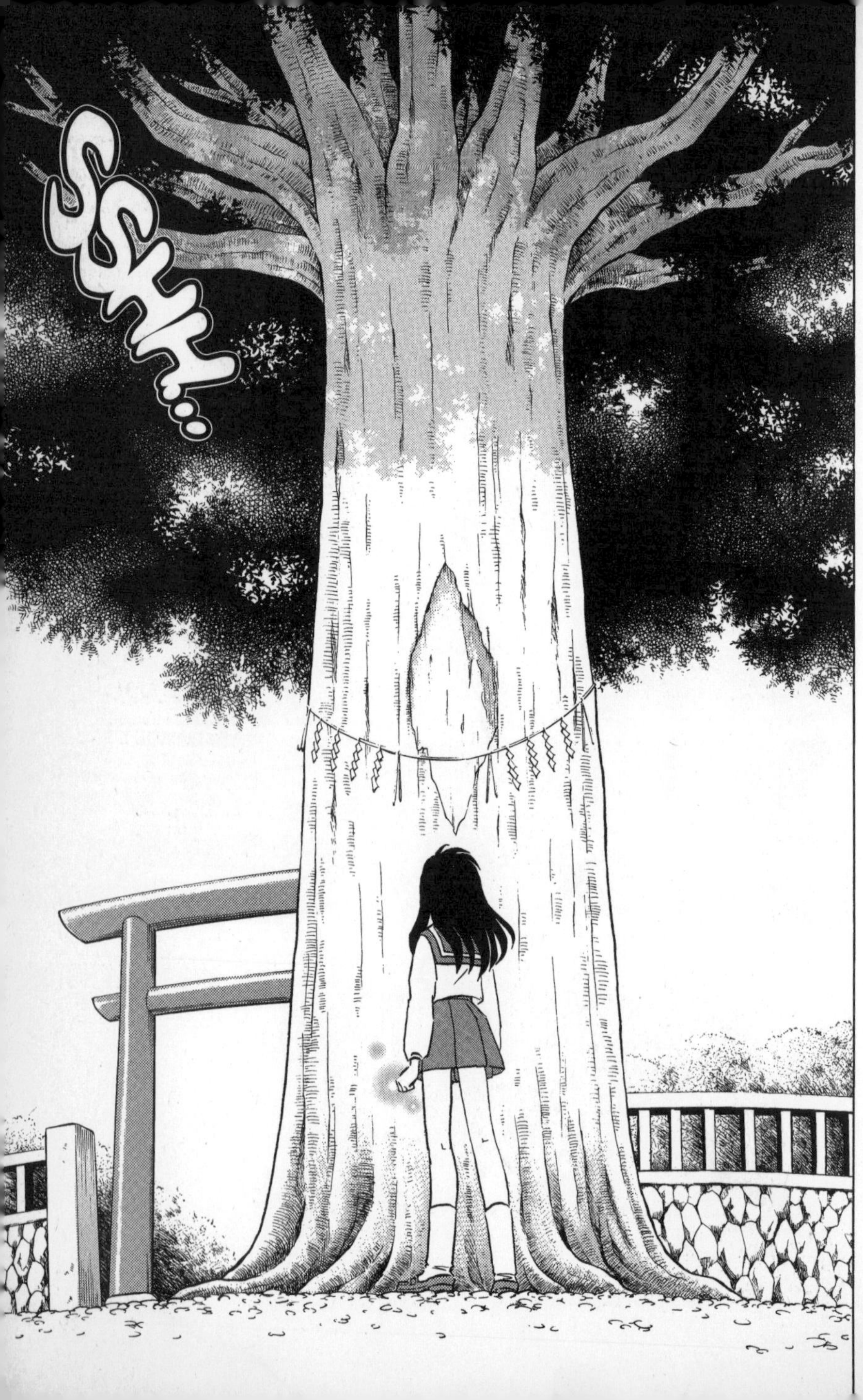
SSHH..

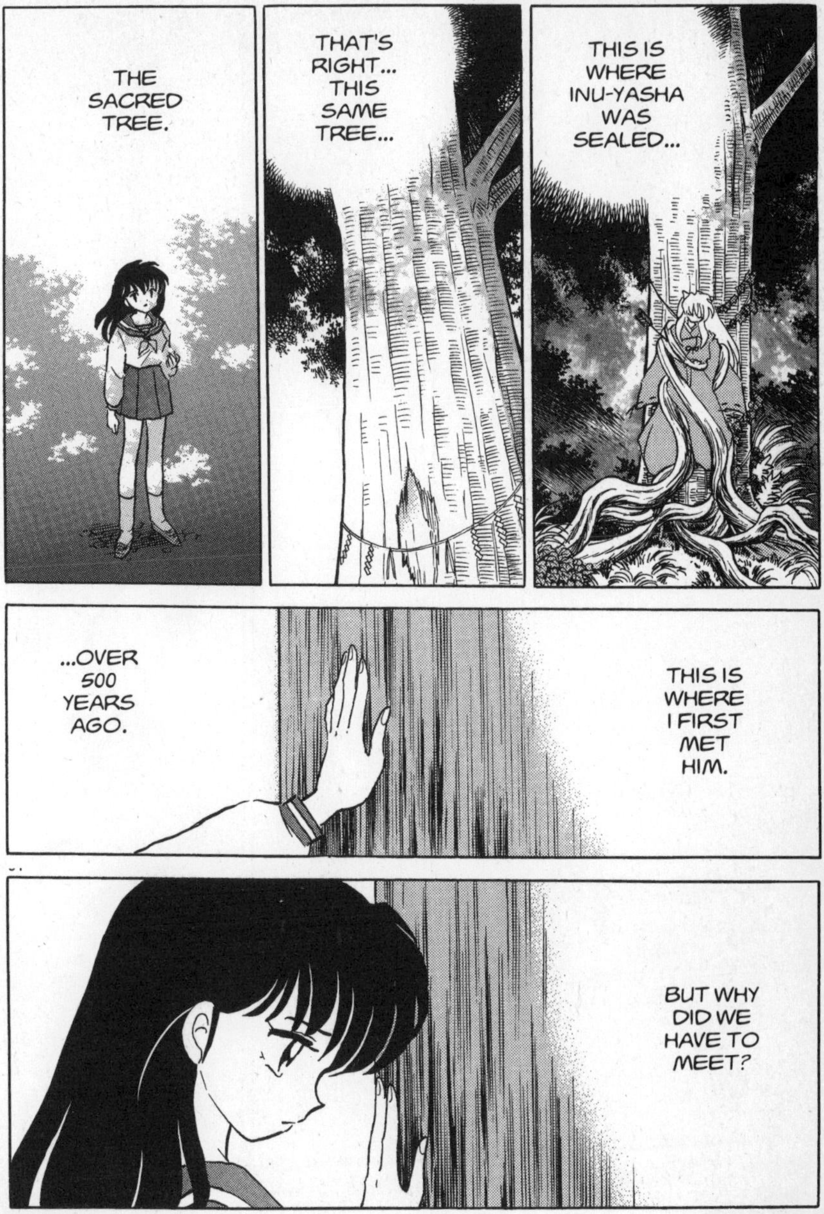
THE SACRED TREE.
THAT'S RIGHT... THIS SAME TREE...
THIS IS WHERE INU-YASHA WAS SEALED...
...OVER 500 YEARS AGO.
THIS IS WHERE I FIRST MET HIM.
BUT WHY DID WE HAVE TO MEET?

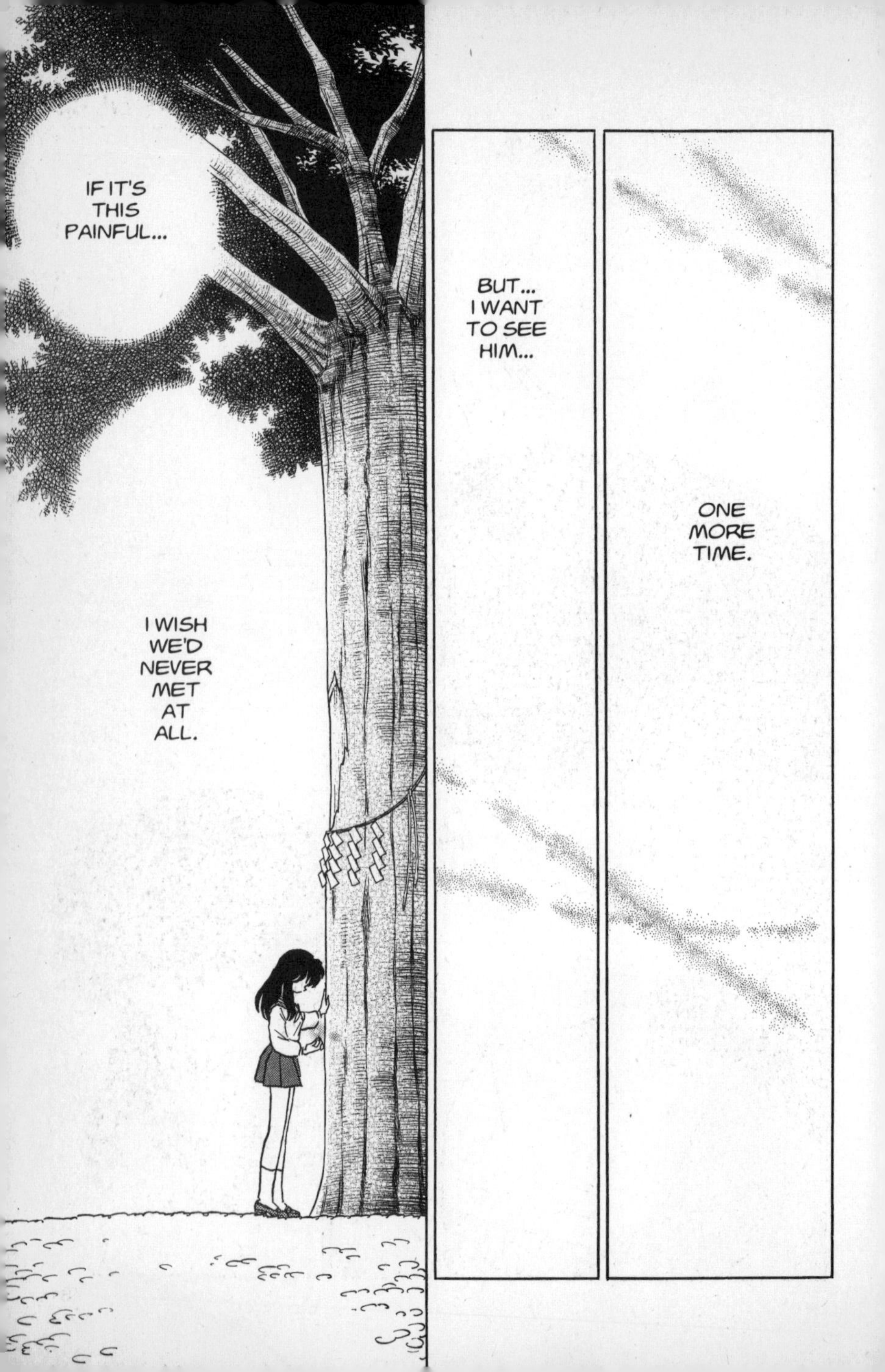
IF IT'S THIS PAINFUL...
I WISH WE'D NEVER MET AT ALL.
BUT... I WANT TO SEE HIM...
ONE MORE TIME.

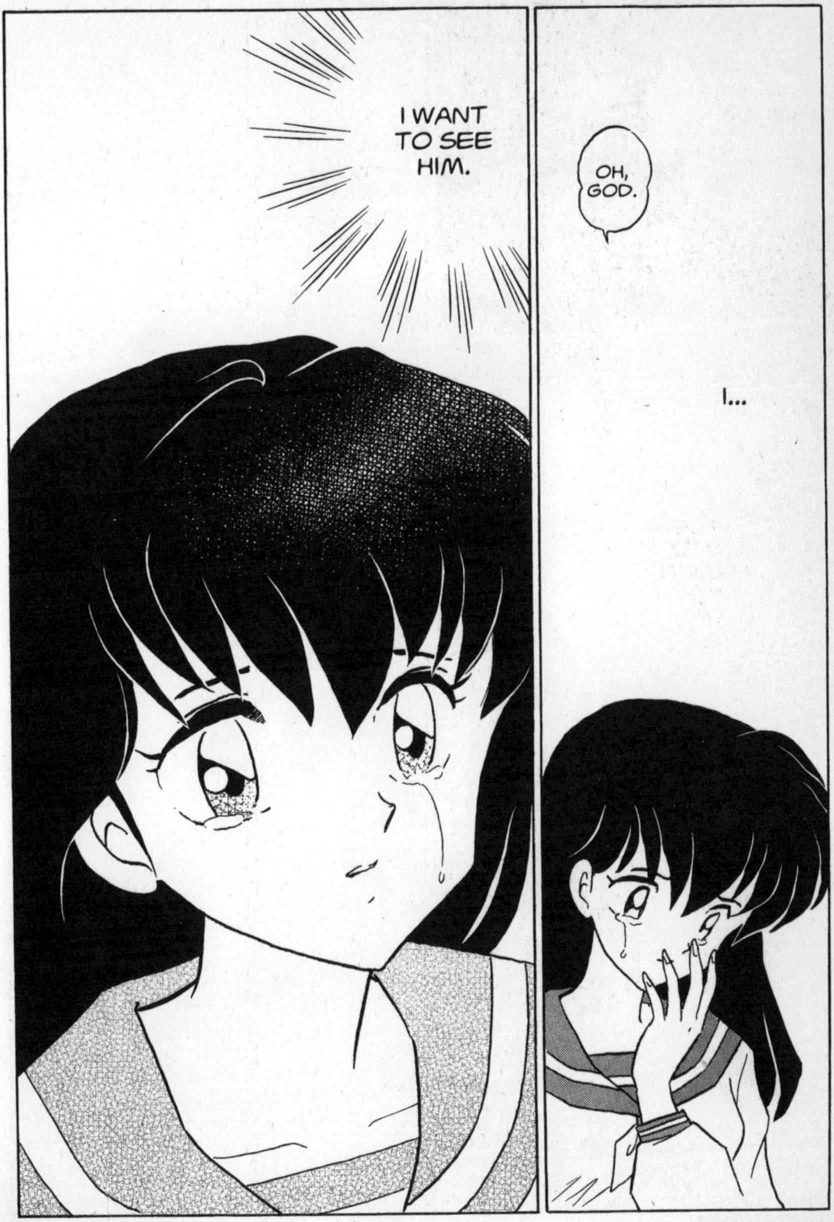
I WANT
TO SEE
HIM.
OH,
GOD.
I...

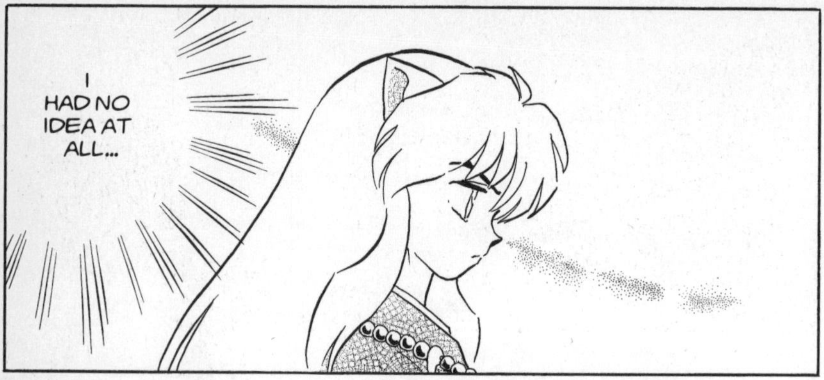
I HAD NO IDEA AT ALL...

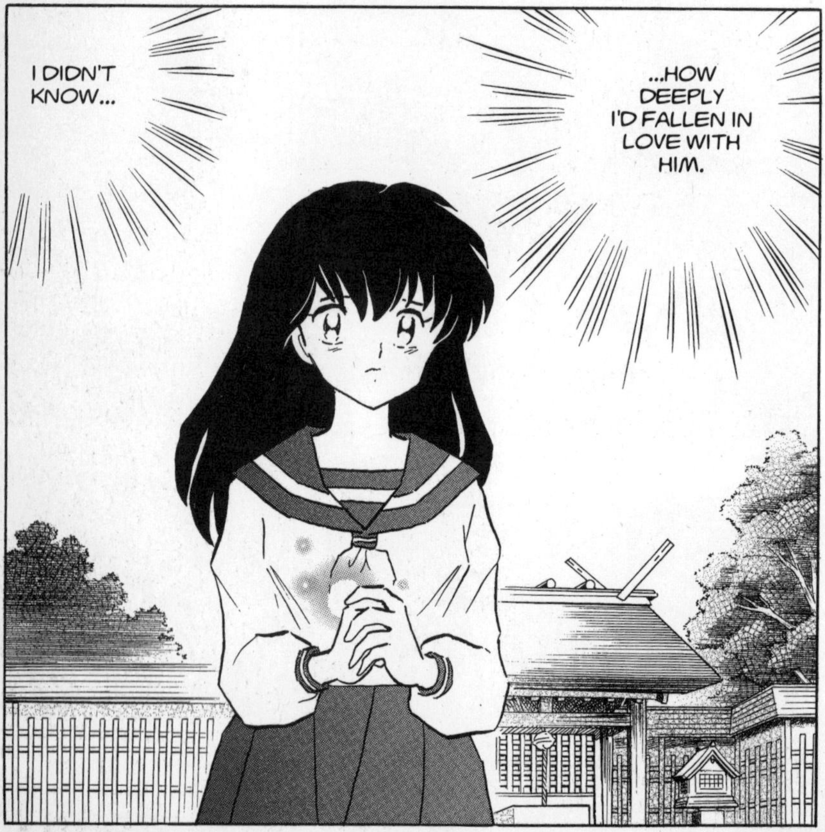
I DIDN'T KNOW...
...HOW DEEPLY I'D FALLEN IN LOVE WITH HIM.

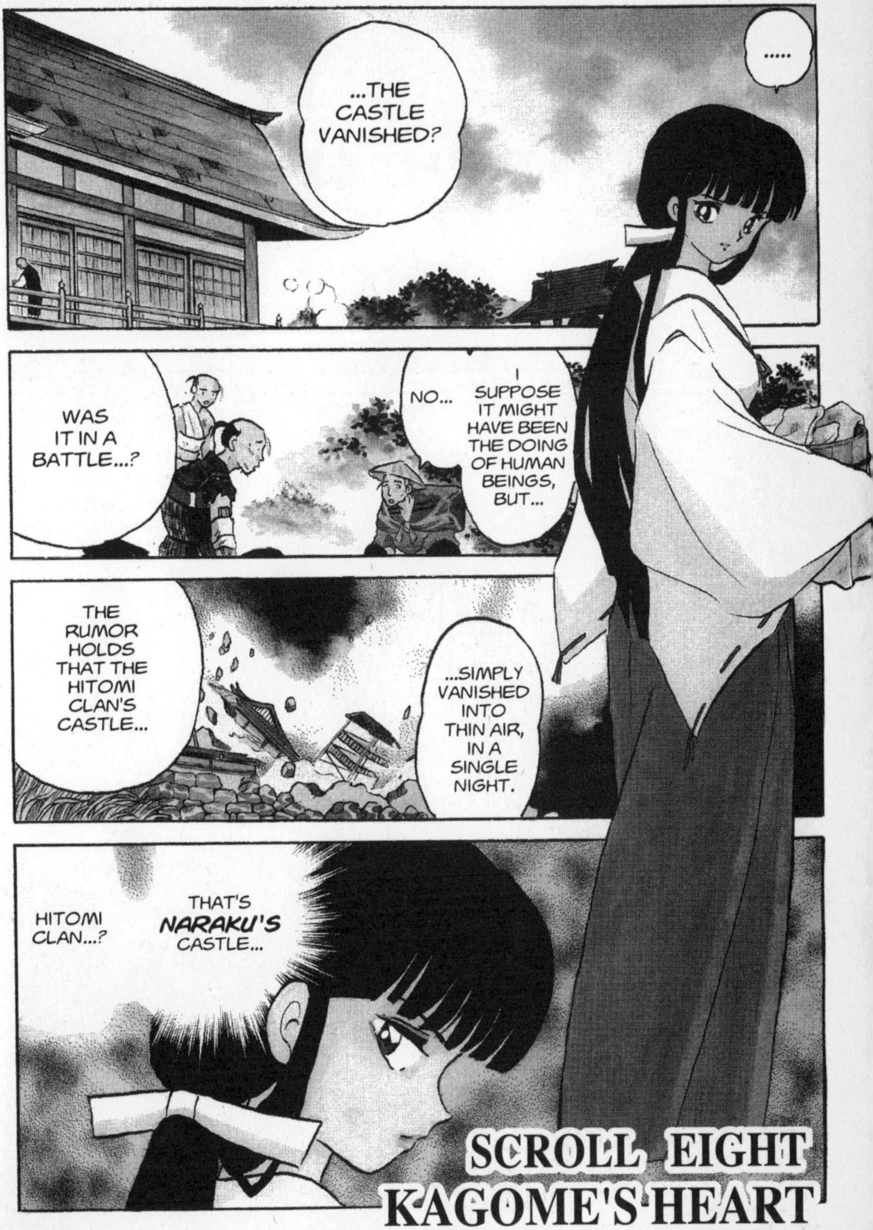
...THE CASTLE VANISHED?
WAS IT IN A BATTLE...?
NO...
I SUPPOSE IT MIGHT HAVE BEEN THE DOING OF HUMAN BEINGS, BUT...
THE RUMOR HOLDS THAT THE HITOMI CLAN'S CASTLE...
...SIMPLY VANISHED INTO THIN AIR, IN A SINGLE NIGHT.
HITOMI CLAN...?
THAT'S ***NARAKU'S*** CASTLE...
.....

SCROLL EIGHT
KAGOME'S HEART

SCROLL EIGHT

KAGOME'S HEART

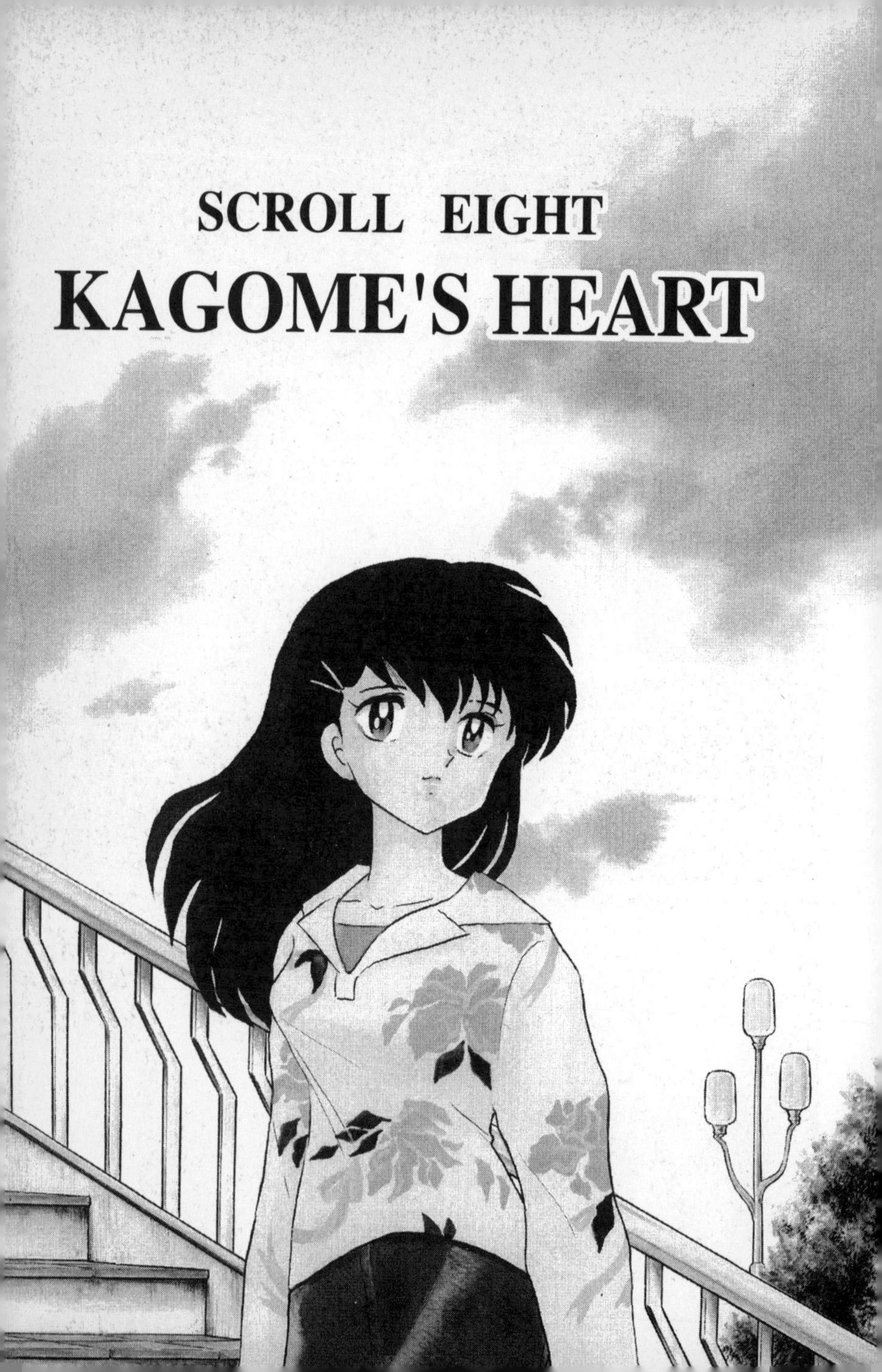

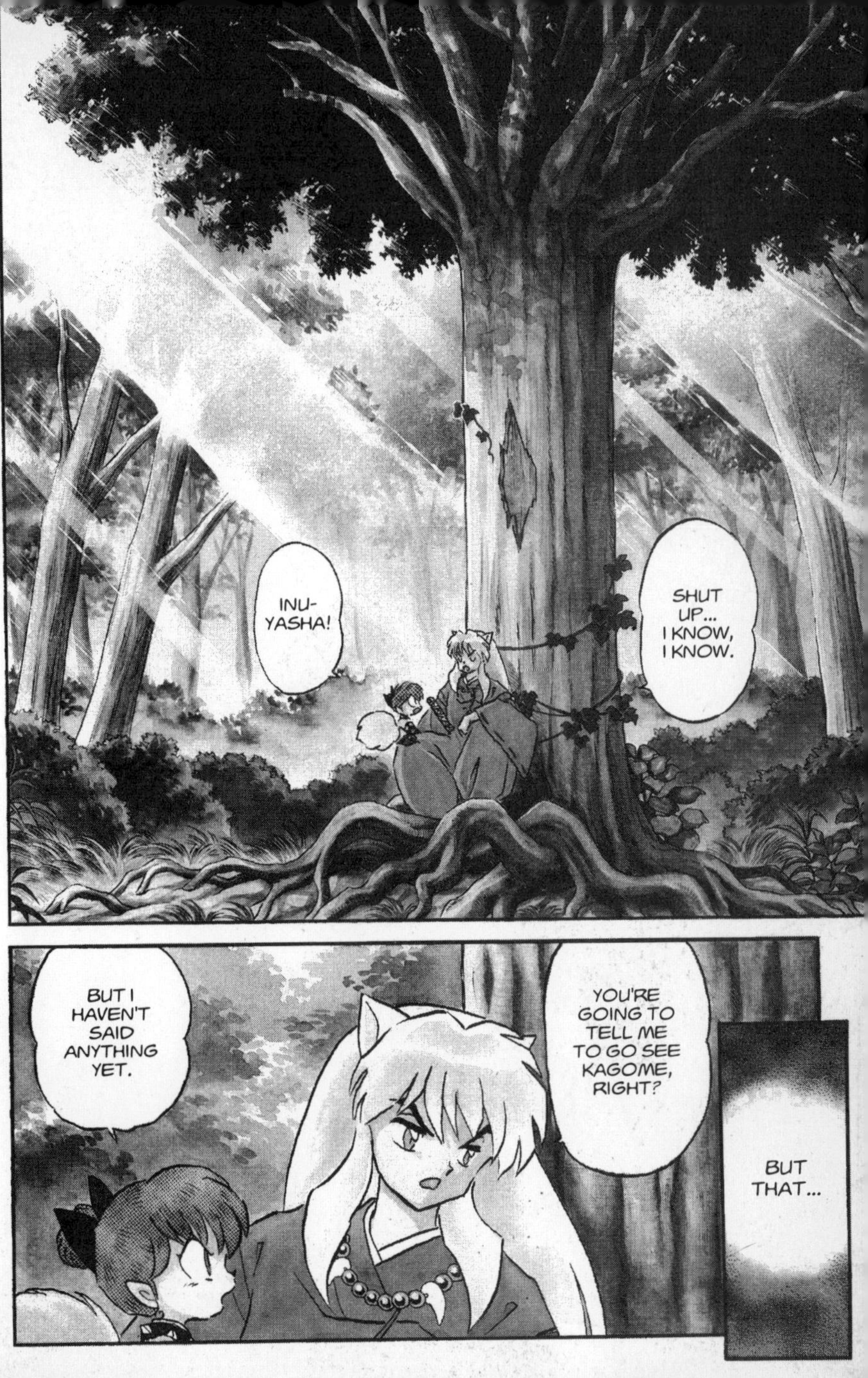
INU-YASHA!
SHUT UP... I KNOW, I KNOW.
BUT I HAVEN'T SAID ANYTHING YET.
YOU'RE GOING TO TELL ME TO GO SEE KAGOME, RIGHT?
BUT THAT...

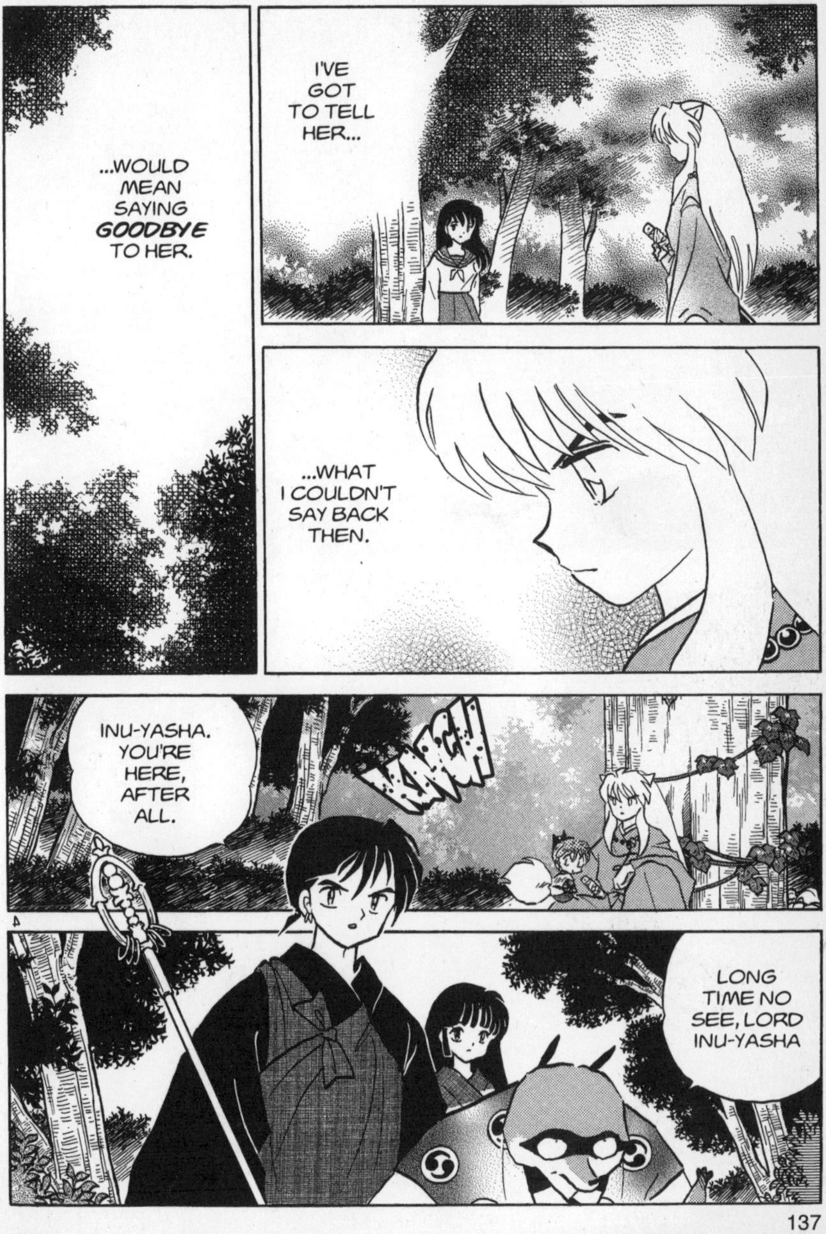
...WOULD MEAN SAYING *GOODBYE* TO HER.
I'VE GOT TO TELL HER...
...WHAT I COULDN'T SAY BACK THEN.
INU-YASHA. YOU'RE HERE, AFTER ALL.
LONG TIME NO SEE, LORD INU-YASHA

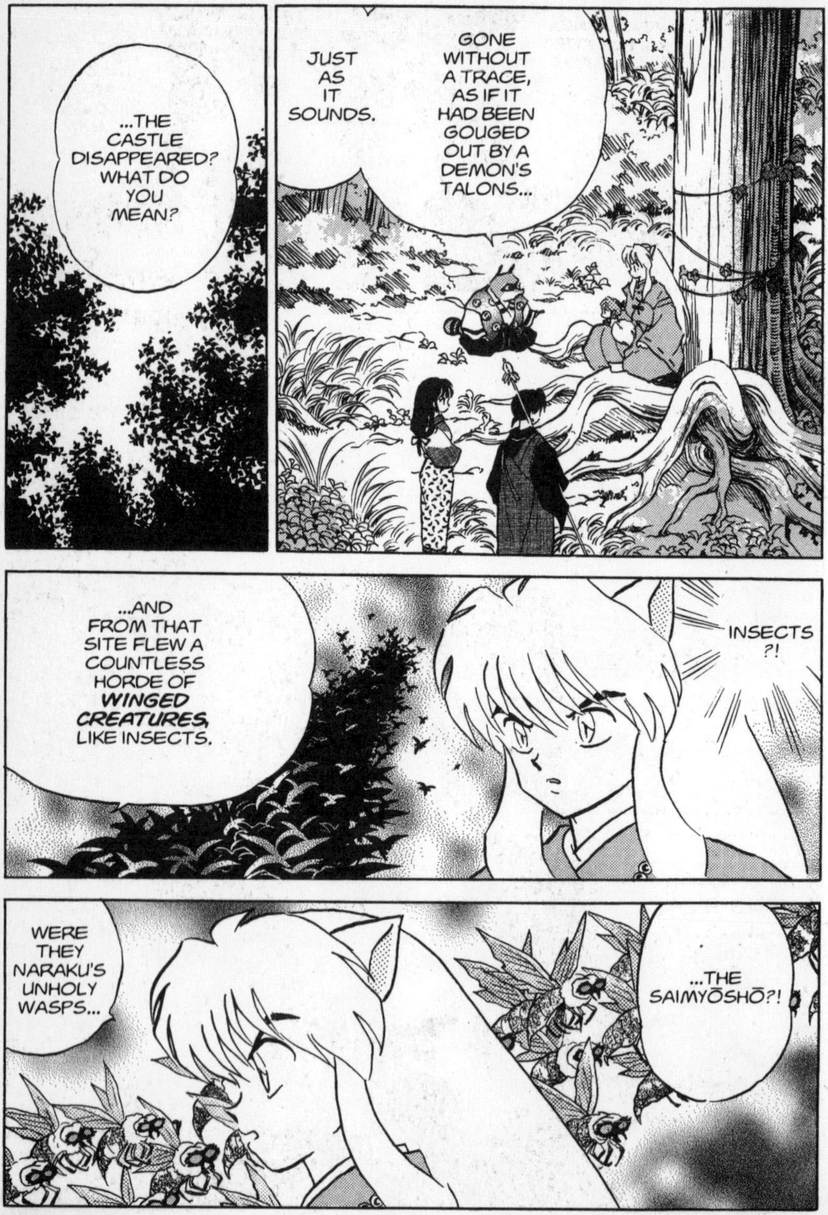
...THE CASTLE DISAPPEARED? WHAT DO YOU MEAN?
JUST AS IT SOUNDS.
GONE WITHOUT A TRACE, AS IF IT HAD BEEN GOUGED OUT BY A DEMON'S TALONS...
...AND FROM THAT SITE FLEW A COUNTLESS HORDE OF ***WINGED CREATURES,*** LIKE INSECTS.
INSECTS ?!
WERE THEY NARAKU'S UNHOLY WASPS...
...THE SAIMYŌSHŌ?!

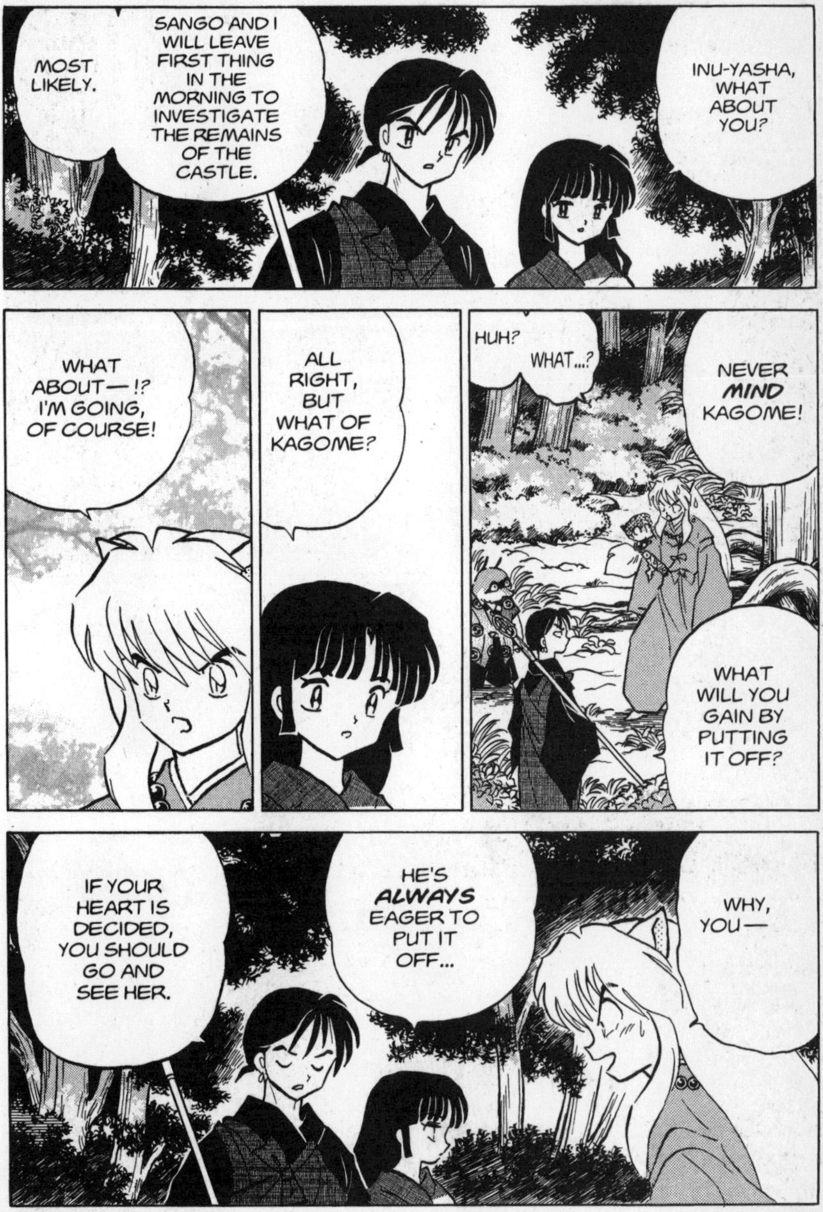
SANGO AND I WILL LEAVE FIRST THING IN THE MORNING TO INVESTIGATE THE REMAINS OF THE CASTLE.
MOST LIKELY.
INU-YASHA, WHAT ABOUT YOU?
WHAT ABOUT—!? I'M GOING, OF COURSE!
ALL RIGHT, BUT WHAT OF KAGOME?
HUH?
WHAT...?
NEVER MIND KAGOME!
WHAT WILL YOU GAIN BY PUTTING IT OFF?
IF YOUR HEART IS DECIDED, YOU SHOULD GO AND SEE HER.
HE'S ALWAYS EAGER TO PUT IT OFF...
WHY, YOU—

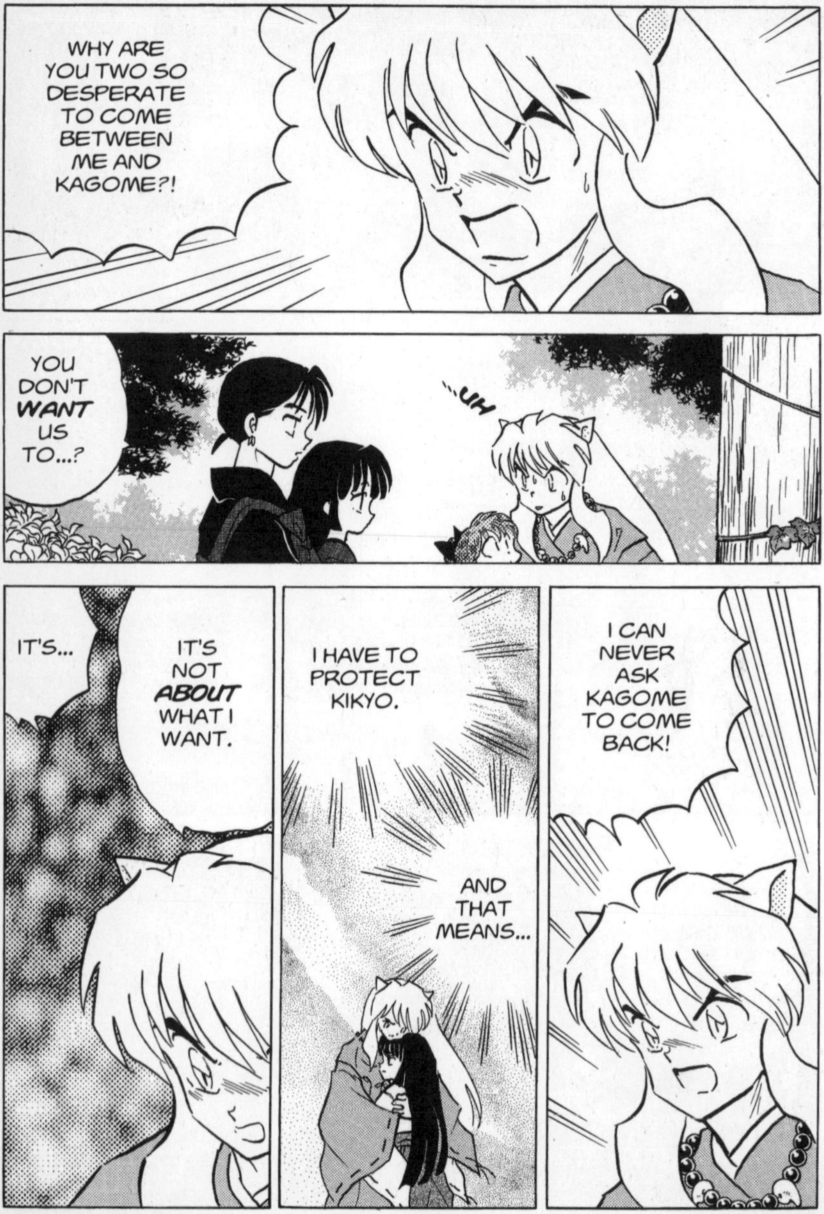
WHY ARE YOU TWO SO DESPERATE TO COME BETWEEN ME AND KAGOME?!
YOU DON'T *WANT* US TO...?
...UH
IT'S...
IT'S NOT *ABOUT* WHAT I WANT.
I HAVE TO PROTECT KIKYO.
AND THAT MEANS...
I CAN NEVER ASK KAGOME TO COME BACK!

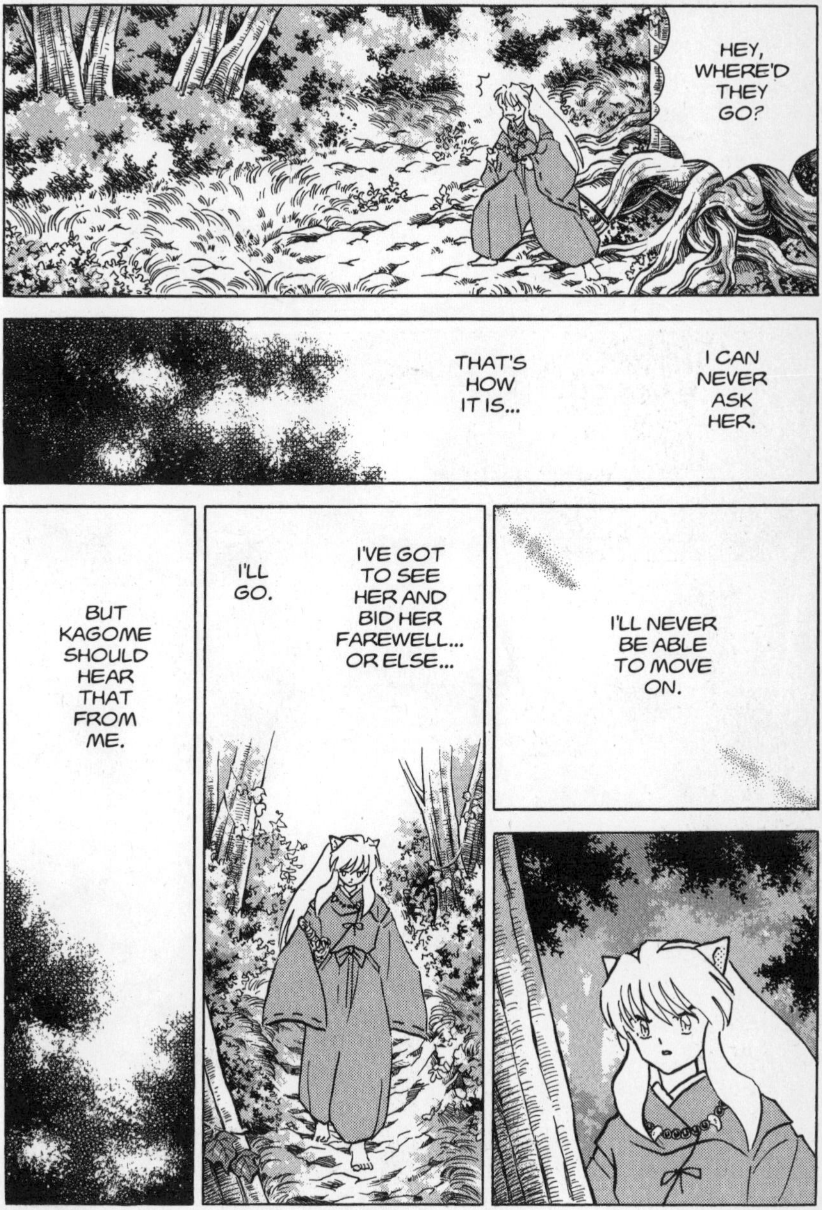
HEY, WHERE'D THEY GO?
THAT'S HOW IT IS...
I CAN NEVER ASK HER.
BUT KAGOME SHOULD HEAR THAT FROM ME.
I'LL GO.
I'VE GOT TO SEE HER AND BID HER FAREWELL... OR ELSE...
I'LL NEVER BE ABLE TO MOVE ON.

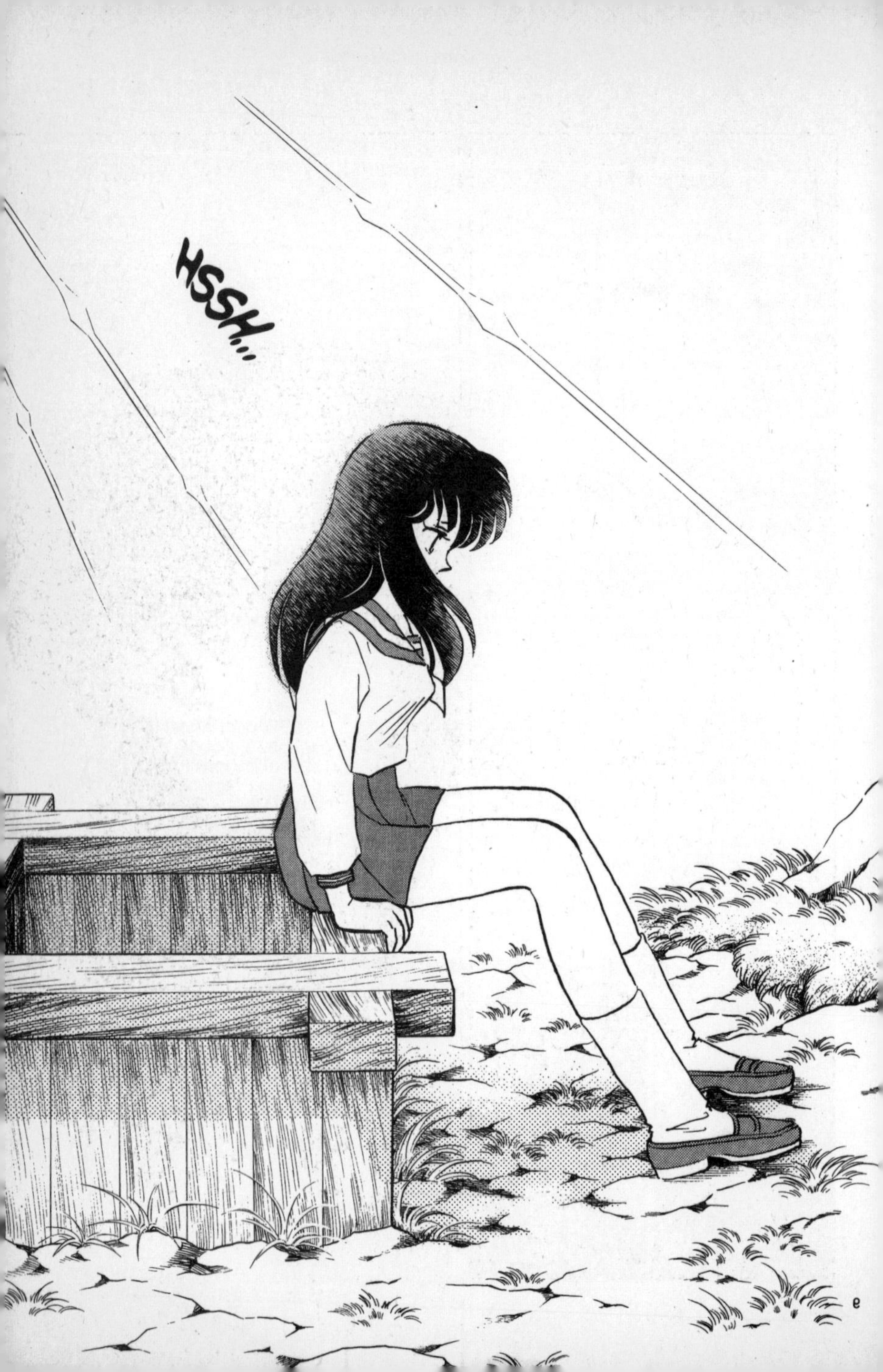
HSSH...

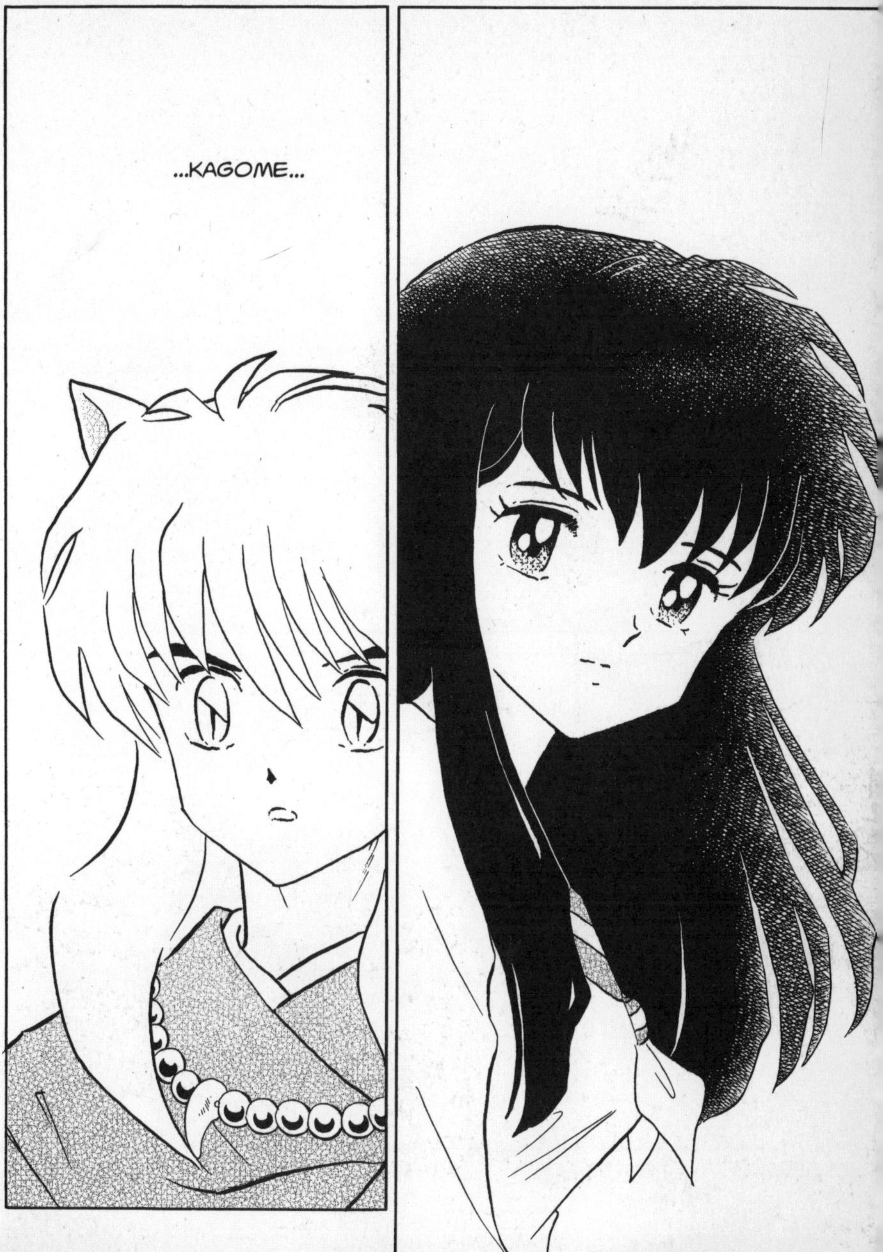
...KAGOME...

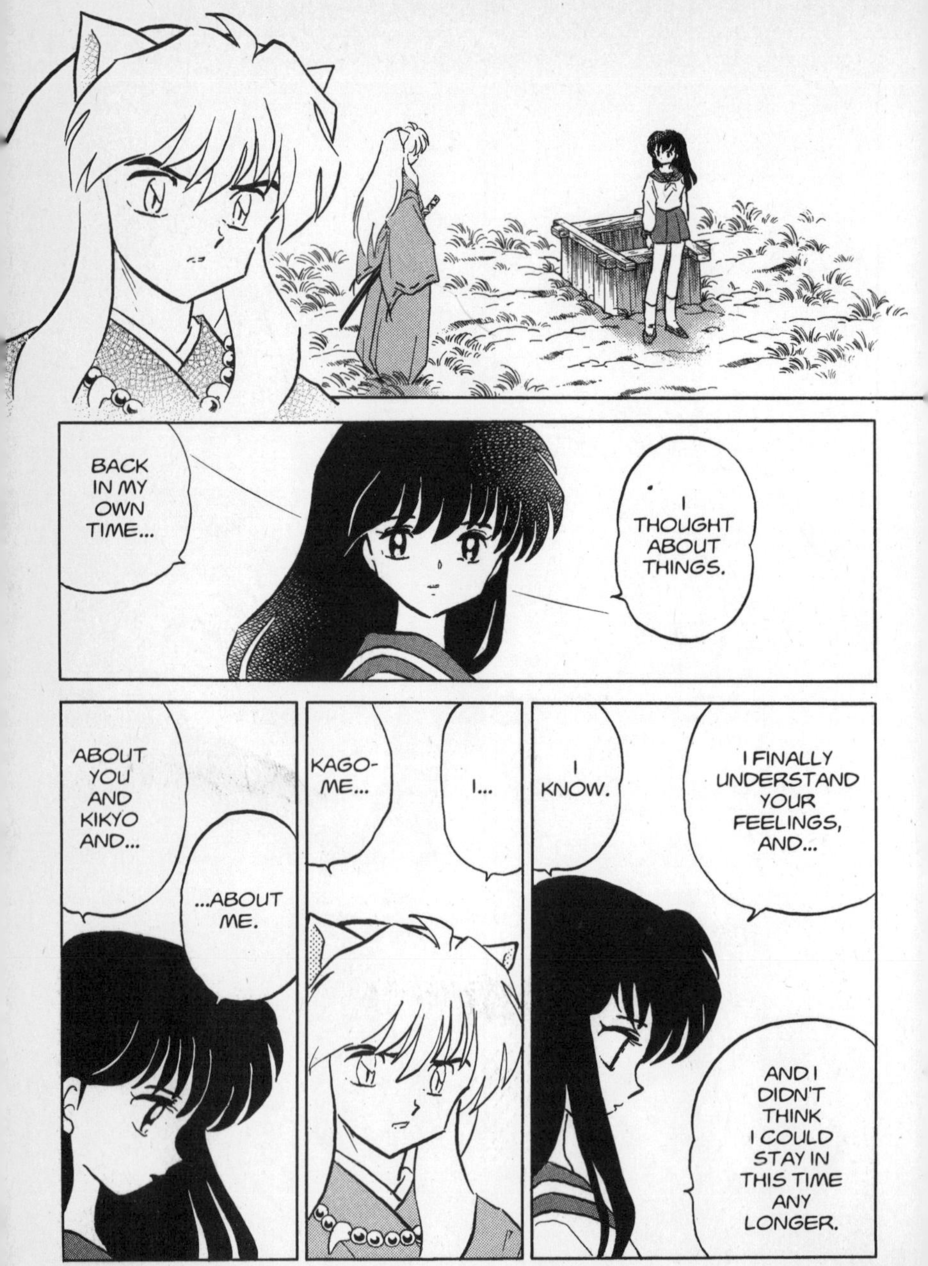
BACK IN MY OWN TIME...
I THOUGHT ABOUT THINGS.
ABOUT YOU AND KIKYO AND...
...ABOUT ME.
KAGO-ME...
I...
I KNOW.
I FINALLY UNDERSTAND YOUR FEELINGS, AND...
AND I DIDN'T THINK I COULD STAY IN THIS TIME ANY LONGER.

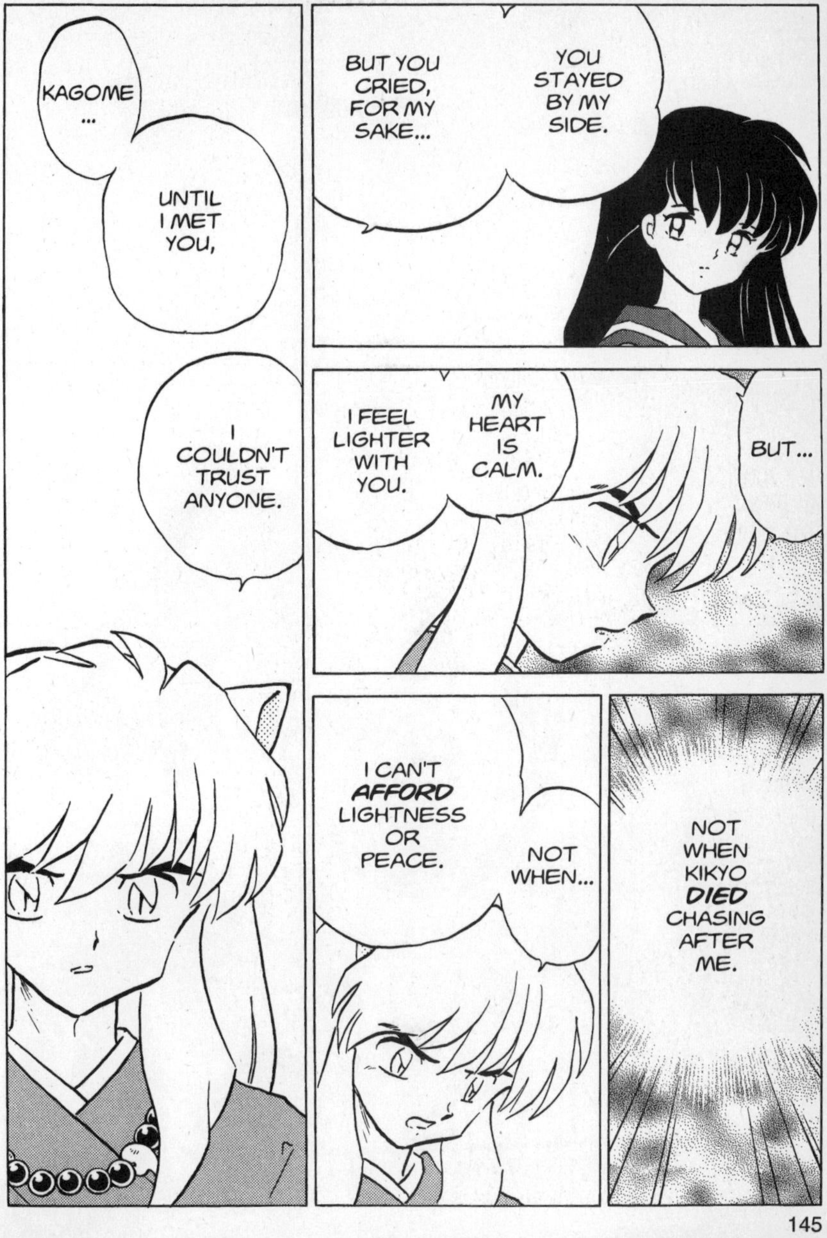
KAGOME ...
UNTIL I MET YOU,
I COULDN'T TRUST ANYONE.
BUT YOU CRIED, FOR MY SAKE...
YOU STAYED BY MY SIDE.
I FEEL LIGHTER WITH YOU.
MY HEART IS CALM.
BUT...
I CAN'T **AFFORD** LIGHTNESS OR PEACE.
NOT WHEN...
NOT WHEN KIKYO **DIED** CHASING AFTER ME.

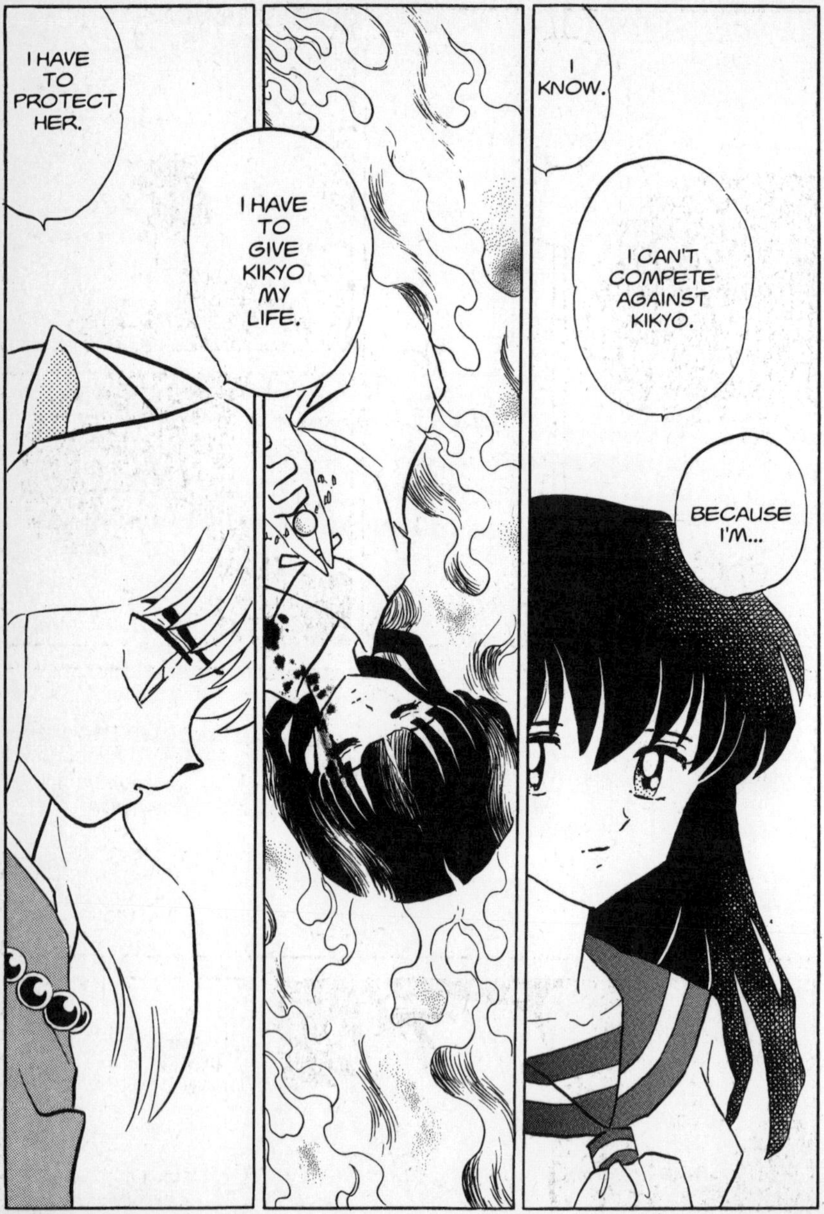
I HAVE TO PROTECT HER.
I HAVE TO GIVE KIKYO MY LIFE.
I KNOW.
I CAN'T COMPETE AGAINST KIKYO.
BECAUSE I'M...

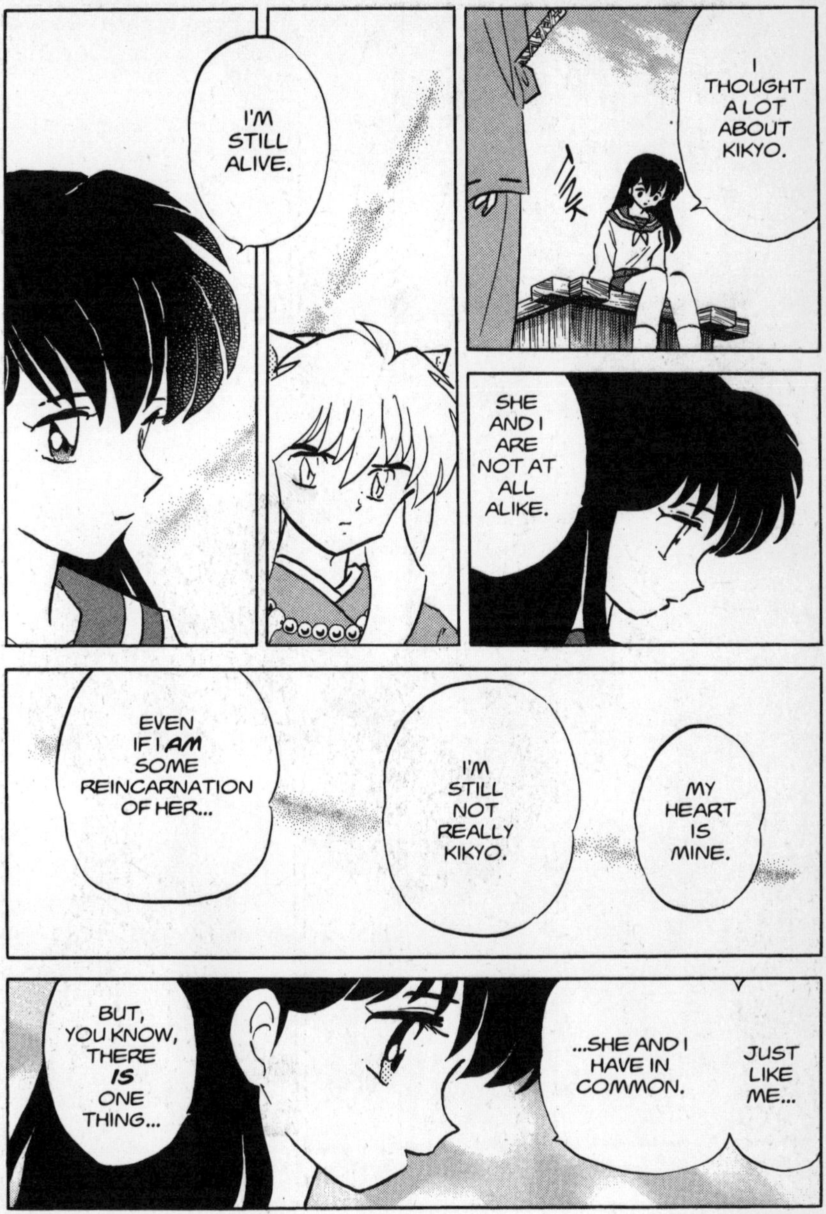
I'M STILL ALIVE.
I THOUGHT A LOT ABOUT KIKYO.
TINK
SHE AND I ARE NOT AT ALL ALIKE.
EVEN IF I *AM* SOME REINCARNATION OF HER...
I'M STILL NOT REALLY KIKYO.
MY HEART IS MINE.
BUT, YOU KNOW, THERE *IS* ONE THING...
...SHE AND I HAVE IN COMMON.
JUST LIKE ME...

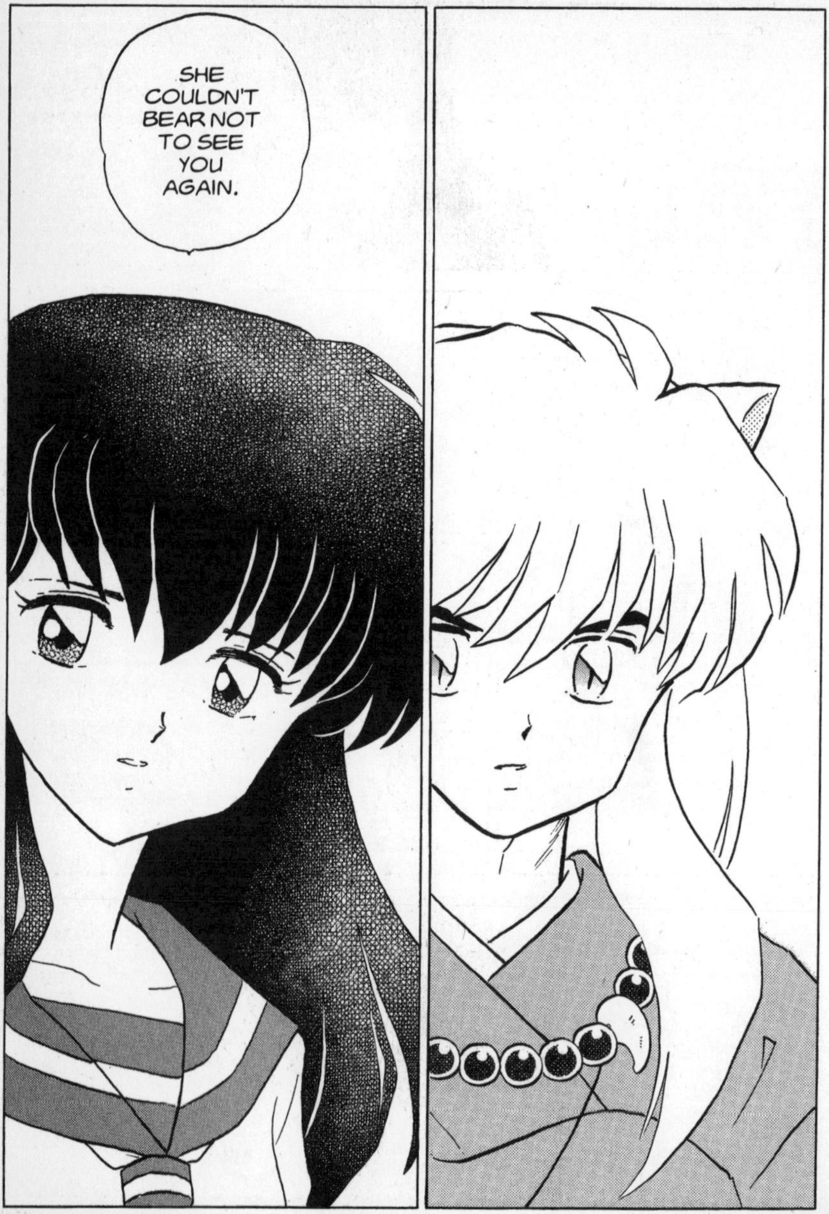
SHE COULDN'T BEAR NOT TO SEE YOU AGAIN.

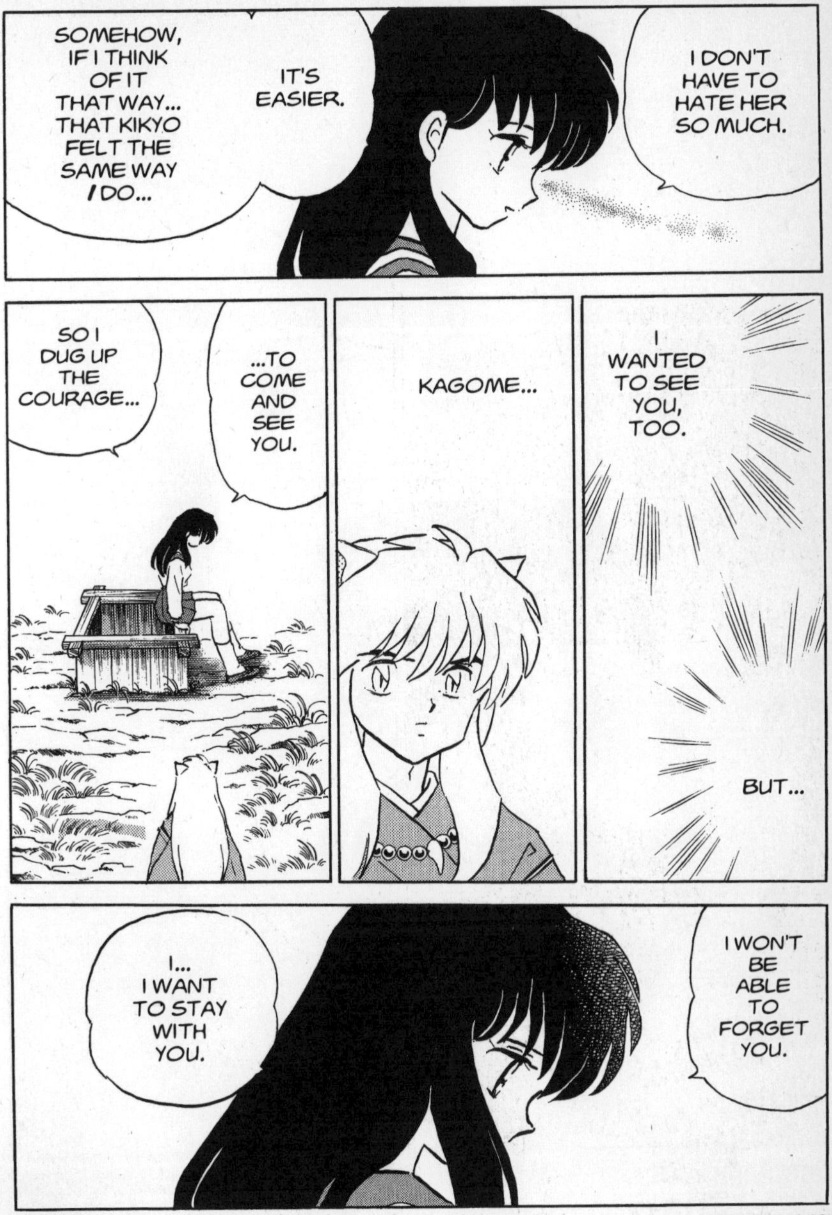
SOMEHOW, IF I THINK OF IT THAT WAY... THAT KIKYO FELT THE SAME WAY I DO...
IT'S EASIER.
I DON'T HAVE TO HATE HER SO MUCH.
SO I DUG UP THE COURAGE...
...TO COME AND SEE YOU.
KAGOME...
I WANTED TO SEE YOU, TOO.
BUT...
I... I WANT TO STAY WITH YOU.
I WON'T BE ABLE TO FORGET YOU.

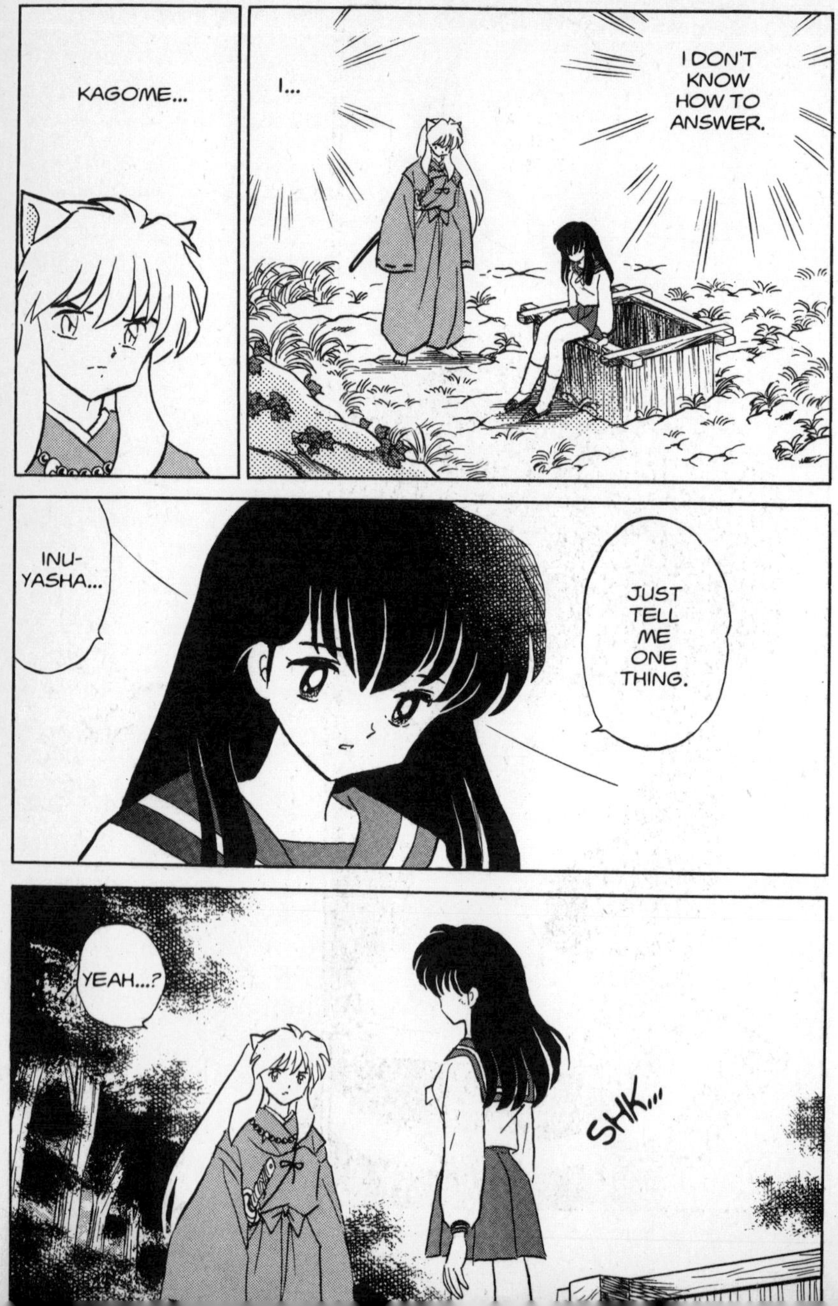
KAGOME...
I...
I DON'T KNOW HOW TO ANSWER.
INU-YASHA...
JUST TELL ME ONE THING.
YEAH...?
SHK...

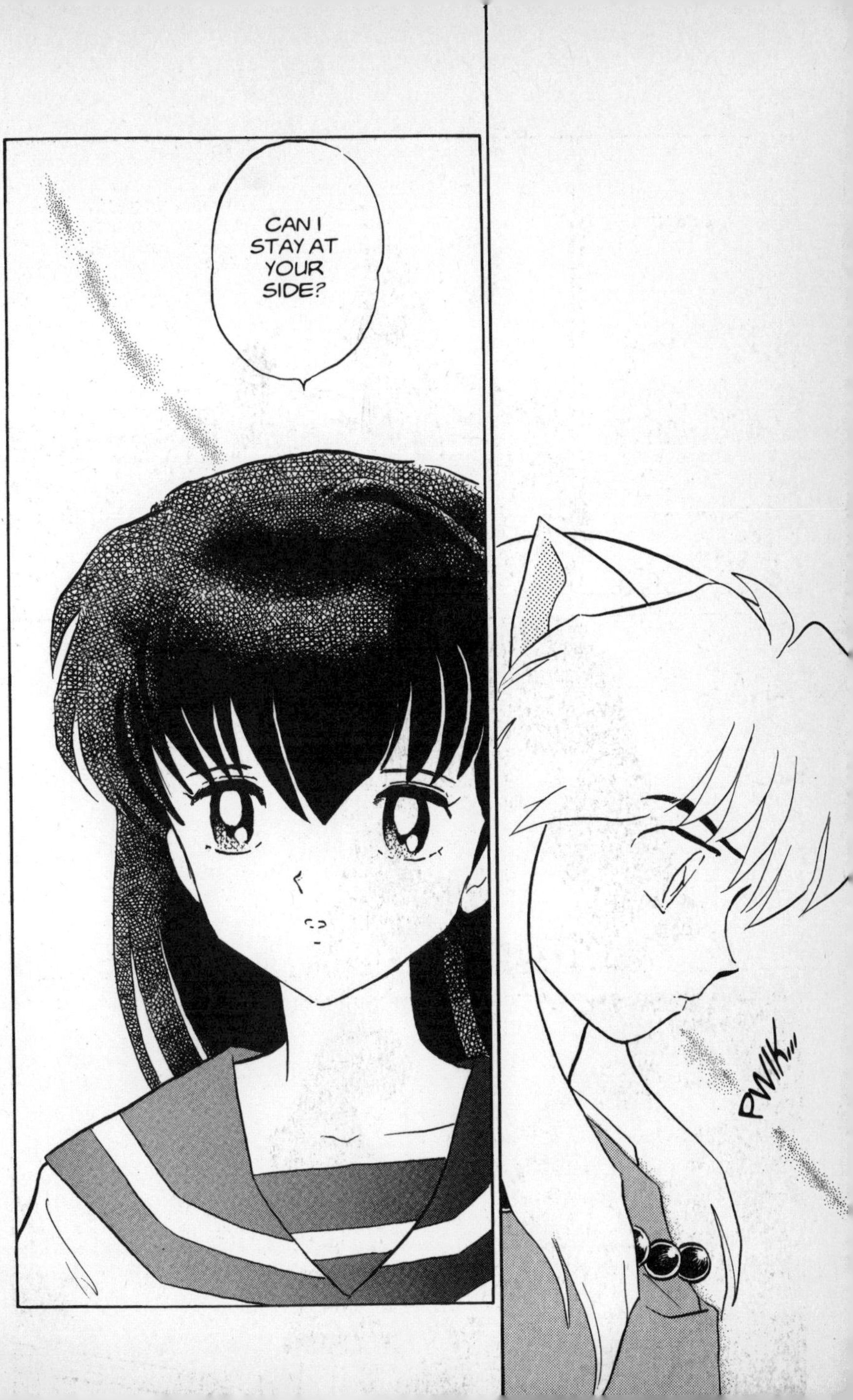
CAN I STAY AT YOUR SIDE?
PWIK....

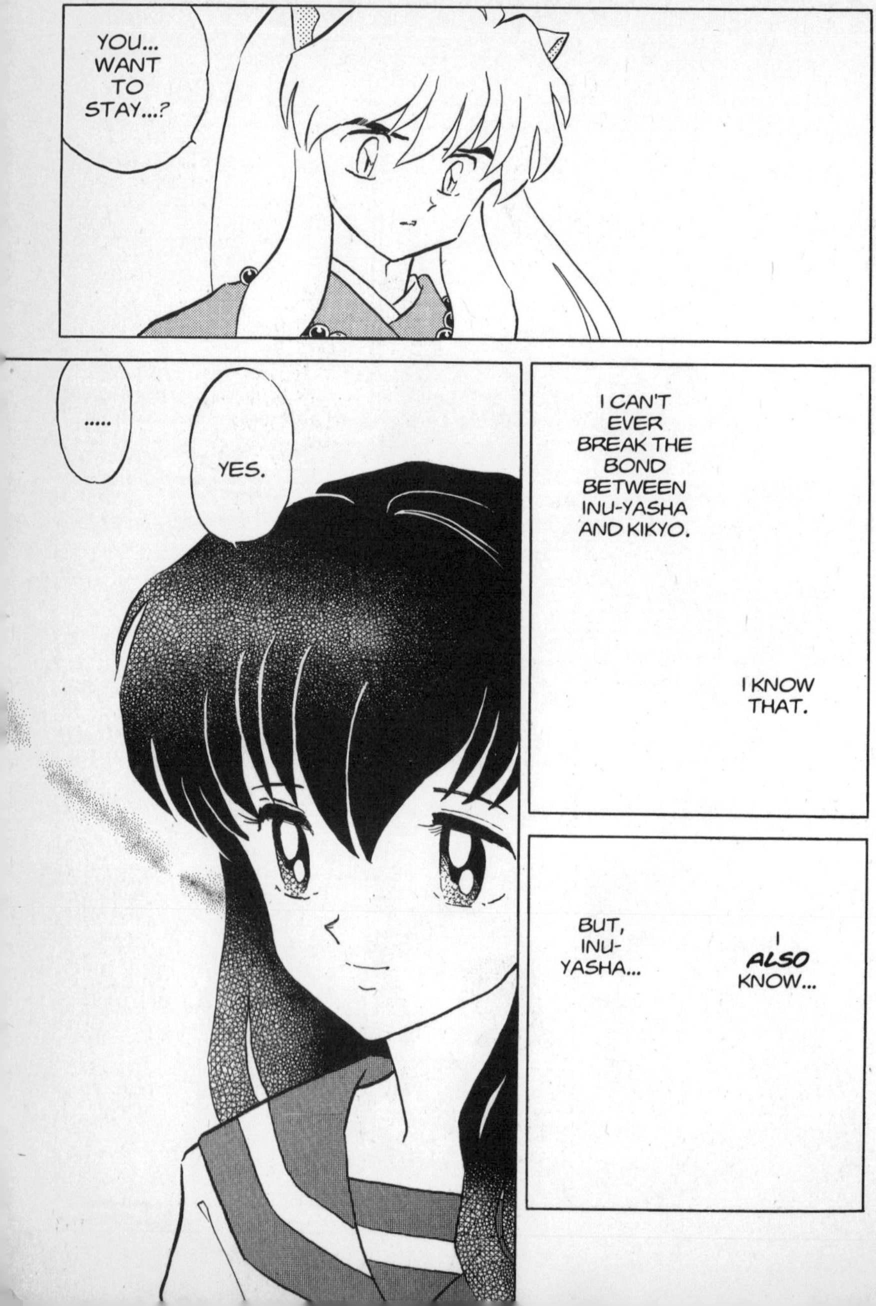
YOU... WANT TO STAY...?
.....
YES.
I CAN'T EVER BREAK THE BOND BETWEEN INU-YASHA AND KIKYO.
I KNOW THAT.
BUT, INU-YASHA...
I *ALSO* KNOW...

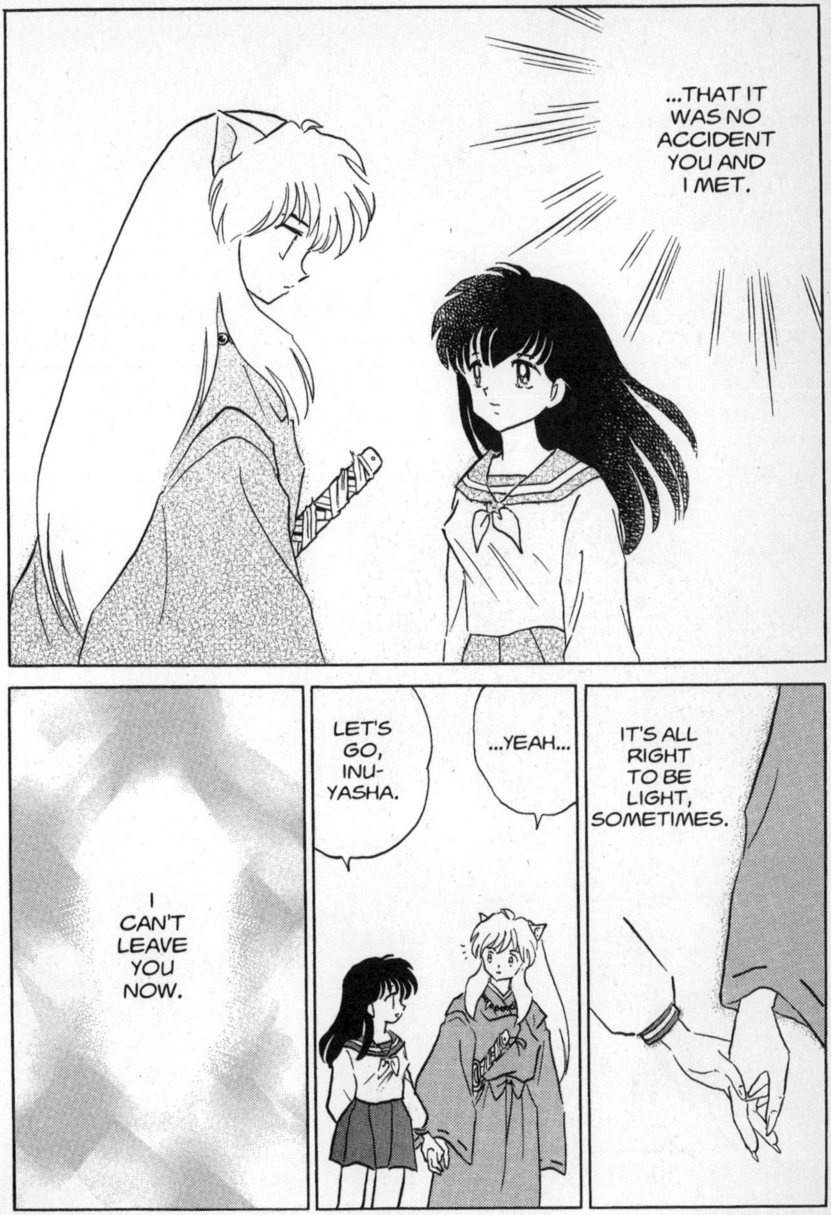
...THAT IT WAS NO ACCIDENT YOU AND I MET.
I CAN'T LEAVE YOU NOW.
LET'S GO, INU-YASHA.
...YEAH...
IT'S ALL RIGHT TO BE LIGHT, SOMETIMES.

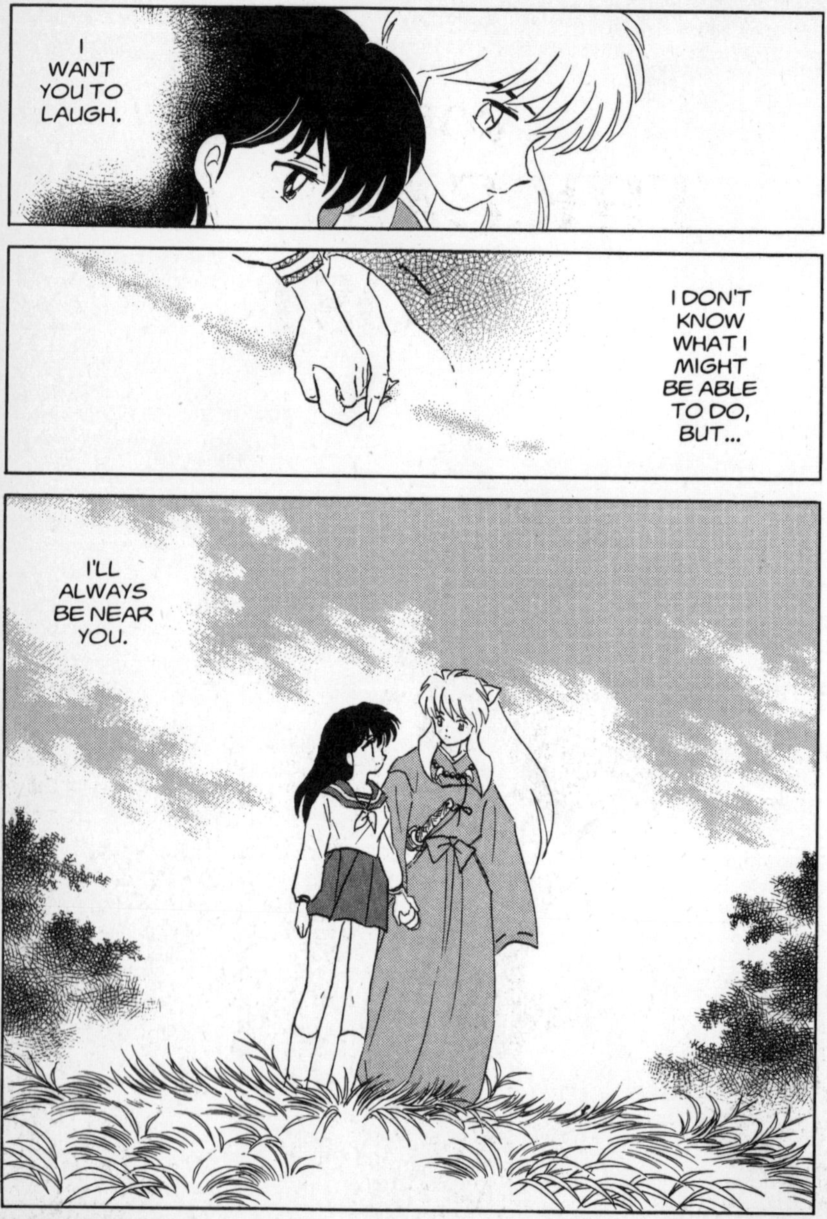
I WANT YOU TO LAUGH.
I DON'T KNOW WHAT I MIGHT BE ABLE TO DO, BUT...
I'LL ALWAYS BE NEAR YOU.

SCROLL NINE
THE CASTLE'S GHOST

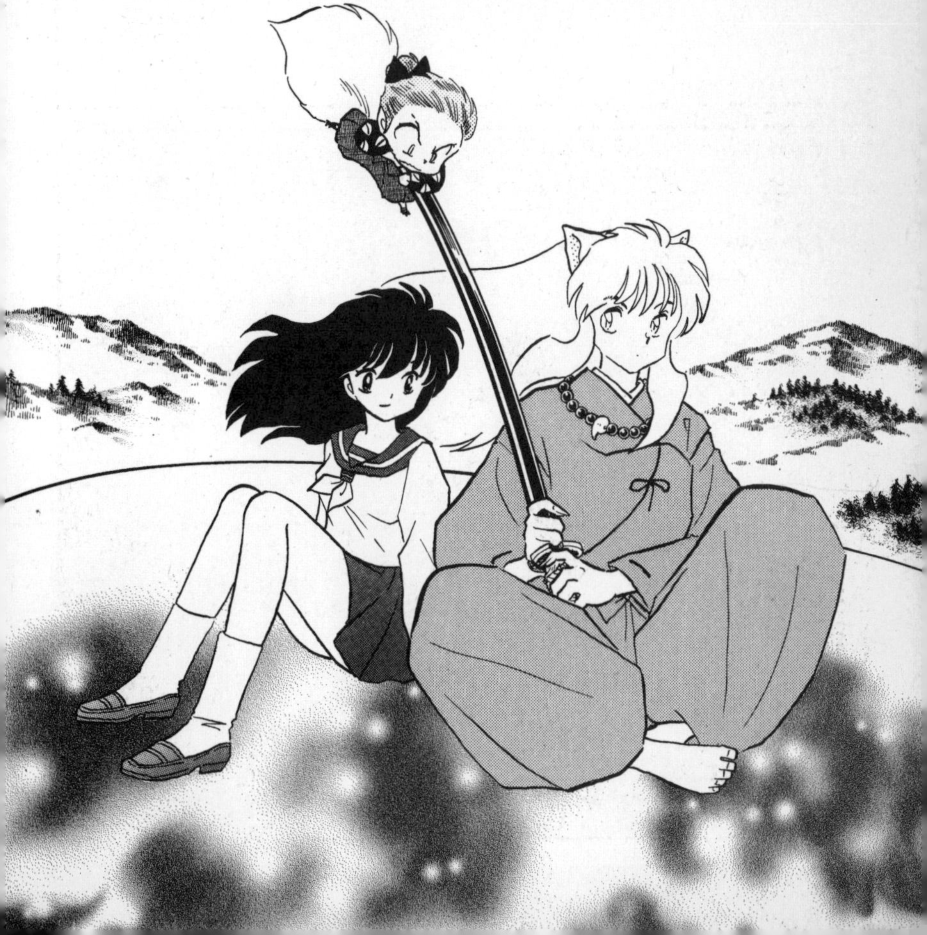

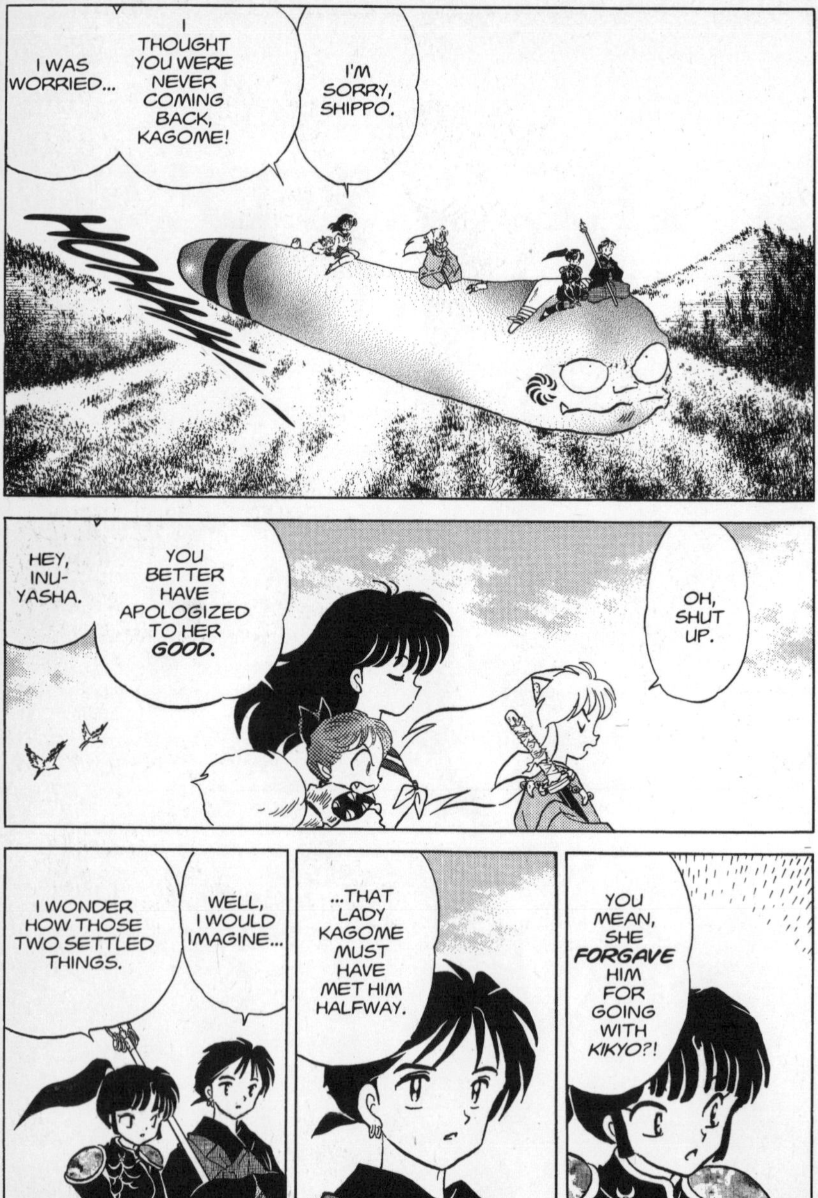
I WAS WORRIED...
I THOUGHT YOU WERE NEVER COMING BACK, KAGOME!
I'M SORRY, SHIPPO.
HEY, INU-YASHA.
YOU BETTER HAVE APOLOGIZED TO HER GOOD.
OH, SHUT UP.
I WONDER HOW THOSE TWO SETTLED THINGS.
WELL, I WOULD IMAGINE...
...THAT LADY KAGOME MUST HAVE MET HIM HALFWAY.
YOU MEAN, SHE FORGAVE HIM FOR GOING WITH KIKYO?!

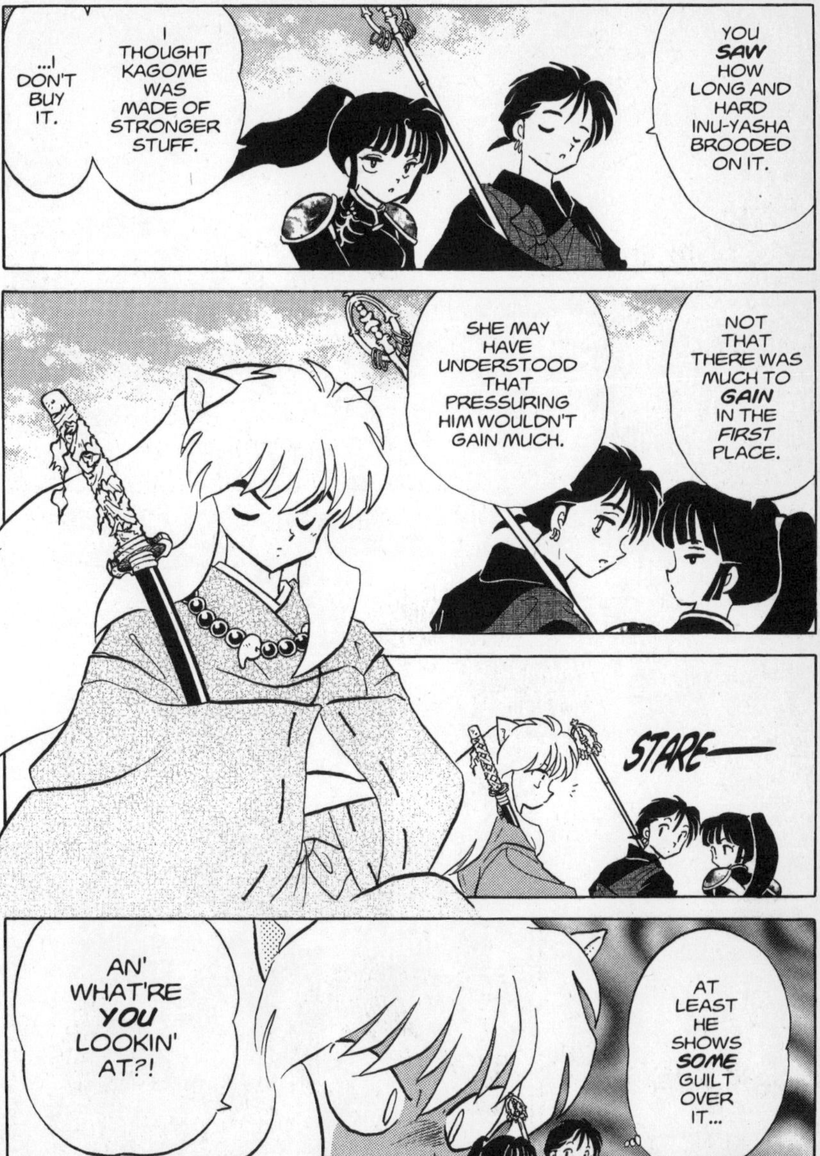
...I DON'T BUY IT.
I THOUGHT KAGOME WAS MADE OF STRONGER STUFF.
YOU SAW HOW LONG AND HARD INU-YASHA BROODED ON IT.
SHE MAY HAVE UNDERSTOOD THAT PRESSURING HIM WOULDN'T GAIN MUCH.
NOT THAT THERE WAS MUCH TO GAIN IN THE FIRST PLACE.
STARE—
AN' WHAT'RE YOU LOOKIN' AT?!
AT LEAST HE SHOWS SOME GUILT OVER IT...

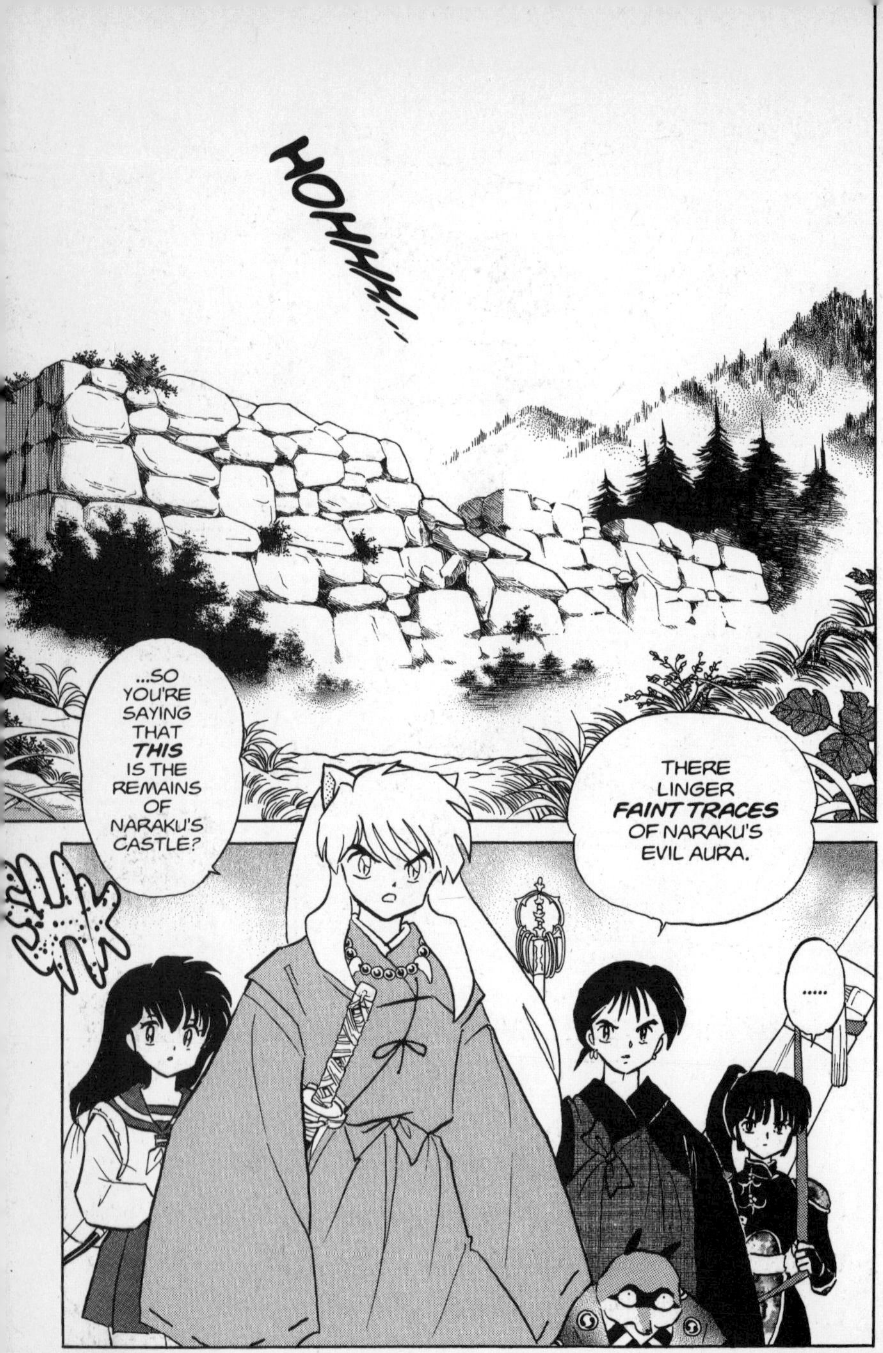
HOHHHH...
...SO YOU'RE SAYING THAT **THIS** IS THE REMAINS OF NARAKU'S CASTLE?
THERE LINGER ***FAINT TRACES*** OF NARAKU'S EVIL AURA.
.....

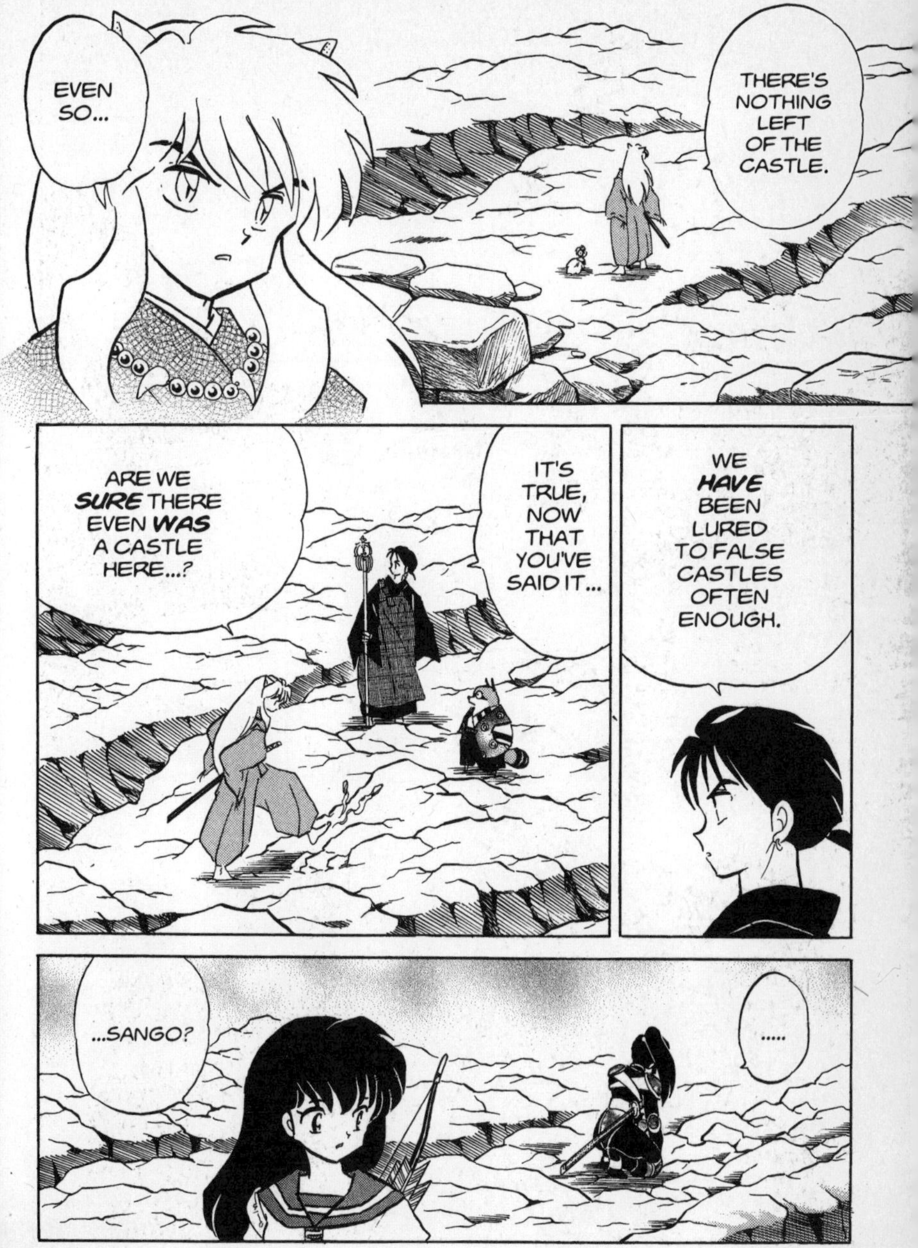
EVEN SO...
THERE'S NOTHING LEFT OF THE CASTLE.
ARE WE SURE THERE EVEN WAS A CASTLE HERE...?
IT'S TRUE, NOW THAT YOU'VE SAID IT...
WE HAVE BEEN LURED TO FALSE CASTLES OFTEN ENOUGH.
...SANGO?
.....

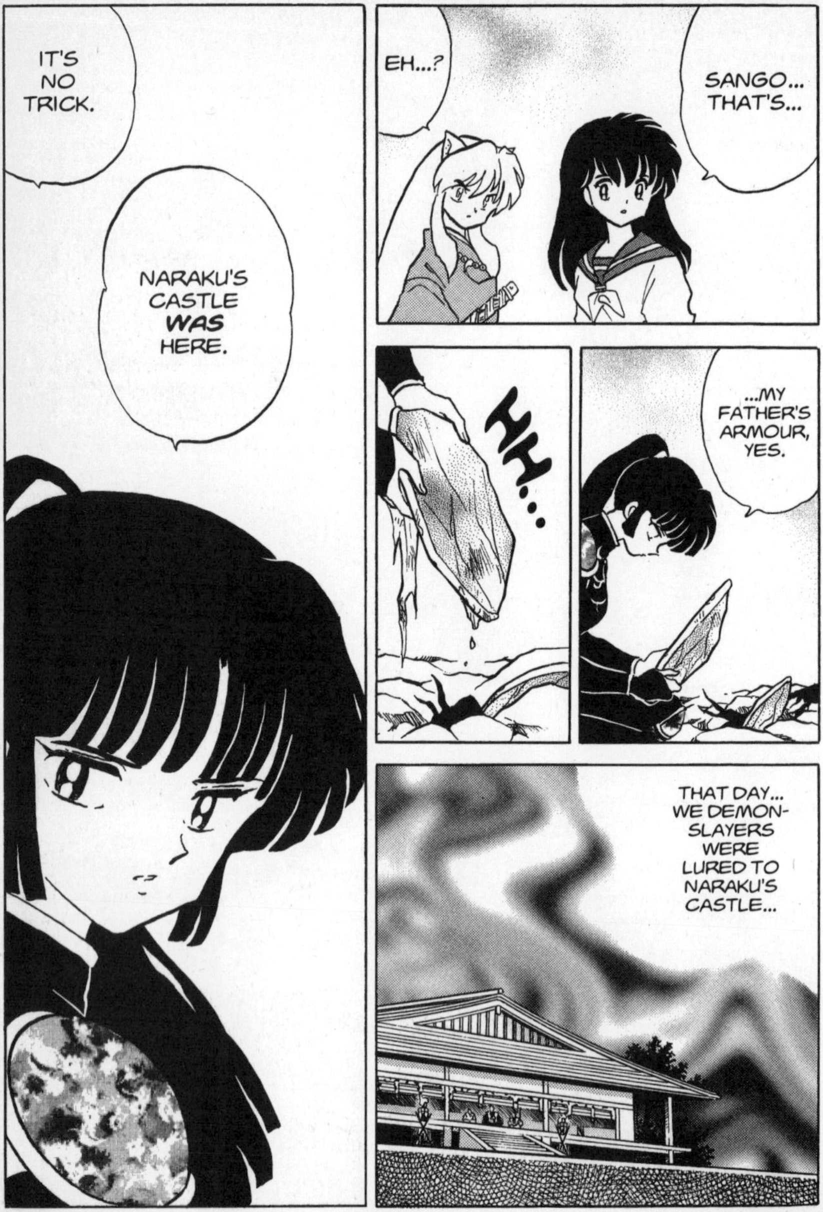
IT'S NO TRICK.
NARAKU'S CASTLE **WAS** HERE.
EH...?
SANGO... THAT'S...
HI...
...MY FATHER'S ARMOUR, YES.
THAT DAY... WE DEMON-SLAYERS WERE LURED TO NARAKU'S CASTLE...

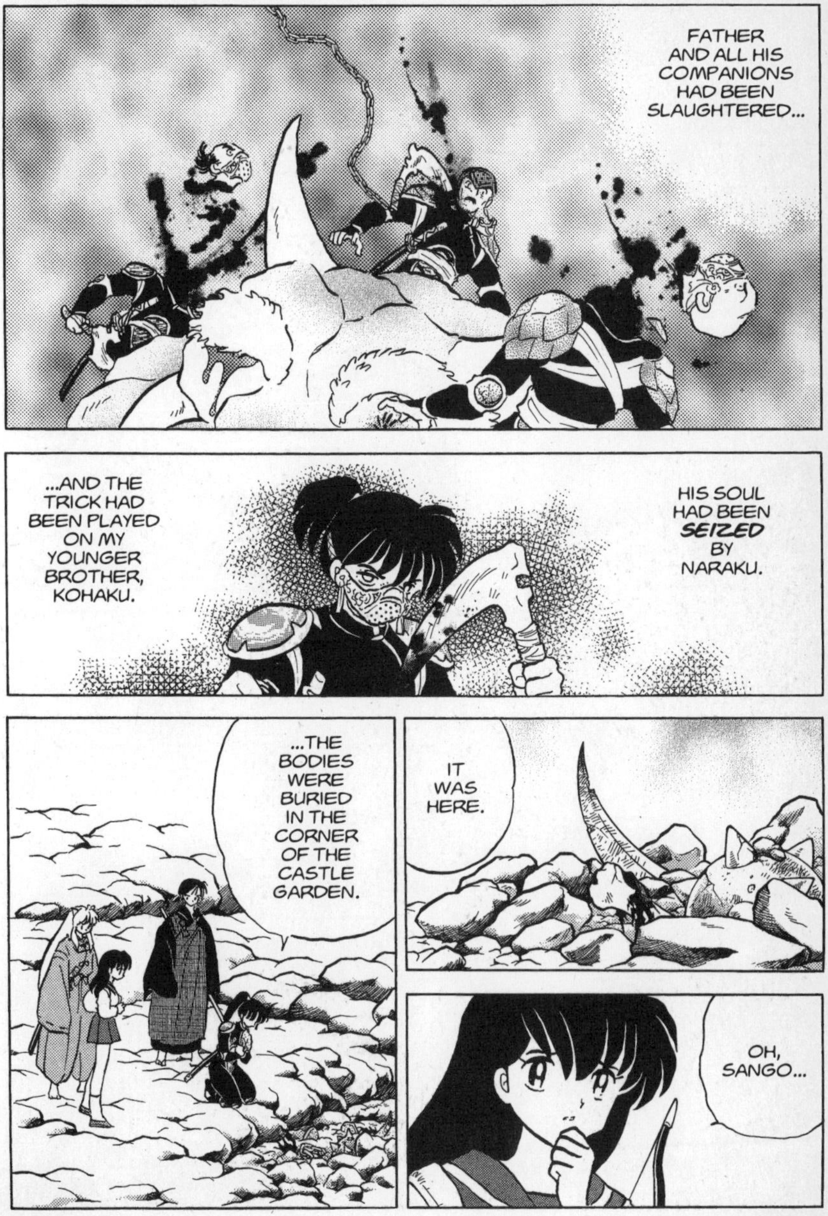
FATHER AND ALL HIS COMPANIONS HAD BEEN SLAUGHTERED...
...AND THE TRICK HAD BEEN PLAYED ON MY YOUNGER BROTHER, KOHAKU.
HIS SOUL HAD BEEN SEIZED BY NARAKU.
...THE BODIES WERE BURIED IN THE CORNER OF THE CASTLE GARDEN.
IT WAS HERE.
OH, SANGO...

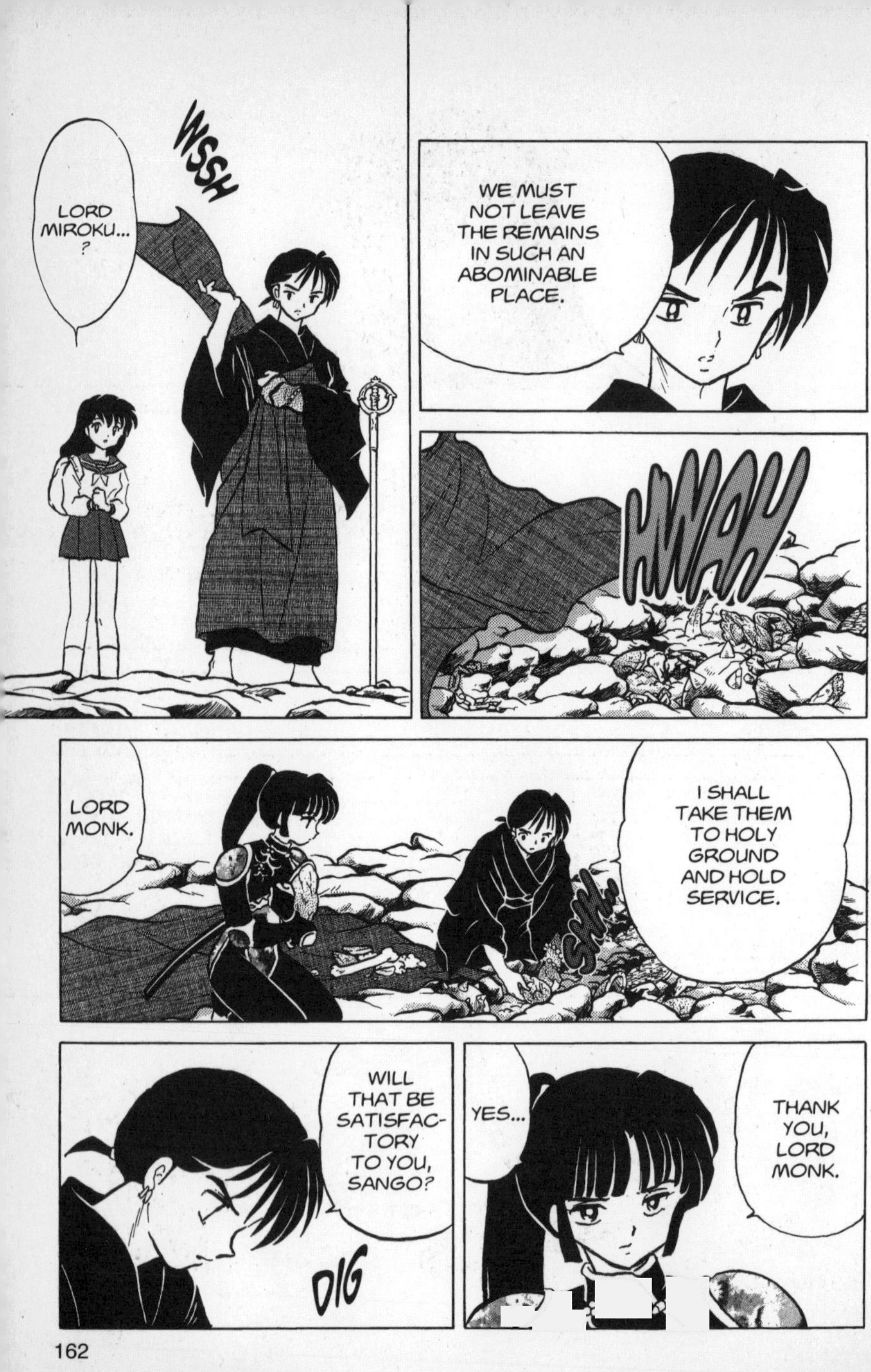
LORD MIROKU...?
WSSH
WE MUST NOT LEAVE THE REMAINS IN SUCH AN ABOMINABLE PLACE.
HWAH
LORD MONK.
I SHALL TAKE THEM TO HOLY GROUND AND HOLD SERVICE.
WILL THAT BE SATISFAC-TORY TO YOU, SANGO?
DIG
YES...
THANK YOU, LORD MONK.

IF THIS **WAS** NARAKU'S CASTLE...

...WHERE ARE THE PEOPLE WHO **LIVED** HERE?

WHERE'S SANGO'S LITTLE BROTHER? WAS HE...

...DESTROYED, ALONG WITH THE BUILDING?

WSSH

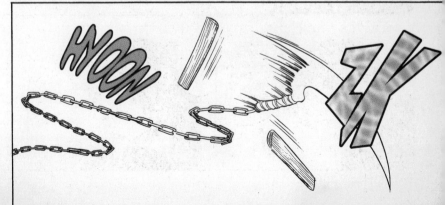

HYOON

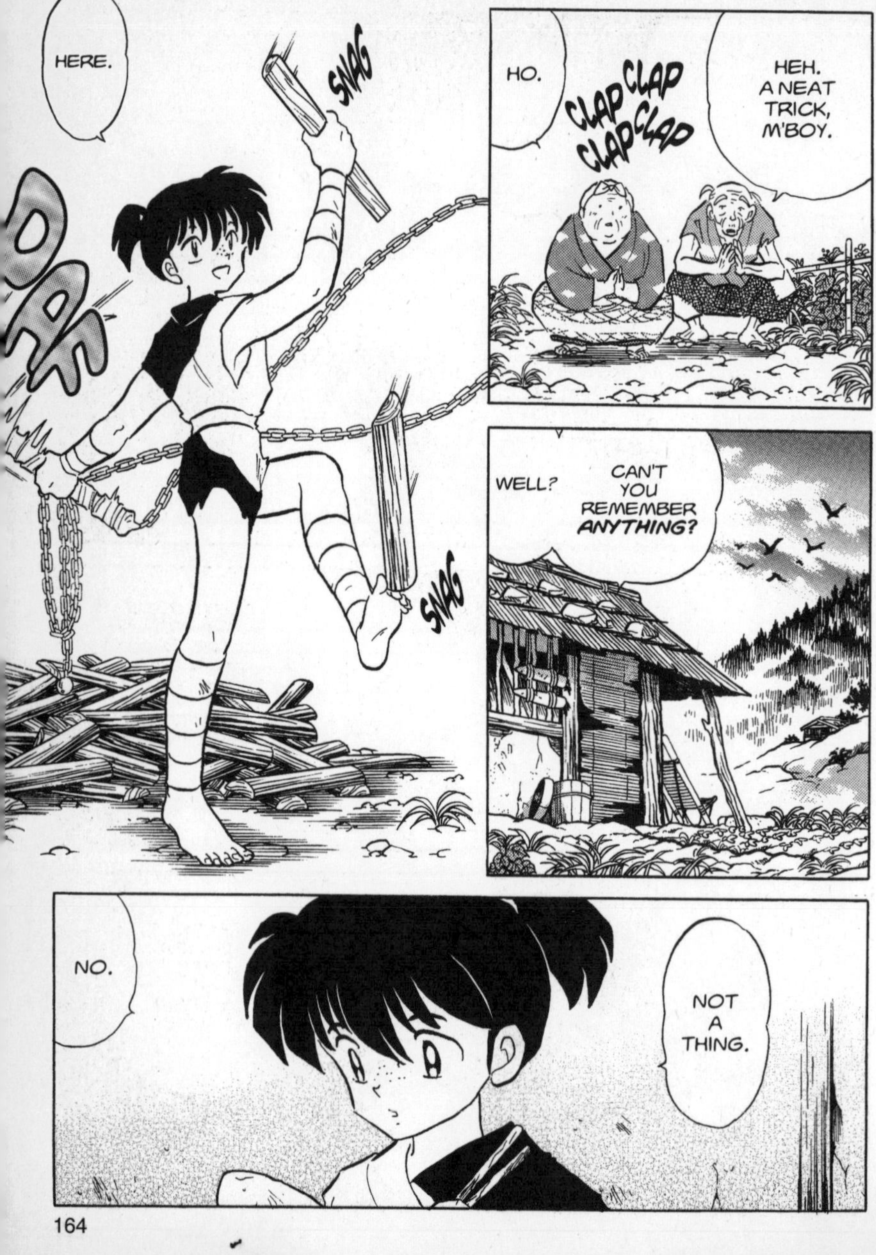
HERE.
SNAG
DAF
SNAG
HO.
CLAP CLAP
CLAP CLAP
HEH. A NEAT TRICK, M'BOY.
WELL?
CAN'T YOU REMEMBER *ANYTHING?*
NO.
NOT A THING.

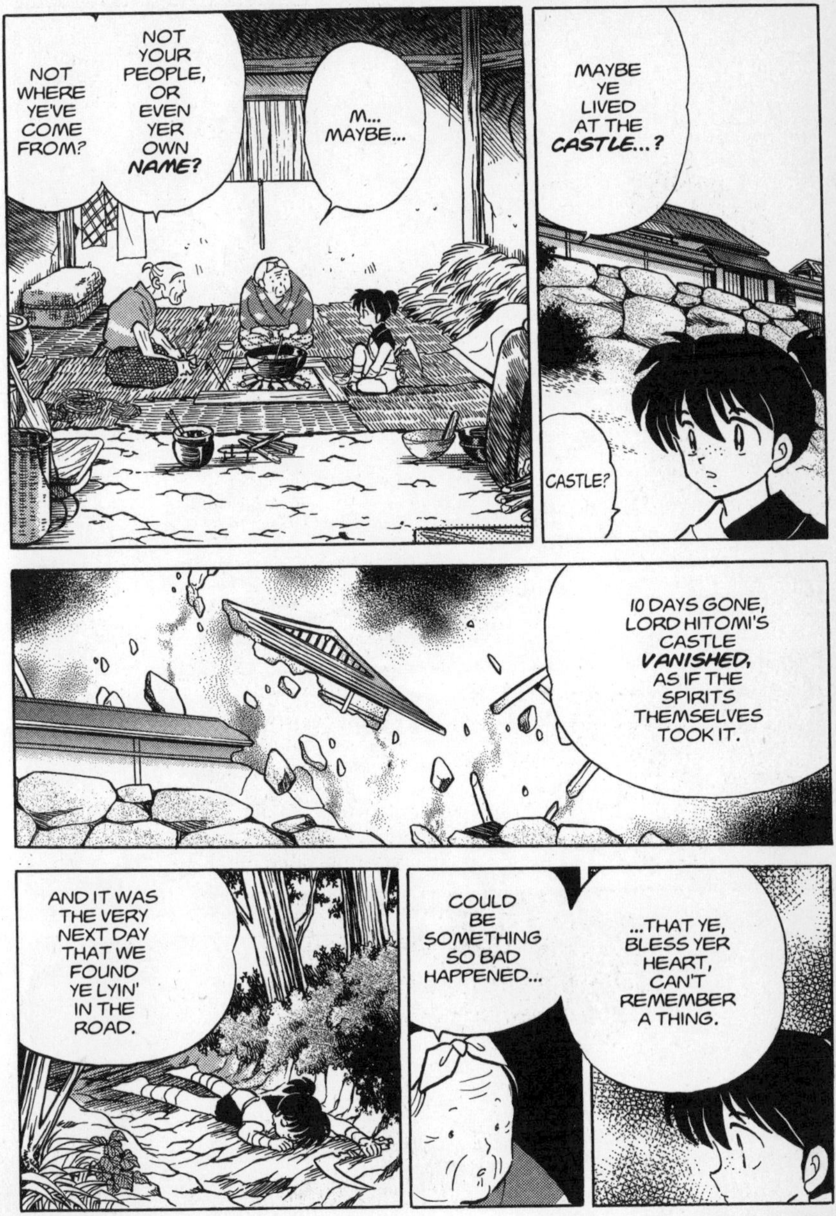
NOT WHERE YE'VE COME FROM?
NOT YOUR PEOPLE, OR EVEN YER OWN NAME?
M... MAYBE...
MAYBE YE LIVED AT THE CASTLE...?
CASTLE?
10 DAYS GONE, LORD HITOMI'S CASTLE VANISHED, AS IF THE SPIRITS THEMSELVES TOOK IT.
AND IT WAS THE VERY NEXT DAY THAT WE FOUND YE LYIN' IN THE ROAD.
COULD BE SOMETHING SO BAD HAPPENED...
...THAT YE, BLESS YER HEART, CAN'T REMEMBER A THING.

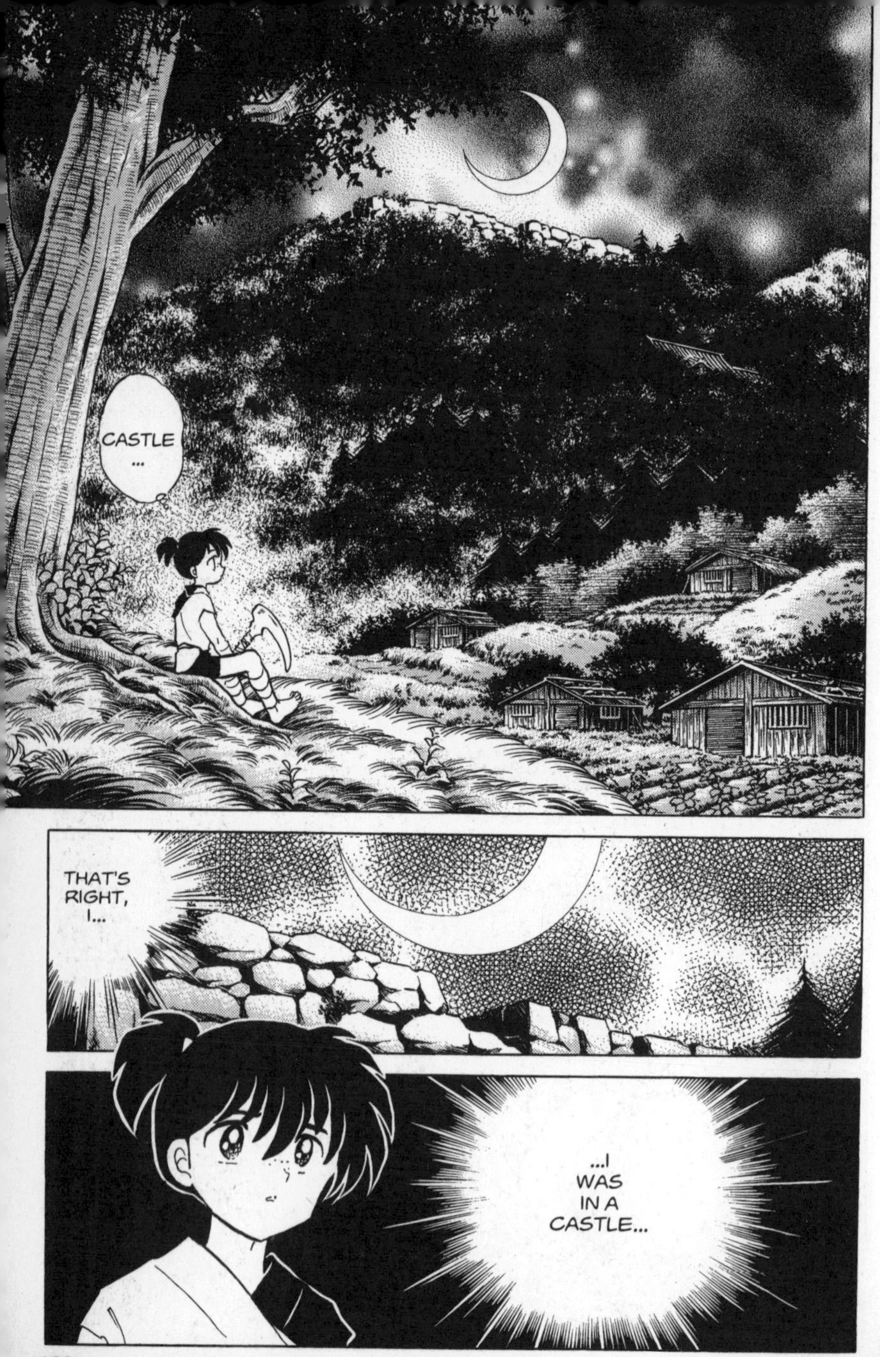
CASTLE ...
THAT'S RIGHT, I...
...I WAS IN A CASTLE...

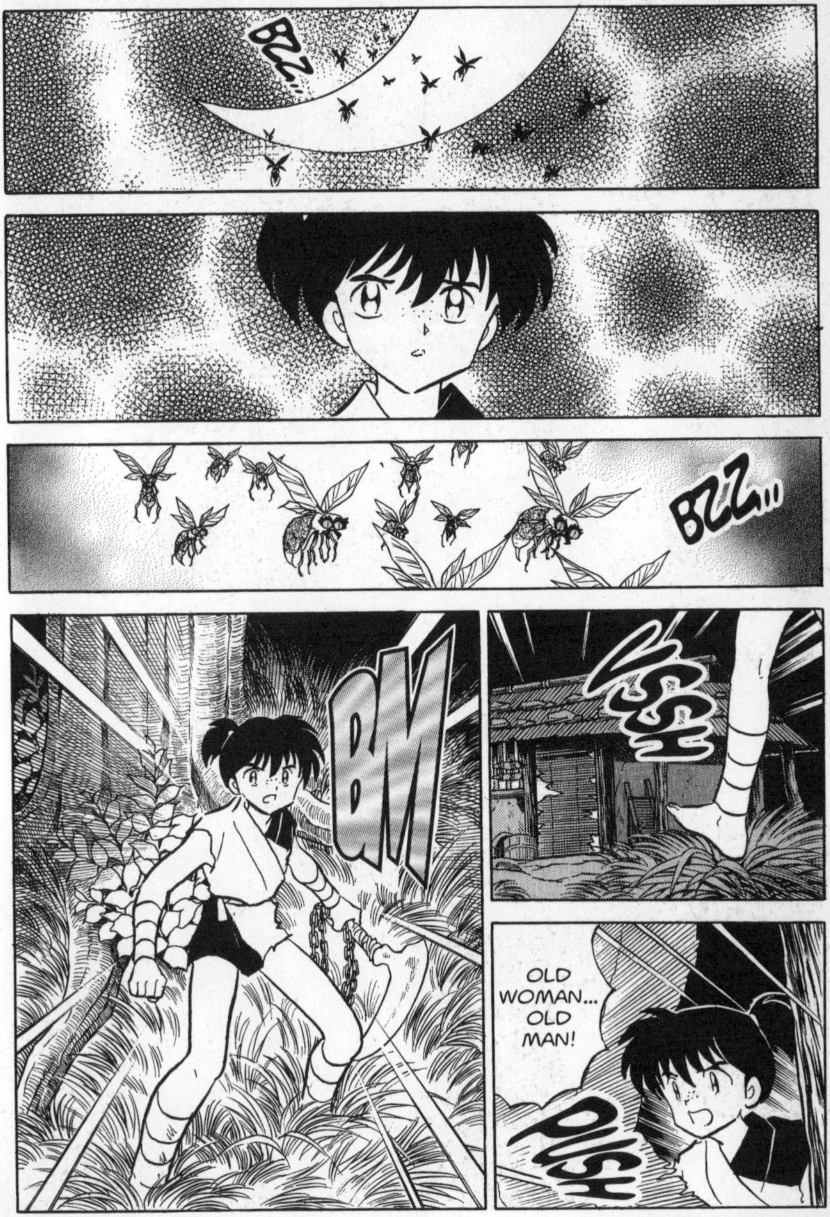
BZZ...
BZZ...
BM
VSSH
OLD WOMAN... OLD MAN!
PUSH

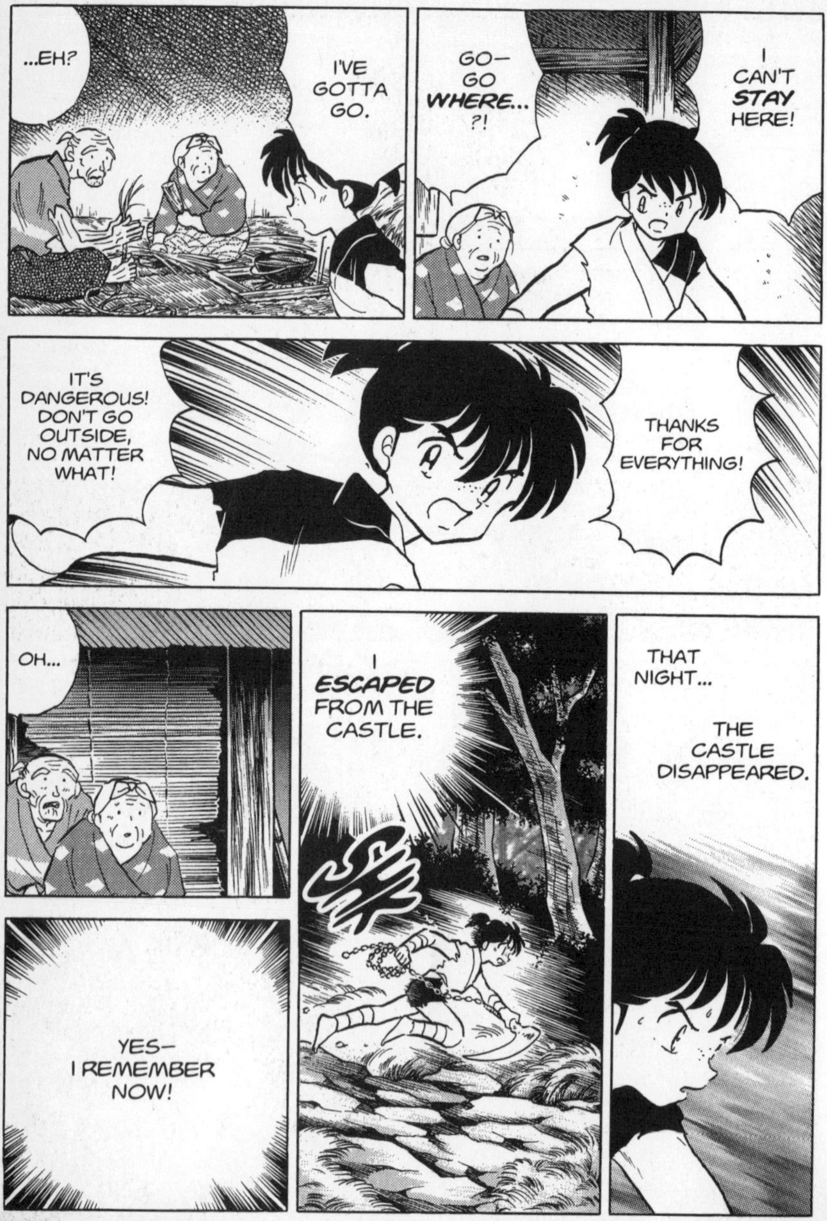
...EH?
I'VE GOTTA GO.
GO— GO WHERE... ?!
I CAN'T STAY HERE!
IT'S DANGEROUS! DON'T GO OUTSIDE, NO MATTER WHAT!
THANKS FOR EVERYTHING!
OH...
YES— I REMEMBER NOW!
I ESCAPED FROM THE CASTLE.
THAT NIGHT...
THE CASTLE DISAPPEARED.

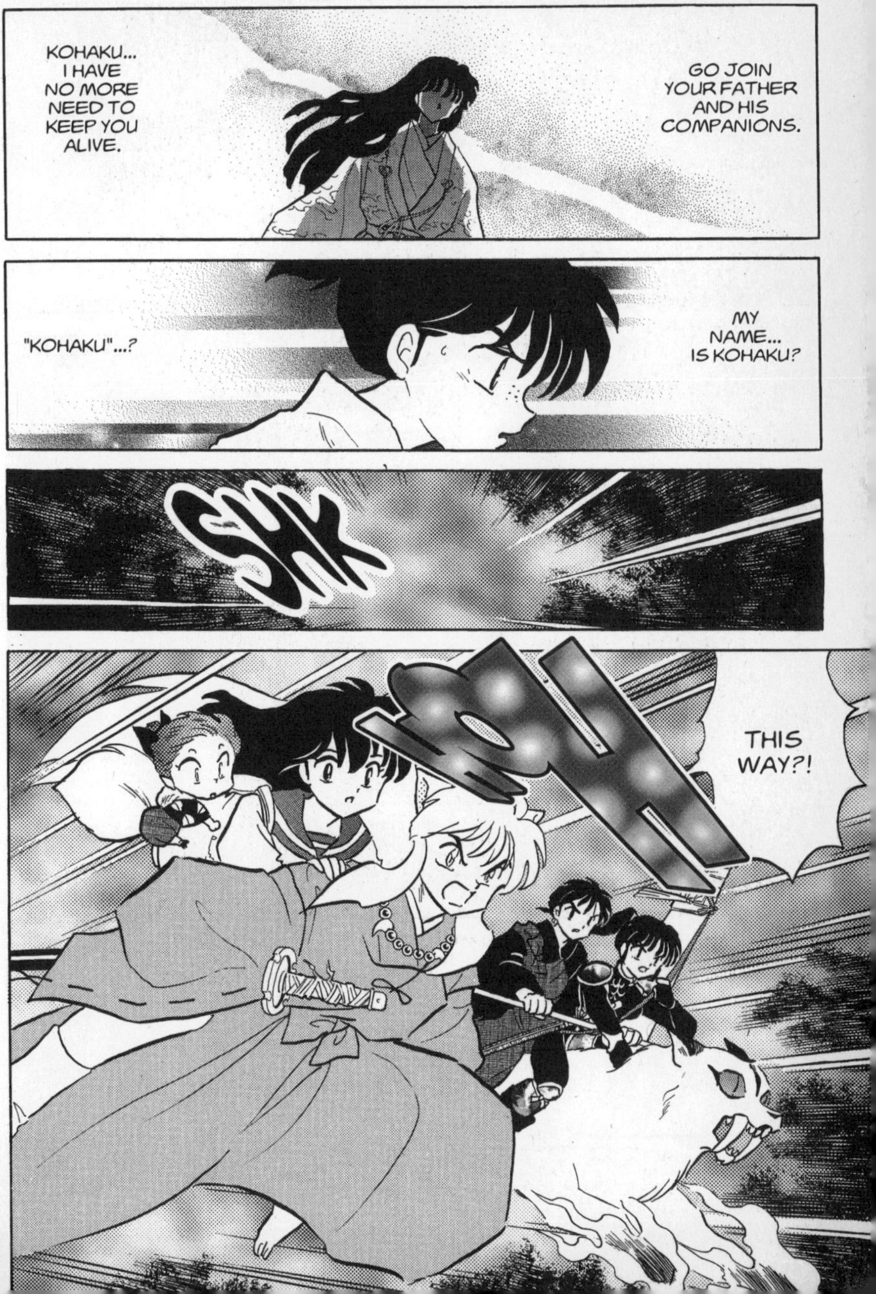
KOHAKU... I HAVE NO MORE NEED TO KEEP YOU ALIVE.
GO JOIN YOUR FATHER AND HIS COMPANIONS.
"KOHAKU"...?
MY NAME... IS KOHAKU?
SHK
THIS WAY?!

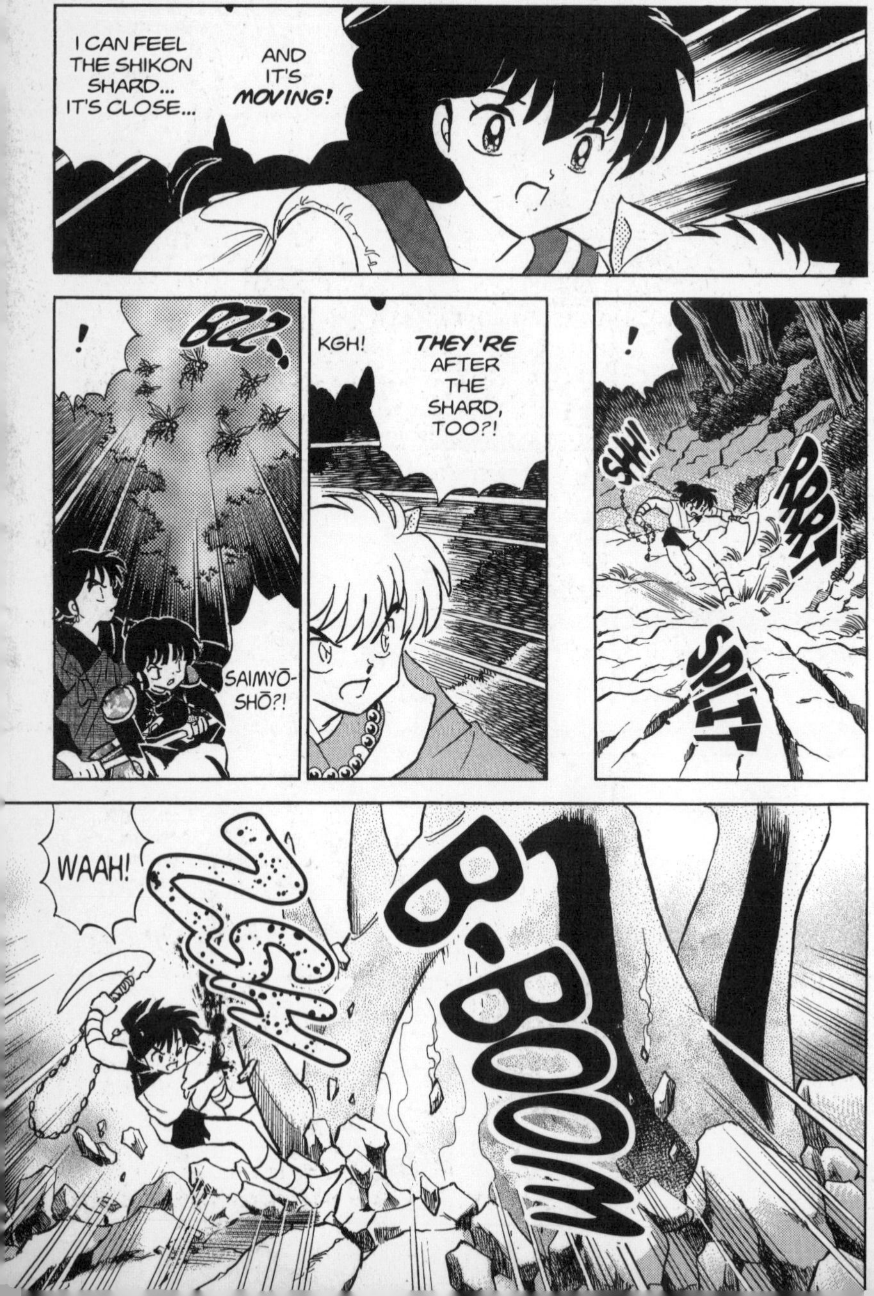
I CAN FEEL THE SHIKON SHARD... IT'S CLOSE...
AND IT'S MOVING!
!
BZZ...
SAIMYŌSHŌ?!
KGH!
THEY'RE AFTER THE SHARD, TOO?!
!
SHH!
RRRRT
SPLIT
WAAH!
ZSH
B-BOOOM

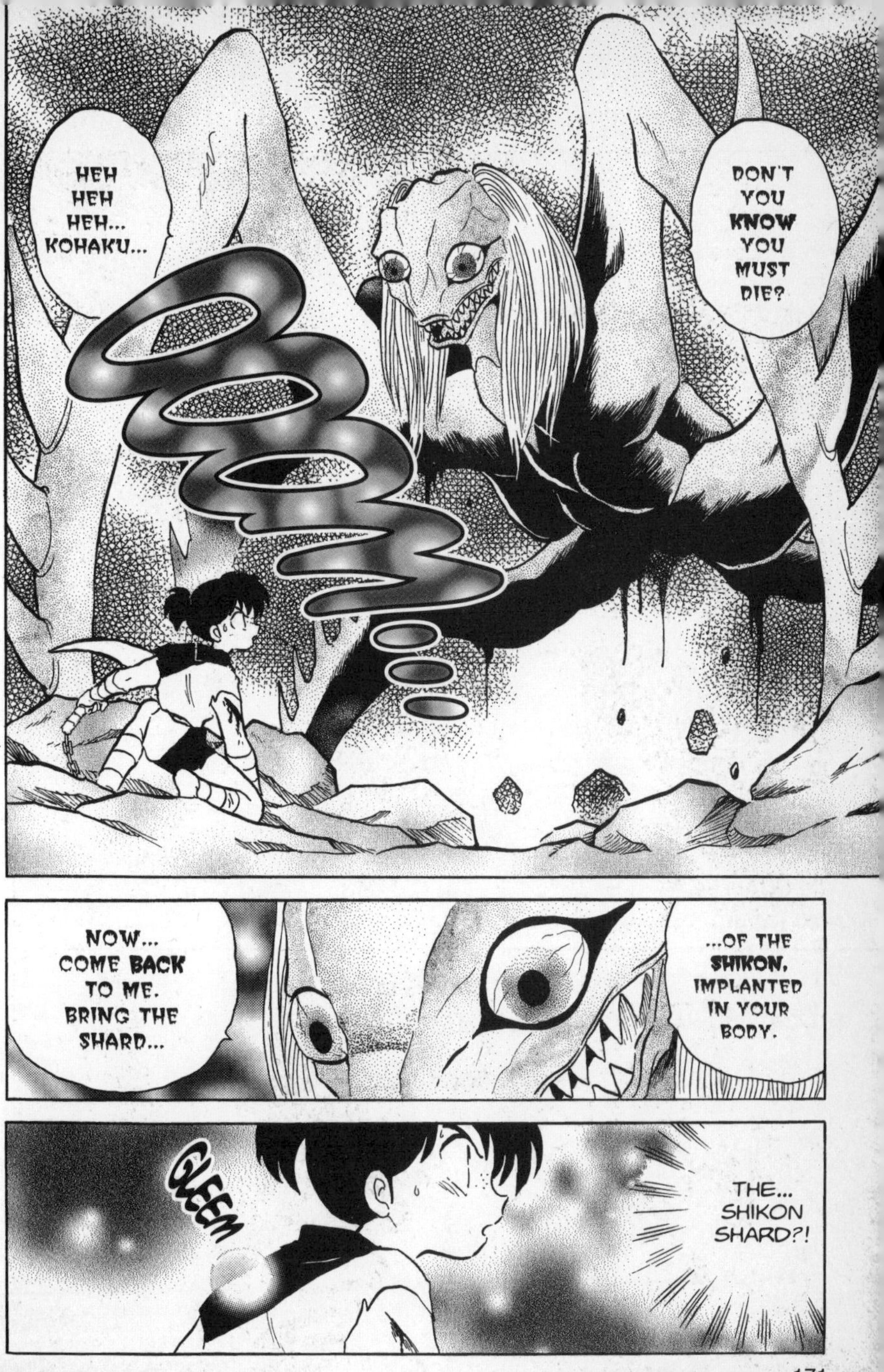
HEH HEH HEH... KOHAKU...
DON'T YOU KNOW YOU MUST DIE?
NOW... COME BACK TO ME. BRING THE SHARD...
...OF THE SHIKON, IMPLANTED IN YOUR BODY.
GLEEM
THE... SHIKON SHARD?!

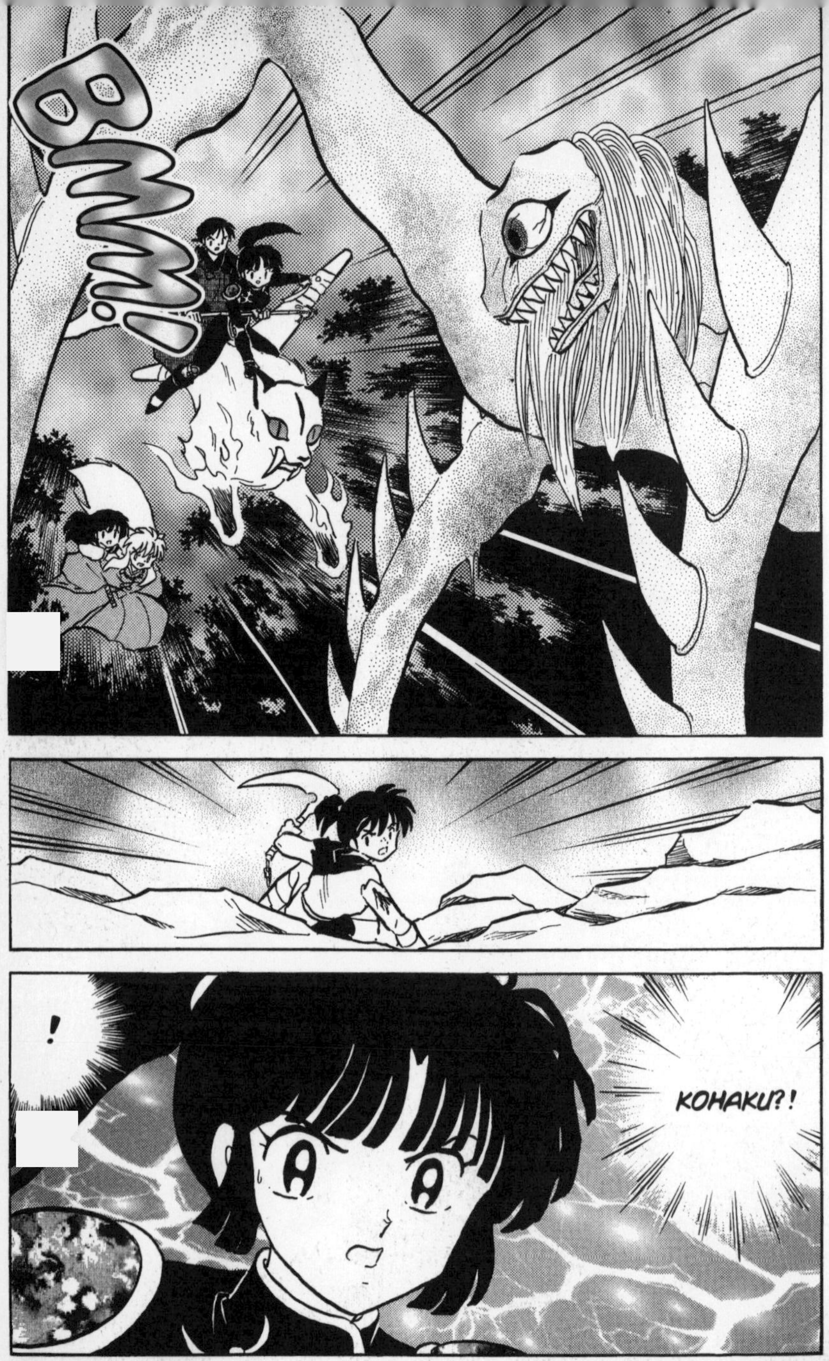
BMM!
!
KOHAKU?!

SCROLL TEN
KOHAKU'S MEMORY

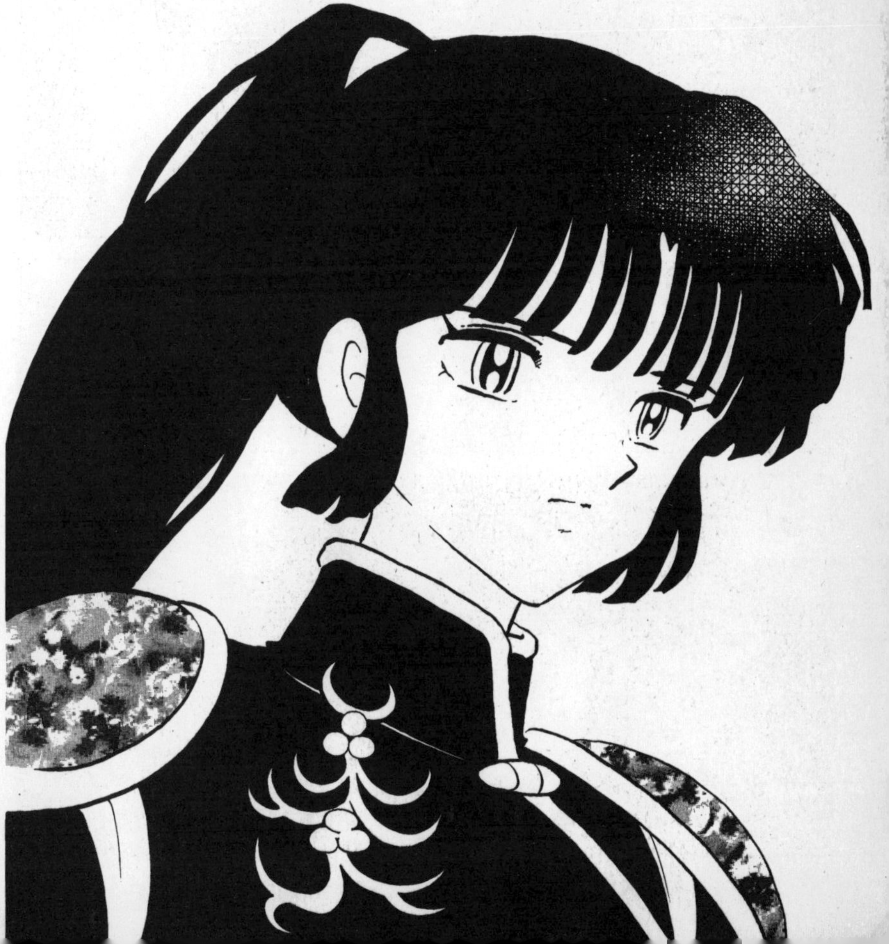

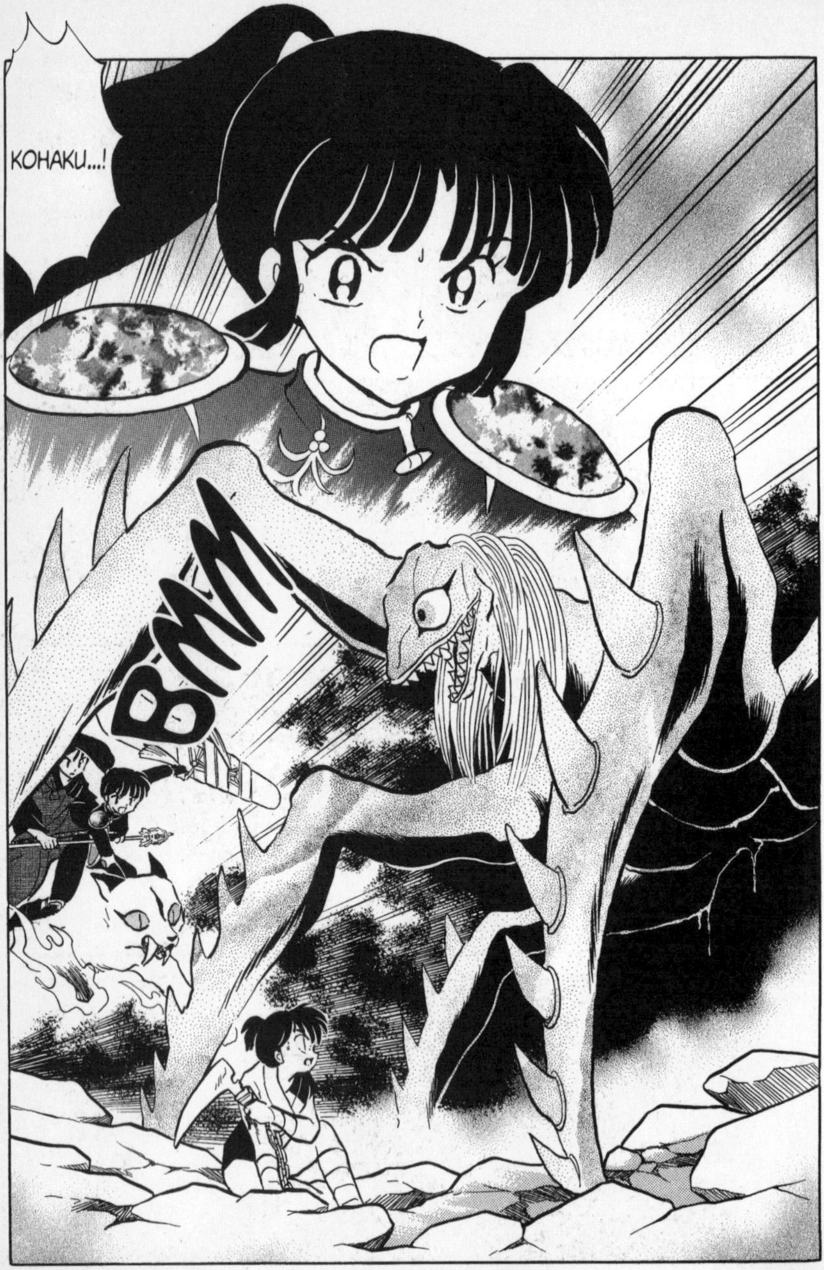
KOHAKU...!
BMM

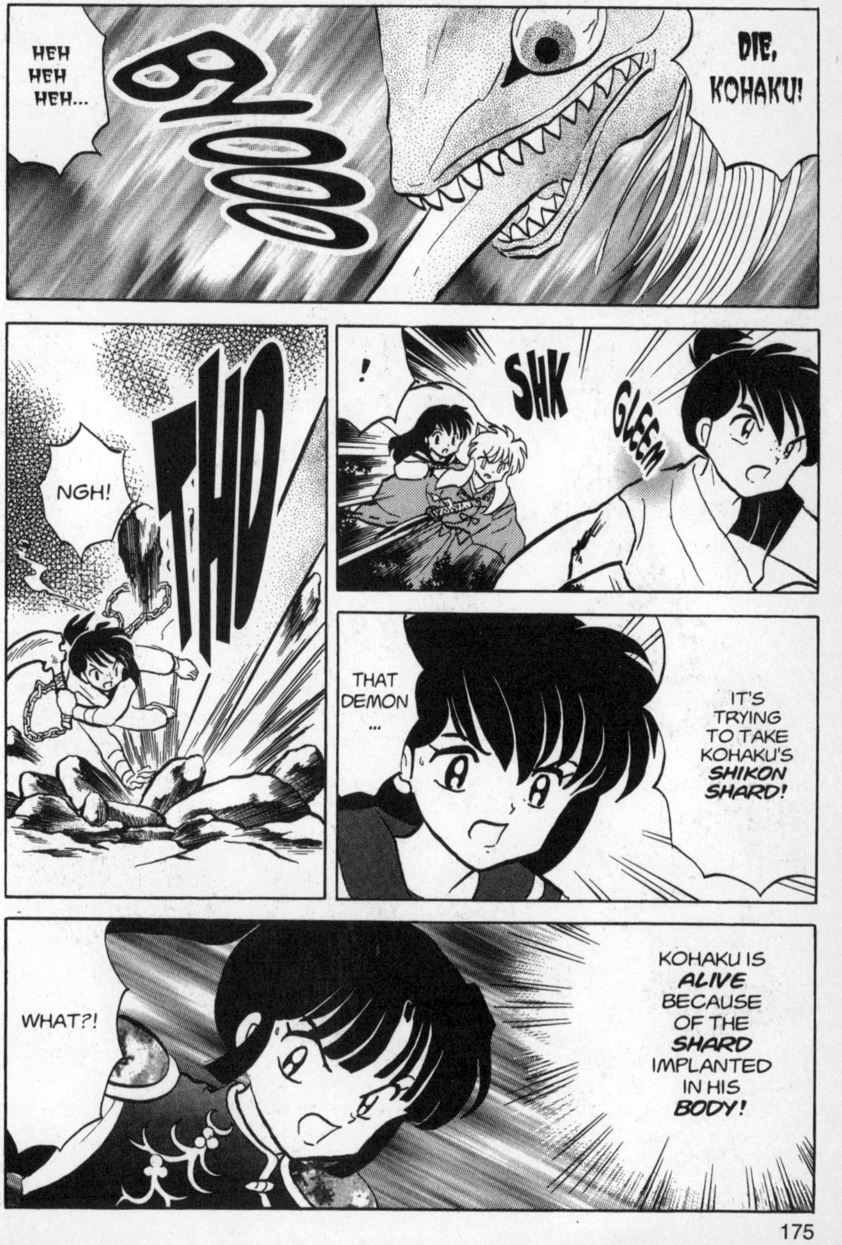
HEH HEH HEH...
BYOOO
DIE, KOHAKU!
NGH!
THD
!
SHK
GLEEM
THAT DEMON ...
IT'S TRYING TO TAKE KOHAKU'S ***SHIKON SHARD!***
WHAT?!
KOHAKU IS ***ALIVE*** BECAUSE OF THE ***SHARD*** IMPLANTED IN HIS ***BODY!***

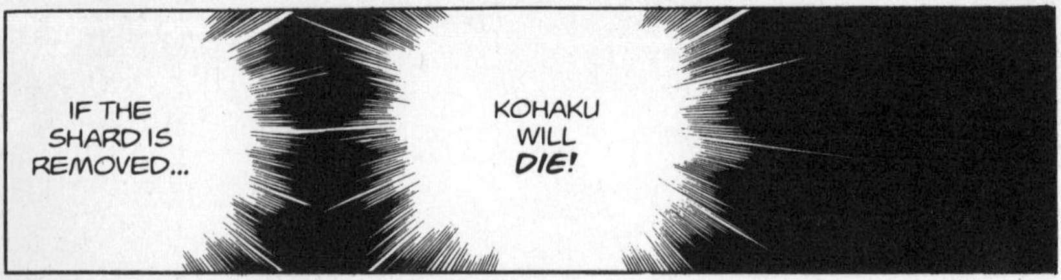
IF THE SHARD IS REMOVED...
KOHAKU WILL ***DIE!***

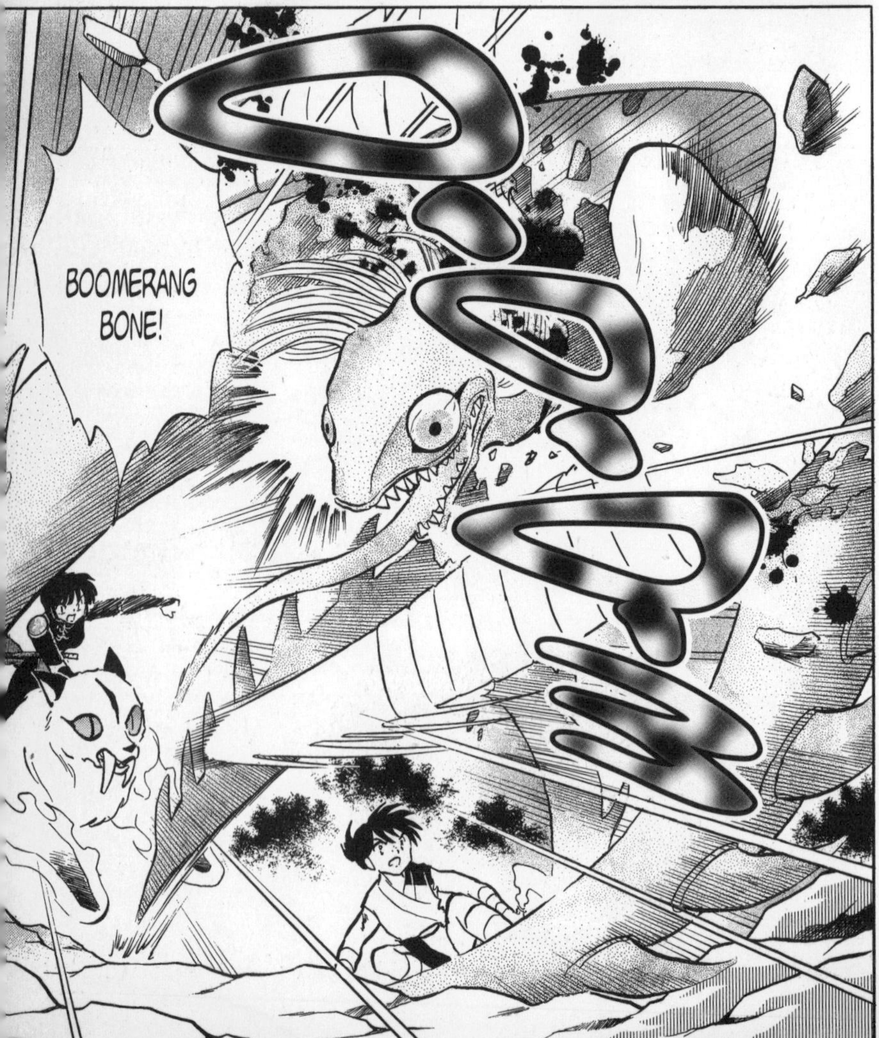
BOOMERANG BONE!

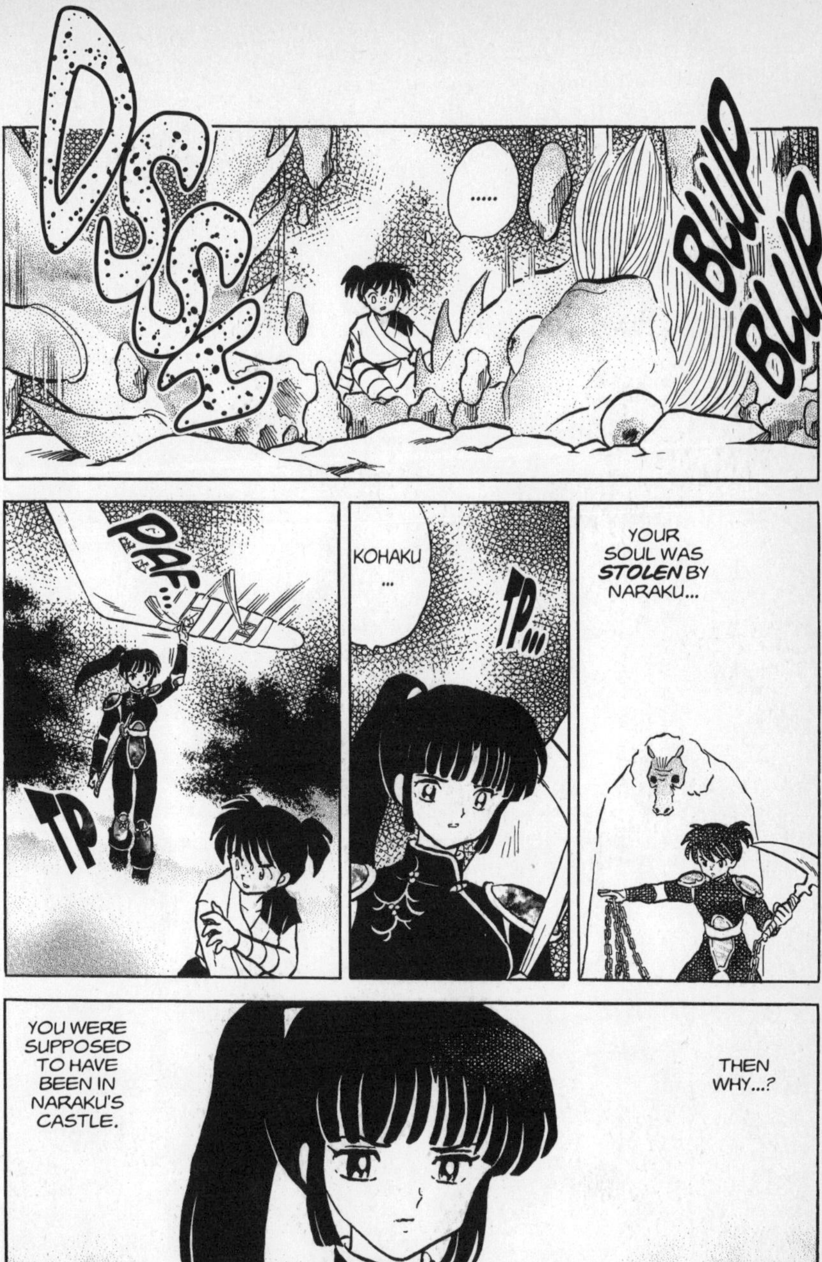
DSSS
.....
BLUP BLUP
PAF...
TP
KOHAKU ...
TP...
YOUR SOUL WAS STOLEN BY NARAKU...
YOU WERE SUPPOSED TO HAVE BEEN IN NARAKU'S CASTLE.
THEN WHY...?

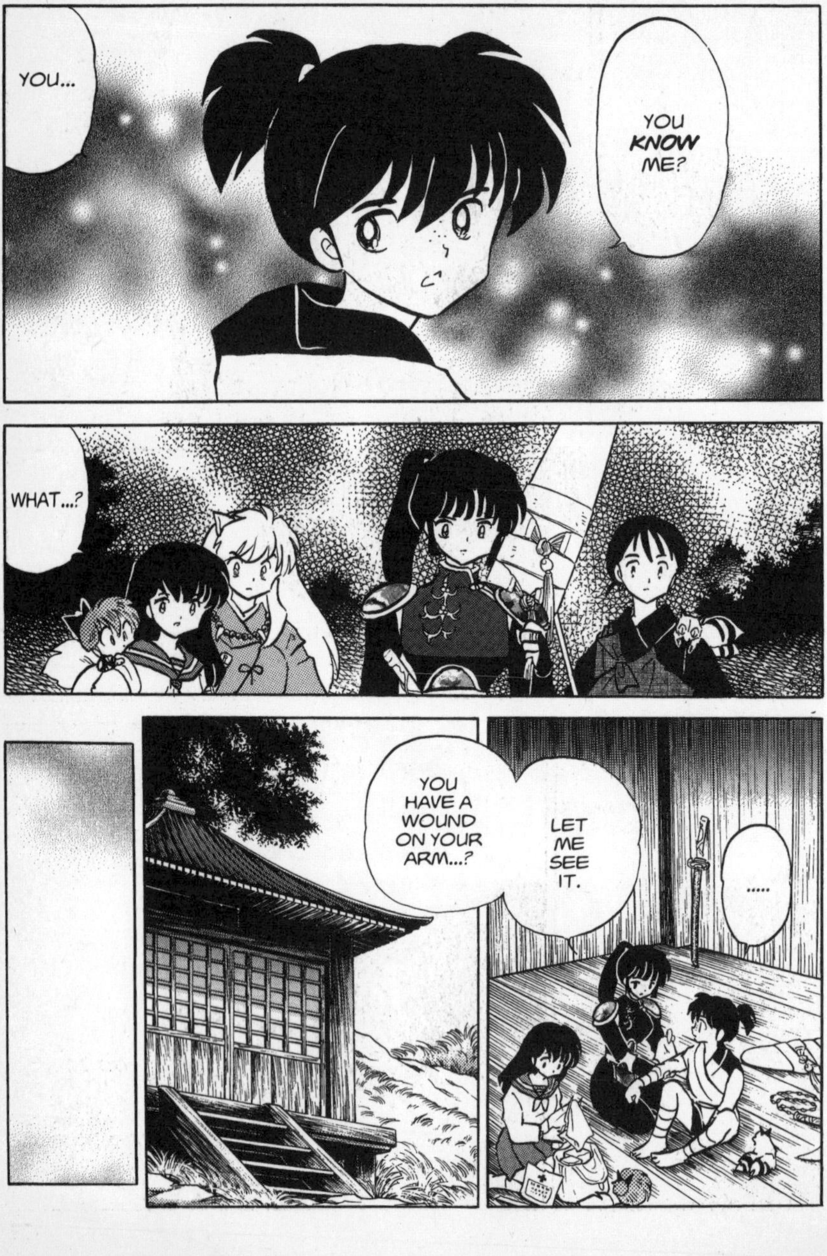
YOU...
YOU **KNOW** ME?
WHAT...?
YOU HAVE A WOUND ON YOUR ARM...?
LET ME SEE IT.
.....

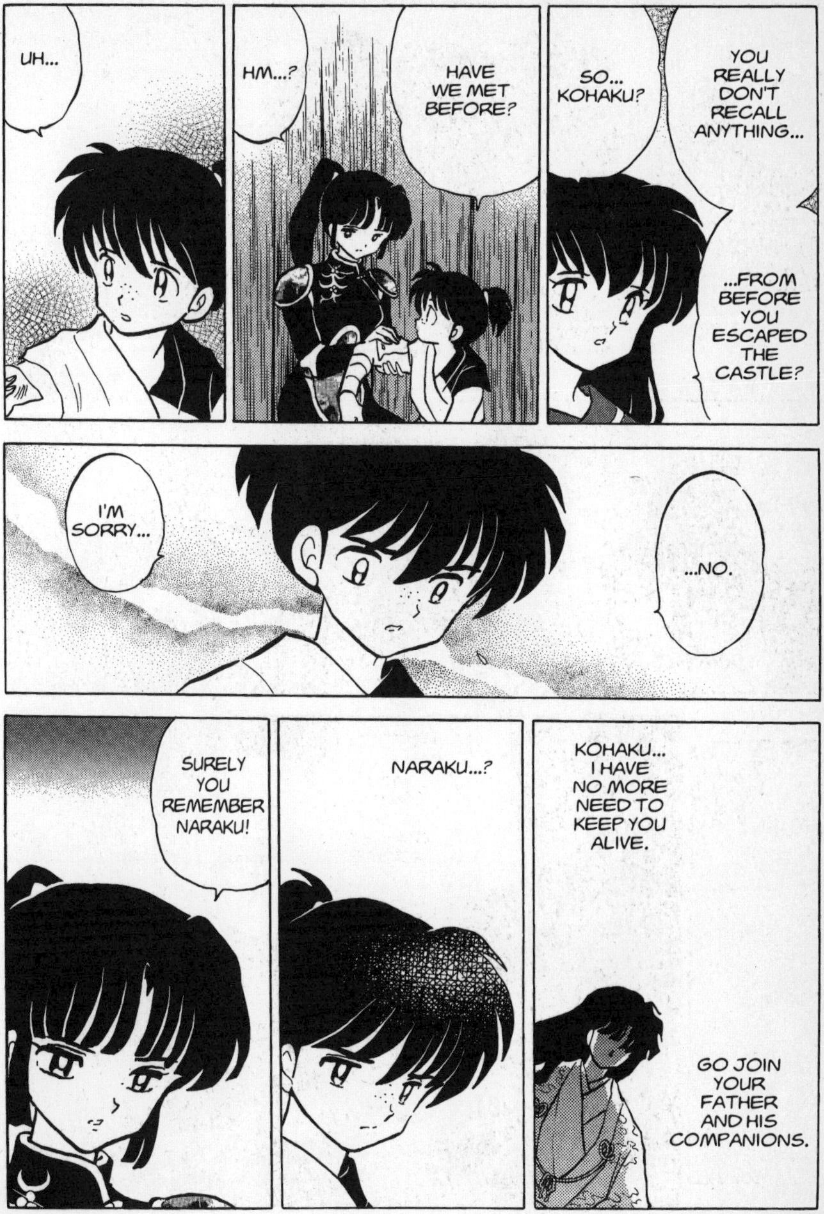
UH...
HM...?
HAVE WE MET BEFORE?
SO... KOHAKU?
YOU REALLY DON'T RECALL ANYTHING...
...FROM BEFORE YOU ESCAPED THE CASTLE?
I'M SORRY...
...NO.
SURELY YOU REMEMBER NARAKU!
NARAKU...?
KOHAKU... I HAVE NO MORE NEED TO KEEP YOU ALIVE.
GO JOIN YOUR FATHER AND HIS COMPANIONS.

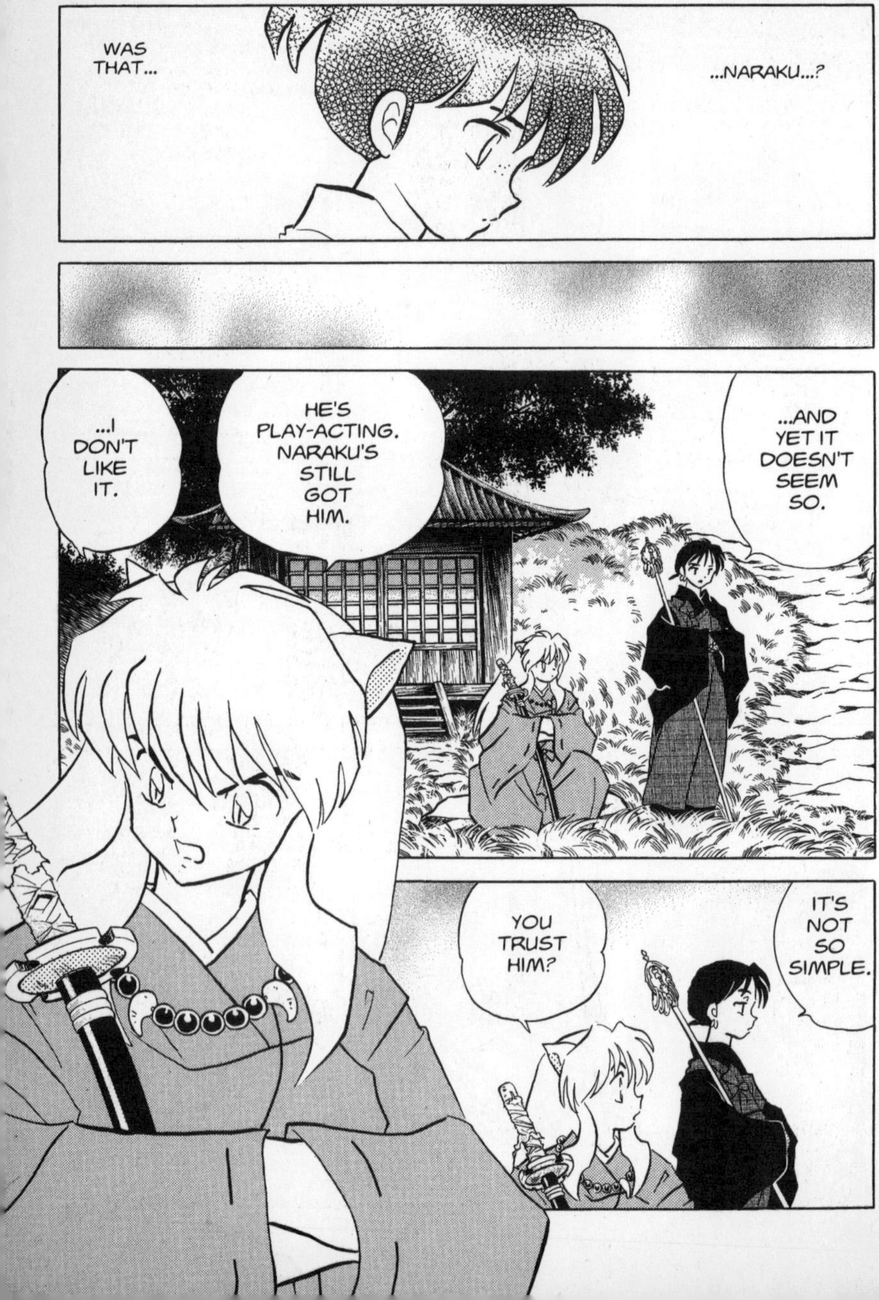
WAS THAT...
...NARAKU...?
...I DON'T LIKE IT.
HE'S PLAY-ACTING. NARAKU'S STILL GOT HIM.
...AND YET IT DOESN'T SEEM SO.
YOU TRUST HIM?
IT'S NOT SO SIMPLE.

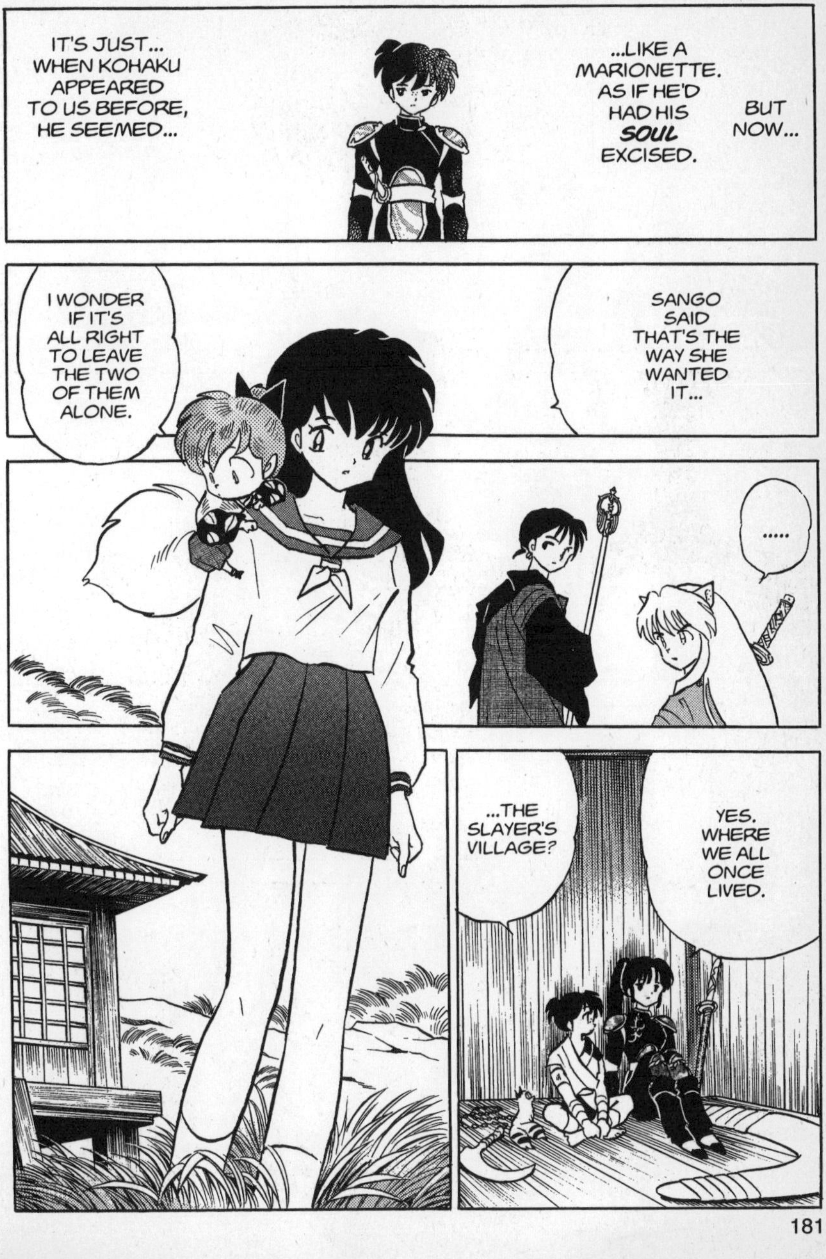
IT'S JUST... WHEN KOHAKU APPEARED TO US BEFORE, HE SEEMED...
...LIKE A MARIONETTE. AS IF HE'D HAD HIS **SOUL** EXCISED.
BUT NOW...
I WONDER IF IT'S ALL RIGHT TO LEAVE THE TWO OF THEM ALONE.
SANGO SAID THAT'S THE WAY SHE WANTED IT...
.....
...THE SLAYER'S VILLAGE?
YES. WHERE WE ALL ONCE LIVED.

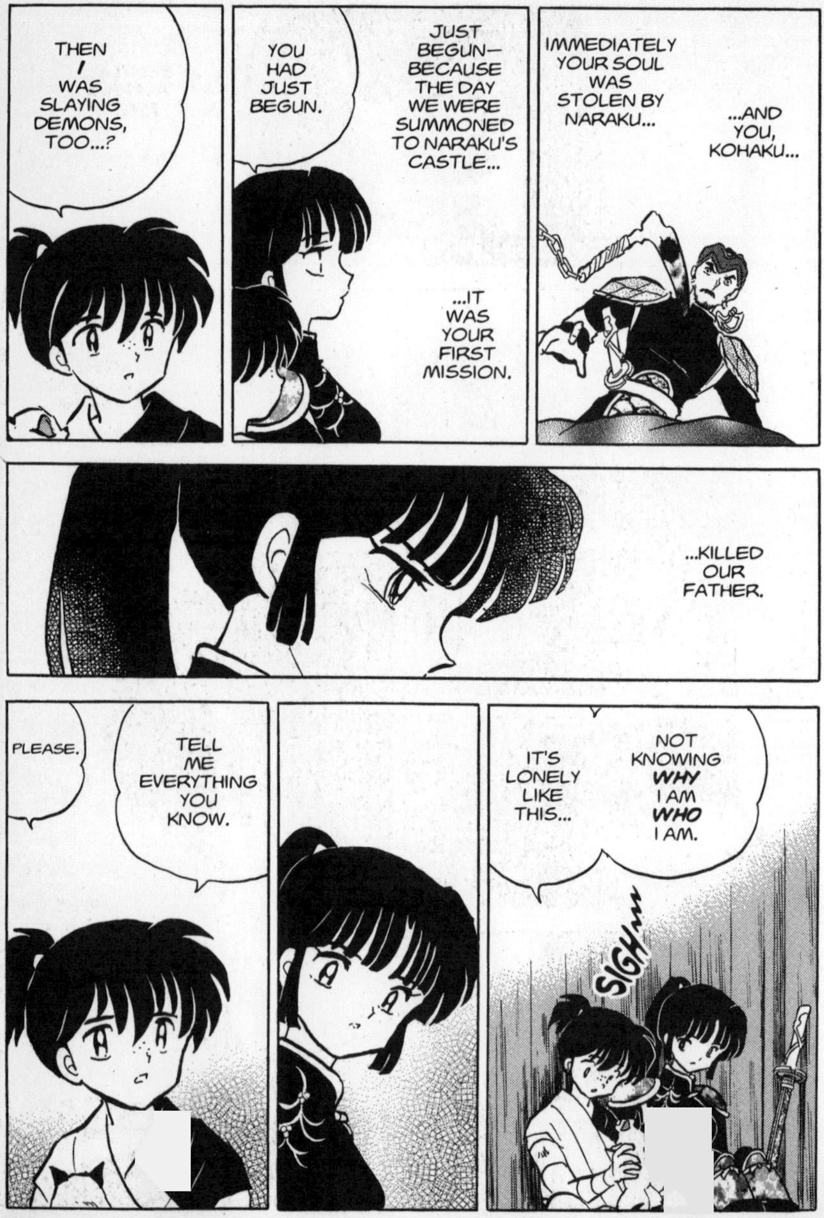
THEN *I* WAS SLAYING DEMONS, TOO...?
YOU HAD JUST BEGUN.
JUST BEGUN— BECAUSE THE DAY WE WERE SUMMONED TO NARAKU'S CASTLE...
...IT WAS YOUR FIRST MISSION.
IMMEDIATELY YOUR SOUL WAS STOLEN BY NARAKU...
...AND YOU, KOHAKU...
...KILLED OUR FATHER.
PLEASE.
TELL ME EVERYTHING YOU KNOW.
IT'S LONELY LIKE THIS...
NOT KNOWING ***WHY*** I AM ***WHO*** I AM.
SIGH

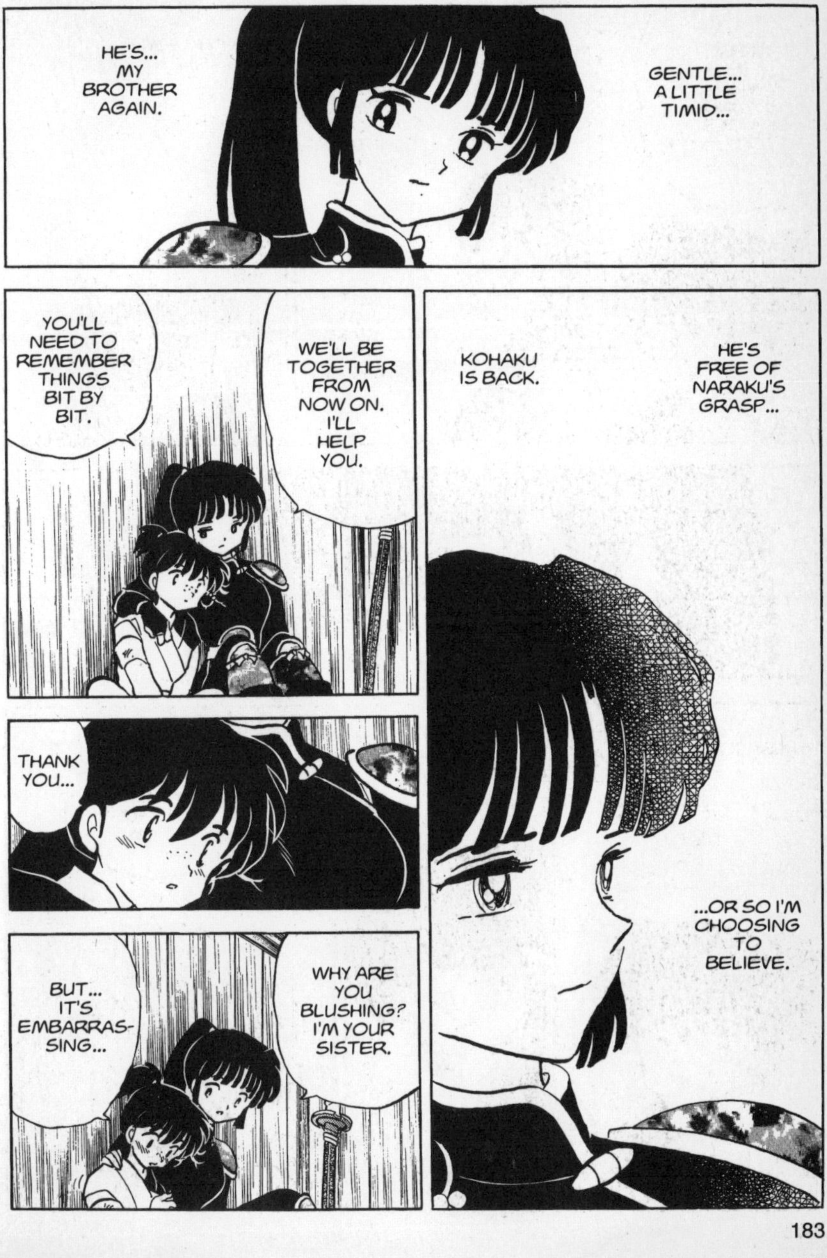
HE'S... MY BROTHER AGAIN.
GENTLE... A LITTLE TIMID...
YOU'LL NEED TO REMEMBER THINGS BIT BY BIT.
WE'LL BE TOGETHER FROM NOW ON. I'LL HELP YOU.
THANK YOU...
BUT... IT'S EMBARRAS-SING...
WHY ARE YOU BLUSHING? I'M YOUR SISTER.
KOHAKU IS BACK.
HE'S FREE OF NARAKU'S GRASP...
...OR SO I'M CHOOSING TO BELIEVE.

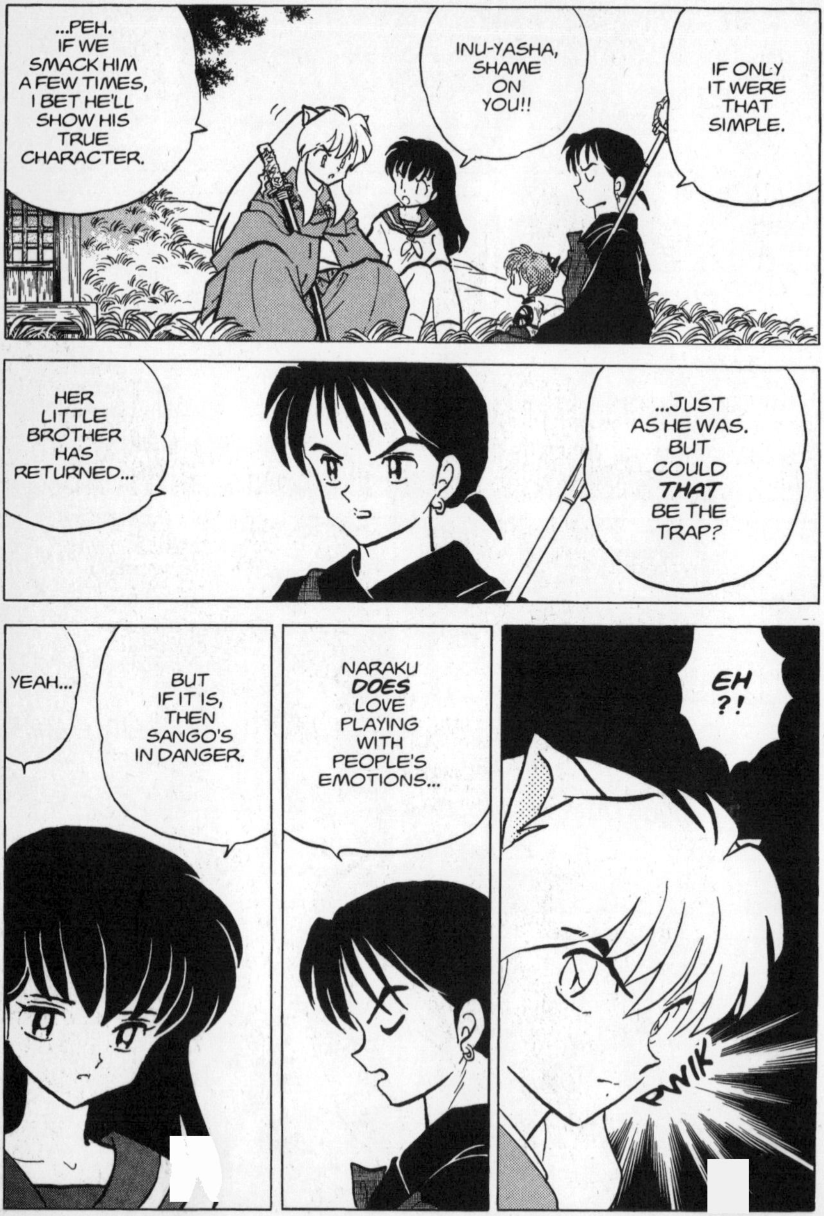
...PEH. IF WE SMACK HIM A FEW TIMES, I BET HE'LL SHOW HIS TRUE CHARACTER.
INU-YASHA, SHAME ON YOU!!
IF ONLY IT WERE THAT SIMPLE.
HER LITTLE BROTHER HAS RETURNED...
...JUST AS HE WAS. BUT COULD **THAT** BE THE TRAP?
YEAH...
BUT IF IT IS, THEN SANGO'S IN DANGER.
NARAKU **DOES** LOVE PLAYING WITH PEOPLE'S EMOTIONS...
EH?!
PWIK

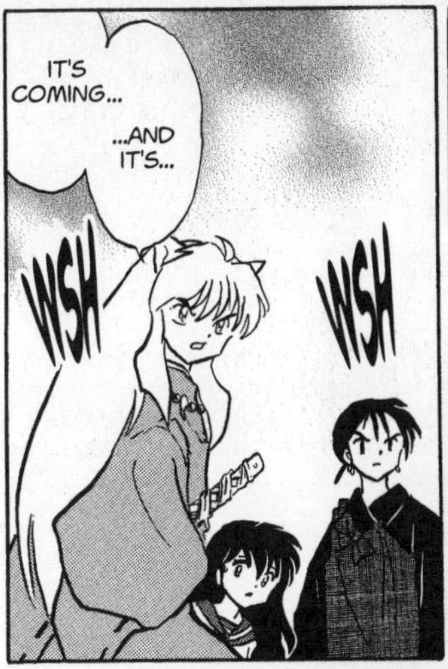
IT'S COMING...
...AND IT'S...
WSH
WSH

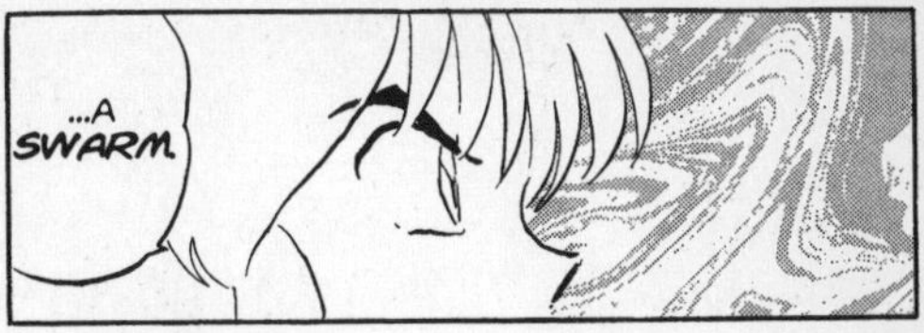
...A SWARM.

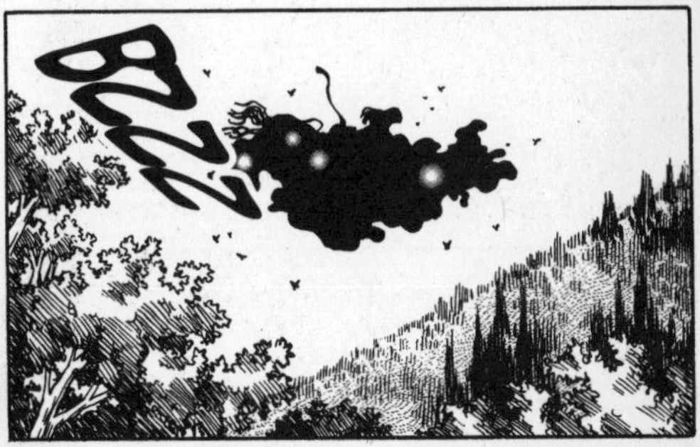
BUZZ

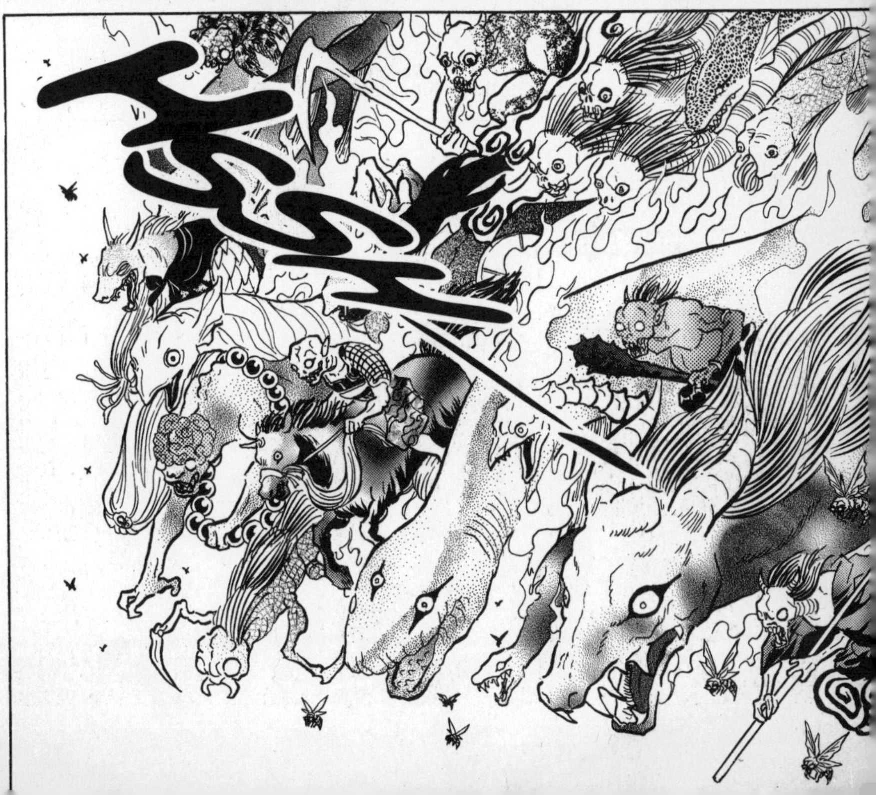

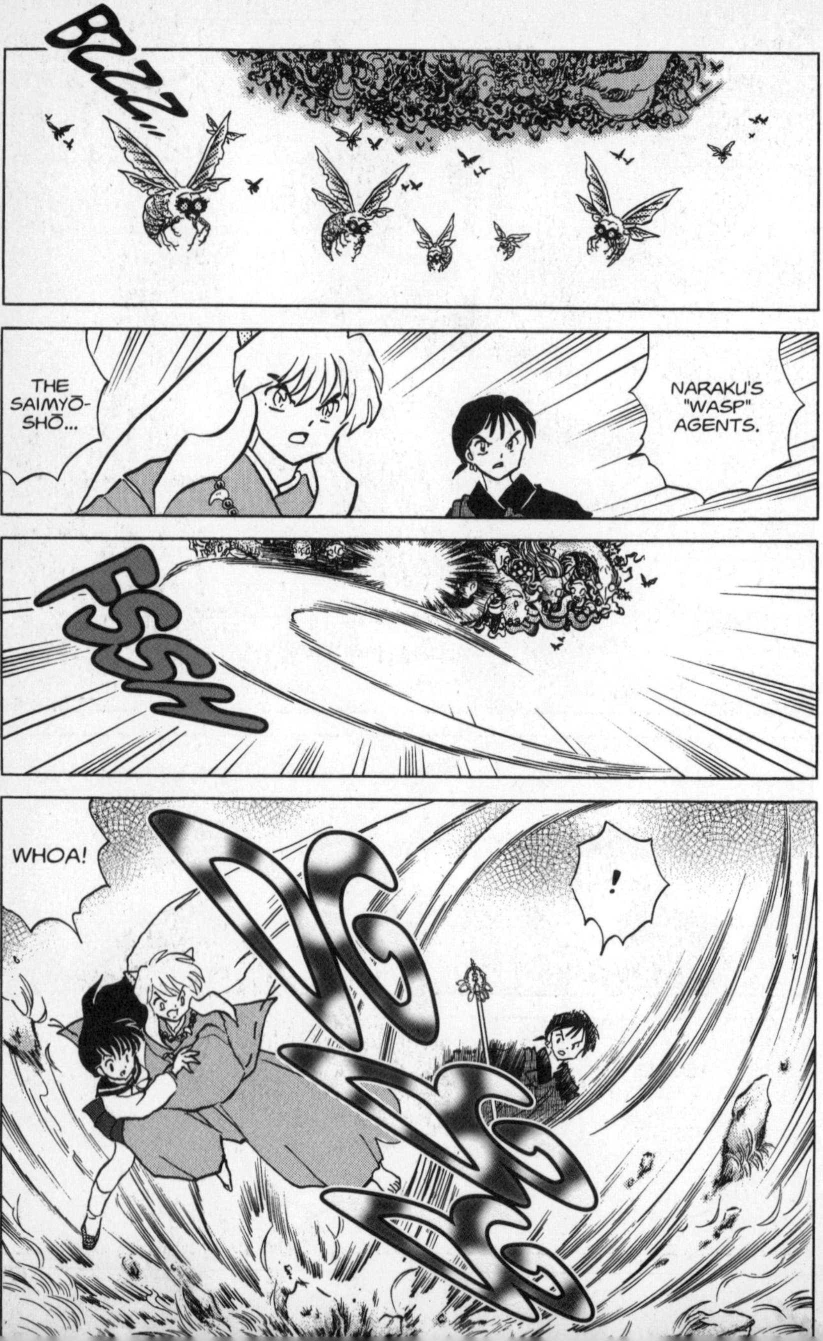
BZZZ!!
THE SAIMYŌ-SHŌ...
NARAKU'S "WASP" AGENTS.
FSSH
WHOA!
!

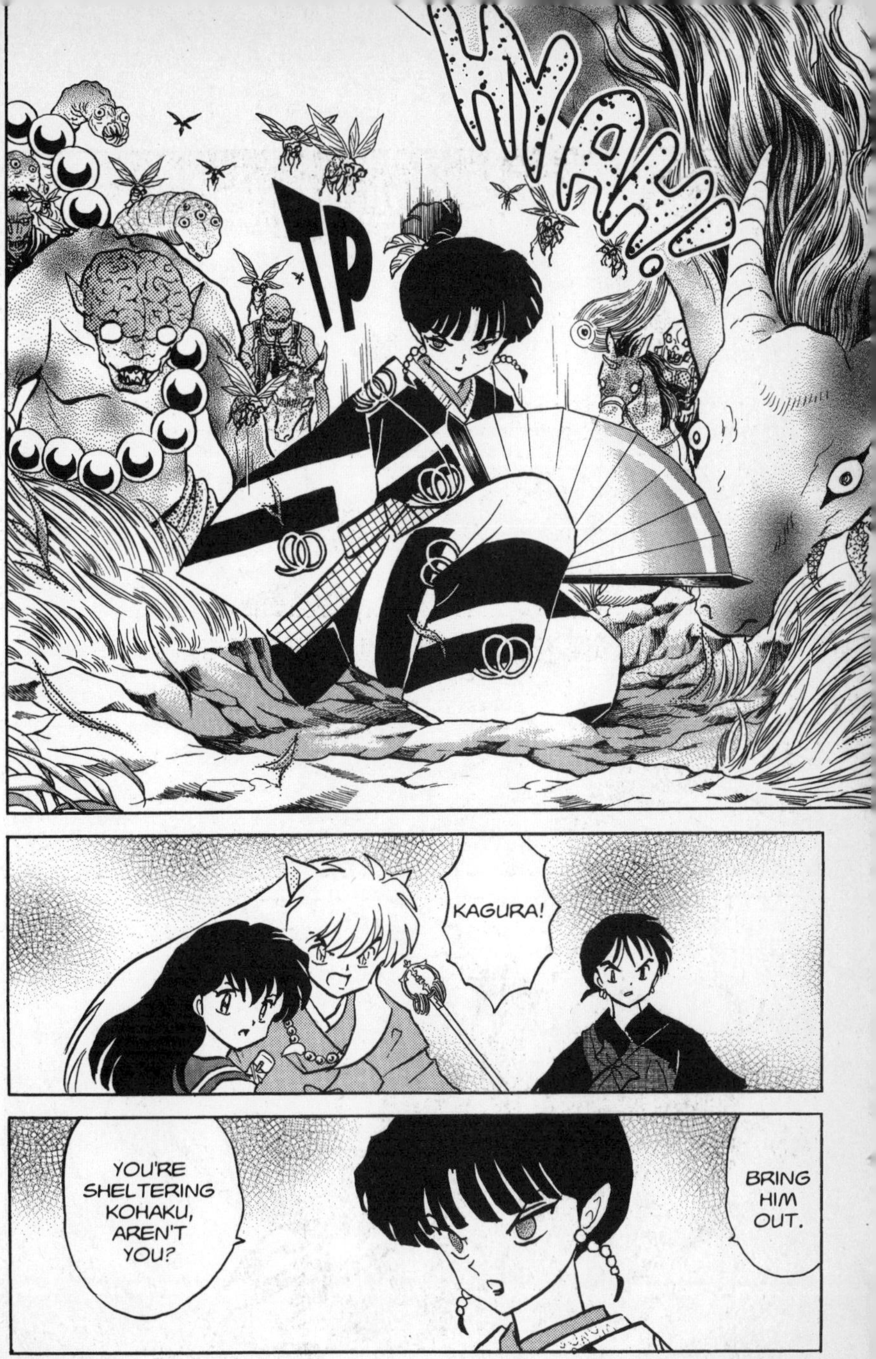

TP
WHAM!!
KAGURA!
YOU'RE SHELTERING KOHAKU, AREN'T YOU?
BRING HIM OUT.

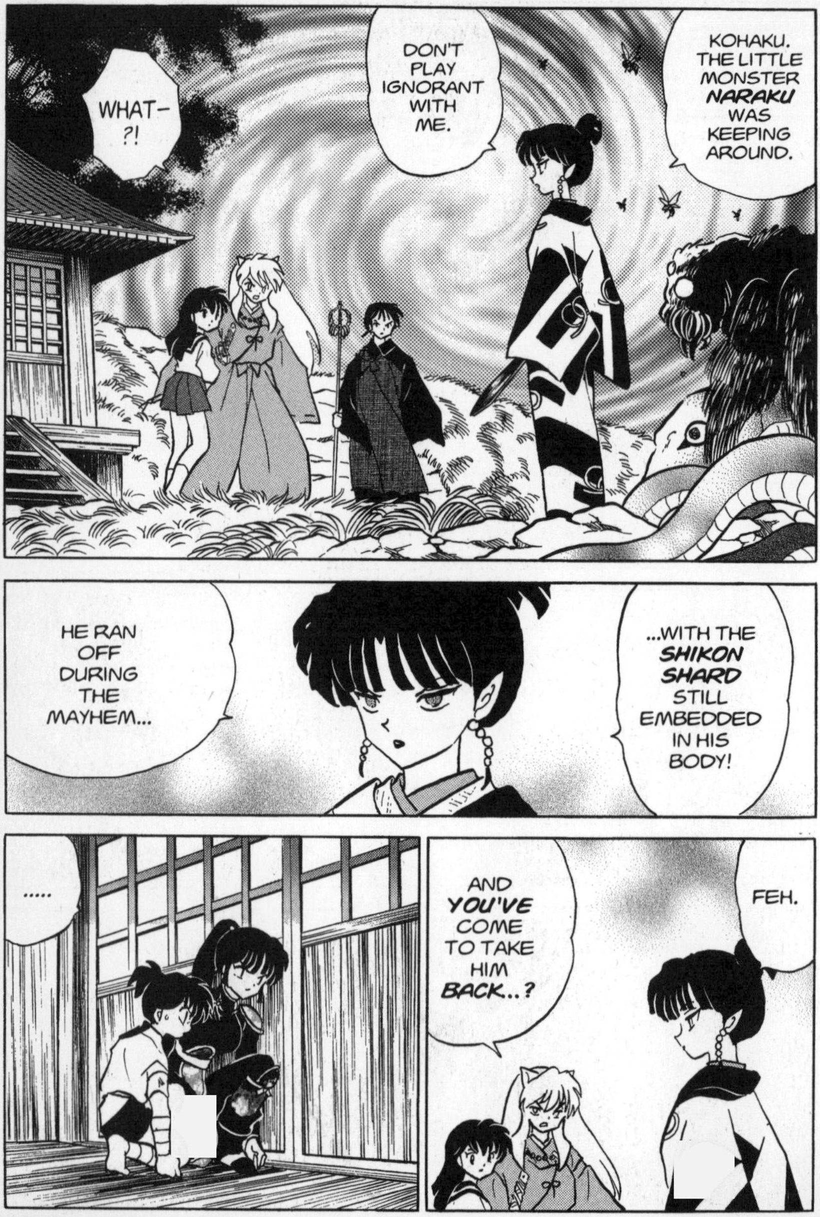
WHAT—?!
DON'T PLAY IGNORANT WITH ME.
KOHAKU. THE LITTLE MONSTER **NARAKU** WAS KEEPING AROUND.
HE RAN OFF DURING THE MAYHEM...
...WITH THE **SHIKON SHARD** STILL EMBEDDED IN HIS BODY!
.....
AND **YOU'VE** COME TO TAKE HIM **BACK**...?
FEH.

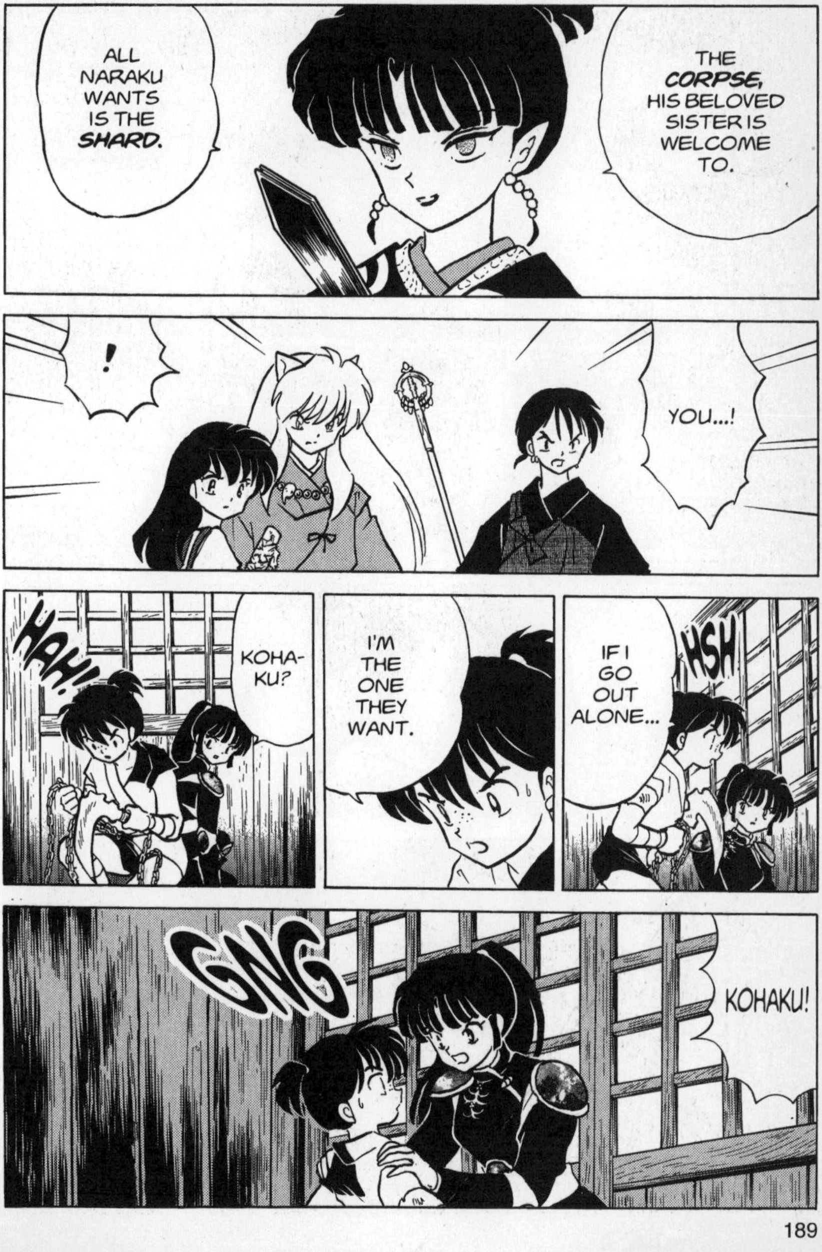
ALL NARAKU WANTS IS THE SHARD.
THE CORPSE, HIS BELOVED SISTER IS WELCOME TO.
!
YOU...!
HAH!
KOHAKU?
I'M THE ONE THEY WANT.
IF I GO OUT ALONE...
HSH
GNG
KOHAKU!

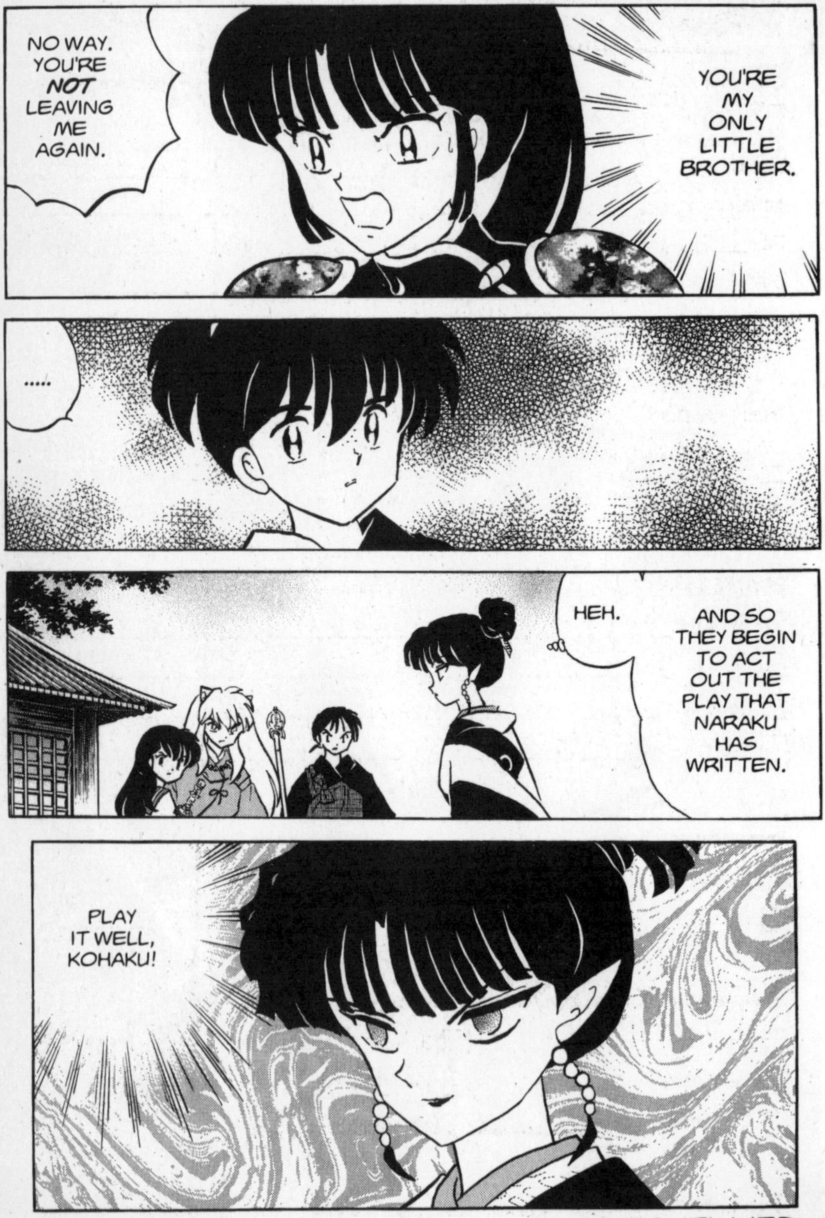
NO WAY. YOU'RE ***NOT*** LEAVING ME AGAIN.
YOU'RE MY ONLY LITTLE BROTHER.
.....
HEH.
AND SO THEY BEGIN TO ACT OUT THE PLAY THAT NARAKU HAS WRITTEN.
PLAY IT WELL, KOHAKU!

TO BE CONTINUED